T0207464

Lecture Notes in Computer Science   13319

Founding Editors

Gerhard Goos
Karlsruhe Institute of Technology, Karlsruhe, Germany

Juris Hartmanis
Cornell University, Ithaca, NY, USA

Editorial Board Members

Elisa Bertino
Purdue University, West Lafayette, IN, USA

Wen Gao
Peking University, Beijing, China

Bernhard Steffen 📵
TU Dortmund University, Dortmund, Germany

Moti Yung 📵
Columbia University, New York, NY, USA

More information about this series at https://link.springer.com/bookseries/558

Vincent G. Duffy (Ed.)

Digital Human Modeling and Applications in Health, Safety, Ergonomics and Risk Management

Anthropometry, Human Behavior,
and Communication

13th International Conference, DHM 2022
Held as Part of the 24th HCI International Conference, HCII 2022
Virtual Event, June 26 – July 1, 2022
Proceedings, Part I

 Springer

Editor
Vincent G. Duffy
Purdue University
West Lafayette, IN, USA

ISSN 0302-9743   ISSN 1611-3349 (electronic)
Lecture Notes in Computer Science
ISBN 978-3-031-05889-9   ISBN 978-3-031-05890-5 (eBook)
https://doi.org/10.1007/978-3-031-05890-5

© The Editor(s) (if applicable) and The Author(s), under exclusive license
to Springer Nature Switzerland AG 2022
This work is subject to copyright. All rights are reserved by the Publisher, whether the whole or part of the
material is concerned, specifically the rights of translation, reprinting, reuse of illustrations, recitation,
broadcasting, reproduction on microfilms or in any other physical way, and transmission or information
storage and retrieval, electronic adaptation, computer software, or by similar or dissimilar methodology now
known or hereafter developed.
The use of general descriptive names, registered names, trademarks, service marks, etc. in this publication
does not imply, even in the absence of a specific statement, that such names are exempt from the relevant
protective laws and regulations and therefore free for general use.
The publisher, the authors and the editors are safe to assume that the advice and information in this book are
believed to be true and accurate at the date of publication. Neither the publisher nor the authors or the editors
give a warranty, expressed or implied, with respect to the material contained herein or for any errors or
omissions that may have been made. The publisher remains neutral with regard to jurisdictional claims in
published maps and institutional affiliations.

This Springer imprint is published by the registered company Springer Nature Switzerland AG
The registered company address is: Gewerbestrasse 11, 6330 Cham, Switzerland

Foreword

Human-computer interaction (HCI) is acquiring an ever-increasing scientific and industrial importance, as well as having more impact on people's everyday life, as an ever-growing number of human activities are progressively moving from the physical to the digital world. This process, which has been ongoing for some time now, has been dramatically accelerated by the COVID-19 pandemic. The HCI International (HCII) conference series, held yearly, aims to respond to the compelling need to advance the exchange of knowledge and research and development efforts on the human aspects of design and use of computing systems.

The 24th International Conference on Human-Computer Interaction, HCI International 2022 (HCII 2022), was planned to be held at the Gothia Towers Hotel and Swedish Exhibition & Congress Centre, Göteborg, Sweden, during June 26 to July 1, 2022. Due to the COVID-19 pandemic and with everyone's health and safety in mind, HCII 2022 was organized and run as a virtual conference. It incorporated the 21 thematic areas and affiliated conferences listed on the following page.

A total of 5583 individuals from academia, research institutes, industry, and governmental agencies from 88 countries submitted contributions, and 1276 papers and 275 posters were included in the proceedings to appear just before the start of the conference. The contributions thoroughly cover the entire field of human-computer interaction, addressing major advances in knowledge and effective use of computers in a variety of application areas. These papers provide academics, researchers, engineers, scientists, practitioners, and students with state-of-the-art information on the most recent advances in HCI. The volumes constituting the set of proceedings to appear before the start of the conference are listed in the following pages.

The HCI International (HCII) conference also offers the option of 'Late Breaking Work' which applies both for papers and posters, and the corresponding volume(s) of the proceedings will appear after the conference. Full papers will be included in the 'HCII 2022 - Late Breaking Papers' volumes of the proceedings to be published in the Springer LNCS series, while 'Poster Extended Abstracts' will be included as short research papers in the 'HCII 2022 - Late Breaking Posters' volumes to be published in the Springer CCIS series.

I would like to thank the Program Board Chairs and the members of the Program Boards of all thematic areas and affiliated conferences for their contribution and support towards the highest scientific quality and overall success of the HCI International 2022 conference; they have helped in so many ways, including session organization, paper reviewing (single-blind review process, with a minimum of two reviews per submission) and, more generally, acting as goodwill ambassadors for the HCII conference.

This conference would not have been possible without the continuous and unwavering support and advice of Gavriel Salvendy, founder, General Chair Emeritus, and Scientific Advisor. For his outstanding efforts, I would like to express my appreciation to Abbas Moallem, Communications Chair and Editor of HCI International News.

June 2022   Constantine Stephanidis

HCI International 2022 Thematic Areas and Affiliated Conferences

Thematic Areas

- HCI: Human-Computer Interaction
- HIMI: Human Interface and the Management of Information

Affiliated Conferences

- EPCE: 19th International Conference on Engineering Psychology and Cognitive Ergonomics
- AC: 16th International Conference on Augmented Cognition
- UAHCI: 16th International Conference on Universal Access in Human-Computer Interaction
- CCD: 14th International Conference on Cross-Cultural Design
- SCSM: 14th International Conference on Social Computing and Social Media
- VAMR: 14th International Conference on Virtual, Augmented and Mixed Reality
- DHM: 13th International Conference on Digital Human Modeling and Applications in Health, Safety, Ergonomics and Risk Management
- DUXU: 11th International Conference on Design, User Experience and Usability
- C&C: 10th International Conference on Culture and Computing
- DAPI: 10th International Conference on Distributed, Ambient and Pervasive Interactions
- HCIBGO: 9th International Conference on HCI in Business, Government and Organizations
- LCT: 9th International Conference on Learning and Collaboration Technologies
- ITAP: 8th International Conference on Human Aspects of IT for the Aged Population
- AIS: 4th International Conference on Adaptive Instructional Systems
- HCI-CPT: 4th International Conference on HCI for Cybersecurity, Privacy and Trust
- HCI-Games: 4th International Conference on HCI in Games
- MobiTAS: 4th International Conference on HCI in Mobility, Transport and Automotive Systems
- AI-HCI: 3rd International Conference on Artificial Intelligence in HCI
- MOBILE: 3rd International Conference on Design, Operation and Evaluation of Mobile Communications

List of Conference Proceedings Volumes Appearing Before the Conference

1. LNCS 13302, Human-Computer Interaction: Theoretical Approaches and Design Methods (Part I), edited by Masaaki Kurosu
2. LNCS 13303, Human-Computer Interaction: Technological Innovation (Part II), edited by Masaaki Kurosu
3. LNCS 13304, Human-Computer Interaction: User Experience and Behavior (Part III), edited by Masaaki Kurosu
4. LNCS 13305, Human Interface and the Management of Information: Visual and Information Design (Part I), edited by Sakae Yamamoto and Hirohiko Mori
5. LNCS 13306, Human Interface and the Management of Information: Applications in Complex Technological Environments (Part II), edited by Sakae Yamamoto and Hirohiko Mori
6. LNAI 13307, Engineering Psychology and Cognitive Ergonomics, edited by Don Harris and Wen-Chin Li
7. LNCS 13308, Universal Access in Human-Computer Interaction: Novel Design Approaches and Technologies (Part I), edited by Margherita Antona and Constantine Stephanidis
8. LNCS 13309, Universal Access in Human-Computer Interaction: User and Context Diversity (Part II), edited by Margherita Antona and Constantine Stephanidis
9. LNAI 13310, Augmented Cognition, edited by Dylan D. Schmorrow and Cali M. Fidopiastis
10. LNCS 13311, Cross-Cultural Design: Interaction Design Across Cultures (Part I), edited by Pei-Luen Patrick Rau
11. LNCS 13312, Cross-Cultural Design: Applications in Learning, Arts, Cultural Heritage, Creative Industries, and Virtual Reality (Part II), edited by Pei-Luen Patrick Rau
12. LNCS 13313, Cross-Cultural Design: Applications in Business, Communication, Health, Well-being, and Inclusiveness (Part III), edited by Pei-Luen Patrick Rau
13. LNCS 13314, Cross-Cultural Design: Product and Service Design, Mobility and Automotive Design, Cities, Urban Areas, and Intelligent Environments Design (Part IV), edited by Pei-Luen Patrick Rau
14. LNCS 13315, Social Computing and Social Media: Design, User Experience and Impact (Part I), edited by Gabriele Meiselwitz
15. LNCS 13316, Social Computing and Social Media: Applications in Education and Commerce (Part II), edited by Gabriele Meiselwitz
16. LNCS 13317, Virtual, Augmented and Mixed Reality: Design and Development (Part I), edited by Jessie Y. C. Chen and Gino Fragomeni
17. LNCS 13318, Virtual, Augmented and Mixed Reality: Applications in Education, Aviation and Industry (Part II), edited by Jessie Y. C. Chen and Gino Fragomeni

http://2022.hci.international/proceedings

Preface

Software representations of humans, including aspects of anthropometry, biometrics, motion capture and prediction, as well as cognition modelling, are known as Digital Human Models (DHM), and are widely used in a variety of complex application domains where it is important to foresee and simulate human behavior, performance, safety, health and comfort. Automation depicting human emotion, social interaction and functional capabilities can also be modeled to support and assist in predicting human response in real world settings. Such domains include medical and nursing applications, education and learning, ergonomics and design, as well as safety and risk management.

The 13th Digital Human Modeling & Applications in Health, Safety, Ergonomics & Risk Management (DHM) Conference, an affiliated conference of the HCI International Conference 2022, encouraged papers from academics, researchers, industry and professionals, on a broad range of theoretical and applied issues related to Digital Human Modelling and its applications.

The research papers contributed to this year's volume spans across different fields that fall within the scope of the DHM Conference. In the context of anthropometry, human behavior, and communication, the physical aspects emphasized build on human modeling lessons of the past, whereas attentional aspects are providing evidence for new theories and applications. The study of DHM issues in various application domains has yielded works emphasizing task analysis, quality and safety in healthcare, as well occupational health and operations management. Digital human modeling in interactive product and service design is also discussed in this year's contributions. There are applications of interest shown across many industries, while multi-disciplinary and systems-related challenges remain for validation and generalizability in future work. Sensors-based modeling, information visualization, collaborative robots, and intelligent interactions are among the human-technology modeling and results reporting efforts this year.

Two volumes of the HCII 2022 proceedings are dedicated to this year's edition of the DHM Conference, entitled Digital Human Modeling and Applications in Health, Safety, Ergonomics and Risk Management: Anthropometry, Human Behavior, and Communication (Part I), and Digital Human Modeling and Applications in Health, Safety, Ergonomics and Risk Management: Health, Operations Management, and Design (Part II). The first volume focuses on topics related to ergonomic design, anthropometry, and human modeling, as well as collaboration, communication, and human behavior. The second volume focuses on topics related to task analysis, quality and safety in health-care, as well as occupational health and operations management, and Digital Human Modeling in interactive product and service design.

Papers of these volumes are included for publication after a minimum of two single–blind reviews from the members of the DHM Program Board or, in some cases, from members of the Program Boards of other affiliated conferences. I would like to thank all of them for their invaluable contribution, support and efforts.

June 2022   Vincent G. Duffy

13th International Conference on Digital Human Modeling and Applications in Health, Safety, Ergonomics and Risk Management (DHM 2022)

Program Board Chair: **Vincent G. Duffy,** Purdue University, USA

- Mária Babicsné Horváth, Budapest University of Technology and Economics, Hungary
- Joan Cahill, Trinity College Dublin, Ireland
- André Calero Valdez, RWTH Aachen University, Germany
- Yaqin Cao, Anhui Polytechnic University, China
- Damien Chablat, CNRS and LS2N, France
- Genett Isabel Delgado, Institución Universitaria ITSA, Colombia
- H. Onan Demirel, Oregon State University, USA
- Martin Fleischer, Technical University of Munich, Germany
- Martin Fränzle, Oldenburg University, Germany
- Afzal Godil, NIST, USA
- Fu Guo, Northeastern University, China
- Michael Harry, Loughborough University, UK
- Sogand Hasanzadeh, Purdue University, USA
- Mingcai Hu, Jiangsu University, China
- Sandy Ingram, University of Applied Sciences of Western Switzerland, Switzerland
- Alexander Mehler, Goethe University Frankfurt, Germany
- Sonja Miesner, KAN - Commission for Occupational Health and Safety and Standardization, Germany
- Fabian Narvaez, Universidad Politecnica Salesiana, Ecuador
- Peter Nickel, Institute for Occupational Safety and Health of the German Social Accident Insurance (IFA), Germany
- T. Patel, North Eastern Regional Institute of Science and Technology, India
- Manikam Pillay, RESMEERTS, Australia
- Qing-Xing Qu, Northeastern University, China
- Caterina Rizzi, Università of Bergamo, Italy
- Joni Salminen, Qatar Computing Research Institute, Qatar
- Beatriz Santos, University of Aveiro, Portugal
- Deep Seth, Mahindra University, India
- Leonor Teixeira, University of Aveiro, Portugal
- Renran Tian, IUPUI, USA
- Alexander Trende, OFFIS - Institute for Information Technology, Germany
- Dustin Van der Haar, University of Johannesburg, South Africa
- Kuan Yew Wong, Universiti Teknologi Malaysia, Malaysia
- Shuping Xiong, Korea Advanced Institute of Science and Technology, South Korea
- James Yang, Texas Tech University, USA

The full list with the Program Board Chairs and the members of the Program Boards of all thematic areas and affiliated conferences is available online at

http://www.hci.international/board-members-2022.php

HCI International 2023

The 25th International Conference on Human-Computer Interaction, HCI International 2023, will be held jointly with the affiliated conferences at the AC Bella Sky Hotel and Bella Center, Copenhagen, Denmark, 23–28 July 2023. It will cover a broad spectrum of themes related to human-computer interaction, including theoretical issues, methods, tools, processes, and case studies in HCI design, as well as novel interaction techniques, interfaces, and applications. The proceedings will be published by Springer. More information will be available on the conference website: http://2023.hci.international/.

General Chair
Constantine Stephanidis
University of Crete and ICS-FORTH
Heraklion, Crete, Greece
Email: general_chair@hcii2023.org

http://2023.hci.international/

Contents – Part I

Collaboration, Communication, and Human Behavior

Contents – Part II

Occupational Health and Operations Management

Digital Human Modeling in Interactive Product and Service Design

Ergonomic Design, Anthropometry, and Human Modeling

Testing of Different Strings for Their Usability in Actuation of Exosuits

Sreejan Alapati and Deep Seth[✉]

Department of Mechanical Engineering, Mahindra University, Hyderabad, India
{sreejan20pmee003,deep.seth}@mahindrauniversity.edu.in

Abstract. Cable driven exoskeletons and exosuits are very popular in rehabilitation and assistive robotics. Exosuits are typically actuated using Bowden cable attached to motors or any other actuators. Bowden cable act as link to activate a joint. However, exosuits because of flexible construction require flexible links or cable. To keep the cost low and for ease of routing, other strings can be explored, instead of using Bowden cables. This work presents the usability of braided nylon fishing lines as an alternative to Bowden cable in exosuit making. An experimental setup is described here for cyclic loading and elongation of string. The results show that both mono nylon string and a braided nylon string can undergo cyclic loading. Due to greater elongation of mono nylon string over braided nylon string, the latter is a better option for use in exosuits.

Keywords: Exouit actuation · Nylon fishing line · Testing · Cyclic loading · Elongation

1 Introduction

Exosuits are wearable robots that are flexible and provides power augmentation to the wearer. Exosuits can be used in rehabilitation, physical therapy and are also to provide assistance [1]. Unlike exoskeletons, exosuits is aimed at easy wearability and are targeted to be a cheaper alternative. The common construction of an exosuit consists of a harness that wraps around the area of actuation which is linked to the actuator with a cable. There are different types of actuators used in exosuits. The most common type of exosuit actuation is cable driven actuation powered with an electric motor [2,3]. Several exoskeletons also use cable driven mechanism for actuation [4]. However, other types of actuators like McKibben actuator [5], pneumatic inflatable actuators [6], shape memory alloys, twisted string actuators [7] are also used. Cable driven exosuit use Bowden cable for power transmission where one end is looped around a spool connected to motor and other end is connected at the actuation point.

Bowden cable has the problem of routing along the suit, as it is not flexible enough for sharp turns in the suit. This limits the number of ways the cable can be incorporated and further limits the design freedom in the suit. This could be one of the reasons why most exosuits that are actuated using bowden cable are

© The Author(s), under exclusive license to Springer Nature Switzerland AG 2022
V. G. Duffy (Ed.): HCII 2022, LNCS 13319, pp. 3–15, 2022.
https://doi.org/10.1007/978-3-031-05890-5_1

limited to few joints. If there are more joints, it is difficult to route cables. Also, the construction of exosuits that are being developed is similar in most cases. Off-the-shelf materials are chosen in the construction, where the service life of different materials and components used is different. For example, as a point of discussion in this paper, the Bowden cable used for actuation may be clamped to the suit using a rivet or is sewn. The riveted or sewn joint may not last as longer as the bowden cable used in the actuation. Metallic bowden cable might outlive the functioning time of the exosuit itself. In this case it is noticeable to choose an alternative cable for actuation, that can be cheaper and has a good service life.

Lot of strings made out of polymers are available and can be chosen, considering longevity of the polymers. One of the widely available string is made out of nylon and is used in fishing lines. In the literature, fishing lines have been used to stabilize the stifle joint of a canine, in a technique called as Lateral Suture Technique [9]. When a ligament of a stifle joint is torn in canines, nylon mono-filament lines are used to surgically stabilise the joint. This is done by making holes in the bones and the nylon mono-filament line ties the bones together, acting as artificial ligament. Several studies have been conducted for the usability of fishing lines in the above procedure [9]. Additionally, biomechanical analysis of using nylon fishing lines has been experimented before [10]. From this it is seen as a promising option to use nylon fishing lines instead of a Bowden cable to actuate the exosuit. Earlier attempts have been made to actuate exosuit with nylon strings [8].

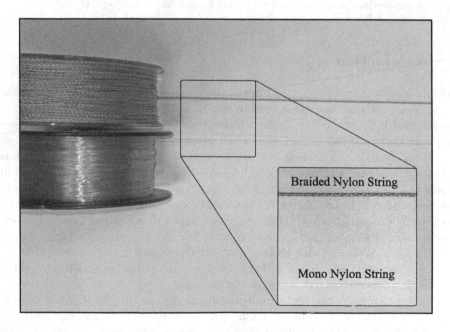

Fig. 1. Strings used in the experimentation

Nylon fishing lines are available in different forms and types, and choosing from them requires testing them for the need and verifying their applicability. Nylon fishing lines [11] come with pre-determined test data for tensile loading and weight capacity. It is not conclusive to say that Nylon fishing lines can be used in the actuation of joints from this data. Bowden cables [12] are previously tested in the actuation of joints. However, nylon fishing lines are only promised to withstand rated tension forces, with testing being required to verify if they can withstand cyclic loading as required in the application for joint actuation of exosuit. Also, nylon strings are prone to elongation when tension is applied. Thus a nylon string with minimal elongation or no elongation needs to be selected. Hence, test for cyclic loading and elongation are done on two kinds of fishing lines. The strings selected are a braided and mono nylon string as shown in Fig. 1, with similar thickness.

Braided string is manufactured by braiding several fibres together. This is done to ensure that the string does not break due to damage or crack formation. In the case of a Mono fishing string any damage will cause the entire string to fail when a load is applied. Additionally, a braided string acts as a composite and the load on individual fibre is not longitudinal. Braided string also have lesser elongation since load on different fibres are in different directions. However, experimentation is required to determine the usability of fishing lines in exosuits.

2 Methodology of Testing

The two tests, one for cyclic loading and another for elongation are chosen. Exo-suits are used for rehabilitation in most cases or are required to assist for lower loads. The testing procedure here considers the tension required for actuation of limbs of an adult. The selection of string and weight to be attached for loading, is also based on this tension force. Once the weight is chosen, a string a with rated tension of more than the load is selected. With this, it is ensured that the string will not break under pure tension loading. This tension force is reversed periodically to check it's capacity to withstand cyclic loading. Elongation is also measured for different length of strings for this chosen tension force/ weight. The different tests done are depicted in the Fig. 2.

The cyclic loading is done with a pre-determined number of cycles. Elongation is measured with a simple Hooke's law setup. This elongation is compared to the theoretical elongation of the string. To calculate theoretical elongation, the modulus of elasticity of the wire is measured with a Universal Testing Machine.

The tension force used for experimentation is determined by finding the weight of the forearm and hand. The parameters of the experiment set are for the purpose of lifting fore arm and hand for elbow actuation. However, later on the experiments can be repeated for any tension force for the actuation of different joints by choosing a string that has a tension capacity greater than the tension required for actuation of that joint. To select the required weight of forearm and hand for elbow actuation, we refer to the anthropometry data [13]. From this, the weight of lower arm and hand of a fully grown adult is around 2.5% (mean

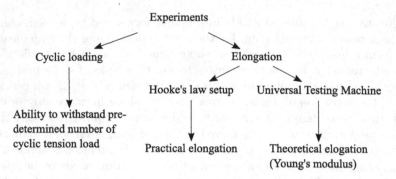

Fig. 2. Experiments on the strings

= 2.521%) of the entire body weight. The test subject chosen is a fully grown adult of around 1.83 m tall with a and weight of about 80 kg. From the data it is estimated that lower arm and hand for this adult would weigh around 2 kg for experiments here. Testing for cyclic loading and elongation is done using three sets of weights below 2 kg, which are 1 kg, 1.5 kg and 2 kg (Table 1).

Table 1. Anthropometric data of forearm and hand

S. No.	Body segment	Segment weight as percentage of body weight
		Mean
1	Forearm	1.818%
2	Hand	0.703%
	Total	2.521%
	Weight	2.521%(80 kg) = 2 kg

2.1 Test for Cyclic Loading

To generate cyclic loading we push and pull the weight against gravity. This is similar to exosuit actuation because the elbow actuator would have to lift weight of fore arm and hand against gravity.

A frame is built out of aluminium profile bars with four columns. Weight is hung inside the frame by the string that is tested. The string is then attached to a pulley which is driven by a DC motor. The weight is lowered and raised in the frame as the direction of the motor is reversed periodically. To set the stroke length and reverse the direction of the motor, two IR proximity sensors have been used as limit switches. The two IR proximity sensors are mounted on one side of the frame, directed into the frame, to detect the presence of the weight. Once the presence of weight is detected, a signal is sent to micro-controller which commands motor driver to change the direction of the motor. It is controlled in such a way that, the motor direction is set clockwise when weight is detected at the upper proximity sensor and vice-versa. It is thus ensured that weight moves between the two sensors, as the string is hung to the right side of the pulley. All the electronic components like micro-controller and motor driver are mounted on the top of the frame. The entire construction can be seen in the Fig. 3.

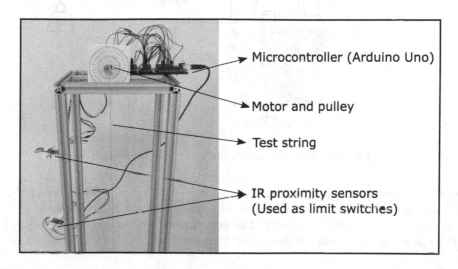

Microcontroller (Arduino Uno)

Motor and pulley

Test string

IR proximity sensors
(Used as limit switches)

Fig. 3. Experimental setup for cyclic loading

The stroke length is set to be 150 mm by the proximity sensors, as the elbow joint actuation doesn't require more length of stroke considering actuation points are kept as close to elbow joint as possible. The stroke length is maintained by adjusting the proximity sensors, as the weights are not of same dimension. The top sensor detects the top portion of the weight and bottom sensor detects the bottom portion of the weight. Because of this, it is necessary to set length considering the vertical dimension of the weight as shown in Fig. 5. It can be seen that the proximity sensors are set at different positions for different loads.

The details of the components used in setup for cyclic loading are described here. The motor used is a Cytron SPG30E-30K (150 rpm), which is connected to an Arduino UNO using a L298N motor driver. The diameter of pulley attached to motor is 60 mm and verticle distance the weights moved is 150 mm. The motor is powered by a 12 V power supply. The Arduino is also powered by this supply. The motor driver and sensors which require 5 V and 3.3 V respectively are powered by the Arduino power pins. The weights are cast in solid concrete. The circuit diagram of the following setup is shown in Fig. 4.

The test setup is run with 1 kg, 1.5 kg and 2 kg. A single strand of the string is taken and is attached to the weight. Then the experiment is turned on and as weight is pulled against gravity and lowered, the string experiences cyclic loading. This loading takes about 5 s for one push-pull cycle and is done for upto 10,000 cycles. Since most electronic components with moving components are rated for

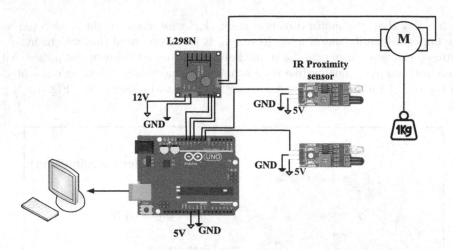

Fig. 4. Circuit diagram of the cyclic loading setup

several thousand cycles, the testing is done for 10,000 cycles. It took around 15 h for each string and weight combination to undergo ten thousand cycles of push and pull strokes against the gravity. The experiments were intentionally stopped after the completion of ten thousand cycles.

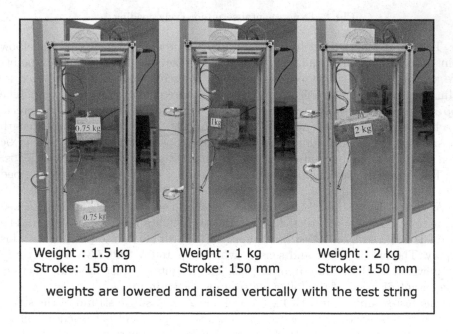

Fig. 5. Cyclic loading with different weights

The Arduino code is written to change the direction of motor when IR proximity sensors detect a signal. One push and pull movement of weight in the stroke length of 150 mm is considered as one cycle. A counter is introduced into the code and is incremented when one cycle is completed. The direction of the motor and the counter data are printed to the serial communication. This data sent with the serial communication is received by a computer with a program 'ArduSpreadsheet' [14] installed into the Arduino IDE. This allows the software to save a CSV (comma seperated values) file with variables read from the serial for all the ten thousand cycles.

2.2 Test for Elongation

Another property that would be important for the usability of the string in exosuit actuation is elongation. If there is elongation in the string, the string would not transfer the tension force but will elongate due to applied force. It is observed that mono nylon fishing line elongates even when the tension is below the rated tension of the string. Therefore it is necessary to determine the elongation due to a certain weight.

A Hooke's law setup is used to test the two strings for elongation. A wall mount is setup with a ruler. One end of the string is attached to the wall mount with a knot. The other end is attached to a snap hook by another knot. The weights are replaced to the snap hook. The length of the string without weights is measured between these knots. The length is initially measured along the scale and to the length after elongation with weight of 1 kg, 1.5 kg and 2 kg. The setup with a weight of 1 kg held against gravity force with a mono nylon string is shown in the Fig. 6.

The string elongation will depend on the length of the string and load, hence strings of different lengths have been taken for testing. For routing the cable in the suit, a string might need to cover a certain distance from actuator to point of actuation. Taking this into consideration, string of length 150 mm to 500 mm are chosen for testing. Each string of certain length is tested with three different loads. For a certain length of string, the elongation is taken in four iterations to minimise the erroneous data. The data collected is shown in Table 2.

To compare the experimental elongation data with theoretical formulation, modulus of elasticity (Young's modulus) of the strings are found using an Universal Testing Machine (UTM). The UTM used is an Instron 5969. The two strings are held in between the clamps, and tensile loading is applied steadily. The load is applied until the strings snap. From the stress strain curves generated during the testing, Young's modulus of the material is calculated. Once the elasticity modulus is known, the elongation can be calculated with the known values of area of cross section, tension force on string and length of the string.

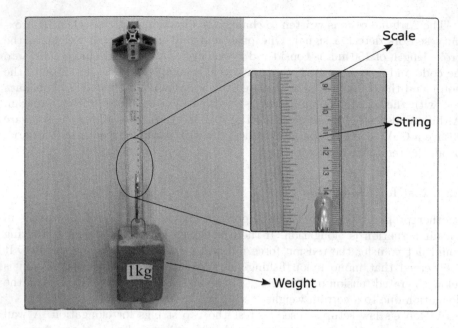

Fig. 6. Hooke's law setup

The equation for Young's modulus is given below [15].

$$E = \sigma/\epsilon = (F/A)/(\delta l/l) \tag{1}$$

where:

E = Young's Modulus
σ = Stress
ϵ = Strain
F = Force
A = Cross section area
δl = elongation
l = original length

2.3   Results

Results of Cyclic Loading. The data saved into the csv file is then plotted as a graph of number of cycles against the time taken (measured in hours) for those number of cycles using Matlab. The details of the weight and type of string are written above each sub-plot.

It can be seen from the Fig. 7 that the two strings could easily go through ten thousand push and pull cycles of cyclic loading without any damage to the string. The time taken for a cycle remains the same and hence the curve is linear. The experiment is manually stopped after ten thousand cycles. Although, the

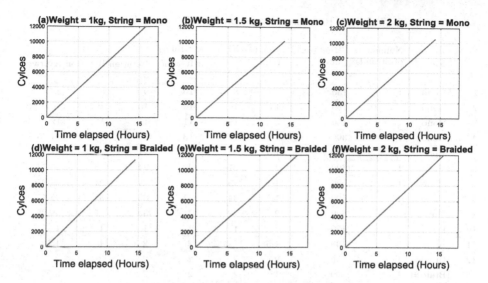

Fig. 7. Cyclic loading results Plot between time taken and number of cycles for cyclic loading for a Mono nylon string with weight of (a) 1 kg (b) 1.5 kg and (c) 2 kg. Plot between time taken and number of cycles for cyclic loading for a Briaded nylon string with weight of (d) 1 kg (e) 1.5 kg and (f) 2 kg

experiment is stopped at ten thousand cycles, the experiment can run further, since no damage was observed in the strings.

Results of Elongation. As shown in Table 2, initially a string of length 150 mm is taken. It is loaded with different weights and elongation is measured. It can be seen that, for mono nylon string of length 150 mm, elongation is around 8 mm. When the length doubled, elongation also doubles to about 15 mm. For a length of sting of 500 mm, the elongation reaches a value of 24 mm. Even though the rated tension of the mono nylon string is around 9 kg, it shows elongation at low weights of 2 kg.

For a braided nylon string of length 150 mm, the elongation is 1 mm for weight of 1 kg. When the length of string is increased to 300 mm, the elongation is around 2 mm and for string length of 500 mm, the elongation is 4 mm. For a weight of 2 kg and length of string of 500 mm, the maximum elongation experienced is about 5 mm. This value of elongation is very low when compared to the Mono nylon string.

From the tests conducted on string with the UTM, the Young's modulus of the material is found. The Young's modulus of the Mono nylon fishing string is 1.64 GPa, and for Braided Nylon is 5.66 GPa.

Table 2. Recorded elongation for different weights

S. No	String type	Number of Strands	String length (mm)	Weight (kg)	Elongation (mm)				
					Iteration 1	Iteration 2	Iteration 3	Iteration 4	Average
1	Mono	1	150	1	8	10	9	8	8.75
2	Mono	1	150	1.5	10	10	10	10	10
3	Mono	1	150	2	15	11	11	11	12
4	Mono	1	300	1	16	13	15	15	14.75
5	Mono	1	300	1.5	22	25	21	20	22
6	Mono	1	300	2	27	29	24	23	25.75
7	Mono	1	500	1	25	23	24	21	23.25
8	Mono	1	500	1.5	34	33	33	31	32.75
9	Mono	1	500	2	42	41	39	35	39.25
10	Braided	1	150	1	1	1	1	1	1
11	Braided	1	150	1.5	1	2	2	1	1.5
12	Braided	1	150	2	2	2	2	2	2
13	Braided	1	300	1	2	2	2	3	2.25
14	Braided	1	300	1.5	2	2	3	3	2.5
15	Braided	1	300	2	3	3	3	4	3.25
16	Braided	1	500	1	4	4	4	3	3.75
17	Braided	1	500	1.5	4	5	4	5	4.5
18	Braided	1	500	2	5	6	5	5	5.25

The theoretical calculations of the elongation are done using Eq. 1. The details of parameters considered in the calculations are listed in Table 3. The necking of the string is omitted during the calculation of elongation. Due to this, the theoretical calculations have an error with the actual elongation recorded during the experiment.

From the Fig. 8, the maximum elongation of Mono nylon string of length 500 mm and for a weight of 2 kg is 40 mm. In other words elongation experienced for this scenario is around 8%. And in case of the braided nylon string of length 500 mm and weight of 2 kg, elongation experienced is about 5 mm. This would be 1% elongation for that weight.

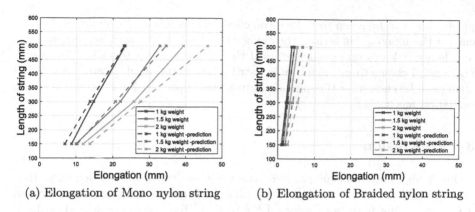

(a) Elongation of Mono nylon string   (b) Elongation of Braided nylon string

Fig. 8. Elongation of strings

Table 3. Theoretical elongation for different weights

S. No	String type	Young's Modulus (GPa)	Length of string (m)	Weight on string (kg)	Tension force (N)	Area of cross section (m^2)	Theoretical Elongation (mm)
1	Mono	1.64	150	1	9.8	0.00000013	6.89
2	Mono	1.64	150	1.5	14.7	0.00000013	10.34
3	Mono	1.64	150	2	19.6	0.00000013	13.79
4	Mono	1.64	300	1	9.8	0.00000013	13.79
5	Mono	1.64	300	1.5	14.7	0.00000013	20.68
6	Mono	1.64	300	2	19.6	0.00000013	27.58
7	Mono	1.64	500	1	9.8	0.00000013	22.98
8	Mono	1.64	500	1.5	14.7	0.00000013	34.47
9	Mono	1.64	500	2	19.6	0.00000013	45.97
10	Braided	5.66	150	1	9.8	0.000000196	1.33
11	Braided	5.66	150	1.5	14.7	0.000000196	1.99
12	Braided	5.66	150	2	19.6	0.000000196	2.65
13	Braided	5.66	300	1	9.8	0.000000196	2.65
14	Braided	5.66	300	1.5	14.7	0.000000196	3.98
15	Braided	5.66	300	2	19.6	0.000000196	5.30
16	Braided	5.66	500	1	9.8	0.000000196	4.42
17	Braided	5.66	500	1.5	14.7	0.000000196	6.63
18	Braided	5.66	500	2	19.6	0.000000196	8.83

The error between theoretical and experimental values are a few millimetres as plotted in Fig. 8. That error is small compared to the length of the string. The calculation of elongation using the Young's modulus of the string can give a reliable value of elongation of the string.

It is assumed that the cause for elongation in braided nylon string is because of the lack of rigidity in the braiding. Since it is braided, there is a scope for sliding in between braided strings. This particular elongation stops after the maximum sliding occurs. So If a braided string is to be used in the exosuit, a pre-tension can be given to reduce the effect of this minimal elongation. But, in case of the mono nylon string, the elongation depends on the material property and hence it keeps on elongation until the wire may start to yield. Hence it is not a good choice to use mono nylon string for actuation of exosuit. A braided string can be chosen for this purpose, given that a pre-tension is provided to the actuation mechanism.

3   Conclusion

Nylon fishing lines are explored here as an alternative to the Bowden cable that are currently used for actuation of exosuits. Two nylon fishing lines, a mono and a braided string have been selected for testing. Tests were conducted on both the strings with tension forces kept below the rated tension of the string. One test is cyclic loading, where both strings have been verified to have capability to undergo cyclic loading for a larger number of cycles. The second test is the elongation test, where mono nylon string was observed to be elongating more even for load within the rated tension force of the string and is not a good choice for actuation of exosuit. Braided nylon string did not undergo high elongation like the mono fishing line and hence could be used for actuation of the exosuit. However, since there is a slight elongation, a pre-tension force is suggested to minimize the effect of under-actuation because of this elongation.

4   Future Scope

There are many other alternatives to using Bowden cable, which can also be explored. The testing procedure can be run for more number of cycles in case of cyclic loading. Both the experiments can be run with higher loads and also, the impact of using double strand or a combination of different strings can be experimented.

Acknowledgement. This work is supported by Mahindra University, Hyderabad, India. All the experiments are conducted in the Center for Robotics at Mahindra University. The material testing is done in Materials laboratory at Mahindra University. We would like to thank all the lab assistants and Junior Research Fellow in Center for Robotics for their support.

References

1. Pons, J.: Wearable Robots: Biomechatronic Exoskeletons. Wiley, Hoboken (2008)
2. Pont, D., et al.: ExoFlex: an upper-limb cable-driven exosuit. In: Iberian Robotics Conference, pp. 417–428 (2019)
3. Samper-Escudero, J., Gimenez-Fernandez, A., Sanchez-Uran, M., Ferre, M.: A cable-driven exosuit for upper limb flexion based on fibres compliance. IEEE Access **8**, 153297–153310 (2020)

4. Gull, M., Bai, S., Bak, T.: A review on design of upper limb exoskeletons. Robotics **9**, 16 (2020)
5. Balasubramanian, S., et al.: RUPERT: an exoskeleton robot for assisting rehabilitation of arm functions. In: 2008 Virtual Rehabilitation, pp. 163–167 (2008)
6. O'Neill, C., et al.: Inflatable soft wearable robot for reducing therapist fatigue during upper extremity rehabilitation in severe stroke. IEEE Robot. Autom. Lett. **5**, 3899–3906 (2020)
7. Gaponov, I., Popov, D., Lee, S.J., Ryu, J.-H.: Auxilio: a portable cable-driven exosuit for upper extremity assistance. Int. J. Control Autom. Syst. **15**(1), 73–84 (2016). https://doi.org/10.1007/s12555-016-0487-7
8. Lessard, S., et al.: CRUX: a compliant robotic upper-extremity exosuit for lightweight, portable, multi-joint muscular augmentation. In: 2017 International Conference on Rehabilitation Robotics (ICORR), pp. 1633–1638 (2017)
9. Igna, C., et al.: In vitro mechanical testing of monofilament nylon fishing line, for the extracapsular stabilisation of canine stifle joint. Bull. Univ. Agric. Sci. Vet. Med. Cluj-Napoca. Vet. Med. **71**, 124–129 (2014)
10. Caporn, T., Roe, S.: Biomechanical evaluation of the suitability of monofilament nylon fishing and leader line for extra-articular stabilisation of the canine cruciate-deficient stifle. Vet. Comp. Orthop. Traumatol. **9**, 126–33 (1996)
11. Gruppo CATALOGO BULK 2019 (2021). https://www.gruppodp.com/wp-content/uploads/2019/07/CATALOGO-BULK-2019.pdf. Accessed 29 Nov 2021
12. Goirlena, A., Retolaza, I., Cenitagoya, A., Martinez, F., Riano, S., Landaluze, J. Analysis of Bowden cable transmission performance for orthosis applications. In: 2009 IEEE International Conference On Mechatronics, pp. 1–6 (2009)
13. Clauser, C., McConville, J., Young, J.: Weight, Volume, and Center of Mass of Segments of the Human Body. Antioch College, Yellow Springs (1969)
14. Circuitjournal - Indrek Luuk Logging Arduino Serial Output to CSV/Excel (2022). https://circuitjournal.com/arduino-serial to-spreadsheet. Accessed 09 Feb 2022
15. Timoshenko, S.: Strength of Materials: Part I. Courier Corporation, Chelmsford (1983)

Utilizing Digital Human Modeling to Optimize the Ergonomic Environment of Heavy Earthmoving Equipment Cabins

Nicholas Anton[✉] and Vincent G. Duffy

Purdue University, West Lafayette 47906, USA
anton5@purdue.edu

Abstract. Among heavy earthmoving equipment operators, extended exposure to the cabin environment presents various ergonomic risks. Accordingly, it is necessary to consider methods to model adjustments to cabin environments to reduce ergonomic risks to operators. Digital human modeling approaches, such as the use of RAMSIS, a computer-aided ergonomic design platform, have been used to effectively improve the ergonomics of workers in a variety of disciplines. A bibliometric analysis was performed on relevant literature, which revealed that these techniques have rarely been applied with heavy machine operators. Accordingly, the purpose of the current project was to utilize RAMSIS to model diverse operators in the cabin environment and perform discomfort analyses to identify methods to reduce ergonomic risk. Digital manikins were created based on anthropometric data for a female operator (5th percentage height), and two male operators (50th and 95th percentile height). Several aspects of the cabin environment were adjusted, and several discomfort analyses were performed to identify optimal adjustments that would reduce the ergonomic risk for diverse providers. Modifications made to the seat, steering wheel, armrests/joystick position, touchscreen, and actuating controls led to significantly reduced ergonomic risk and discomfort.

Keywords: Digital human modeling · Ergonomics · Discomfort · Heavy earth moving equipment

1 Introduction and Background

1.1 Ergonomic Risks of Heavy Earthmoving Equipment Operators

Heavy earthmoving equipment (HEME) (e.g., excavators) are vital to major construction projects. Operators of HEME are stationary in the cabin for lengthy periods, so poor environmental design may present significant ergonomic risks. Indeed, previous research involving postural evaluations of HEME operators has shown that operators are required to assume awkward trunk, neck, and shoulder postures while working [1]. Furthermore, researchers have identified HEME cabin ergonomic risk factors such as the height of the seat, which can lead to musculoskeletal disorders [2]. Accordingly, it is necessary to consider methods to optimize HEME cabin environments to reduce ergonomic risks.

© The Author(s), under exclusive license to Springer Nature Switzerland AG 2022
V. G. Duffy (Ed.): HCII 2022, LNCS 13319, pp. 16–31, 2022.
https://doi.org/10.1007/978-3-031-05890-5_2

1.2 Digital Human Modeling and Analysis

The field of ergonomics is becoming increasingly reliant on digital human modeling of workers to optimize the physical ergonomics of workstations given this modality's relative inexpensiveness and enhanced efficiency compared to physical ergonomic modeling methods [3]. Computer-aided design software programs, such as RAMSIS (RAMSIS NextGen Ergonomics, Human Solutions, Kaiserslautern, Germany), can allow engineers to make environmental adjustments to workstations and assess their ergonomic impact on human operators. It is unclear, however, if digital human modeling software would be helpful to reduce ergonomic risks for HEME operators.

1.3 Bibliometric Analysis

To determine the existing literature and trends of ergonomics, digital human modeling, and HEME operators, three bibliometric analysis methods were used.

Vicinitas Engagement Search. Twitter has become an important platform for researchers and laypeople to share their opinions on myriad topics. Vicinitas is an analytics platform that allows researchers to assess the engagement (e.g., tweets, retweets, comments, etc.) of posts made on certain topics. This approach can be used to identify current trends in a field for the past 10 days of the search. To assess current trends in the field of ergonomics, the search term "ergonomics" was used. Results of the search are shown in Fig. 1. Based on the resulting word cloud, it appears that "improved design" and "chair" were among the most popular words in recent tweets about ergonomics. Thus, focusing on design improvements to the excavator seat may be an important consideration.

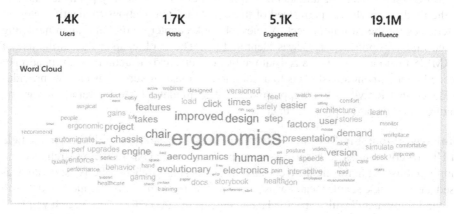

Fig. 1. Vicinitas analytics word cloud from Twitter posts on "ergonomics".

Co-authorship Analysis. To identify the leading authors in the field of digital human modeling, a co-authorship analysis was performed. Using the Scopus database, a search was performed using the keywords "digital human modeling" and "ergonomics". A total of 579 references were identified and exported to VOS Viewer in .CSV format. VOS viewer is a software tool used to visualize bibliometric connections. Using VOS viewer, a co-authorship analysis was performed using the exported Scopus metadata. A threshold of 5 publications was set as the minimum number of publications needed to be included in the co-authorship analysis (Fig. 2).

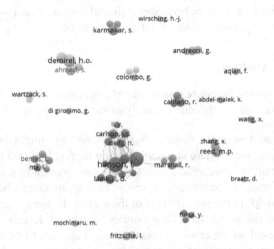

Fig. 2. Co-authorship network visualizing the most published authors on ergonomics and digital human modeling.

Based on this analysis and identification of the most commonly-published authors in the field, a search was performed of these authors' publications to identify relevant references for the current project. A relevant book chapter on digital human modeling based on anthropometric data was identified [4]. The book chapter details the use of RAMSIS to model variously-sized automobile drivers, and the authors' identification of needed environment adjustments to accommodate these drivers. This chapter provides evidence that RAMSIS is an appropriate tool to model HEME operators of varying stature based on anthropometric data.

BibExcel Authorship Review. To determine which researchers are leaders in the field of HEME ergonomics, it was necessary to perform an analysis of the researchers commonly publishing in this field. Accordingly, the Harzing Publish or Perish software was used, and a google scholar search was performed on the terms "Ergonomics" and "Earth Moving Equipment" with a specified date range from 2000–2021. This search yielded a total of 302 papers. These citations were exported in Web of Science format to BibExcel, which is freely available software that allows users to convert literature searches to .CSV Microsoft Excel files. Following extraction of author names and citation count into Microsoft Excel, a pivot chart was created to visualize this data (Fig. 3).

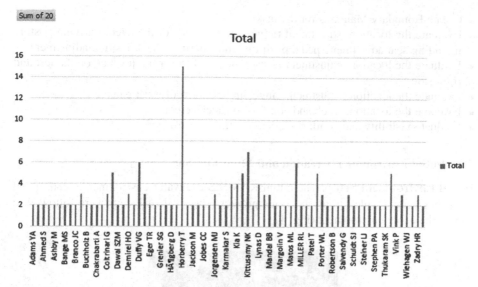

Fig. 3. Pivot chart displaying authors with most citations on ergonomics and digital human modeling.

Following identification of the leading authors in this area, Publish or Perish was again consulted to review the leading authors' publications to determine if relevant insights could be gleaned for this project. A literature review on construction equipment operators' postural stress was identified [5]. The authors of this review found that few studies had attempted to quantify awkward postures among HEME operators. However, those researchers in this area did find that postural stress contributed to the low back pain of operators and lumbar disk herniation. These findings offer further attestation that ergonomic improvements to the HEME cabin environment are needed.

1.4 Problem Statement

Currently, there is a lack of literature on the use of digital human modeling to optimize the HEME cabin environment for human operators of varying statures. Given the ergonomic risks for HEME operators, this project focused on assessing the level of discomfort by diverse operators (i.e., 5th percentile height female, 50th percentile height male, 95th percentile height male), and the adjustment ranges needed for several aspects of the cabin environment to reduce discomfort to an appropriate level for all manikins.

2 Procedure

2.1 Statement of Work

For this project, the following statement of work was requested, which guided the analyses used in this project:

- Create Boundary Manikins for the tasks
- Evaluate the location, adjustment range, and comfort for the overall driving posture including seat adjustment, pedal position, and steering wheel position/adjustment
- Evaluate the location, adjustment range, and comfort for the joystick on the left and right side
- Evaluate the location, adjustment range, and comfort of wrist pads
- Evaluate the location, reach and comfort to touch screen
- Evaluate visibility and comfort while actuating controls.

2.2 Initial Environment Creation and Manipulation

Initial Environment Setup. The initial RAMSIS excavator environment creation and setup has been detailed in my previous project report [6]. All steps were followed to isolate the cabin environment (Fig. 4).

Fig. 4. Isolated excavator cabin environment.

Initial Environment Manipulation. To affix the manikins' hands in the correct locations on the steering wheel, joysticks, touchscreen, and control panel, it was necessary to "group" environment components as needed and create geometry points.

Grouping of Components. For the steering wheel (i.e., base, pedestal, steering wheel), joysticks (i.e., armrests, wrist pads, joysticks), touchscreen (i.e., housing and screen), and controls (i.e., control buttons and jousting), all components of each respective "group" were combined. While holding down the "Ctrl" key, all components of each group were selected using the left mouse button. Then, the right mouse button was used, then the function "Group" was selected.

Placement of Geometry Points. To affix the manikins' hands to positions on the steering wheel at the "9-o'clock" and "3-o'clock" positions and on the control buttons, it was necessary to add geometry points in these positions on the steering wheel. Accordingly, "Geometry" was selected from the top of the software's menu, and "Point" was selected. Then, the drop-down menu was selected and the option "Create on Object" was selected. Finally, using the left mouse button, points were added to the steering wheel as appropriate.

Creation of Geometry Kinematics. The final element of initial environment manipulation involved the creation of object kinematics to be able to manipulate the direction of elements. First, the user selects "Geometry", then "Object Kinematics". Once on this screen, the user selects the starting point (i.e., the surface of the object to be moved) using the left mouse button, then the direction of movement (i.e., x-, y-, or z-axis), and finally the minimum and maximum amount of movement for the object. For the steering wheel, the steering wheel and pedestal were hidden, and two geometry points were added on opposite sides of the top of the base. Then, a point was added in between the two created points to serve as a joint for the steering wheel adjustments (Fig. 5).

Fig. 5. Joint created at top of steering wheel base.

A degree of freedom was added to this joint to angle the steering wheel -30° (i.e., upward away from the driver) and 30° (i.e., towards the driver). The steering wheel and pedestal were then added back to the scene, and a degree of freedom was added to extend the steering wheel to extend it towards the driver (i.e., at a 45° angle). For the operator's seat, armrests, and touchscreen in the positive x- and z-axes (i.e., positive and negative), and controls in the negative x-axis.

2.3 Boundary Manikin Creation

To create manikins for the present project, NextGen Body Builder was selected, and the "Define Typology" button was selected from the "Anthropometry" menu. The "Germany 2004" anthropometry database was used for the creation of both male and female manikins. Then, under the anthropometry tab, "Control Measurements" was selected to define the unique typology for each manikin. For the first manikin, a male, the age group was defined as 18–70, the reference year was defined as 2034, and the body height, waist circumference, and sitting height were defined by values. Since I wanted the first manikin to represent a 95th percentile male in height, I set the percentile of body height to 95, waist circumference to 35, and sitting height to 44.87. I repeated this process to create a second typology to represent a 50th percentile male in height, so I set the percentile of body height to 50, waist circumference to 50, and sitting height to 50. Finally, I created a third typology to represent a 5th percentile female in height, so I set the percentile of body height to 5, waist circumference to 46.75, and sitting height to 43.74.

Following the creation of these body typologies, a single role of "operator" was created by selecting the item "Role Definition", which indicates what role is being defined, and indicates the prepositioning point is "PHPT".

2.4 Evaluate the Location, Adjustment Range, and Comfort for the Overall Driving Posture Including Seat Adjustment, Pedal Position, and Steering Wheel Position/Adjustment

Initial Positioning. All manikins were individually positioned in the seat using the following protocol. The manikins were positioned in the seat by creating "Target" restrictions which position certain skin points of the manikin in specific points in the environment. The following target restrictions were created:

– H-point (the center of the manikin's buttocks) was affixed to the surface of the seat
– Right heel was affixed on the surface of the floor behind the pedals
– Left heel was affixed on the surface of the floor behind the pedals
– Right ball offset was affixed in the centerline of the right pedal
– Left ball offset was affixed in the centerline of the left pedal
– The points between the index and thumb were placed on geometry points on the steering wheel at 3 and 9-o' clock.

Following initial positioning, a "Pelvis Rotation" restriction was defined to prevent the manikin from rotating their trunks in the seat. Finally, directional restrictions for line-of-vision were imposed to enable the manikins to focus their eyes forward in a natural plane (Fig. 6).

Fig. 6. Initial positioning of all manikins.

Modifications. Following an iterative process of making modifications and assessing the impact of those changes on the manikins' comfort for various elements of the body, unique modifications were made to the seat and steering wheel for each manikin. All final modifications are specified for each manikin below (Fig. 7).

Fig. 7. From left to right, final steering wheel position for 5th percentile female, 50th percentile male, and 95th percentile male.

5th Percentile Female. Seat modifications for the 5th percentile female included lowering the seat in the negative z-axis by 50 mm (mm). Steering wheel modifications included tilting the steering wheel forward by 20° and extending the wheel to the operator by 100 mm.

50th Percentile Male. Seat modifications for the 50th percentile male included raising the seat in the positive z-axis by 50 mm. Steering wheel modifications included tilting the steering wheel forward by 9° and extending the wheel to the operator by 110 mm.

95th Percentile Male. Seat modifications for the 95th percentile male include raising the seat in the positive z-axis by 100 mm and moving the seat backward (i.e., in the positive x-axis). Modifications to the steering wheel include tilting the steering wheel forward by 12° and extending towards the operator by 185 mm.

Analysis. In the current project, discomfort analyses were performed to determine the impact of changes to the cabin environment on operators' comfort. The RAMSIS ergonomics manual defines the discomfort analysis as the assessment of manikins' discomfort in various body elements and the body as a whole, and any value above 3.5 is considered uncomfortable [7]. A baseline discomfort analysis was performed for each manikin in the origin position. A second discomfort analysis was performed for each manikin at the final modified position for comparison.

Results. The results of the discomfort analyses are presented in Table 1. At the original position, all manikins experienced discomfort in several body elements. Specifically, the 5th percentile female experienced discomfort in the neck, legs, and overall. The 50th and 95th percentile males experienced discomfort in the neck, shoulders, legs, and overall. After adjustments were made, no manikins experienced discomfort in anybody elements. However, all manikins still experienced discomfort overall, but the reductions in discomfort are still appreciable.

The range of modifications to the seat was − 50 mm–100 mm in the z-axis and 0 mm–100 mm on the x-axis. The range of modifications to the steering wheel includes tilting the wheel down toward the operator from 9–20° and moving toward the operator from 100–185 mm.

Table 1. Differences in discomfort from baseline to post-modifications to the steering wheel and seat.

Body element	5th% female		50th% male		95th% male	
	Origin	Modified	Origin	Modified	Origin	Modified
Neck	4.22*	3.1	4.7*	3.4	4.9*	3.4
Shoulders	3.12	2.5	4.5*	2.8	4.9*	2.8
Back	2.7	2.2	3.4	2.7	3.45	2.6
Buttocks	2.4	1.7	2.8	2.1	3.3	2
Left leg	3.6*	2.4	4.6*	3.1	5.2*	3
Right leg	3.6*	2.4	4.5*	3.1	5.2*	2.9
Left arm	3.45	2.6	3.3	2.8	3.3	2.9
Right arm	3.4	2.5	3.45	2.8	3.4	2.8
Discomfort feeling	5.51*	4.3*	6.5*	4.9*	7*	4.8*

*Indicates a value is above 3.5 and is uncomfortable.

Design Changes. Based on this data, I believe it is necessary to make the seat adjustable to move back up to 100 mm and have the ability to depress downward up to 50 mm and raise to 100 mm. The steering wheel should be made telescopic to allow egress and ingress into and out of the cabin by keeping the steering wheel at its original position and then moving it toward the operator from 100–185 mm. Furthermore, the steering wheel should have the ability to tilt downward to the operator from 9–20°.

2.5 Evaluate the Location, Adjustment Range, and Comfort for Joystick on the Left and Right Side

Initial Positioning. With the manikin in the previously-discussed initial position (see Sect. 2.4), the manikin's hands were placed on the joysticks in points just below the top of the joystick (Fig. 8).

Fig. 8. Operator with hands affixed to joysticks.

Modifications. Following an iterative process of making modifications and assessing the impact of those changes on the manikins' comfort for various elements of the body, unique modifications were made to the armrests for each manikin.

5ᵗʰ Percentile Female. For the 5ᵗʰ percentile female, the armrests were moved up in the z-axis by 200 mm and backward in the x-axis by 150 mm.

50ᵗʰ Percentile Male. For the 50ᵗʰ percentile male, the armrests were moved up in the z-axis by 200 mm and backward in the x-axis by 150 mm.

95ᵗʰ Percentile Male. For the 95ᵗʰ percentile male, the armrests were moved up in the z-axis by 175 mm and backward in the x-axis by 135 mm.

Analysis. A baseline discomfort analysis was performed for each manikin in the origin position. A second discomfort analysis was performed for each manikin at the final modified position for comparison.

Results. The results of the armrest discomfort analyses are presented in Table 2. At the original position, all manikins experienced discomfort in several body elements. The 5ᵗʰ percent female experienced discomfort in the neck, legs, and overall, and the 50ᵗʰ and 95ᵗʰ percentile males experienced discomfort in the neck, shoulders, legs, and overall. All manikins experienced reductions in discomfort in all body elements and overall (i.e., to the point of being unremarkable aside from overall discomfort).

Table 2. Differences in discomfort from baseline to post-modifications to the armrests.

Body element	5ᵗʰ% female		50ᵗʰ% male		95ᵗʰ% male	
	Origin	Modified	Origin	Modified	Origin	Modified
Neck	4.45*	3	4.7*	3	4.7*	3.1
Shoulders	3.32	2.4	4.1*	2.7	4.6*	3
Back	3.8*	2.3	3.8*	3	4.2*	3.2
Buttocks	2.9	1.8	3.4	2.4	3.4	2.2
Left leg	3.8*	2.3	4.1*	3	5.2*	4.4*
Right leg	3.7*	2.3	4*	3	5.2*	4.3*
Left arm	3.4	2.9	3.6*	2.6	3.8*	2.4
Right arm	4*	2.1	3.6*	2.6	3.8*	2.4
Discomfort feeling	6.4*	4.2*	6.9*	5*	7.3*	5.1*

*-Indicates a value is above 3.5 and is uncomfortable.

The range of modifications to the armrests was 175–200 mm on the z-axis and 135–150 mm on the x-axis.

Design Changes. Based on this data, I recommend making the armrests adjustable in the z- and x-axes, by 25 and 15 mm, respectively, and moving them upwards in the z-axis by 175 mm and backward in the x-axis by 135 mm.

2.6 Evaluate the Location, Adjustment Range, and Comfort of Wrist Pads

Initial Positioning. With the manikin in the previously-discussed position (see Sect. 2.5) and the armrests positioned accordingly, the wrist pads were manipulated to determine the optimal position just behind the wrist.

Modifications. Following manipulation of the wrist pads only (i.e., by grouping them, and establishing degrees of freedom in the z- and x-axes), the optimal position for each manikin was determined.

5th Percentile Female. For the 5th percentile female, the wrist pads were moved down in the negative z-axis by 30 mm, and forwards in the negative x-axis by 50 mm.

50th Percentile Male. For the 50th percentile male, the armrests were moved down in the negative z-axis by 15 mm, and forwards in the negative x-axis by 60 mm.

95th Percentile Male. For the 95th percentile male, the armrests were moved down in the z-axis by 10 mm, and forwards in the x-axis by 50 mm.

Design Changes. Based on this data, I recommend making the wrist pads adjustable in the z- and x-axes, by at least 20 and 10 mm, respectively, and moving them downwards in the negative z-axis by 10 mm and forwards in the negative x-axis by 50 mm.

2.7 Evaluate the Location, Reach and Comfort to Touch Screen

Initial Positioning. With the manikin in the previously-discussed initial position (see Sect. 2.4), the manikin's right index finger and line of vision were placed on the center of the touch screen (Fig. 9).

Fig. 9. Position of index and line of vision on the touchscreen.

Modifications. Following an iterative process of making modifications and assessing the impact of those changes on the manikins' comfort for various elements of the body, unique modifications were made to the touchscreen for all manikins. Unlike the previous modifications, a single modification was made to the touchscreen that appropriately reduced discomfort for all manikins. The touchscreen was raised in the z-axis by 200 mm and was moved toward the operator in the x-axis by 210 mm.

Analyses. In addition to the discomfort analysis, a reach analysis was performed for the manikins' right arms, which provides a visual indicator of what aspects of the environment fall within a manikin's reach (Fig. 10) [7].

Fig. 10. Reach analysis of what environmental elements are within the manikin's reach.

Results. The results of the touchscreen discomfort analyses are presented in Table 3. The modifications to the touchscreen location led to remarkable reductions in discomfort for all manikins. The 95th percentile male did retain some neck discomfort, but this was borderline uncomfortable given the threshold for this value.

Table 3. Differences in discomfort from pre- to post-modifications to the touchscreen.

Body element	5th% female		50th% male		95th% male	
	Origin	Modified	Origin	Modified	Origin	Modified
Neck	4*	3.1	4.84*	3.1	4*	3.5*
Shoulders	4.4*	2.8	4.9*	2.8	4.6*	3.2
Back	2.8	2.1	3.5*	2.1	2.5	2.2
Buttocks	3.2	1.3	3.5*	1.4	2.6	1.9
Left leg	3.4	2.6	4.9*	2.8	3.3	2.8
Right leg	3.1	2.4	4.4*	2.7	3	2.6
Left arm	2.9	2.2	3.6*	1.9	2	1.8
Right arm	3.5*	2.2	3.5*	2.5	3.2	3
Discomfort feeling	5.8*	4*	6.8*	4*	5.4*	4.5*

*-Indicates a value is above 3.5 and is uncomfortable.

Regarding the reach analysis, the touch screen was partially within reach at its origin but fell within reach for all manikins following the modifications.

Design Changes. Based on this data, I recommend a fixed position of the touchscreen by increasing it in the z-axis by 200 mm and moving it in the x-axis by 210 mm towards the operator.

2.8   Evaluate Visibility and Comfort While Actuating Controls

Initial Positioning. With the manikin in the previously-discussed initial position (see Sect. 2.4), the manikin's right index finger and line of vision were placed on a point on the actuating controls (Fig. 11).

Fig. 11. Position of index and line of vision on actuating controls.

Modifications. Through several modifications to the actuating controls' location and assessing the impact of those changes on the manikins' comfort for various elements of the body, unique modifications were made to the actuating controls for all manikins. Again, a single modification was made to the actuating controls that appropriately reduced discomfort for all manikins. The controls were moved in the negative x-axis by 150 mm.

Analyses. A discomfort analysis was performed before and following the modifications. Additionally, an analysis of operators' visual field was conducted by selecting the "Analysis" tab on the menu, then selecting "Vision", and finally "Limits of Visual Field". The vision analysis provides visual insights into the limits of sharp ($\pm2.5°$), optimum ($\pm15°$), and maximum ($\pm50°$) sight areas [7]. The purpose of the visual field analysis was to determine whether or not the manikins were able to maintain the touch screen and the front window of the excavator within their optimal and/or maximum visual fields of vision.

Results. The results of the actuating controls discomfort analyses are presented in Table 4. The modifications to the actuating controls' location led to reductions in discomfort for all manikins, yet there was still discomfort in the male operators' legs. However, given the limited amount of time likely needed to operate the actuating controls, this discomfort is likely minimal.

Table 4. Differences in discomfort from pre- to post-modifications to the controls.

Body element	5th% female		50th% male		95th% male	
	Origin	Modified	Origin	Modified	Origin	Modified
Neck	3.6	3.1	4.6*	3.4	4.1*	3.2
Shoulders	2.2	2	2.5	2.2	4.6*	2
Back	3.2	2.9	4*	3.48	3.7*	3.2
Buttocks	1.5	1.7	2.3	1.9	2.1	1.6
Left leg	2.9	2.9	4.4*	3.92*	4*	3.6*
Right leg	3.1	2.8	4.1*	3.7*	3.7*	3.3
Left arm	2.9	2.8	2.9	2.3	2.6	2.1
Right arm	1.6	2.1	4*	3.3	3.9*	3.2
Discomfort feeling	4.6*	4.6*	6.22*	5.3*	5.7*	4.9*

*-Indicates a value is above 3.5 and is uncomfortable.

In regards to the visual field analysis, all manikins were unable to maintain the touchscreen in the optimal field of vision and the front of the excavator in the maximum field of vision when focusing on the actuating controls in their original position (Fig. 12). However, after modifications were made to the actuating controls' location, all manikins were able to maintain the touchscreen in their optimal field of vision and increased their vision of the front of the excavator.

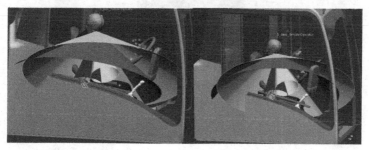

Fig. 12. The difference in optimal (red) and maximum (blue) visual fields of 5th percentage female with controls at original (left) and final positions.

Design Changes. Based on this data, I recommend a fixed position of the actuating controls by moving them in the negative x-axis by 150 mm.

3   Discussion

3.1   Impact of Prior Experience on Assignment Completion

Previously, I have been a teaching assistant in an undergraduate-level ergonomics course, and I taught students to use a digital modeling program to assess the postural impact of various lifts on joints and the workers' spine. Despite the differences between this program and RAMSIS, this experience helped me learn to navigate RAMSIS efficiently. This experience also helped me understand that I need to be mindful of realism when modeling manikins using digital modeling software, as an unrealistic manikin position will impact my ability to provide meaningful suggestions for ergonomic improvements.

3.2   Challenge Overcome During Assignment

One issue I faced during this assignment was making realistic modifications to the environment based on the joint capacity analysis. When using this analysis tool to modify aspects of the environment, I frequently encountered situations where the manikins' backs would be forced through the seatback to attain a more comfortable posture (Fig. 13). Since this approach is unrealistic and limits my ability to meaningfully interpret the data, I elected to utilize the discomfort analysis for the work requested in Andre's statement of work, as I could reliably model realistic manikin positions and make appropriate suggestions for modifications. While not ideal, I felt this was the best way to proceed with this project given the limitations I faced.

Fig. 13. Unrealistic manikin position using joint capacity analysis to modify the environment.

3.3   Future Considerations for RAMSIS Users

Future users of RAMSIS should be provided a comprehensive list of issues faced when using the software (e.g., unrealistic manikin positioning like the problem above), and potential solutions to the problem. Following the completion of an initial demonstration, this information would be helpful to have is addition to a question and answer session with a RAMSIS representative, as users could troubleshoot any unresolved issues with their assistance. Furthermore, further discussion is needed on the various analyses ran, and how to properly interpret the data. Specifically, the visual field analysis was not discussed during the demonstrations for the current study, so my interpretation of this information may be skewed from its intended application.

4 Future Work

4.1 Limitations of RAMSIS

Currently, RAMSIS does not allow for the assessment of machine vibration on operators. For excavator operators, this is an important consideration, as research has shown that vibrations are a major source of ergonomic risk to operators [5]. Perhaps RAMSIS could assess the estimated vibrations experienced by the operator, and display how modifications to the materials surrounding the engine or cabin or modifications to the seat pedestal structure could impact vibrations felt by the operators.

References

1. Kittusamy, N.K.: Assessment of ergonomic risk factors among operators of heavy earthmoving machinery. In: ASSE Professional Development Conference and Exposition. OnePetro (2003)
2. Pałęga, M., Rydz, D.: Work safety and ergonomics at the workplace an excavator operator. Trans. Motauto World 3(1), 25–29 (2018)
3. Duffy, V.: Human digital modeling in design. In: Salvendy, G. (ed.) Handbook of Human Factors and Ergonomics, pp. 1016–1030. John Wiley & Sons, Hoboken (2012)
4. Hanson, L., Högberg, D.: Use of anthropometric measures and digital human modeling tools for product and workplace design. In: Handbook of Anthropometry, pp. 3015–3034. Springer, New York, NY (2012)
5. Kittusamy, N.K, Buchholz, B.: Whole-body vibration and postural stress among operators of construction equipment: a literature review. J. Saf. Res. 35(3), 255–261 (2004)
6. Anton, N.: Reducing Ergonomic Risk and Discomfort of Excavator Operators Using RAMSIS. IE 578 Project 1 Report (2021)
7. RAMSIS NextGen 1.8 Ergonoics User Guide, pp. 1–243. Human Solutions, Germany (2021)

An Early Design Method to Quantify Vision Obstruction: Formula One (F1) Halo Case Study

H. Onan Demirel[✉], Alex Jennings, and Sriram Srinivasan

Oregon State University, Corvallis, OR 97331, USA
{onan.demirel,jenninal,srinivsr}@oregonstate.edu

Abstract. This paper introduces a proactive ergonomics methodology to quantify vision obstruction by integrating computer-aided design (CAD), digital human modeling (DHM), and image processing. The "rough and rapid" approach presented in this study uses an image analysis macro to measure forward field of view (FoV) obstruction based on the snapshots collected from DHM software. The proof-of-concept design study presented in this research investigates the quantification of the obstruction caused by halo-type cockpit safety and protection equipment introduced into Formula 1 (F1) race cars in 2018. Halo is a curved bar that surrounds the driver's head over the cockpit opening and offers additional protection to drivers. However, the halo's introduction has raised obstruction-related concerns due to its vertical and horizontal bars (pillar-like elements) sitting in front of the cockpit. In this case study, a low-fidelity digital F1 race car model, including halo safety equipment, was constructed along with the manikins representing generic F1 drivers with different anthropometric characteristics. A low-fidelity DHM simulation setup, consisting of the F1 vehicle and simplified race track model, was used to collect forward FoV vision snapshots of drivers. The snapshots were then sent to an image processing software to quantify the area obscured by the halo. Overall, the results show how the methodology can supply designers with quantitative data to gain more insight into visibility concerns regarding obstruction caused by body frame and cockpit components early in preliminary design. This approach discussed in this study is particularly noteworthy during the preliminary design, where designers demand robust concept evaluation tools to evaluate concepts variants before building time-consuming and costly physical mockups.

Keywords: Digital human modeling · Human factors engineering · Ergonomics · Vehicle design · Vision obstruction · Safety engineering

1 Introduction

Considering human product interactions early and often throughout the engineering design process improves product quality and facilitates user safety [1,2].

© The Author(s), under exclusive license to Springer Nature Switzerland AG 2022
V. G. Duffy (Ed.): HCII 2022, LNCS 13319, pp. 32–44, 2022.
https://doi.org/10.1007/978-3-031-05890-5_3

However, design tasks involving human factors engineering (HFE) early in design are challenging since many design attributes related to human factors are vague and require testing, re-testing, and human participant studies [3]. Typically, these studies are carried out on full-scale physical mockups, which are time-consuming to conduct experiments and require significant financial investments [4,5]. Although several digital tools and techniques have been proposed to improve early design human factors interventions, designers still lack computational tools to quantify human factors requirements during preliminary design. For example, drivers' forward field of view (FoV) is one of the many important topics requiring better early design computational HFE tools to assess human performance concerns and the feasibility of the design variants.

It is vital to provide a clear and unobstructed forward FoV to drivers for safe driving. As driving is a highly visual activity, the dashboard and body frame of a vehicle should not block or occlude the driver's vision [6,7]. Any obstruction within the drivers' forward FoV increases the possibility of drivers not seeing other vehicles, pedestrians, or traffic signs [8]. Thus, obstructed FoV negatively affects traffic safety and well-being and leads to fatal accidents or costly mishaps [9]. Understanding obscuration-related needs and discovering potential issues early in design can minimize the risk of injuries or fatalities and reduce the total number of design iterations and human participant experiments.

Exploring how the vehicle packaging causes obstruction requires evaluating drivers' FoV in different driving conditions, ideally during the preliminary design phase. Most design methodologies and practices applied to vision obstruction problems require significant prototyping and human-subject experiments. Thus, they are often conducted towards the embodiment and detail design phases, where significant design specifications and decisions are already committed. This approach is prone to excess time and cost once problems about the proposed design are encountered. Hence, retrofitting or iterating on physical prototypes becomes a hurdle [4]. In contrast to the above approach, this study proposes a computational approach based on digital human modeling (DHM) research. Unlike other late design approaches requiring extensive empirical studies, we propose that DHM linked to an image processing macro can supply a "rough and rapid" solution to quantify drivers' obstruction early in the design.

This paper presents a proof-of-concept design case study to demonstrate how approach proposed in this research can assist designers in quantifying vision obstruction. The case study investigates the quantification of the forward FoV obstruction caused by halo-type cockpit safety and protection equipment—a curved bar that surrounds the driver's head over the cockpit opening—introduced into Formula One (F1) race cars in 2018. Halo equipment provides an additional layer of protection by preventing drivers from getting head and neck trauma from flying debris or larger projectiles. However, the halo's central vertical pillar joint, which sits in front of the driver's FoV, proposes obstruction-related questions. The quantification methodology presented in this study uses an image analysis macro to measure forward FoV obstruction based on the snapshots collected from DHM software. Overall, this study demonstrates how the framework can supply designers with early quantitative data to gain more insight into visibility concerns regarding obstruction caused by vehicle structures and components.

2   Literature Review

2.1   Halo Safety Equipment and Concerns About Visibility

Occupant safety is perhaps the highest priority in automotive design today, and vehicles are designed to have essential safety standards to protect the driver and occupants [7]. Likewise, racing vehicles abide by much stricter regulations to accommodate safety. For example, sudden accelerations/deceleration, extreme driver postures, and physiological stressors associated with very high-speed F1 racing demand sophisticated driver protection systems, including but not limited to specialized carbon fiber survival cells, roll structures, and head and neck support (HANS) equipment. As the driver's head and neck pose a primary concern in an open canopy racing, the Fédération Internationale de l'Automobile (FIA)—the governing body for F1—adopted the halo safety equipment in 2018. The primary objective was to reduce the injuries resulting from severe head trauma after cranial impacts with foreign objects [10]. Halo safety equipment is a lightweight truss member made of high-strength titanium composed of thin bars and sits over the open cockpit (See Fig. 1. It protects the driver against significant risks of injuries due to vehicle-to-vehicle contact, vehicle-to-environment contact, and external object hit [11].

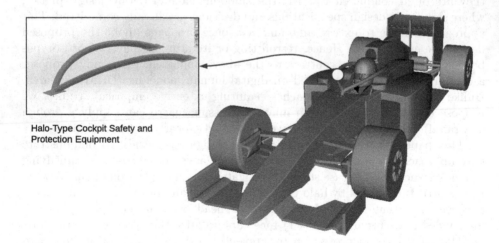

Halo-Type Cockpit Safety and
Protection Equipment

Fig. 1. The figure illustrates a concept halo-type cockpit safety equipment that sits over the open cockpit and provides additional protection to drivers.

Until the introduction of halo safety equipment, F1 race cars did not include a cockpit canopy that could protect the driver from a foreign object impact. The lack of additional safety barriers around the open cockpit often resulted in severe driver injuries and fatalities [12]. With the introduction of the halo equipment, an additional layer of safety has been implemented to protect drivers. However, manufacturers and drivers expressed concerns about whether the halo equipment affects drivers' safety and performance due to obscuration zones caused by the truss design. The vision obstruction concern was mostly concentrated around the central vertical pillar. Halo safety equipment is attached to the frame of the F1 car at three points, and the two side joints of the curved bar are located at a height outside the drivers' peripheral vision. The central vertical pillar is designed very thin; thus, the assumption is that it vanishes from sight when drivers look straight ahead. Before the official introduction, drivers and manufacturers were doubtful whether the vertical pillar in front of the driver could block a portion of the driver's sight by causing a vision obstruction or blind spot [13].

Before adopting the final halo design specifications and unraveling the concerns about racing performance, manufacturers and regulators conducted exhaustive research and field tests, which included F1 drivers to evaluate concept halo designs and check safety-related measures [14]. These studies suggested no immediate danger or concern about halo equipment causing significant occlusion that adversely affects driver safety and performance. Although some drivers find halo equipment intrusive and discomforting, the common consensus is that it does not cause a significant problem regarding drivers' forward FoV. However, drivers expressed minor concerns about the overhead visibility regarding seeing pit lights and other reference points. Overall, it is concluded that halo equipment only restricts a minimal area of monocular vision [11].

2.2 Proactive Ergonomics via Designing with Digital Humans

Prior studies suggest that driver's vision should be considered early and often during the design process to improve driver safety and overall driving comfort and performance. Significant time and resources are dedicated to identifying the body structures and fixtures to provide a clear FoV to drivers [7,15,16]. Besides, accessories and safety equipment, such as helmets, can also contribute to loss in forward FoV by reducing the driver's peripheral vision, around $18\,°C$ ($\pm 5\,°C$) while driving [17]. Therefore, tackling obstruction-related issues should start with employing a holistic approach early in occupant packaging planning to minimize elements blocking drivers' vision. Typically, transportation design studies employ long laboratory and field tests, where human subjects assess the obstruction issues on physical mockups and functional prototypes. This reactive approach enables designers to retrofit vehicles once obstruction issues are identified on physical mockups [1,5]. One caveat about this practice is that it increases the overall time and cost spent on product development. Studies show that computational design tools allow designers to evaluate obstruction issues early and often based on digital mockups. This proactive approach can bring potential savings by mitigating costly late-stage design changes associated with retrofitting and redesigning [4,18]. One of the computational tools used in proactive ergonomics arsenal, DHM, can help design teams identify potential obstruction issues via creating "what-if" scenarios [19,20].

Digital human modeling is a computational method for visualizing and simulating the human body based on mathematical constraints [21]. It incorporates anthropometric databases, human motion simulation, and posture prediction modules to create manikins and position them in digital or virtual environments to assess ergonomics. The empirically-validated ergonomics analyses toolkits allow designers to evaluate the risk of injury or comfort based on physiological and musculoskeletal methods such as metabolic energy expenditure, lower back, and fatigue. Overall, DHM facilitates the prediction of safety and comfort early in design by executing ergonomics analysis based on CAD models [22].

Digital human modeling software packages include computational analysis modules to help designers gain insight into obstruction-related safety concerns through simulating driver monocular and binocular views, peripheral coverage zones, and FoV. For example, a vehicle design study by Gilad and Byran (2015) presented a quantitative method to measure the FoV of a tractor driver using Siemens Jack software. The results showed that the percent available FoV ranged from 30 to 50% due to differences in tractor cabin and chassis design [23]. The suggested method enabled designers to rank concept variants based on FoV results. Another study investigated how postural preferences and manikin size affect the line-of-sight of mining vehicle drivers by exploring the percent area visible using a forward visibility plane in DHM software. The study suggested that driver posture and manikin size significantly affect the percent visual ground area obscured, with the smallest manikin (1st percentile) only able to see 10% visual area and the largest manikin (99th percentile) able to see 33% of the considered visual area [24].

3   Methodology

This research proposes an early design approach to quantify obstruction caused by halo safety equipment. The proposed methodology employs a *rough and quick* computational approach by integrating computer-aided design (CAD), digital human modeling (DHM), and image processing tools. The study aims to assess vision obstruction resulting from halo safety equipment early in design—before committing to physical prototyping and field tests. A low-fidelity digital mockup of a typical F1 race car, including halo safety equipment and driver's helmet, was constructed as a light CAD model using surface and solid modeling techniques. Manikins representing F1 drivers with different anthropometric characteristics were created to illustrate generic F1 drivers. The vehicle setup was used to capture binocular vision snapshots of manikins through the eye-view module within Siemens Jack. The snapshots were sent to ImageJ, an image processing software, to quantify the area obscured by the frame of the F1 race car (e.g., cockpit) and safety equipment (e.g., helmet and halo). The overall data flow is illustrated in Fig. 2.

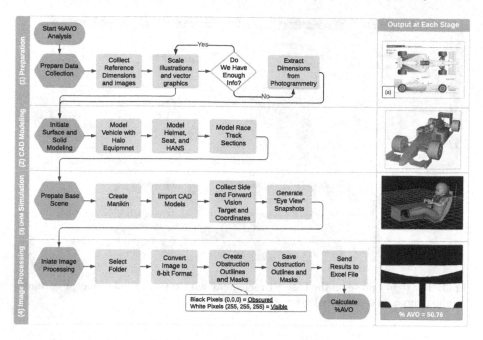

Fig. 2. The data flow diagram illustrates the stages of the methodology, including (1) Preparation: gathering data [25], (2) CAD Modeling: developing digital mockups, (3) DMH Simulations: creating manikins, scenarios, and capturing eye-view snapshots, and (4) Image Processing: quantifying obstruction zones.

4   Case Study

4.1   Simulation Setup - Base Vehicle and Halo Models

A base F1 race car digital mockup was modeled based on information gathered from FIA F1 technical regulations and approximate illustrations [25]. This approach also involved extracting photogrammetric measurements from representative photos when necessary. It is also important to note that intricate aerodynamics details such as diffusers, deflectors, wingtips, and brake ducts were not included in CAD modeling purposefully. Since this study focused on vision obstruction-related research inquires, aerodynamics and structures related elements of the vehicle design were omitted during CAD modeling purposefully. Overall, the CAD modeling used in this study generated a rough representation of the base vehicle and halo models to establish quick and dirty modeling and analysis, which better suits the preliminary design. Along with the concept halo variants, three halo bar cross-sections were used with a circular, 0.9 major to minor axis ratio ellipse, and a more exaggerated 0.7 minor to major axis ratio ellipse. Figure 3 shows the base F1 car that was used throughout this study with halo concepts and cross-sections.

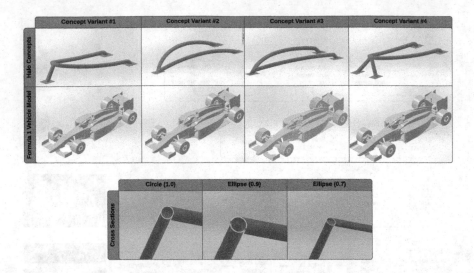

Fig. 3. The figure presents the base F1 racing car with different halo concept variants, including three cross-sectional geometries.

4.2 Simulation Setup - Generic Manikins and Safety Equipment

This study used three different manikins representing small-extreme (166 cm, 59 kg), average (177 cm, 66 kg), and large-extreme (186 cm, 66 kg) anthropometric populations based on the German anthropometric database. Each digital manikin was positioned within the cockpit accordingly based on the FIA technical regulations [25]. We used the suggested cockpit entry and cross-section templates as reference plans for cockpit packaging. First, we overlayed the plans as 2D sketches and used representative coordinate points to place the DHM manikin within the cockpit. Then, the driver posture was adjusted using the human control panel, where we manipulated each body joint separately based on the reference points illustrated on the templates. When positioning manikins, Siemens Jack's collision detection utility was used to detect whether manikin causes interference with the CAD models, including the seat, survival cell, helmet, and HANS device (See Fig. 4).

4.3 Simulation Setup - Racing Scenarios

Two scenarios representing typical driving settings from F1 racing were modeled: (1) driving straight and (2) taking a left turn. Each scenario demanded manikins take a specific gaze direction depending on the driving tasks executed (see Fig. 5). For example, the first scenario illustrates that the driver is on a long straight section of the race track, looking "forward"—both eyes are targeted at an object or a reference point at the "center" of the race track. The second scenario considers the driver taking a high-speed left turn, looking to the "side"—both eyes are targeted on an object or a reference point located at

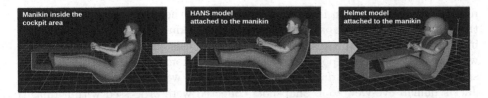

Fig. 4. The cockpit setup used in this study includes DHM manikins, HANS equipment, and a racing helmet.

the "left" side of the race track. The track models were constructed in CAD and used as visual references in Siemens Jack when setting up the scenes and collecting eye-view (both eyes) snapshots.

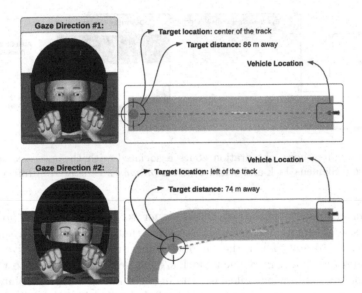

Fig. 5. The image represents the manikin's postural change based on two scenario setups: Gaze Direction #1 and Gaze Direction #2

5 Results

This study consisted of 72 unique vision obstruction simulations, including four halo variants, three pillar cross-sections, two scenarios, and three manikins. An additional six simulations that incorporated three manikins and two scenarios with a blank F1 car were also added to the simulation. These scenes represented the control group where the F1 race car did not include the halo safety equipment. The base F1 car model with halo variants, helmet, and HANS device models were rooted upon import and anchored to the center or global origin of the Siemens Jack design space. All model and manikin coordinates were recorded in a Microsoft Excel spreadsheet to check the consistency of the manikins and working model reference points throughout simulation creation. After setting the simulation scenes, vision data regarding driver FoV were collected using Siemens Jack's human eye-view tool. Snapshots collected were processed within ImageJ software via a macro that was created for automating vision analysis calculations. Figure 6 shows a sample set of results for Gaze Direction #1 for average manikin scenarios considering the halo design with the circular cross-section geometry. In ImageJ macro, the outline geometry was used for tracing the obscuration area perimeter. Further, the mask was implemented as a visual confirmation means to illustrate areas blocked by the halo structure. Later, the mask was used for quantifying the percent obstruction area via the ImageJ macro.

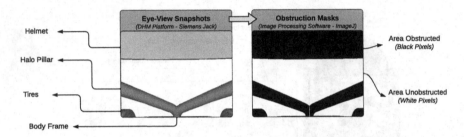

Fig. 6. The figure shows obscuration zones associated with the *eye-view snapshots* collected from Siemens Jack and vision *obstruction masks* generated in ImageJ.

The ImageJ macro prompted the designer to determine which folders to access to save Siemens Jack snapshots. After that, first, all vision snapshots were converted to 8bit. Then, the car model and driver manikin (driver's FoV) were set absolute black in Siemens Jack's color setting to eliminate the need for thresholding calibration. Likewise, the background was kept absolute white. Therefore, F1 car models, the manikin, and the helmet's color value were set to (0,0,0—black) and the background to (255,255,255—white) in Jack to avoid thresholding calibration. This way, all black pixels in the snapshot image represented "obstruction zones" while white pixels represented "visible" areas. In this macro, the percent area visual obscuration (AVO) was quantified by the following equation:

$$\text{Percent Area Visual Obscuration (\% AVO)} = \frac{\text{Obscured Pixels}}{\text{Total Pixels}} \times 100 \quad (1)$$

The preliminary findings showed that the proposed methodology enables designers to assess the performance of the concept halo variants based on the % AVO approach. For example, the proof-of-concept study illustrated in Fig. 7 presents how designers can generate rough and rapid assessments to compare vision obstruction with and without the presence of halo equipment. With the addition of halo concept variant #3, the % AVO increased from % 34.5 to % 45.4 due to halo bars blocking additional areas on the driver's forward FoV. Furthermore, ImageJ macro also allows designers to bring automation when assessing obstruction zones. For example, after collecting eye-view snapshots from Siemens Jack in batches, ImageJ macro supplied automated image processing capabilities where outputs can be directly imported in Microsoft Excel. Figure 8 presents preliminary results where Gaze Direction #2 yielded a higher % AVO for halo variant compared to Gaze Direction #1.

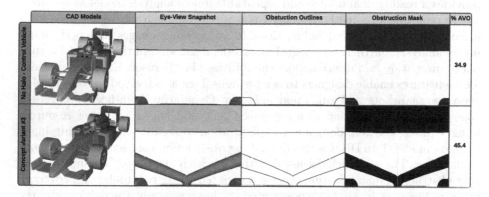

Fig. 7. With the introduction of halo-type safety equipment, the % AVO jumped from % 34.5 to % 45.4 due to bars blocking areas on the driver's forward FoV.

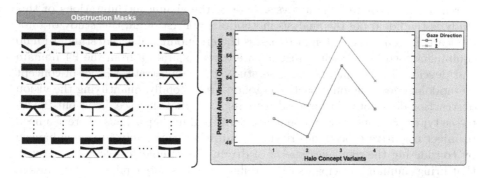

Fig. 8. The figure presents early findings about vision obstruction in different racing scenarios, where Gaze Direction #2 yielded a larger % AVO for each halo variant compared to Gaze Direction #1.

6 Discussions

The aim this study was to demonstrate an alternative approach to obstruction analysis with DHM. We developed a macro within ImageJ software to calculate percent area visual obscuration from the forward FoV binocular eye-view snapshots. The results illustrate that the proposed approach is repeatable for a wide range of vision obstruction studies, such as assessing obstructions caused by halo safety equipment and F1 race care cockpit elements, as demonstrated via a case study in this paper.

The macro-based obstruction analysis approach represented in this study provides a readily quantifiable and repeatable image analysis model as an alternative quantification method. ImageJ is a reputable open-source software used in scientific peer-reviewed publications for processing images and performing image analysis. Further, the ImageJ macro demonstrated in this study also supplies automation and direct import capabilities via Microsoft Excel integration. These features enable designers to use Siemens Jack as a testbed to collect quick eye-view snapshots and run rapid analysis. Generating high-fidelity coverage zone analysis and working with complex CAD models is a computer resource-hungry process. Often, designers complain about difficulties in importing high-polygon models into DHM software, making obstruction zone analysis even more challenging. The approach discussed in this research allows speeding up the percent obstruction quantification process compared to existing tools (e.g., coverage zones in Siemens Jack). As demonstrated in this case study, the quick-and-dirty approach via low-fidelity CAD models would allow designers to create rapid vision analysis studies suitable for early design activities.

This study provided only a glimpse into quantifying drivers' vision obstruction via DHM. Other aspects of the DHM-based vision analysis tool for engineering design and computational ergonomics require further research beyond increasing the speed of the analysis. One of the significant limitations of this study is the fidelity of the analysis methodology. First of all, this study did not replicate F1 vehicles or attempt to assess the ergonomics of actual standard halo equipment used in F1 racing. Instead, we took inspiration from the F1 domain and developed a computational case study to demonstrate a proof-of-concept methodology focusing on proactive ergonomics. Secondly, quantifying the vision obstruction does not tell whether drivers register what they see. Look-but-failed-to-see type accidents are common in accidents and mishaps. Thus, there is a need to inject cognitive aspects of drivers. In addition, this study can be enhanced by considering the dynamic aspects of driving. An immersive simulation setup that brings human participants to try different halo safety equipment variants in virtual or augmented environments can significantly increase the fidelity of data collection. Another shortcoming is that the research methodology discussed in this paper can be improved by further automating the scene and driver setup process. For example, the scene setup within DHM, including manikin creation, posture configuration, and generating eye-view snapshots, can be automated. This capability would allow designers to generate a large pool of scenarios without manually arranging different layouts or postures.

References

1. Chaffin, D.B.: Improving digital human modelling for proactive ergonomics in design. Ergonomics **48**(5), 478–491 (2005)
2. Onan Demirel, H., Duffy, V.G.: Building quality into design process through digital human modelling. Int. J. Digit. Hum. **1**(2), 153–168 (2016)
3. Demirel, H.O., Ahmed, S., Duffy, V.G.: Digital human modeling: a review and reappraisal of origins, present, and expected future methods for representing humans computationally. Int. J. Hum.-Comput. Interact. 1–41 (2021)
4. Ahmed, S., Irshad, L., Gawand, M.S., Demirel, H.O.: Integrating human factors early in the design process using digital human modelling and surrogate modelling. J. Eng. Des. **32**(4), 165–186 (2021)
5. Ahmed, S., Irshad, L., Demirel, H.O., Tumer, I.Y.: A comparison between virtual reality and digital human modeling for proactive ergonomic design. In: Duffy, V.G. (ed.) HCII 2019. LNCS, vol. 11581, pp. 3–21. Springer, Cham (2019). https://doi.org/10.1007/978-3-030-22216-1_1
6. Obeidat, M.S., Altheeb, N.F., Momani, A., Al Theeb, N.: Analyzing the invisibility angles formed by vehicle blind spots to increase driver's field of view and traffic safety. Int. J. Occup. Saf. Ergon. **28**, 1–10 (2020)
7. Bhise, V.D.: Ergonomics in the Automotive Design Process. CRC Press, Boca Raton (2011)
8. Sivak, M., Schoettle, B., Reed, M.P., Flannagan, M.J.: Body-pillar vision obstructions and lane-change crashes. J. Saf. Res. **38**(5), 557–561 (2007)
9. Pipkorn, B., Lundström, J., Ericsson, M.: Safety and vision improvements by expandable a-pillars. In: 22nd International Technical Conference on the Enhanced Safety of Vehicles (ESV) National Highway Traffic Safety Administration, no. 11–0105 (2011)
10. Rosalie, S.M., Malone, J.M.: Effect of halo-type frontal cockpit protection on overtaking. Case Reports (2018)
11. FIA. F1 - Why halo is the best solution—Federation Internationale de l'Automobile (2017). https://www.fia.com/news/f1-why-halo-best-solution. Accessed 03 Jan 2022
12. Watkins, S.: Beyond the Limit. Macmillan (2001)
13. Silvestro, B.: Formula 1 driver explains exactly how the new halo impacts driver vision (2018). https://www.roadandtrack.com/motorsports/a19496576/formula-1-driver-explains-halo-vision-impact/. Accessed 03 Mar 2022
14. FIA. Halo breaks cover in Barcelona—Federation Internationale de l'Automobile (2016). https://www.fia.com/news/halo-breaks-cover-barcelona. Accessed 03 Jan 2022
15. Castro, C.: Human Factors of Visual and Cognitive Performance in Driving. CRC Press, Boca Raton (2008)
16. Peacock, B., Karwowski, W.: Automotive Ergonomics. Taylor & Francis, London (1993)
17. McKnight, A.J., McKnight, A.S.: The effects of motorcycle helmets upon seeing and hearing. Accid. Anal. Prevent. **27**(4), 493–501 (1995)
18. Ahmed, S., Gawand, M.S., Irshad, L., Demirel, H.O.: Exploring the design space using a surrogate model approach with digital human modeling simulations. In: International Design Engineering Technical Conferences and Computers and Information in Engineering Conference, vol. 51739, p. V01BT02A011. American Society of Mechanical Engineers (2018)

19. Duffy, V.G.: Modified virtual build methodology for computer-aided ergonomics and safety. Hum. Factors Ergon. Manuf. Serv. Ind. **17**(5), 413–422 (2007)
20. Demirel, H.O.: Digital human-in-the-loop framework. In: Duffy, V.G. (ed.) HCII 2020. LNCS, vol. 12198, pp. 18–32. Springer, Cham (2020). https://doi.org/10.1007/978-3-030-49904-4_2
21. Chaffin, D.B.: Digital human modeling for workspace design. Rev. Hum. Factors Ergon. **4**(1), 41–74 (2008)
22. Demirel, H.O., Duffy, V.G.: Digital human modeling for product lifecycle management. In: Duffy, V.G. (ed.) ICDHM 2007. LNCS, vol. 4561, pp. 372–381. Springer, Heidelberg (2007). https://doi.org/10.1007/978-3-540-73321-8_43
23. Gilad, I., Byran, E.: Quantifying driver's field-of-view in tractors: methodology and case study. Int. J. Occup. Saf. Ergon. **21**(1), 20–29 (2015)
24. Godwin, A., Eger, T., Salmoni, A., Grenier, S., Dunn, P.: Postural implications of obtaining line-of-sight for seated operators of underground mining load-haul-dump vehicles. Ergonomics **50**(2), 192–207 (2007)
25. FIA. Formula 1 Technical Regulations 2021 (2020). https://www.fia.com/sites/default/files/2021_formula_1_technical_regulations_-_iss_7_-_2020-12-16.pdf. Accessed 03 Mar 2022

Redesigning an Excavator Operator's Seat and Controls Using Digital Human Modelling in RAMSIS

Bishrut Jayaswal(✉)

Purdue University, West Lafayette, IN 47906, USA
bjayaswa@purdue.edu

Abstract. This paper aims to ergonomically analyze and improve an excavator operator's seat design for comfort and reachability. Anthropometric diversity considerations uncover glaring oversights in the seat's initial design and serve as a potential for improvement before actual production begins. Three manikins - 2 males and 1 female - of different sizes were used in all assessments to simulate even demographic spread and identify boundary conditions. The 3D CAD software RAMSIS was used to perform all simulations, dichotomized into operators performing two key actions from their seat – Driving and Digging. The three fundamental analyses that were covered in this report are Comfort Feeling, Joint Capacity, and Reach assessment. Results demonstrate that the neck and shoulder joints face maximum discomfort while performing digging tasks and a simple design change like raising the armrests showed considerable improvement in comfort feeling. Some variation in discomfort was seen when the manikin type was altered. Reachability analysis unveiled another crucial design flaw as a controls shaft near the steering wheel was out of reach of all three manikins. Some of the recommended modifications in seating include height-adjustable armrests (discomfort feeling dropped by 28% for the medium Male) and slide-mounted steering, which can move forward and backward (a translational movement of 100–130 mm along the x-axis was required to get the touchscreen and driving controls within arm's reach of all manikins). Procedure and challenges are discussed, and some operator-specific customizations have been incorporated along with the scope for further design improvement. As a motivation for the problem statement, literature surveys, and bibliometric analyses have been included in this report, which highlights the importance of cultural change in higher-order decision making to push for design improvements that promote employee well-being. Relative movement of repositioned controls has been tabulated at the end, in a table for each case, to access the range of movement needed for each object/control. Findings and studies from this paper can be referenced by design teams to aid in ergonomically optimizing operator seats and controls of excavators or similar construction equipment.

Keywords: RAMSIS · Comfort · Reach · Manikin · Ergonomics

© The Author(s), under exclusive license to Springer Nature Switzerland AG 2022
V. G. Duffy (Ed.): HCII 2022, LNCS 13319, pp. 45–58, 2022.
https://doi.org/10.1007/978-3-031-05890-5_4

1 Introduction and Background

1.1 Problem Statement and Objective

Repositioning controls for improved ease of access and minimizing strain to make sensible recommendations considering a broader perspective than the last paper. The same 3 manikins were used to run all simulations, providing a range of values for customizing the positions of the seat and controls. Apart from the usual driving and digging tasks, the manikin is simulated to access the touchscreen and control knobs near the right armrest as well. Foot pedal positions and angles, which were largely ignored in the previous analysis have been taken into consideration. Also, eye and head movements have been introduced to get a holistic sense of vision and barriers to the line of sight. Individual objects for the armrests, foot pedals, touch screen, and steering wheel were defined to identify the best positions for each manikin, and boundary conditions were identified.

1.2 Motivation

Boosting employee health and safety. Jobs like those of an excavator operator require prolonged shifts repeated actions under stressful operating conditions. Cases of employees suffering from Work-related musculoskeletal disorders (WMSDs) are prevalent in a job line like theirs. This issue has ballooned, even in developed countries like the US. Conservative figures estimate that WMSDs cost the US a total of $45 to $54 billion annually [1].

Moreover, a press release by the Bureau of Labor Statistics shows that there were 1000 cases of WMSDs each day on average during 2014, at a rate of 34 cases per 10 000 full-time workers [2]. This can be seriously debilitating for businesses as these are not only lost work hours but seriously crippling cases can also lead to lawsuits and compensation charges. Software like RAMSIS can largely assist in solving this problem by suggesting smarter workplace and job designs through CAD models and simulations.

Another motivating factor was that as of today very few engineers have been trained in human factors and ergonomics, and only a small percentage of human factors and ergonomics specialists have the opportunity to learn about DHM (Digital Human Modeling) as a part of the course curriculum [3]. Increasing awareness and demonstrating the benefits of HMI modeling to inculcate these indispensable aspects of engineering in future generations is a strong motivating factor for corporations and educational institutes.

2 Systematic Review

Change beings from the top. Leaders are often the drivers of positive change that is reflected in safe and employee-friendly workplace practices. Initially, my literature surveys were heavily focused on ergonomics in corporate decision-making and how culture creates a dialog that reflects in design changes. These changes aimed at improving employee health and safety trickle down to the grass-root level to benefit frontline workers. As engineers, our challenge is not only to push for implementing best practices but also to understand if corporations introduce effective policies to improve work conditions and if they really take into account workers' issues [4]. The next steps in my systematic review approach covered finer topics pertinent to this project. 3 out of the 8 conducted analyses have been included below.

2.1 MAXQDA Wordcloud Analysis

I chose 4 random articles across a spread of sources (SpringerLink, ResearchGate, and GoogleScholar) and Chapter 15 from the Handbook of Human Factors to identify buzzwords and popular terms used in publications. The overarching theme of all these papers revolved around Human Machine interface and computer aided-simulation. The wordcloud in Fig. 1 indicates trending hot topics and as expected, some popular terms repeated across multiple publications are – **analysis, model, disability, design,** and **measurement.**

Fig. 1. Literature analysis: Word-cloud to identify main topics of discussion from publications

2.2 Pivot Chart of Authors for Selected Search Terms

A keyword search for the terms "accessibility" and "ergonomics" was performed on Google Scholar to identify key contributing authors whose publications encompass these fields as shown in Fig. 2. The time range was set to 2010–2021 to filter out obsolete trends.

2.3 Cluster Analysis Using WoS Extract on CiteSpace

For the next analysis, I wanted to narrow my search down towards a specific application of ergonomics, that was related to my project work. My search terms on Web

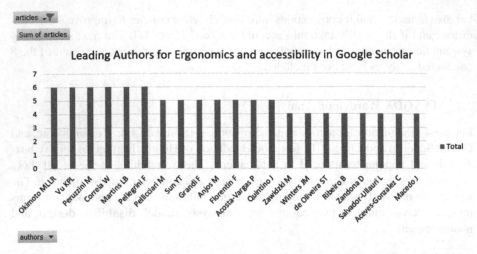

Fig. 2. This chart displays the leading authors who've published articles pertaining to the fields of ergonomics and accessibility. Values above 4 have been retained.

of Science were "driver", "seat" and "ergonomics". Time slicing for the years 2016–2021 was performed in CiteSpace to visualize the attached cluster diagram. As seen in Fig. 3, "Automotive Ergonomics" and "Seat design" are prominent clusters amongst the 6 identified. Some popular authors also came up from this analysis.

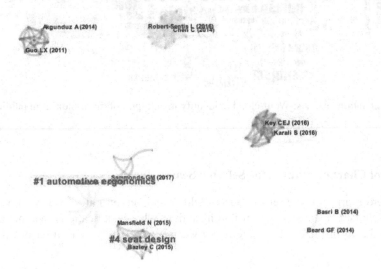

Fig. 3. This image was generated using Citespace and the Metadata was sourced from Web of Science.

3   Statements of Work – RAMSIS Simulations

3.1   Creating Boundary Conditions for the Tasks

Using the Germany2004 dataset available in RAMSIS, I created 3 manikins to simulate all experiments, representative of almost 90% of the entire population. Anthropometric measurements were retained from my last paper [5]. The 95%tile male and 5%tile female were used to determine upper and lower bounds. Initial runs were carried out on the Medium Male and to ascertain upper and lower limits of motion, these were then replicated on the Tall Male and Short Female. The process to group and name objects and define kinematics can be referenced in my previous paper. A walkthrough of those procedures would be repetitive and hence those have purposefully been omitted from this paper.

3.2   Evaluating Location, Adjustment Range, Comfort for the Overall Driving and Digging Posture Including Seat Adjustment, Pedal Position, and Steering Wheel Position/adjustment

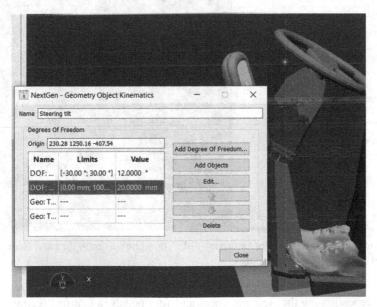

Fig. 4.   Creating the steering tilt object and defining Kinematics.

The new Steering wheel geometry splits the steering mount into 2 parts. After the new steering wheel geometry file was copied to the project folder, 2 degrees of freedom were added for the upper part. The first changed the angle of tilt between 0° to 30° as shown in Fig. 4 above. The second translational degree of freedom moves the upper joint up and down for improved reach.

The pedals were grouped into a common object called Pedals. This was then assigned a rotational degree of freedom to adjust angle of tilt and a translation one to move it up and down as seen in Fig. 5.

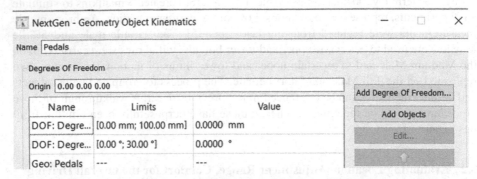

Fig. 5. Creating the Pedals object and defining Kinematics.

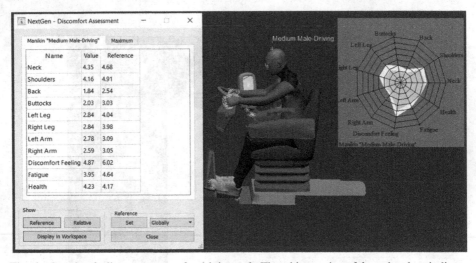

Fig. 6. Comfort feeling assessment for driving task. The white portion of the radar chart indicates discomfort values before repositioning

After repositioning the steering wheel and foot pedals, a comfort feeling analysis was done for the medium male manikin (Fig. 6). The reference values were set before relocating pedals and steering wheel to compare the change in comfort levels. Splitting the steering wheel and lifting the foot pedals has resulted in an improvement of comfort feeling from my previous paper [5].

As an improvement from my last paper [5], The armrests were assigned now assigned an additional translational degree of freedom along the x-axis apart from the pre-existing one for the z-axis (Fig. 7).

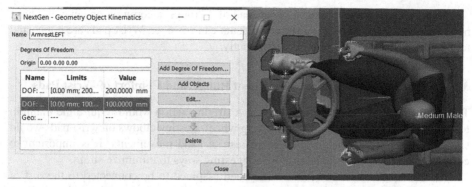

Fig. 7. Creating the ArmrestLEFT object and defining Kinematics. Similarly, ArmrestRIGHT was also created

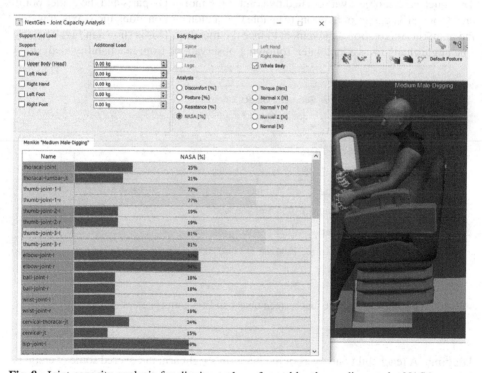

Fig. 8. Joint capacity analysis for digging task performed by the medium male. NASA zero-g posture is used to compute discomfort percentages. Apart from the shoulder joints and fingers, all values were green. (Color figure online)

Both armrests move in unison, so instead of 2 groups, a common object could have been created. This is something future students can consider. Wrist pads are connected to the armrests and do not move independently.

3.3 Evaluating the Location, Adjustment Range, and Comfort of Wrist Pads

This part only applies to the digging task. A driving action would require the manikin to free its elbows while rotating the steering wheel. Resting elbows on wrist pads would show an increase in comfort feeling but restrict hand movements. It is important to consider what the task demands before suggesting ways to minimize strain.

For all experiments, wrist pads have been assumed to be connected to the rest of the armrest. The manikin's elbows have been made to touch the wrist pads to reduce discomfort % as seen in the joint capacity analysis image in Fig. 8 for the medium male manikin.

3.4 Evaluating the Location, Reach, and Comfort of Touchscreen

The touch screen object was created by combining individual parts and the center point and assigned 3 degrees of freedom to enable translation motion along the x-axis, towards the manikin and rotational movement to face the manikin. This is shown in Fig. 9 below. The angle change was added later, following observations from reachability analysis.

NextGen - Geometry Object Kinematics

Name Touchscreen

Degrees Of Freedom

Origin 0.00 0.00 0.00

Name	Limits	Value
DOF: Degre...	[0.00 mm; 6...	400.0000 mm
DOF: Degre...	[0.00 °; 40.0...	40.0000 °
DOF: Degre...	[0.00 mm; 1...	100.0000 mm
Geo: Touchs...	---	---

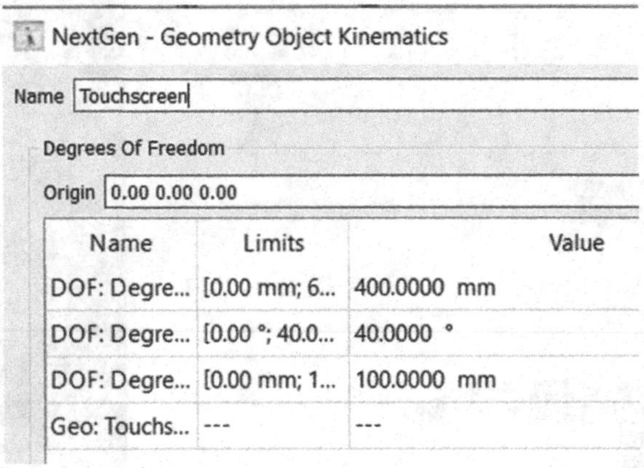

Fig. 9. Creating the touchscreen object and assigning degrees of freedom

Digging. A reachability analysis of the manikin's right arm uncovered some oversights in initial touchscreen placement. For this analysis, the touchscreen object was moved by 200 mm along the z-axis and 500 mm along the x-axis. The inner green sphere in Fig. 10 indicates "comfort reach" which was created under Reach Definitions by using points on the manikin's right shoulder and index finger. This is an improvement from the change of 250 mm suggested for the medium manikin in my mid-term paper [5].

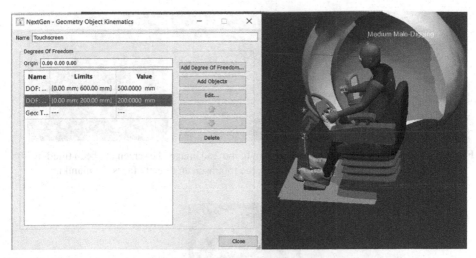

Fig. 10. The green envelope indicates comfort reach of the manikin's right arm. The touchscreen is now within comfortable reach (Color figure online)

Another key observation from this exercise the touchscreen was not only found to be out of reach of the short female manikin's right arm but also partially blocked, beyond her line of sight (Fig. 11).

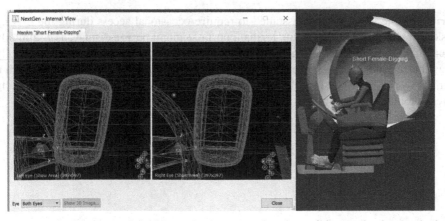

Fig. 11. For the touchscreen's initial position, the short female manikin was simulated to look at that general direction. Her vision is captured in the image on the left

Once the touchscreen position is changed, it is also desirable to alter the viewing angle to ensure that it faces the operator (Fig. 12). Additional head movement, if avoidable would reduce the chances of neck injuries or strain. Hence, 3 degrees of freedom were finally assigned to the touchscreen and the final position is shown below, in reference to the medium male mannikin. The final touchscreen position is shown in Fig. 13.

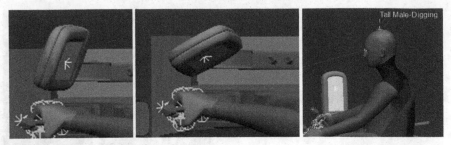

Fig. 12. Touchscreen position post-relocation. In the 2nd image, the screen has been tilted by 40° towards the operator for better viewing. Now, the touchscreen directly faces the manikin.

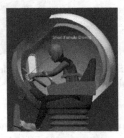

Fig. 13. Final touchscreen position for the short female manikin. The touchscreen is within comfortable reach of her right arm

Driving. The touchscreen is assumed to require occasional access during the driving task as it would cause distraction. Its main purpose might be as a display, as commonly seen on car dashboards. It is highly unlikely that the operator would need to periodically press buttons on the touchscreen while driving. For the driving task as well, although it isn't shown in Fig. 14 for the sake of brevity, the touchscreen was repositioned following a reachability analysis.

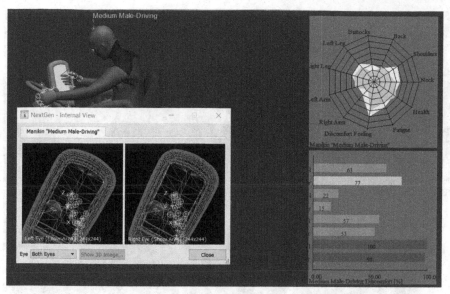

Fig. 14. The manikin is simulated to reach the mid-point on the touchscreen with one hand on the steering. Comfort feeling (radar diagram, joint capacity (color-coded bar plot), and vision are also displayed (Color figure online)

3.5 Evaluating Comfort While Actuating Controls

A key observation from Fig. 15 is that while actuating the control knobs/buttons on its right, the manikin's right shoulder joint is under considerably less stress as opposed to its left shoulder. Outstretched arms exert more load on the shoulder joint and this is directly proportional to the object's proximity.

4 Results and Recommendations

For each of the 3 manikins, unique combinations of repositioning metrics have been calculated from RAMSIS simulations and tabulated in Table 1. For digging, joint capacity analysis was used to compute (NASA) discomfort percentage levels and comfort feeling analysis for driving. The optimum levels of comfort were reached when all objects were moved in unison.

Office-chair-like armrest adjustments that go up-down and slide forward and backward need to be installed on the seat. The steering wheel needs to be angle adjustable as well as movable towards the operator's seating direction. This can be achieved by splitting the steering joint and adding a telescopic arm connecting the 2 parts. This arm would then be placed on a hinge-joint to facilitate angular motion. To accommodate height differences among operators, foot pedals should move up-down but angle adjustment is largely insignificant. Adding an additional movable part on the pedals for a minuscule improvement in comfort wouldn't be prudent. There is a further need to simulate the manikins' feet under flexion while pressing the pedals. Hanging pedals can also

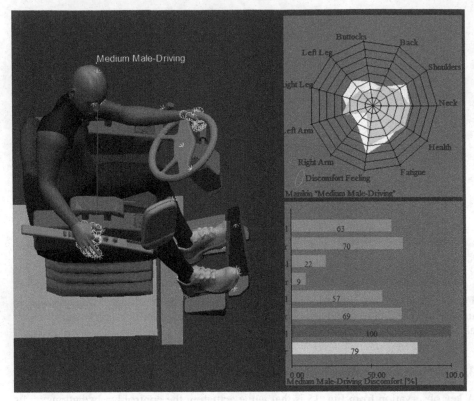

Fig. 15. Comfort feeling and joint capacity analysis while actuating controls

Table 1. Recommended changes in object placement. All non-angle values are in mm.

Object	Direction	Digging			Driving		
		Tall Male	Medium Male	Short Female	Tall Male	Medium Male	Short Female
Armrests	x-axis	100	50	0	NA	NA	NA
	z-axis	250	200	170	NA	NA	NA
Steering	Angle	NA	NA	NA	0°	5°	12°
	Away from mast	NA	NA	NA	200	180	70
Foot pedals	Angle	0°	5°	5°	0	0	0
	x-axis	0	30	40	0	0	0
Touch screen	x-axis	400	500	450	300	400	250
	Away from manikin	100	100	40	100	100	100
	Angle towards manikin	40°	40°	40°	40°	40°	40°

be tested. The touchscreen needs to be mounted on a movable arm with multiple degrees of freedom. It should allow for rotation as well as front-back and side-side translational motion. Ideally, a 2-stage arm connected by ball and socket joints would suffice.

5   Discussion

5.1   Prior Experience

My prior analytics experience came in handy and I could understand concepts pertinent to systematic review quite well. I have worked as a freelance tutor in the past, helping master's and doctorate students with their dissertations and reports. I am well versed with literature review concepts and have performed text mining, bibliometric analyses, natural language processing, and created interactive visuals like word clouds, clusters, and network diagrams using R.

5.2   Overcoming Challenges

I took this course online alongside my full-time co-op which is scheduled to end in January 2022. As my company is still in a relatively nascent stage, my team is putting in the hard yards to get ahead of the curb. For a significant portion of my co-op, I ended up working overtime. Balancing and distributing my time was quite challenging but my multitasking abilities helped me overcome this challenge. I deployed the Agile project management strategy to deliver this project on time - breaking down deliverables into sequential daily tasks to keep myself on track.

At least 6 software were required to perform bibliometric and literature analyses as a pre-requisite for this project. RAMSIS in itself is quite bulky and combined with these, I had to clear out quite some space on my laptop to install all of them. Future students should clear out at least 8 GB of space on their computers beforehand to successfully install and run these without lag. It would help if a consolidated download manual with all links is provided at the very start of the course rather than scattering setup instructions across pdfs on TopHat.

6   Future Work

A bottom-up approach can be tested where students get to reverse engineer ideal seating position by defining restrictions first and then repositioning the manikin on the seat. This approach might give better results in terms of joint stresses and reach.

Amongst several data points that are missing, perhaps the most critical piece is data on resistance to motion. Additional insight on motion resistance of the steering wheel, foot pedals, and joysticks to the force exerted by the operator. The closest approach for simulating this is by adding additional weights on the manikin's joints under joint-capacity analysis.

A myriad of practical considerations come into play when a redesign is discussed in depth. HVAC aspects like the positioning of cooling vents have not been considered in the cab design at all. Accelerated fatigue on hot sunny days needs to be simulated to understand actual field conditions. Ingress-egress and ladder placement were not taken into account in this paper.

References

1. Marcum, J., Adams, D.: Work-related musculoskeletal disorder surveillance using the Washington state workers' compensation system: recent declines and patterns by industry, 1999–2013. Am. J. Ind. Med. **60**(5), 457–471 (2017)
2. Bureau of Labor Statistics (BLS): http://www.bls.gov/news.release/pdf/osh2.pdf (2015a). Last accessed 11 Dec 2021
3. Duffy, V.G.: Human digital modeling in design. In: Handbook of Human Factors and Ergonomics, pp. 1016–1030. John Wiley & Sons, Inc, Hoboken, NJ, USA (2012)
4. Bolis, I., Brunoro, C.M., Sznelwar, L.I.: Work in corporate sustainability policies: the contribution of ergonomics. Work (Reading, Mass.) **49**(3), 417–431 (2014)
5. Jayaswal, B.: Ergonomic Analysis of Excavator Operator's Seat using RAMSIS. Purdue University, IN, USA (2021)

Research on the Index System for Evaluating the Ergonomics Design of Helicopter Cockpits

Xiaodong Li[1], Hao Yu[2], Youchao Sun[2(✉)], Honglan Wu[2], and Xia Zhang[2]

[1] China Aeronautical Radio and Electronics Research Institute, Shanghai 200233, China
[2] Nanjing University of Aeronautics and Astronautics, Nanjing 211106, China
sunyc@nuaa.edu.cn

Abstract. Helicopter cockpit ergonomic evaluation is a process of judging whether the matching relationship design of pilot-related displays, controllers and auxiliary components in cockpit design meets ergonomic requirements based on helicopter cockpit design specifications and pilots' operating experience. Based on the analysis and trade-off study of the influencing factors of helicopter ergonomics, combined with the design features of the cockpit and the pilot's operating procedures, this paper initially establishes an index system for evaluating the ergonomics. The index system for evaluating the ergonomics was screened and optimized according to the results of expert consultation. Finally, 3 first-level evaluation objectives, 9 second-level evaluation objectives, 23 third-level evaluation objectives, and 78 evaluation indexes were obtained. The evaluation methods and evaluation rules of the indexes have formed a scientific and reasonable index system for evaluating the ergonomics of helicopter cockpits. It lays a foundation for the comprehensive evaluation of helicopter cockpit ergonomics with multiple indexes.

Keywords: Ergonomics · Modified Delphi Method · Helicopter cockpit · Evaluation index system

1 Introduction

1.1 Research Content

The purpose of the ergonomic evaluation of helicopter cockpit is to discover the defects in the design in time and feedback to the design department for modification, to improve the ergonomic characteristics of the cockpit. Helicopter cockpit ergonomic evaluation is a multi-attribute problem that needs to be comprehensively considered. It involves many factors, and the evaluation process often contains many uncertainties, randomness and ambiguity. Therefore, a comprehensive evaluation system needs to be established. Only by constructing a pilot-centered evaluation model that fits the cockpit mechanism can the ergonomic evaluation be effectively carried out according to the characteristics of the cockpit.

In the past, ergonomic evaluation was often carried out at the end of the cockpit design or during the test flight of the aircraft, which not only made it difficult to improve

© The Author(s), under exclusive license to Springer Nature Switzerland AG 2022
V. G. Duffy (Ed.): HCII 2022, LNCS 13319, pp. 59–76, 2022.
https://doi.org/10.1007/978-3-031-05890-5_5

the found ergonomic design problems, but also caused a waste of manpower and material resources. Therefore, the ergonomic evaluation of the helicopter cockpit should be carried out synchronously with the cockpit design process. In the past, ergonomic evaluation was often carried out at the end of the cockpit design or during the test flight of the aircraft, which not only made it difficult to improve the found ergonomic design problems, but also caused a waste of manpower and material resources. Therefore, the ergonomic evaluation of the helicopter cockpit should be carried out simultaneously with the cockpit design process. At each stage of the cockpit design, there should be a corresponding ergonomic evaluation process. In this way, the ergonomic problems existing in the design of the cockpit can be discovered and solved in time through the evaluation, so as to ensure that the ergonomics level at this stage meets the design requirements. The common ergonomic evaluation has high requirements on the experience and knowledge background of the evaluators, and has defects such as strong subjectivity, and it is difficult to comprehensively consider the human–machine-environment factors. Based on the research on the influencing factors of helicopter ergonomics, combined with the characteristics of cockpit design and pilot operating procedures, this paper uses the Modified Delphi Method (MDM) to establish an ergonomic evaluation index system and gives the evaluation methods and evaluation rules for each index. This research lays the foundation for the comprehensive evaluation of the multi-index ergonomics of the helicopter cockpit.

1.2 Related Work

In the early stage of the development of aviation ergonomics, most of the research on the ergonomics of the cockpit was based on the analysis and evaluation of a certain ergonomic problem, and there were few systematic ergonomic evaluation studies on the cockpit. However, with the development of disciplines such as complex systems, the evaluation research on cockpit ergonomics has become more comprehensive and comprehensive.

As early as 1984, the U.S. Army and the National Aeronautics and Space Administration (NASA) jointly launched a research project called the Army-NASA Aircrew/Aircraft Integration Interface Design and Analysis (A3I). The Man–machine Interface Design and Analysis System (MIDAS) [1] is used in the conceptual design of the advanced rotorcraft cockpit. NASA's Gomes et al. [2] studied the automatic evaluation method of ergonomics based on expert knowledge, developed a software called TAKE to collect and analyze human factors related evaluation intentions, and implemented it on the MH-53 J helicopter. application. In addition, NASA has established a guideline on human–machine systems (NASA-STD-3000) [3], and through a series of investigations and studies, it has clarified the ergonomic data, methods and related tools needed in the design process. Grant et al. [4] aimed at the back muscle pain problem of HH-60G helicopter pilots, measured the occupant's working posture size, and compared it with the anthropometric data of the US Air Force pilots. The ergonomic design was evaluated. Craig and Burrett [5], researchers at the British Institute of Defense Appraisal, conducted research on the ergonomic factors of the C-130 J cockpit of a large transport aircraft. The ergonomic design of the cockpit was evaluated in the form of a questionnaire.

Estock et al. [6] studied the impact of F-16 fighter visual ergonomics on pilot performance. The United States and other countries have also applied computer technology virtual simulation technology to the ergonomic evaluation of the human–machine interface of the aircraft, studied the development of digital prototypes and human models, the construction of simulation environment, and the methods of ergonomic simulation and evaluation, and developed COMBIMAN, DELMIA, JACK and RAMSIS and other ergonomic design analysis software.

China's research on cockpit ergonomic evaluation has largely benefited from the research results of computer-aided design, using advanced computer-aided design methods, combined with ergonomics, robotics, aviation ergonomics and other borderline interdisciplinary knowledge, on CATIA, ProE, RAMSIS, JACK and other platforms, the use of secondary development languages VB, VC++ and other functions to achieve the corresponding pilot manipulation action simulation, vision inspection, visual simulation, accessibility calculation and manipulation force calculation.

Nanjing University of Aeronautics and Astronautics has established an ergonomic index system and a comprehensive evaluation model for aircraft driving ergonomics and maintenance ergonomics, and has studied ergonomic design, analysis and evaluation technology based on virtual simulation [7]. Based on the changes of the pilot's physiological index parameters, a comprehensive price model of the pilot's task load was constructed [8]. Beijing University of Aeronautics and Astronautics proposed a comprehensive evaluation method system based on the ergonomic evaluation of the human–machine interface of the fighter cockpit [9]. In the indexes, 100 evaluation indexes were selected through two rounds of expert consultation [10], and then the G1 method was used to determine the weight coefficient of each index [11], and finally the eigenvalues of each index were quantified, and then the fuzzy weighted average operator was used as a comprehensive method. The mathematical model of the evaluation calculates the evaluation result. Northwestern Polytechnical University has carried out research on the ergonomic design and evaluation of UAV ground control stations and civil aircraft cockpits, and used the fuzzy comprehensive evaluation method to comprehensively evaluate the reliability of human–machine interface design [12]. The CATIA model was imported into the ergonomic analysis software JACK and optimized, and the layout of equipment such as seats, instrument meals, hoods, rudder pedals, and joysticks (handwheel) was evaluated [13].

China has developed rapidly in cockpit ergonomic design, analysis and evaluation technology, but due to its late start, there is a lack of systematic and in-depth research on helicopter cockpit ergonomic evaluation technology, mainly in the following aspects:

- Ergonomic analysis and evaluation are mainly based on the subjective feelings of experts (including experienced pilots, ergonomic experts, etc.) or the experience data of similar equipment, which lacks scientificity and normativeness.
- Ergonomic analysis and evaluation are mainly carried out on a certain aspect of ergonomic problems, which lacks systematicness and comprehensiveness, which may easily lead to the better level of some ergonomic indexes, but other ergonomic indexes have obvious defects.
- The ergonomic analysis and evaluation methods corresponding to the index system often rely on physical prototypes, resulting in a serious delay in the timing of analysis

and evaluation, and high economic costs. When using virtual prototypes for ergonomic analysis and evaluation, it relies on imported computer software. Some of the functional modules (such as anthropometric data) do not conform to the actual situation in our country and cannot be directly used in the ergonomic analysis and evaluation of the helicopter cockpit.

- For the research on cockpit ergonomics, foreign countries generally take specific models as the research objects, and carry out a series of method research and software development, and the models are relatively comprehensive. Relatively speaking, domestic research is mostly concentrated on civil transport aircraft, lacking applicable Methods and tools for helicopter cockpit ergonomics.

2 Overall Framework

By the requirements of safety, comfort, efficiency and system optimization of the ergonomic design of the helicopter cockpit, the index system for evaluating the ergonomics of helicopter cockpit shall be established according to the following principles:

- Scientific and objective. The selection, screening and optimization of evaluation indexes must be scientific and reasonable, not only to meet the basic requirements of ergonomics, but also to be combined with the specific background of helicopter cockpit design. The establishment of the index system for evaluating must be based on the theory and method of multi-index comprehensive evaluation and be objective.
- Comprehensive and comprehensive. If only a single index is considered, and the relationship between each index is not comprehensively considered, it is prone to the problem that some indicators are better, but the overall work efficiency level is not good. Therefore, the ergonomics requirements of all aspects should be considered as comprehensively as possible, and an index system should be established.
- Hierarchy and independence. When establishing an index system, in order to facilitate analysis and comparison, the evaluation indexes should be divided into different levels; at the same time, each index should be as independent as possible to avoid adverse effects caused by overlapping indexes.
- Operability. Each evaluation index should have a clear meaning and be easy to understand, determine reasonable qualitative or quantitative index values, and give the corresponding single-index evaluation method.

The establishment of the index system for evaluating is a process of gradually deepening, improving and systematizing the understanding of the evaluation target. Generally, the establishment of an index system needs to go through the steps of determining the evaluation objectives, familiarizing with the basic theories in the relevant fields, establishing an evaluation index framework, and optimizing and improving the evaluation indexes. Among them, the comprehensiveness and comprehensiveness of the evaluation indexes should be ensured first when constructing the evaluation index framework and preliminary screening evaluation indexes, and repeated or even unnecessary evaluation indexes can be allowed. Then based on mathematical statistics and other methods to analyze the relationship between the indexes, further select the evaluation indexes, optimize and improve the index system structure, and finally form a scientific and reasonable index system for evaluating the ergonomics of helicopter cockpit.

The overall framework of the index system for evaluating the ergonomics of helicopter cockpit is shown in Fig. 1.

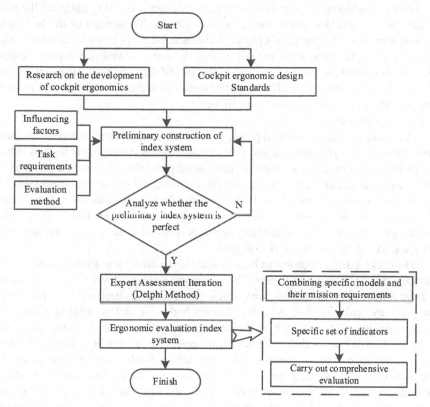

Fig. 1. Overall framework on the index system for evaluating the ergonomics design of helicopter cockpits

3 Basis for Constructing the Index System

3.1 Influencing Factors of Ergonomics

Good ergonomic design can enable pilots to quickly and accurately obtain various visual, auditory and tactile signals reflecting the working state of the aircraft without feeling fatigued, and make correct manipulation and control instructions as needed. It can also reduce the probability of erroneous operations as much as possible, so as to complete the flight mission safely and smoothly. In the design process, the layout and arrangement of airborne system equipment such as manipulation, control, communication, and navigation should be reasonably planned according to the aircraft development indexes and the pilot's cognition, physiology, psychology and other factors.

The factors affecting the ergonomics of helicopter pilots are mainly divided into the following three aspects.

- Pilot's factors

  Human psychological, physiological characteristics and ability limits are the basis of all "human–machine-environment" system design. The design of the helicopter cockpit must consider the pilot's physical characteristics, perception characteristics, behavior characteristics, work reliability, ability limits, as well as the pilot's cognitive, physiological, psychological characteristics and their changes during the driving process. Whether the design of the cockpit takes into account the above requirements directly affect the ergonomics of the helicopter.

- Cockpit design factors

  The cockpit is the pilot's workplace, which is characterized by small space, many instruments, and high functional and safety requirements. Arranging numerous instruments in a very limited space requires consideration of the ergonomic aspects of the basic structure, size and layout of the cockpit. Only when these devices are designed to fit the characteristics of the human body can pilots be able to fly the aircraft efficiently and in a comfortable working posture without premature fatigue. Therefore, whether the design of the cockpit structure and layout is reasonable has a direct impact on the pilot's work efficiency and work comfort.

  The cockpit design factors can be attributed to the layout and arrangement, control devices, display devices and seats. The ergonomics design level of the cockpit has a great influence on the pilot's work efficiency. The space design size requirements are given by analyzing factors such as human body size and the field of view in the cockpit. Require. The research on the arrangement of the control device shows that both the throttle lever and the joystick arrangement range should be arranged within the comfort zone of hand operation. The research on display arrangement shows that the main factors influencing the pilot's observation and identification of the displayed content are the physical characteristics of the display. The display should clearly and unambiguously indicate and direct the appropriate response of the controller. The response of the display to the movement of the controller should be consistent, measurable, and consistent with the operator's expectations. The character recognition effect on the display is closely related to the observation angle. Within a certain range, there is a compensatory relationship between the observation angle and the viewing angle of the characters. The layout of the console and the instrument panel and its markings are closely related to the pilot's observation, identification of various information in the cockpit, and comfortable operation of various devices.

- Cockpit environmental factors

  The working environment directly affects people's work efficiency and physical health. Helicopter cockpit environmental factors mainly include light, noise, vibration, acceleration and thermal environment. Studies have shown that glare can cause pilots to distract, reduce visibility, and affect visual performance; long-term repeated noise effects can cause pilots to have dizziness, headache, tinnitus, heart palpitations, nervousness, irritability, inattention, insomnia and other neurasthenic syndromes; vibration will have a physiological and psychological response to the pilot, thereby affecting the pilot's visual recognition, voice call quality and hands-on ability; excessive acceleration will cause The pilot had difficulty breathing, difficulty speaking, chest pain, loss of touch, and periodic total loss of vision. Measures must be taken to control the light, noise, vibration, color, acceleration, temperature and humidity in the cockpit within a reasonable range to protect the pilot's health and improve the pilot's work efficiency.

3.2 Human–Computer Interaction Equipment

Helicopter cockpit human–computer interaction equipment includes two categories: control device and display device. Taking the display device as an example, the display device provides the pilot with various display information such as flight data and system working status, including instrument panels, head-up displays and multi-function displays, visual warning systems and auditory warning systems.

- Dashboard
    The instrument panel refers to the board that is located in the pilot's field of vision and is used to install instruments, electronic displays, control devices, and light signal devices. According to the requirements of GJB 1560–1992 Helicopter Dashboard Layout, the ergonomics of helicopter dashboard layout have the following index factors: viewing angle, accessibility, consistency, correspondence, preventing interference with visual reading and emergency use.
- Head-up display and multi-function display
    With reference to GJB-T 5062–1991 General requirements for ergonomics of information display devices, HB 7270–1996 General specifications for helicopter head-up display systems and other relevant standard requirements, the ergonomic design index factors of head-up displays and multi-function displays mainly include brightness, Field of view, character and glare.
- Visual warning system
    The ergonomics of the cockpit visual warning system is mainly determined by the coding of the warning signal, and the influencing factors mainly include the position of the warning signal and the color coding of the warning signal. When comprehensively considering the ergonomics of the cockpit warning system, attention should also be paid to the ergonomics of the warning response operation.
- Audible warning system
    In the display and control system of the helicopter cockpit, a lot of information is transmitted to the pilot in the form of sound. Hearing is an important information transmission channel second only to vision. Auditory information transmission has the advantages of quick response, the transmission device can be configured in any direction, and the response performance is good when talking in language. The influencing factors of sound alarm ergonomics are: signal strength, signal coding and signal alarm reliability.

3.3   Pilot Operating Procedures

There is a direct relationship between Pilot Operation Procedures (POP) and driving ergonomics. It is a technical document that describes and explains the relationship between avionics system functions, pilot operations, aircraft status, and the environment from the human–machine interface, that is, the display interface-pilot-control interface, in the environment-aircraft-pilot system. The pilot operation procedure is related to how the pilot operates to make the entire avionics system and even the entire aircraft enter the optimum state required by the pilot, so that the pilot can complete the task quickly, easily and effectively.

Pilot operating procedures are divided into standard procedures and abnormal emergency procedures. Modern aircraft are highly sophisticated and complex. The aircraft operates close to the limit of its capability, and the allowable variation range of flight parameters is very small. Pilots are required to accurately grasp various parameters, and the flight crew controls many systems, each of which has multiple control links, each link has multiple options. Various manipulation combinations, or even different manipulation sequences of the same combination, will affect the work of the system and affect the flight status. The environmental conditions at that time will ultimately have different consequences for flight safety. Especially for highly automated aircraft, the severity of the consequences of many combinations is difficult to predict. The standard operating procedure is flight specification. It is an industry consensus that has been rigorously analyzed, carefully designed and tested in practice. It takes into account the optimization of performance, ease of operation and sufficient safety margin. Deviation from the standard operating procedure will reduce the efficiency and reduce the safety margin, sometimes creating potential trouble for the operator, increased workload and the possibility of additional errors.

4   Construction and Optimization of Index Systems Based on MDM

There are two commonly used methods for establishing an index system. One is the statistical analysis method of data, which establishes the index system through statistics and analysis of data, so it is only suitable for quantitative indexes; the other is the combination of expert subjective evaluation and comparative judgment. The method is to establish an index system through expert knowledge and experience, which is suitable for indexes that are relatively lacking in data and difficult to obtain statistical data. Due to the numerous elements of helicopter cockpit ergonomic evaluation indexes, most of which are qualitative indexes, it is difficult to carry out quantitative processing, and similar research data and statistical data are rare. Based on the MDM, we solicit and refine the opinions of expert groups, select indexes, and establish an index system.

4.1   Implementation Steps of MDM

The steps of establishing an index system based on the MDM are shown in Fig. 2.

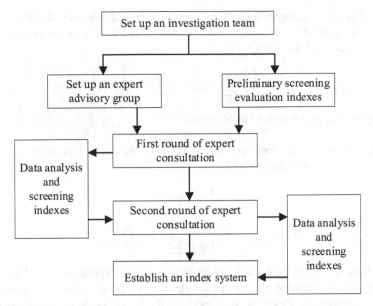

Fig. 2 Implementation steps of establishing index system based on MDM

4.2 Statistical Method of Expert Consultation Results

In practice, statistical parameters such as the degree of concentration, degree of dispersion, and degree of coordination are often used to analyze the consulting results of the MDM.

- Concentration of expert opinion

  The degree of concentration can be represented by the mean value $\overline{E_i}$ and the full frequency K_i.

$$\overline{E_i} = \sum_{i=1}^{5} E_j m_{ij}/d, i = 1, 2, \cdots, n \tag{1}$$

In the formula, E_j represents the degree of influence of the index on the ergonomics of the helicopter cockpit (the value is $1 \sim 5$); m_{ij} represents the number of experts who rate the index I at level j; d represents the total number of experts; n represents the number of indexes.

$$K_i = \frac{m_{ij}}{d}(j = 5) \tag{2}$$

The full-score frequency K_i can be used as a supplement to $\overline{E_i}$ in the evaluation. It represents the ratio of the number of experts who give the index i full marks to the total number of experts, and the value is between 0 and 1. The larger the K_i, the more important the index is.

- The degree of dispersion of expert opinion

The degree of dispersion can be represented by the standard deviation σ_i. The smaller the value of σ_i, the smaller the dispersion degree of experts' opinions on the evaluation result of the index i.

$$\sigma_i = \left[\sum_{i=1}^{5} m_{ij}\left(E_j - \overline{E_i}\right)/(d-1) \right]^{\frac{1}{2}} \tag{3}$$

- The degree of coordination of expert opinions

The degree of coordination can be represented by the coefficient of variation V_i and the coefficient of coordination W.

$$V_i = \frac{\sigma_i}{\overline{E_i}} \tag{4}$$

$$W = \frac{12}{d^2\left(n^3 - n\right) - d \sum_{k=1}^{d} T_k} \sum_{i=1}^{n} s_i^2 \tag{5}$$

In the formula, V_i represents the coordination degree of experts on index I, the smaller the coefficient of variation, the higher the degree of coordination; W represents the degree of coordination of experts on all indexes, the larger the coordination coefficient, the higher the degree of coordination of expert opinions; T_k is the correction coefficient; s_i represents the difference between the level sum of index I and the arithmetic mean of the sum of all index levels.

The significance of the coordination coefficient can be tested by the χ^2 test:

$$\chi_R^2 = \frac{\sum_{i=1}^{n} s_i^2}{dn(n+1) - \frac{1}{n-1} \sum_{k=1}^{d} T_k} \tag{6}$$

According to the degree of freedom and significance level, the critical value χ_α^2 can be found from the χ^2 distribution table. If $\chi_R^2 > \chi_\alpha^2$, it means that the coordination coefficient is significant, and the coordination degree of expert opinions is better, and the result is desirable; otherwise, the smaller the χ_R^2 is. It shows that there is a high probability of non-accidental coordination of expert opinions. When the confidence level is 95%, if $P > 0.05$, it indicates that the reliability of the evaluation conclusion is poor, and the result is not desirable.

4.3   Evaluation Index Screening Method

After two rounds of consultation, the coordination coefficient of expert opinions was calculated, and based on the boundary value method, the indexes were selected by calculating the full score frequency, average value and the boundary value of the coefficient of variation of each indexes influence degree score. The boundary-value of the full score frequency and the average value is A_1, which is defined as the difference between the arithmetic means and the standard deviation, and the indexes whose scores are higher than the boundary value are screened out; the boundary value of the coefficient of variation is A_2, which is defined as the sum of the arithmetic means and the standard deviation, and filter out the index whose scores are lower than the threshold.

After two rounds of consultation, the coordination coefficient of the expert opinion was calculated. Based on the boundary value method, the full score frequency, average value and the boundary value of the coefficient of variation of each index's influence degree score were calculated. The boundary-value of the full score frequency and the average value is A_1, which is defined as the difference between the arithmetic mean and the standard deviation, and the indexes with a score higher than the boundary value are selected. The cutoff value of the coefficient of variation is A_2, which is defined as the sum of the arithmetic mean and the standard deviation, and indexes with scores below the cutoff are selected.

$$A_1 = \bar{x} - \sigma \tag{7}$$

$$A_2 = \bar{x} + \sigma \tag{8}$$

In order to ensure the comprehensiveness and comprehensiveness of the index system, the indexes that do not meet the requirements of the above three measurement scales are eliminated; one and only one that does not meet the requirements shall be reserved; there are only two indexes that do not meet the requirements, which need to be comprehensively considered in combination with expert opinions, and the choice should be made after repeated weighing.

5 Case Study

5.1 Preliminary Establishment of Index System

Based on analyzing the relevant standard (Chinese military standards, Aviation industry standards, US military standards, SAE standards, FAA standards, airworthiness standards, NASA standards, ISO standards, etc.) requirements of cockpit ergonomics, combined with the design characteristics of helicopter cockpit, the ergonomic evaluation index of helicopter cockpit was preliminarily screened out with the analysis and trade-off results of cockpit ergonomics influencing factors as input. Establish a multi-level index system for evaluating.

The index system for evaluating the ergonomics of helicopter cockpit is composed of evaluation objectives and evaluation indexes. O represents the overall evaluation objective (the ergonomic level of helicopter cockpit), Oi represents the first-level evaluation objective, Oi-j represents the second-level evaluation objective, and Oi-j-k represents the third-level evaluation target, and Ui-m represents the evaluation index. The initially established helicopter cockpit ergonomic evaluation index system includes 3 first-level evaluation objectives, 9 s-level evaluation objectives, 23 third-level evaluation objectives, and 80 evaluation indexes. The sources of each index have a relevant basis. For example, the evaluation index of perception ability is a qualitative index, derived from psychological and physiological research, and the evaluation method is subjective evaluation; the evaluation index of rotor brake control logic is derived from MIL-STD-1472G-2012 Department Defense Design Criteria Standard: Human Engineering, etc.

5.2 Screening and Optimizing the Index System

According to actual needs, 15 active helicopter pilots were selected as consultants in the research. Their average age is 38 years old (SD = 3.99), and average flight time is 3160 h (SD = 1126.40). They have piloted several types of helicopters and have rich experience and professional knowledge. In the implementation of the MDM, each expert judged the degree of influence of each index on the ergonomics of the helicopter cockpit based on their own knowledge and experience.

According to the preliminary constructed index system, a questionnaire was designed. During the first round of consultation, experts need to judge the degree of influence of 80 indexes on the ergonomics of the helicopter cockpit and their confidence in their judgment based on their own experience.

Statistics obtained from the questionnaire include:

- Parameters $\overline{E_i}$ (average value), K_i (full score frequency), and η (the percentage of experts who believe that the degree of influence is greater than 3 to the total number of experts) that describe the degree of concentration of expert opinions.
- The parameter σ_i describing the dispersion degree of expert opinions.
- The parameter V_i representing the degree of coordination of expert opinions.
- The parameter GCR describing the average confidence of expert opinions.

In addition, consider the degree of freedom $= n - 1$ (n is the number of evaluation indexes).

When the degree of freedom is greater than 30, $Z = \sqrt{(2\chi^2)} - \sqrt{(2n - 1)}$ should be calculated, and the statistical significance limit should be determined according to the standard normal distribution law. If the value of P corresponding to Z is less than 0.01 or P is less than 0.05, it indicates that the coordination of expert evaluation is good, and the result is desirable; If the value of P corresponding to Z is larger than 0.05, the result is not desirable.

According to the statistical data of the expert questionnaire, the evaluation indexes are screened.

Set the data with GCR $\geq$ 3 as valid data for statistics. It is considered that the index with $\eta < 0.4$ has a low degree of influence, the index with $\sigma \geq 1$ has a larger degree of dispersion, and the index with V > 0.3 has a poor degree of coordination. Screen out the indexes with low confidence in expert judgment, low degree of influence of indexes, large degree of dispersion, and poor degree of coordination, and feed them back to each expert. After the experts consider these situations, they will conduct a second round of evaluation of each index. The selected indexes will be marked in the questionnaire, the second round of expert consultation will be carried out, and the index system will be adjusted and optimized according to the consultation results.

First round of expert consultation. In general, in the implementation of the MDM, the responses of experts in the first round of consultations were scattered.

In subsequent rounds, through information feedback, the responses of experts will be gradually concentrated, and the group opinion (average of all expert judgments) of the expert group from the previous round to the next round will be more and more accurate.

Generally, through two rounds of consultation, the opinions of experts have converged.

Therefore, according to the second round of opinions, the evaluation indexes were selected. The unanimous opinion of experts is defined as: no less than 2/3 (about 67%, hereinafter referred to as P33) of the expert judgment level is the judgment result above "big". The "big" in it indicates the degree of influence of the index on the ergonomics of the cockpit.

A total of 15 questionnaires were received in this survey. Statistical data include the degree of concentration, average confidence, dispersion and coordination of expert opinions. The statistical results corresponding to some index parameters are shown in Table 1:

Table 1. Statistical table for the first round of expert consultation

Index name	Degree of concentration			Average confidence	Degree of dispersion	Degree of coordination
	$\overline{E_i}$	K_i	η	GCR	σ_i	V_i
Perception	4.533	0.600	0.933	4.400	0.640	0.141
Quality of attention	4.400	0.467	0.933	4.533	0.632	0.144
Memory	3.933	0.267	0.667	4.200	0.799	0.203
Judgment	4.267	0.400	0.867	4.467	0.704	0.165
...	...	...	...	...	...	...
Differential pressure Protection	3.667	0.200	0.600	3.933	1.047	0.285
Temperature range	3.933	0.267	0.800	4.000	0.961	0.244
Humidity range	3.533	0.133	0.600	4.000	0.990	0.280
Thermal regulation	4.333	0.600	0.800	4.333	0.976	0.225

After completing the first round of expert consultation, the indexes with higher discrete values were screened as shown in Table 2:

It is considered that the index with $V > 0.3$ has a poor degree of coordination, and the indexes with a poor degree of coordination are shown in Table 3.

The second round of expert consultation was conducted for the indexes in Tables 2 and 3.

Second round of expert consultation. The results of the second round of expert consultation showed that η were all greater than 0.4, indicating that experts believed that

Table 2. Indexes with greater dispersion in the first round of expert consultation

First-level index	Second-level index	Third-level index	Index name	Degree of dispersion σ
Human	Comprehensive ability	Environmental tolerance	Overload endurance	1.060
			Heat and humidity endurance	1.014
Machine	Layout and arrangement	Equipment layout	Rotor brake installation location	1.014
			Wheel brake installation location	1.014
	Control device	Rotor brake	Rotor brake control logic	1.404
		Wheel brake	Wheel brake control logic	1.438
Environment	Air environment	Pressure environment	Differential pressure protection	1.047

Table 3. Indexes of poor coordination in the first round of expert consultation

First-level index	Second-level index	Third-level index	Index name	Degree of coordination V
Machine	Control device	Rotor brake	Rotor brake control logic	1.060
		Wheel brake	Wheel brake control logic	1.014

the 80 indexes had a high degree of influence. Indexes with a GCR < 3 are considered to have low confidence.

The results of the first round of expert consultation showed that GCR > 3, indicating a high degree of confidence in expert judgment. It is considered that the dispersion degree of the influence degree of the index with σ ≥ 1 is larger. The indexes with larger dispersion are shown in Table 4.

It is considered that the degree of coordination of the index influence degree of V > 0.3 is poor. Indexes of poor coordination are shown in Table 5.

Recommendations of the Advisory Group of Experts. In order to give full play to the experience advantages of experts, during the second round of expert consultation

Table 4. Indexes with greater dispersion in the second round of expert consultation

First-level index	Second-level index	Third-level index	Index name	Degree of dispersion σ
Machine	Control device	Rotor brake	Rotor brake control logic	1.280
		Wheel brake	Wheel brake control logic	1.320

Table 5. Indexes of poor coordination in the second round of expert consultation

First-level index	Second-level index	Third-level index	Index name	Degree of coordination V
Machine	Control device	Rotor brake	Rotor brake control logic	0.436
		Wheel brake	Wheel brake control logic	0.347

in this survey, the following two additional subjective questions were added to the questionnaire:

1. Do you think this questionnaire can fully cover the ergonomic evaluation of helicopter cockpit entry? If not, what other indexes do you think should be added?
2. On the basis of the current helicopters, in what areas do you think the cockpit of high-speed helicopters should be improved or optimized? What are your suggestions for the development of high-speed helicopter cockpits?

By summarizing and analyzing the experts' replies to the first question, some unreasonable indexes in the research process were screened out, and the statistical results during the expert consultation process were verified to be correct.

For example, in the initially established index system, one of the indexes is the control logic of the rotor brake, which means that the movement direction of the rotor brake is consistent with the direction of the helicopter's movement. In the first and second rounds of expert consultation, this index has a larger degree of dispersion and a lower score of influence degree. For this index, two experts believe that the setting of this index is unreasonable and that the movement direction of the rotor brake is not directly related to the direction of the helicopter's movement. The same goes for wheel brakes.

The answer to the second question is that the experts gave suggestions on the ergonomic optimization design of modern helicopter cockpits from the perspective of pilots. Combined with the actual flight experience, the expert advisory group gives optimization suggestions for the ergonomic design of the helicopter cockpit. In the future, the ergonomic design optimization of the helicopter cockpit can be carried out from these aspects, such as solving the problem of heat supply and physiological needs of

Table 6. The index system for evaluating the ergonomics design of helicopter cockpits

First-level evaluation target	Second-level evaluation target	Third-level evaluation target	Evaluation index	Index description
O1Human	O1-1 Comprehensive ability	O1-1–1 cognitive ability	U1-1 Perception	The ability to quickly and accurately respond to in-flight information (including speed, altitude, three-dimensional distance, ground and air targets, flight status, and spatial orientation) through vision, hearing, touch, vestibular and other sensory organs
		⋮	⋮	⋮
		O1-1–4 environmental tolerance	U1-12 Overload endurance	The ability to maintain coordinated movements of the hands, feet, and head during acceleration overloads
		⋮	⋮	⋮
O2Machine	O2-1 layout and arrangement	O2-1–1 General layout		
		⋮		
	⋮			
O3 Environment	O3-1 Lighting environment			
	⋮			

long-range pilots, improving seat comfort to reduce fatigue caused by long-term flight, reducing cockpit noise and vibration, and improving cockpit vision conditions. Solving potential ergonomics problems can create a safer and better cockpit environment for pilots.

5.3 The Index System for Evaluating the Ergonomics Design of Helicopter Cockpits

In two rounds of expert consultation, the concentration of expert opinions, the degree of coordination, and the average self-confidence are counted. Among the 80 evaluation indexes, 78 indexes that have a high degree of influence on the ergonomics of the helicopter cockpit are selected, and the two indexes with less influence, the rotor brake control logic and the wheel brake control logic, are removed. Finally, the index system for evaluating the ergonomics design of helicopter cockpits contains 3 first-level evaluation targets, 9 s-level evaluation targets, 23 third-level evaluation targets, and 78 evaluation indexes.

Some contents of the index system are shown in Table 6.

6   Conclusion

The comprehensive evaluation of helicopter cockpit ergonomics is an extremely important step in the development of the cockpit. In the past, during the development of the cockpit, the comprehensive evaluation of ergonomics may have been neglected due to various engineering quality measures, resulting in many ergonomic problems in the designed cockpit. Therefore, the research on cockpit ergonomics evaluation method is of practical significance. This paper conducts a systematic and in-depth study on the index system for evaluating the ergonomics design of helicopter cockpits from the aspects of the index system construction method based on the MDM and the initial construction of the index system.

From the aspects of scientificity and objectivity, comprehensiveness and comprehensiveness, hierarchy and independence, and operability, the top-level principles for constructing the index system for evaluating the ergonomics design of helicopter cockpits are determined.

The factors affecting the work efficiency of helicopter pilots, the design standards and specifications for human factors in the helicopter cockpit, the development trend of the human–machine interaction in the helicopter cockpit, and the pilot operating procedures are considered comprehensively. The general idea of constructing the index system for evaluating the ergonomics design of helicopter cockpits based on the MDM is formed.

The construction method of the index system is studied from the aspects of improving the implementation steps of MDM, the statistical method of expert consultation results, and the selection method of evaluation indexes. The implementation method of screening the evaluation indexes and optimizing the index system is given.

A multi-level index system for evaluating the ergonomics design of helicopter cockpits was initially constructed from the aspects of pilots, cockpit design and cockpit environment, a questionnaire for expert consultation was designed, and the selection principle of evaluation indexes were proposed. The initially constructed index system includes 3 first-level evaluation objectives, 9 second-level evaluation objectives, 23 third-level evaluation objectives, and 80 evaluation indexes. Based on the MDM, the initial construction index system was screened, and finally 3 first-level evaluation objectives, 9 second-level evaluation objectives, 23 third-level evaluation objectives, and 78 evaluation indexes were obtained.

In this paper, by researching and analyzing the ergonomic design standards of helicopter cockpit and the influencing factors of helicopter cockpit ergonomics, based on the MDM which has the advantage of expert group decision-making, an index system for evaluating the ergonomics design of helicopter cockpits is established, which can provide technical support for evaluating the ergonomics of helicopter cockpits.

References

1. Smith, B.R., Banda, C.P.: Use of a knowledge-based system to assess aircrew training requirements as part of conceptual design. In: IEEE International Conference on Systems, Man and Cybernetics, pp. 105–110 (1989)
2. Gomes, M.E., Lind, S., Snyder, D.E.: A human factors evaluation using tools for automated knowledge engineering. In: Proceedings of the IEEE 1993 National Aerospace and Electronics Conference, pp. 661–664 (1993)
3. NASA-STD-3000 Man-system Integration Standards. National Aeronautics and Space Administration (1995)
4. Grant, K.A.: Ergonomic assessment of a helicopter crew seat: the HH-60G flight engineer position. Aviation Space & Environmental Medicine 73(9), 913–918 (2002)
5. Craig, J.R., Burrett, G.L.: The design of a human factors questionnaire for cockpit assessment. In: International Conference on Human Interfaces in Control Rooms, Cockpits and Command Centres, pp. 16–20 (1999)
6. Estock, J.L., et al.: Impact of visual scene field of view on F-16 pilot performance. Proc. Hum. Fac. Ergono. Soc. Ann. Meet. 51(2), 75–79 (2007)
7. Liu, Q.: Research on Ergonomic Evaluation Method of Civil Aircraft Cockpit. Nanjing University of Aeronautics and Astronautics (2013).
8. Zhang, Y.: Research on Some Key Technologies of Ergonomic Design of Civil Aircraft Cockpit. Nanjing University of Aeronautics and Astronautics (2014)
9. Li, Y., et al.: Comprehensive evaluation of aircraft cockpit ergonomics and its application. J. Beijing Univ. Aero. Astr. 31(6), 652–656 (2005)
10. Li, Y., Yuan, X., Du, J.: Research on the evaluation index of human-machine geometric fitness of aircraft cockpit. Chinese J. Safety Sci. 15(12), 25–28 (2005)
11. Li, Y., et al.: Determination of weight coefficient of ergonomic evaluation index of fighter cockpit. J. Aero. Astr. 27(3), 370–373 (2006)
12. Yi, H., Song, B., Wang, Y.: Comprehensive evaluation of reliability of human-machine interface design of UAV control station. Ergonomics 12(1), 28–29 (2006)
13. Su, R., Xue, H., Song, B.: Evaluation of ergonomic layout of civil aircraft cockpit based on virtual design. Aero. Comp. Technol. 38(2), 69–73 (2008)

A Design Method of Sports Protective Gear Based on Periodic Discrete Parameterization

Kaice Man$^{(\boxtimes)}$, Wenda Tian, and Fei Yue

Tsinghua University, Beijing, People's Republic of China
mkc18@tsinghua.org.cn

Abstract. In cycling accidents, head injuries have been one cause of high injury rates. Therefore, the protection of the head from injuries is essential to any cyclist. Helmets are an effective head protective system. The protective capabilities of helmets are provided by inner liners made of expanded polystyrene foams (EPS). However, it is not easy to adopt this material to obtain more protective capabilities, limited by weight requirements and wearing comfort. Therefore, it is still significant to propose a new helmet design method. The honeycomb structure is a structure with excellent properties such as lightweight and energy absorption. The use of honeycomb structures in helmet design can improve energy absorption. This also does not add extra weight to a helmet. Since helmets are curved in shape, the design of honeycomb structures needs to adapt to curved surfaces. This paper proposes a new parametric design method. It enables the more flexible creation of honeycomb structures on curved surfaces. Finally, we apply the developed method to complete the design of a honeycomb-shaped helmet.

Keywords: Helmet design · Honeycomb structure · Algorithm design · Generative design

1 Introduction

The protection of the head from injuries is essential to the safety of cyclists. Cycling helmets are the head protection system that reduces impact injury severity or prevents such injuries. A typical cycling helmet consists of a rigid outer shell, an impact-absorbing liner, a comfort pad, and a retention system. The protective functions are mainly provided by the outer shell and the inner liner, the latter of which plays an essential role in head protection by absorbing impact energy. Expanded polystyrene foams (EPS) are often used to produce helmet liners due to their impact resistance and low costs [1]. The liners made of EPS perform energy absorption by deforming and crushing the structures within. The energy-absorbing performance provided by EPS can be adjusted by changing the material's density and the foam's thickness [2]. However, the density is limited by weight requirements, while the thickness is limited by wearing comfort constraints [3]. Newman [4] showed the theoretical thickness required to prevent serious concussion at two impact speeds. At 16 kph, the 3.8-cm (1.5-in.) liner is able to absorb enough energy to prevent concussion. At 32 kph, at least 12.7-cm (5-in.) liner is required to prevent concussion. These results give us an insight into the design challenge, which is to provide enough protection without creating a large helmet that the user may not accept.

© The Author(s), under exclusive license to Springer Nature Switzerland AG 2022
V. G. Duffy (Ed.): HCII 2022, LNCS 13319, pp. 77–89, 2022.
https://doi.org/10.1007/978-3-031-05890-5_6

2 Motivation

Within helmet design, the use of honeycomb structures can improve energy absorption [1]. This does not add extra weight and bulk to a helmet. For the purpose of a lightweight and energy-absorbing helmet, the design of honeycomb structures is required to adapt curved surfaces. For a long time, honeycomb structures have been used in freeform structural design to reduce material usage without losing structural strength. Therefore, the methods to construct honeycomb structures in an interactive way have also become an issue worth exploring.

Ways of interactive geometry modeling are often used in freeform structural design. Designers can use constrained optimization algorithms to realize design goals [5]. Tang et al. [6] proposed an effective method. They developed a system that has a graphical interface. This system is suitable for the interactive design of meshes and other structures. A user can create and modify a geometry by setting constraints such as boundary alignment and equilibrant forces. This approach is useful to design a freeform structure consisting of similar elements.

When designing honeycomb structures and others, it is common to start by creating planar meshes (like triangle meshes or quad meshes). Meshes with various additional properties (like equal angles, equal sides) are available for interactive geometry modeling [5]. A typical example is Lobel meshes, which are a type of structure composed of equilateral triangle meshes. Lobel meshes can be used to create the corresponding honeycombs [5]. Schiftner et al. [7] showed that hexagonal torsion-free structures could be derived from Lobel meshes. Their work also showed that Lobel meshes could be used to create other patterns or structures, such as circle patterns and sphere packings. These show the extensibility of Lobel meshes in structural design.

Jiang et al. [8] proposed a design method for structural design. It allows constructing torsion-free structures aligned with hexagonal meshes on a curved surface. In their work, the focus is an analysis of the flexibility of using honeycomb structures to cover a curved surface. They applied the developed method to design a freeform shade structure with honeycomb structures. Their work shows the applicability of honeycomb structures in freeform structural design.

The methods in the above works can efficiently realize the creation of honeycomb structures. But these methods involve complex coding and algorithms. These may not be easy for designers who do not have a specific programming foundation. Rhino (RH) and Grasshopper (GH) are design software commonly used by industrial designers. We need to propose a parametric design method for creating honeycomb structures by using RH and GH.

3 Design Issue

The research aims to propose a parametric design method, which is flexible to create honeycomb structures on curved surfaces. Our method should have two capabilities. The first is that the creation of honeycomb structures cannot be constrained by the UV lines on a curved surface. The secondary is that uncontrolled deformations can be reduced in creating honeycomb structures. This method can be easily applied to create honeycomb structures on different shapes of curved surfaces. This is an important quality. It means that designers can create suitable shapes of honeycomb structures according to different design goals, such as a helmet, elbow pad, or knee pad. This research also aims to complete the design of a sports helmet through the developed method. The key point of this design is to create a honeycomb helmet liner based on the morphological features of the human skull.

4 Building the Design Program

We used GH to build a generative design program for creating honeycomb structures. GH is a graphical program editor which is integrated into RH. In the program, the key point is the combined use of two GH plugins, ShapeMap and Kangaroo. To illustrate the essence of the program, we first briefly describe the functional advantages of the two plugins.

ShapeMap is a parametric plugin developed by the Shaper3D®. Designers can quickly map a 2D or 3D geometric grid to a curved surface by using this plugin. The advantage of using this plugin is that the grid mapped to a surface reduces uncontrolled deformation. In addition, the operation of mapping grids is not constrained by the UV lines on a surface. The combined use of Shapmap and other GH plugins can adjust and change the shape of grids in real-time and intuitively. Therefore, we applied this plugin, which is used to map a hexagonal grid to a surface. The mapped grid is used to generate honeycomb structures.

Kangaroo is a parametric plugin for shape design. Now, there are many ways to manipulate digital geometry. Still, one significant advantage of physically-based approaches is that we have a natural feel for them, and this quality makes itself ideal for the parametric design [9]. Using the Kangaroo plugin, designers can shape geometric forms in real-time by inputting parameters such as applied forces and material properties. Simulation is nonlinear in Kangaroo. Therefore, it helps design structures involving large deformations [9]. We applied the Kangaroo plugin to carry out shape design and optimization for hexagonal grids.

We developed the generative design program by mainly using these two plugins. The program enables the creation of honeycomb structures on a curved surface, and the process is intuitive and real-time. To illustrate how the design of honeycomb structures is generated, we explain the key points of the program created for this research. As seen in Fig. 1, this is the program created for our research.

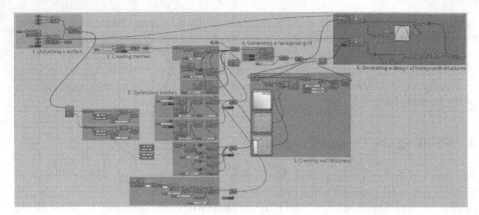

Fig. 1. The program is created for generating honeycomb structures.

A curved surface was created in Rhino, representing the target used to map grids. Based on the shape of this surface, The program would first generate the design of a hexagonal grid. In our process, the first step is to unfold the curved surface, as seen in Fig. 2. The way to unfold surfaces uses ShapeMap components, including ShapeSolver and ShapeMap, as seen in Fig. 2 pink group. The unfolding of surfaces is done to make it easier to create grids. The program allows generating a hexagonal grid on the unfolded surface and then mapping it to the curved surface. Compared to creating grids directly on curved surfaces, this indirect approach is useful to improve the quality of grids created.

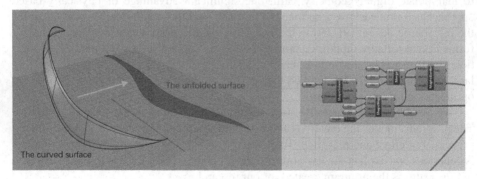

Fig. 2. The curved surface is converted to the unfolded surface.

The program created for this research only accepts geometry converted to meshes as input. As seen in Fig. 3, The initial mesh is created using the non-parametric method, which is that designers create meshes manually in RH. Based on the shape of the unfolded surface, we applied the Mesh tool to create the initial mesh composed of triangle meshes. And then, the initial mesh is subdivided using the Refine and Mesh Triangulate components, as seen in Fig. 3 green group. The result is that triangle meshes in the initial mesh are converted into a large number of smaller meshes. As seen in Fig. 3, this is the final mesh used to prepare it for creating a hexagonal grid.

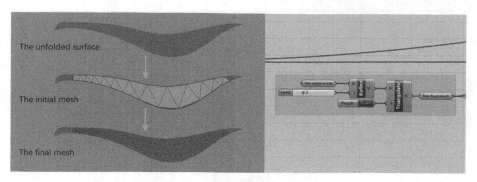

Fig. 3. The process of creating meshes

The final mesh consists of a lot of triangle meshes, each of which contains three vertices. Therefore, the essence of manipulating meshes is to adjust the positions of all vertices. In our research, the vertices are divided into outer points and inner points, as seen in Fig. 4. The final mesh is manipulated mainly using Kangaroo forces, including tensile forces and gravity, as seen in Fig. 4 purple group. The tensile forces are applied to pull the outer points to the boundary of the unfolded surface. The gravity is applied to keep all points on a plane. We required that each triangle mesh should be shaped into an equilateral triangle. This was useful for our program to generate a regular hexagonal grid. Therefore, the final mesh is also shaped using Kangaroo constraints, such as rest angles and equal angles, as seen in Fig. 4 purple group. After setting the requirements above, we solved it with the Kangaroo solver to obtain the mesh with an optimized shape.

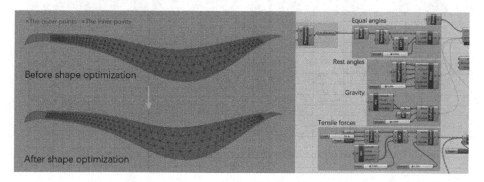

Fig. 4. The shape optimization for the final mesh

The way to generate hexagonal grids use Weaverbird's Dual graph component, which allows extracting center points of triangle meshes and creating polylines from these points to form closed graphs. As seen in Fig. 5, this is the hexagonal grid created. The gaps between the hexagons represents the wall thickness of honeycomb structures. After the hexagonal grid is obtained, it is mapped to the curved surface by the MapToShape component.

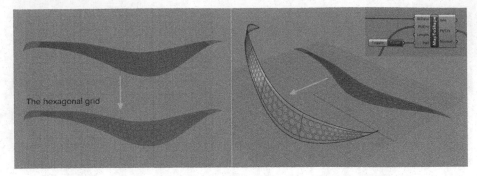

Fig. 5. The hexagonal grid and the state of mapping it to the curved surface

The final phase addresses creating honeycomb structures based on the hexagonal grid mapped. It is divided into two parts: extruding hexagonal prisms from the grid and then cutting honeycomb structures out of a solid. In the first part, the hexagonal prisms were generated by extruding planar surfaces along vectors. The program created each planar surface from the edge curves, which were converted from every hexagon boundary. In addition, each planar surface was matched an individual vector, involving the direction and the length. As seen in Fig. 6, these are the hexagonal prisms created. In the second part, the honeycomb structures were cut out of a solid by the Boolean difference command. The solid was created by offsetting the curved surface. As seen in Fig. 6, It partially intersects with the hexagonal prisms.

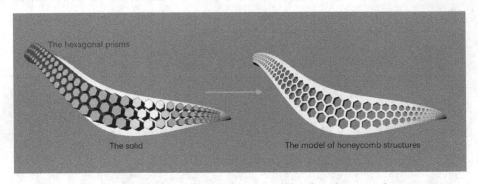

Fig. 6. The hexagonal prisms intersect with the solid to form honeycomb structures.

5   Generating the Design

5.1   Understanding Human Skull

The human skull, which consists of twenty-two bones, is a complex structure in human skeleton. The skull is generally divided into the cranium and the facial skeleton. The cranium, which consists of eight bones, encloses and protects the brain, meninges, and cerebrovascular system. In anatomy, the cranium can be subdivided into the cranial roof and the cranial base. The cranial roof is composed of the frontal bone, the pairs of parietal bones, and the occipital bone. The bones that make up the cranial roof form the three most important sutures in the human skull: coronal, sagittal, and chevron sutures. In addition, two important junctions are pterions where the frontal, parietal, sphenoid, and temporal bones meet. The pterions are the thinnest parts in the cranium, with an average thickness of about 1–2 mm. Compared to the pterions, the other parts in the cranium are thicker, about 5~10 mm.

Typical head injuries are skull fracture, cerebral contusion, concussion, and intracranial hematoma. The skull fracture is the most common type of head injury caused by traffic accidents. It is caused by three main injury mechanisms: contact force, head acceleration, and rotational motion [10]. The fracture will occur when the impact force exceeds the tolerance level of the skull. Depending on the severity of the skull fractures, there are four typical types of skull fractures, including linear fracture, depressed fracture, comminuted depressed fracture, and compound fracture. In the linear fracture, the bone breaks but does not move from its original position, while in the compound fracture, the bone is severely fractured with a skin laceration. Skull fractures mainly occur in the parietal and frontal bones, followed by the occipital and temporal bones.

As seen in Fig. 7, we divide six protective areas based on the anatomy of the skull and the biomechanics. Four protective areas (A1, A2, A3, A4) cover the coronal, sagittal, and herringbone sutures. Two protective areas (A5, A6) cover the two pterions with their surrounding areas. In the design of the helmet liner, we would apply the developed method to design suitable honeycomb structures for each protective area.

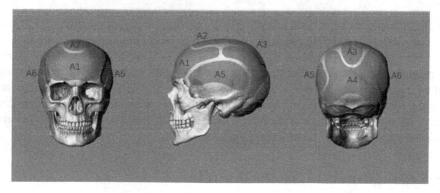

Fig. 7. The six protective areas

5.2 Ergonomic Elements Related to Helmet Design

The European EN 960 is the widely accepted international standard that specifies the performance of the head forms used in helmet design [11]. This standard identifies four reference planes for head dimensions. These are the basic plane, the longitudinal plane, the transverse plane, and the reference plane. The protective range of a helmet needs to be

arranged regarding these planes. As seen in Fig. 8, the basic plane, roughly in the center
placement of the head, is defined by the points of the lower edge of the eyelid and the
upper edge of the ear canal. The longitudinal plane is perpendicular to the basic plane.
The transverse plane is perpendicular to the two previous planes, through the center of
the ear hole. The reference plane is parallel to the basic plane and above it, approximately
2.5 cm from the basic plane. In addition, the definitions of four reference planes are also
adopted in the Chinese GB 24429–2009, which is the current design standard for sports
helmets in China. The helmet sizing for this project is set with reference to the GB
24429–2009.

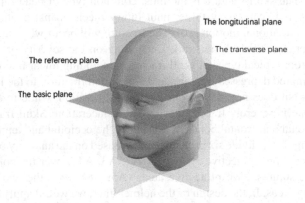

Fig. 8. The four reference planes in helmet design

The helmet sizes are divided according to the head circumference, including 520 mm,
540 mm, 560 mm, and 580 mm [12]. In addition to head circumference, we collected
other head dimensions required for helmet design. As seen in Table 1, these are the
reference head dimensions. The data are derived from the anthropometric study of the
3000 Chinese workers of different ages by Wang et al. [13]. These dimensions are
essential for adjusting the digital head model we bought. Referring to head dimensions
at P90, we adjusted the shape of the digital head model in RH. The adjusted head model
was used as the reference for modeling the helmet.

5.3 Creating Honeycomb Liner for Helmet Design

In Sect. 3 of the paper, we have detailed the essence of the developed program. Therefore,
in the discussion of helmet lining design, we briefly show the generative process of the
honeycomb liner through multiple sets of pictures.

As seen in Fig. 9, these are six curved surfaces created with reference to the head
model, each of which represents a protective area of the head. The first step in our process
is to unfold these surfaces. The unfolded surfaces can make it easier for the program to
create hexagonal grids.

Table 1. The head dimensions required for helmet design

Dimension	Mean	Standard deviation	Percentiles		
			P10	P50	P90
Male					
Head circumference	567.0	13.6	541	567	586
Head length	185.7	5.8	175	186	194
Head breadth	157.2	5.3	147	157	165
Bitragion frontal arc	311.7	10.1	292	312	326
Bitragion coronal arc	358.7	11.8	335	360	376

Source: Head-and-face anthropometric survey of Chinese workers [J].

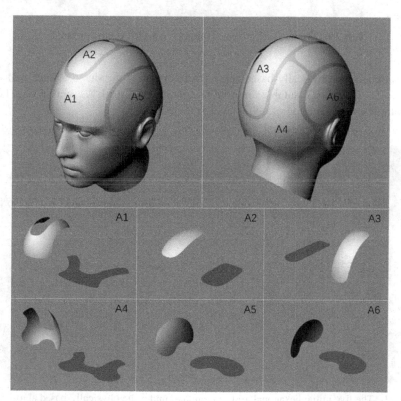

Fig. 9. The six curved surfaces are used to create hexagonal grids.

The program only accepts geometry converted to meshes as input. As seen in Fig. 10, the unfolded surfaces are converted into five collections of meshes, each composed of a lot of triangle meshes.

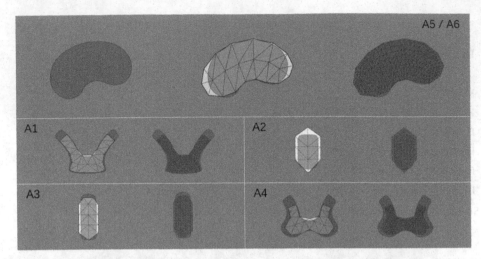

Fig. 10. The five collections of meshes (A5 and A6 are mirrored)

We applied the physically-based approach to optimize the shape of each collection of meshes so that it was suitable for creating a hexagonal grid. As seen in Fig. 11, we have completed the creation of initial hexagonal grids.

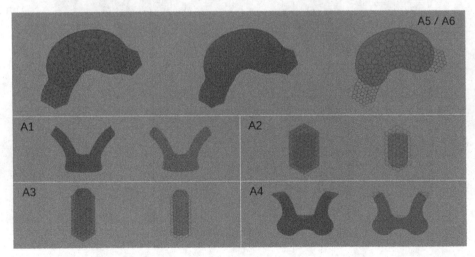

Fig. 11. The five initial hexagonal grids are created under the physically-based algorithm.

As seen in Fig. 12, the final grid used for mapping is created based on the initial hexagonal grid. The gaps between the hexagons represent the wall thickness of honeycomb structures. The average gap widths are different among the final grids. This is because the thickness of the bones is different in different parts of the cranium. For example, the two protective areas (A5, A6) cover the pterions, the thinnest parts of a cranium. Therefore, the gaps in the final grids for A5 and A6 are thicker than the other ones. It has the potential to enhance the protection of pterions.

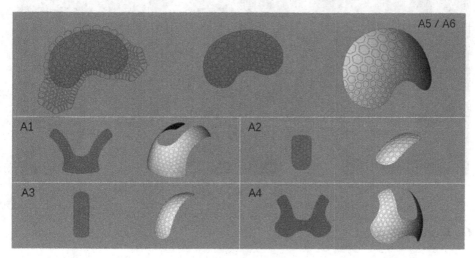

Fig. 12. Each final grid and the state of mapping it to the corresponding curved surface

As seen in Fig. 13, each part of the honeycomb liner is created from the corresponding mapped grid. For each part, prisms are extruded from the mapped grid, and then honeycomb structures are cut out of the solid. As seen in Fig. 14, this is the design model of the helmet with the honeycomb liner.

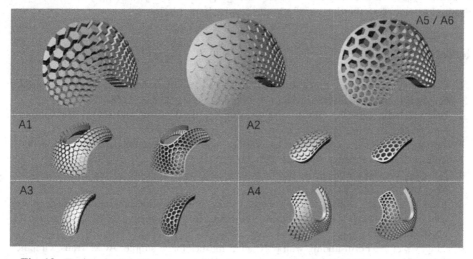

Fig. 13. Each part of the honeycomb liner is created by the Boolean difference command.

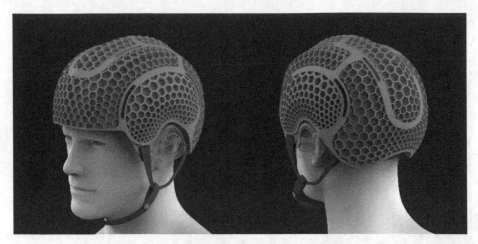

Fig. 14. Helmet rendering

6 Conclusion

We propose a new parametric design method. It enables the more flexible creation of honeycomb structures on curved surfaces. This method has two main advantages. The first advantage is that the creation of honeycomb structures is not constrained by UV lines on a curved surface. The second advantage is that uncontrolled deformations can be reduced in the creation of honeycomb structures. Using this method, we create honeycomb structures based on different shapes of surfaces. This shows that our method has a certain generality. It means that other designers may refer to our method to create honeycomb structures according to different design goals. Finally, we apply the developed method to complete the design of a honeycomb-shaped helmet.

References

1. Caserta, G.D., Iannucci, L., Galvanetto, U.: Shock absorption performance of a motorbike helmet with honeycomb reinforced liner. Compos. Struct. **93**(11), 2748–2759 (2011)
2. Di Landro, L., Sala, G., Olivieri, D.: Deformation mechanisms and energy absorption of polystyrene foams for protective helmets[J]. Polym. Testing **21**(2), 217–228 (2002)
3. Yettran, A.L.: Materials for motorcycle crash helmets-a finite element parametric study. Plast. Rubber Compos. Process. Appl. **22**, 215–221 (1994)
4. Newman, J.A.: Biomechanics of human trauma: head protection. Accidental Injury. Springer, New York, NY, pp. 292-310 (1993)
5. Jiang, C., et al.: Interactive modeling of architectural freeform structures: combining geometry with fabrication and statics. Advances in Architectural Geometry 2014. Springer, Cham, pp. 95-108 (2015)
6. Tang, C., et al.: Form-finding with polyhedral meshes made simple. ACM Trans. Graphics (TOG) **33**(4), 1–9 (2014)
7. Schiftner, A., et al.: Packing circles and spheres on surfaces. ACM SIGGRAPH Asia 2009 papers, 1–8 (2009)

8. Jiang, C., et al.: Freeform honeycomb structures. Computer Graphics Forum. **33**(5), 185–194 (2014)
9. Piker, D.: Kangaroo: form finding with computational physics. Archit. Des. **83**(2), 136–137 (2013)
10. Yang, J.: Review of injury biomechanics in car-pedestrian collisions. Int. J. Veh. Saf. **1**(1–3), 100–117 (2005)
11. Ball, R.: 3-D design tools from the SizeChina project. Ergonomics in Design **17**(3), 8–13 (2009)
12. China National Institute of Standardization: CNIS GB 24429–2009. Sports helmets -Safety requirements for sports helmets for cyclists and users of skateboards and roller skates. General Administration of Quality Supervision, Inspection and Quarantine of the People's Republic of China, Beijing, China (2009)
13. Du, L., et al.: Head-and-face anthropometric survey of Chinese workers. Ann. Occup. Hyg. **52**(8), 773–782 (2008)

Feasibility Study for the Physical Load Evaluation of Construction Machine Ingress and Maintenance

Tsubasa Maruyama[1]([✉]) [iD], Takeshi Furuya[2], Mistunori Tada[1] [iD], Haruki Toda[1] [iD], Ippei Suzuki[2], and Yuka Wada[2]

[1] Artificial Intelligence Research Center, National Institute of Advanced Industrial Science and Technology (AIST), Tokyo, Japan
{tbs-maruyama,m.tada,haruki-toda}@aist.go.jp
[2] Development Division, Komatsu Ltd., Osaka, Japan
{takeshi_furuya,ippei_suzuki,yuka_yw_wada}@global.komatsu

Abstract. Construction machine ingress and maintenance is burdensome. Evaluating the operator's physical load is thus important according to individual differences of the operators and machines. This paper presents a feasibility study for the physical load evaluation of two real-life operators of two excavator machines by motion measurement experiment in actual construction fields. Wearable inertial measurement units are used to capture the full-body posture of the operator. Insole foot pressure sensors and a strain gauge on the machine are used for measuring the contact forces. Physical load indices such as joint torques, the Ovako working posture analyzing system (OWAS), and the base-of-support (BoS) are calculated by kinematic and dynamic analysis of the digital human (DH). Applicability and effectiveness of evaluating physical load based on measurement in actual construction fields were discussed. Our results indicated that the joint torque evaluation is applicable to almost cases, however, the BoS and the OWAS are effective for a part of works.

Keywords: Digital human · Construction machine · Ergonomics · Inertial measurement unit

1 Introduction

Construction machines are widely used by people with a variety of body shapes. However, construction machine-related work, such as ingress and maintenance, is burdensome. Apart from safety-related standards, there are no detailed specifications for working postures, which differ among operators and machines.

Evaluating operator's physical loads can improve machine design and posture instructions. Laboratory-based evaluation using digital humans (DHs) have been conducted; however, there remains an unavoidable gap between actual construction equipment and the imitated environment [1, 2]. In the laboratory setting, it is basically infeasible to use actual construction machine. Thus, we are forced to use mock-ups for experiments. In addition, the operators are required to wear a special clothing and markers for

© The Author(s), under exclusive license to Springer Nature Switzerland AG 2022
V. G. Duffy (Ed.): HCII 2022, LNCS 13319, pp. 90–99, 2022.
https://doi.org/10.1007/978-3-031-05890-5_7

motion capture system. Therefore, the laboratory-based method does not always capture the actual motion in the construction fields although it is useful for revealing human basic characteristics. On the other hand, recent advances in inertial measurement unit (IMU) enables the wearable motion capture in various environments. For example, Greco et al. utilized the IMU-based motion capture for ergonomic assessment during manufacturing task [3]. Caputo et al. applied the IMU-based motion capture for car assembly task [4]. However, no research has been done to evaluate the operator's physical load by capturing their full-body motion in actual construction fields.

Therefore, this paper presents a feasibility study for the physical load evaluation of two real-life operators of two excavator machines. The operators perform eight work items (W1–W8) shown in Fig. 1. Full-body postures and external forces during ingress and maintenance were measured by IMU-based motion capture [5], insole foot pressure sensors, and machine-mounted force sensors. Several physical load indices such as joint torques, the Ovako working posture analyzing system (OWAS), and the base-of-support (BoS) were calculated by kinematic and dynamic analysis of the DH, and their applicability is discussed.

2 Method

2.1 Motion Measurements

As shown in Fig. 2, the full-body posture and the external forces during performing the work items in Fig. 1 were measured as follows.

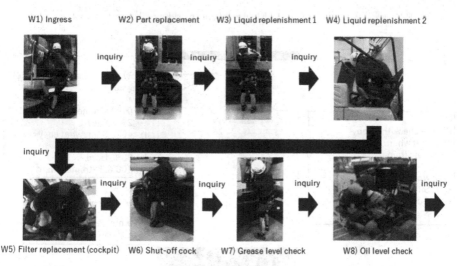

Fig. 1. Work items

- Full-body motion: To avoid occlusions and ambient light effects, an IMU-based motion-capture [6] was used. 15 IMUs (Xsens, MTw2) were attached on the body segments of the subject, pelvis, trunk, upper arms, forearms, hands, upper legs, lower legs, feet, and head. At the begging of the measurement, the subject was asked to take a calibration pose for calculating the relative sensor orientation with respect to the body segment. To reduce the effect on sensor drift error, the measurement was performed within 10 min per trial.

- External forces: The forces in both feet were measured by insole pressure sheet sensors (Novel, Pedar). During ingress (W1), the hand forces were measured by a strain gage on the handrail (Kyowa, KFGS series). The conversion equation from the strain to the force has been calculated using a spring scale prior to the experiment.

After the operator completed each work item, the operator is asked to fill a questionnaire about the physical load shown in Fig. 3. In the questionnaire, the operators answered the physical load they felt in percentages.

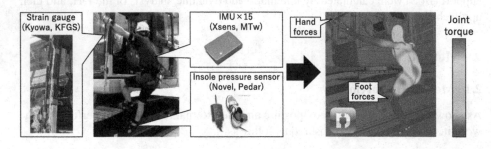

Fig. 2. Measurement overview

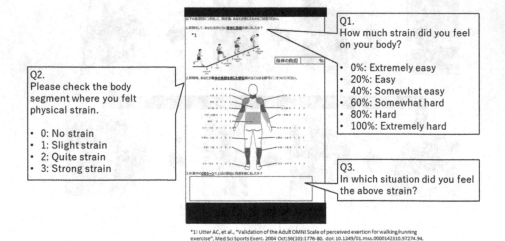

*1: Utter AC, et al., "Validation of the Adult OMNI Scale of perceived exertion for walking/running exercise", Med Sci Sports Exerc. 2004 Oct;36(10):1776-80. doi: 10.1249/01.mss.0000142310.97274.94.

Fig. 3. Subjective evaluation

2.2 Motion Analysis

The measured motions and forces were then reconstructed by our in-house DH software, DhaibaWorks [2], and the following physical load indices were calculated.

- Joint torque: Although the joint torque requires both motion and force measurements for calculation, it can be applied to several ergonomics assessments [6]. In this study, it is calculated by an inverse-dynamics calculation [2], where the torque is estimated by solving an optimization calculation under the assumptions of the equilibrium of gravity, inertial, and contact forces and the equilibrium of moment. The details are described in our previous paper [2].
- OWAS: The OWAS evaluates a four-level physical load by classifying posture and load forces [7]. When the hand forces were not measured (W2–W8), they were estimated by the difference between the body weight and the foot forces.
- BoS: The BoS represents the posture stability from the kinematic aspects [8]. The convex hull coverings of both feet were calculated. Then, the point-to-line distance, d_b, between the center-of-mass (CoM) projected onto the floor and its nearest hull polyline was calculated. This was represented as a signed value, where a positive or negative d_b represented the CoM inside or outside the hull, respectively. The posture became more unstable as d_b decreased.

3 Results

3.1 Experiment Overview

We conducted an experiment with two male operators (S1 and S2), who have experience of construction machine-related works in Fig. 1. They were 1.69 and 1.75 m tall, and they weighed 59 and 70 kg, respectively. They performed the work items with two excavators, M1 and M2. During the experiment, 15 IMUs and insole pressure sensors were attached to the operators. Safety management during the experiment and protection of personal information were carried out in compliance with the internal regulations of the organizations to which the subjects and the experimenters belonged (Komatsu Ltd.).

3.2 Subjective Evaluation Results

The subjective evaluation results are shown in Fig. 4. As shown in Fig. 4, there is no difference between two excavators for the ingress (W1). For the shut-off cock (W6), both operators answered that the physical load of the excavator M1 is greater than that of M2. In contrast, their answers showed the opposite trend for the liquid replenishment work 1 (W3). Thus, it was confirmed that the subjective physical loads for different machines and work items did not necessarily coincide even for the operators with similar body heights. The subjective evaluation results were compared with the physical load evaluation results in the following subsections.

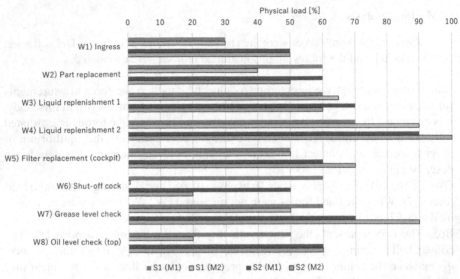

Fig. 4. Subjective evaluation results. S1 and S2 are the operators, and M1 and M2 are the machines.

3.3 Physical Load Evaluation Results

Figure 5 shows the joint torque estimation results during the ingress (W1). The ingress to the excavator was carried out in three steps. No difference was observed in the subjective evaluation; however, the estimated torso joint torque differed between the operators and the excavators. For operator S1, the joint torque at step 1 for excavator M1 was larger than that of M2. As shown in Fig. 6, this is caused by the operator's different postures for each excavator. In particular, the angle between the upper leg and the trunk during the ingress to M1 was larger than that of M2. This led the increases in the joint torque for M1. Since the ingress posture was easily affected by the body dimensions and the arrangement of the handrails and steps, the evaluation using the joint torque might be considered to be suitable. In addition, it should be evaluated for individual operators on individual machines.

Figure 7 shows the physical load evaluation results for the shut-off cock work (W6). As shown in Fig. 7 (a), this work was performed while standing. In this work, both joint torque and the OWAS corresponded to the subjective evaluation. In addition, the postures with M1 seemed to be unstable. As shown in Fig. 7 (b), the BoS evaluation results also indicated the work with M1 was unstable both operators. Thus, applying the BoS analysis for such maintenance work with unstable reaching posture is considered as reasonable.

Figure 8 shows the physical load evaluation results for the liquid replenishment (W3). As shown in Fig. 8 (a), this work was performed by different postures for each excavator (Fig. 8). In this case, although applying joint torque and the OWAS seemed reasonable, they did not correspond to the subjective evaluation.

Our results indicated that the joint torque evaluation is effective for clarifying the difference in physical load during the ingress. In addition, the BoS-based evaluation has a potential for quantifying the unstable posture during the maintenance. However, evaluating the work items in which the working posture differs greatly depending on the machine, i.e., the work W3, remains challenging.

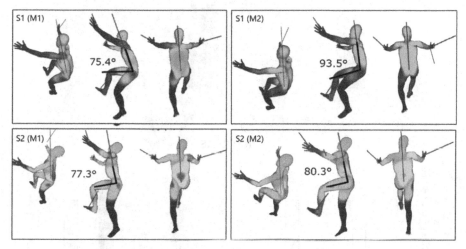

Fig. 5. Ingress step-1 postures

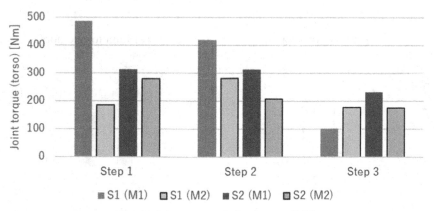

Fig. 6. Joint torques during ingress (W1)

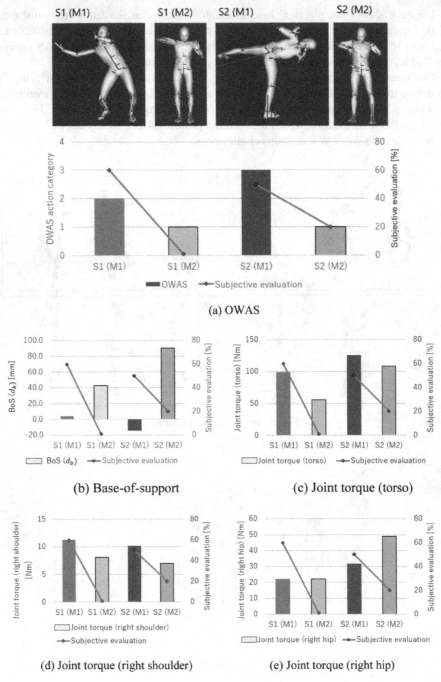

(a) OWAS

(b) Base-of-support

(c) Joint torque (torso)

(d) Joint torque (right shoulder)

(e) Joint torque (right hip)

Fig. 7. Results for shut-off cock (W6)

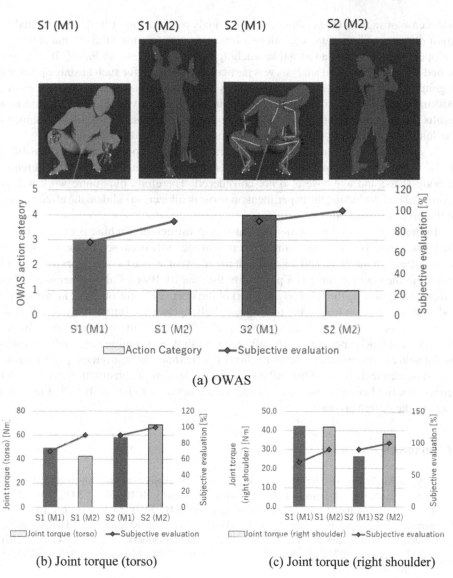

(a) OWAS

(b) Joint torque (torso)   (c) Joint torque (right shoulder)

Fig. 8. Results for liquid replenishment 1 (W3)

4 Conclusion

This paper presented a feasibility study for physical load evaluations based on the measurement in actual construction fields. The wearable IMU-based motion capture, the
insole foot pressure sensors, and the strain gauge were used to capture the actual operators. From the posture and force measurements, the joint torque, BoS, and OWAS were
calculated for real-life operators using construction machines. It was confirmed that the
joint torque evaluation could be used to clarify the physical load differences especially

in the case of ingress (W1). This is because analysis by the joint torque is affected by slight differences in posture and external forces. In construction machine maintenance, the operator might take an unstable reaching posture as shown in Fig. 7. It was confirmed that the BoS-based analysis was particularly effective for such unstable postures. In general, the OWAS has been used to clarify the physical load differences between the working postures differed greatly as shown in Fig. 8. However, the OWAS evaluation results did not correspond to the subjective evaluation results. Therefore, it remained a challenge to evaluate physical loads when working postures differed greatly.

It should be noted that only two operators joined the experiment in this feasibility study. Therefore, the statistical validity has not been shown. In addition, differences in body shape and age have also not considered. Therefore, our future work will be addressed for conducting the experiment on various subjects to validate the effectiveness of the proposed method.

In this study, the maneuvering motion of a construction machine is excluded from the work items. This is because the drift error of the IMU is caused by the vibration of the construction machine, and it is difficult to remove it. Since the operators do not walk around in the cockpit, there is a possibility that the RGB or RGBD cameras could be utilized for capturing the full-body or a part of the operator's motions. The measurement and analysis of the maneuvering motion are challenges in our future study.

On the other hand, it is difficult to cover all types of the operators only by the evaluation of field experiments. Therefore, it is desirable to combine the analysis results by the field experiments with the simulation of body shape and movement patterns using digital human technology. This will enable the evaluation of construction machine that reflects the field context and various types of the operator to be conducted at the early stage of the design process.

References

1. Dorynek, M., Zhang, H., Hofmann, N., Bengler, K.: New Approaches to Movement Evaluation Using Accurate Truck Ingress Data. In: Duffy, V.G. (ed.) HCII 2021. LNCS, vol. 12777, pp. 110–121. Springer, Cham (2021). https://doi.org/10.1007/978-3-030-77817-0_10
2. Maruyama, T., Toda, H., Endo, Y., Tada, M., Hagiwara, H., Kitamura, K.: Digital Human Simulation for Fall Risk Evaluation When Sitting on Stepladders. In: Duffy, V.G. (ed.) HCII 2021. LNCS, vol. 12777, pp. 58–66. Springer, Cham (2021). https://doi.org/10.1007/978-3-030-77817-0_5
3. Greco, A., Caterino, M., Fera, M., Gerbino, S.: Digital twin for monitoring ergonomics during manufacturing production. Appl. Sci. **10**, 7758 (2020). https://doi.org/10.3390/app10217758
4. Caputo, F., Greco, A., Fera, M., Macchiaroli, R.: Digital twins to enhance the integration of ergonomics in the workplace design. Int. J. Ind. Ergono. **71**, 20-31 (2019). ISSN 0169-8141, https://doi.org/10.1016/j.ergon.2019.02.001
5. Maruyama, T., Tada, M., Toda, H., Riding motion capture system using inertial measurement units with contact constraints, Int. J. Auto. Technol. **13**(4), 506–516 (2019). https://doi.org/10.20965/ijat.2019.p0506
6. Menychtas, D., Glushkova, A., Manitsaris, S.: Analyzing the kinematic and kinetic contributions of the human upper body's joints for ergonomics assessment. J. Ambient. Intell. Humaniz. Comput. **11**(12), 6093–6105 (2020). https://doi.org/10.1007/s12652-020-01926-y

7. Veikko, L., Timo S.: OWAS: a method for the evaluation of postural load during work, In: Pavi H. (ed.) Training Publication 11. Institute of Occupational Health, Topeliuksenkatu, pp. 2–20 (1992)
8. Yang, B.-S., Ashton-Miller, J.A.: Factors affecting stepladder stability during a lateral weight transfer: a study in healthy young adults. J. App. Ergonomics. **36**, 601–607 (2005). https://doi.org/10.1016/j.apergo.2005.01.012

Computer-Aid Ergonomic Analysis of Excavator Driver's Body Posture Model

Chuqing Ni[✉]

Purdue University, West Lafayette, IN 47907, USA
ni45@purdue.edu

Abstract. The two main objectives of this project are to understand the menu and basic functions of RAMSIS. The other purpose of this project is to implement the understanding of the software and used those skills to improve the design of an excavator by doing ergonomic analysis. This report talks about several main functions used to create manikins, discomfort assessment, and the future improvement of the project based on the result. The project mainly focuses on a 50 percentile American male body size manikin. After running several iteration and analyses, by raising the armrest height, the result shows it is necessary to improve the excavator in order to make the product more user-friendly. This report also compared and contrasted with another paper with a similar project done by Sinchuk et al. The comparison allows the author to think further about the project and also learned serval new ways that will lead to the same result.

Keywords: Discomfort assessment · Excavator · RAMSIS

1 Computer- Aided Ergonomic Analysis

"Ergonomics (or human factors) is the scientific discipline concerned with the understanding of interactions among humans and other elements of a system, and the profession that applies theory, principles, data, and other methods to design in order to optimize human well-being and overall system performance" [1]. Many product designers devoted themselves to ergonomics in order to create a comfortable and user-friendly environment for people to live in. A properly designed product may improve people's productivity and also make them enjoy, not endure, the long time work [4]. Thus, project one focuses on improving the excavator in the factory, which helps the worker to mitigate the accumulation of stress over a long time repetitive working situation.

The method used to achieve this goal in this project is by doing a computer simulation on RAMSIS. RAMSIS is a 3D Digital Human Modeling tool that permits the user to create specified manikins. Then, by adjusting the gesture of the manikins, and use the analyzing tool that comes with the system. The discomfort assessment will run automatically and provide a discomfort score for each joint. Thus, the ultimate goal of project one is to adjust the excavator to make it more comfortable for drivers to use.

© The Author(s), under exclusive license to Springer Nature Switzerland AG 2022
V. G. Duffy (Ed.): HCII 2022, LNCS 13319, pp. 100–111, 2022.
https://doi.org/10.1007/978-3-031-05890-5_8

2 Problem Statement

There are two main purposes of Project 1. The first part is to learn how to use RAMSIS and to understand the use of some of the functions in the software menu. This includes how to build a manikin with specific values (e.g. height, bust, age, gender, region, etc.); how to select points on the manikin and connect them to the environment or the object used; and how to analyze the comfort level when they were using the object in a specific position in order to help the designer better adjust the product parameters and improve the design. The other goal of this project is to do research on the excavator's driving seat and find the ergonomic risks. In the project, the original idea was to create 3 sets of manikins: one very tall American male, one 50 percentile size American male, one 5 percentile size American female. The reason to run the project with different sizes and genders of people is intended to design the workstation better while minimizing the number of people being excluded [2]. Each sets includes two roles: one driving and one digging. Then each set was altered to sit on the excavator while having the hand either hold on the steering wheel or the joystick, while the eye line looks to the front. Finally, derive the discomforting number for each manikin and diagnose the ergonomic risk factor of the joints. However, due to the author don't have access to the RAMSIS, the result based on Andre's sample only shows the simulation and the result of the 50 percentile men. Thus, the simulation was only done for one set and been repeated three times. The reason that this project is important is that the driving situation is a commonly seen situation in the real-life, and many people have stated that a comfortable chair could is one of the most essential facilities in a working place, which helps them relieve stress and maintain independence [3]. Therefore, what has been explored in this project, can also be put into practice in the real world situation.

3 Procedure

3.1 Loading the Software

After following the instruction of installing RAMSIS correctly, after launching into the software, it should look similar to Fig. 1. Next, by clicking the (File > Load Session > Find Session Folder > OK), the model of the excavator should pop up as shown in Fig. 2.

Fig. 1. (Left): The panel after launch in RAMSIS   **Fig. 2.** (Right): The model of the excavator without manikins

3.2 Hide and Show Unnecessary Parts

The concealment feature allows the user to see a separate part of a complex product simply and directly after all the parts have been mounted. This not only ensures that the user can easily select the widget they want after installation but also provides a more visual representation of the relationship between each piece and the product. In RAMSIS, there are two ways to achieve this goal. The first is to right-click on the component that needs to hide and select the (Hide/Show) option, refer to Fig. 3, then the component will be hidden. Alternatively, one can find the corresponding parts on the general structure tree and shift the active to inactive. Besides, one can hide the unhidden part while showing the hidden part by selecting the (Swap Visible Space) option after right click on the features. More specific details of the selection on the menu can be found in Fig. 4 and Fig. 5.

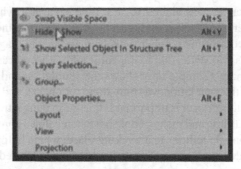

Fig. 3. The panel for selecting the parts visibility.

Fig. 4. (Left): The sitting section of the excavator. All other parts are being hidden.

Fig. 5. (Right): Figure under Swap Visible Space.

3.3 Create Manikins with Specified Role and Gender

There are two methods to create manikins by RAMSIS. The first way is to click the blue circle button indicate in Fig. 6, then adjust the necessary feature on the screen that pops up. First, under the "Anthropometry" section adjust the feature to a very tall male, medium waist, and long torso. Then, move to "Role Assignment" and click the green circle in Fig. 6 for generating new roles. Adjustig the features as shown in Fig. 7 and name the role as Driving. Following the same steps while keeping everything else the same as Driving, generating another role called Digging. By doing those steps, a set of manikins is produced. If the generated manikins are formed by lines only, then click the red circle as shown in Fig. 1. The other way to create a new manikin is by click (Start > NextGen Body Builder). Then following (Anthropometry > Typology > Control Measurement) to input percentile of the size of the manikin, the data shown in Fig. 8. Comparing with the first method, this method can generate a more precise manikin, the difference can be found in Fig. 9. Repeating the step and create a 5 percentile female and a 50 percentile male. Following the step in the next few sections to add restrictions, and the final view looks like Fig. 10.

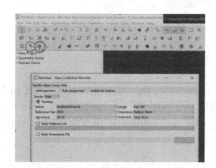

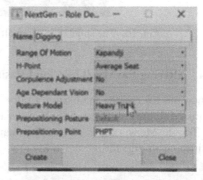

Fig. 6. (Left): Panel for creating manikins.

Fig. 7. (Right): Properties selection when creating roles for manikins.

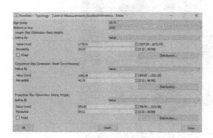

Fig. 8. (Left): The data input to create a male manikin with a 50 percentile size.

Fig. 9. (Right): Difference between use Anthropometry (right) and Body Builder (left) to create manikins

Fig. 10. The simulation when all the 3 manikins been placed on the seat.

3.4 Altering the Manikin's Joint Position

Since the role of the manikin is to drive the excavator, thus the manikins need to be adjusted to the sitting position. In order to fulfill this goal, by clicking (Anthropometry > Toggle Measuring Posture). The manikin will automatically change to the sitting poition as in Fig. 11.

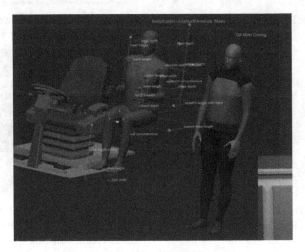

Fig. 11. Manikins in sitting gesture.

3.5 Manikins-Object Interaction

Manikins- object interaction allows the user to adjust the gesture and position of manikins as they want. This function could be regarded as the fundamental that supports RAMSIS to perform the necessary analysis and deduct the conclusion on whether the manikin is in a comfortable situation. This function can be accessed by click on the yellow circle shown in Fig. 1 (Define Restriction > Input as Fig. 12). The "Manikin Comp." is the yellow dots (Fig. 13) shown on the manikins which represent the joint of the model. There are various kinds of restrictions that can be added between the object and the manikins. In this project, the commonly used restrictions are Target, Pelvis Rotation, and Direction.

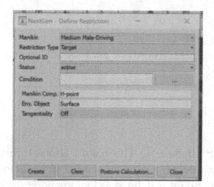 

Fig. 12. (Left): The panel for adding the restriction between the manikins and the object

Fig. 13. (Right): The example of manikin components (yellow dots) on the hands. (Color figure online)

Target Restrictions. Target restriction meaning having the body in contact with the surface. For example, if add a target restriction between the manikin's hand and the steering wheel, it will result in that hand hold on the steering wheel. The list of target restrictions need to create between the manikin and the object is shown in Fig. 14.

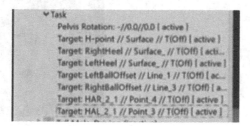

Fig. 14. The list of target restriction

Pelvis Rotation. Pelvis rotation in this project prevents the manikin tilt in the seat, which makes sure the manikin is sitting straight on the seat. The properties selected are shown in Fig. 15. After set as Fig. 15, click create for adding this restriction to the general structure tree.

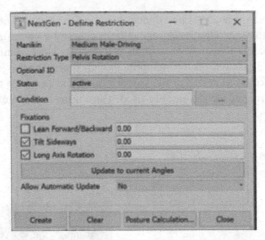

Fig. 15. The input properties for pelvis rotation.

Direction. This feature is also under the Restriction menu. This feature allows the user to constrain certain movements by defining the direction of the movement. For example, in the case of this project, the eye line of the manikins is defined as looking horizontally forward by setting the restriction as shown in Fig. 16. Then press the Posture Calculation, and the manikin will eventually look like Fig. 17.

Fig. 16. (Left): The setting panel of changing the direction of the line of vision.   **Fig. 17.** (Right): The manikin posture after adding the restriction of the line of vision.

Create Surface Point. Create surface point is used to add additional restrictions between the object and the manikin, this feature is mainly used when some objects are not directly selectable by the user, therefore, the user needs to create a new contact point on the object to meet the interaction between the manikin and the object (Geometry > Point > Change the point type to "create on object" > Select the position on the surface that need to add point).

Posture Calculation. The posture calculation function can be found in the grey box of Fig. 1, then click the start button. After the user adds all the restrictions, this function does iterations to make sure all restrictions could be satisfied. If there is an error, the system will indicate the error by marking the restriction in red. The final posture with the manikin's hand on the steering wheel looks similar to Fig. 18. By following the same steps with adding points to the joystick, the posture with manikin holding the joystick looks like Fig. 19. The restriction type for the joystick should be Target at first, and then add a Manual Grasping restriction to the same point of the manikin and the object. This will result in the hand of the manikin hold on the stick. Besides, by changing the grasping model, the way to hold could also be modified.

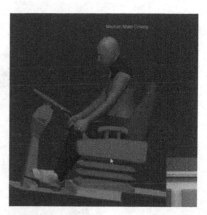

Fig. 18. (Left): Manikin hold the steering wheel

Fig. 19. (Right): Manikin hold the joystick

3.6 Position Adjustment and Analysis Tool

The Position Adjustment feature helped the designer to improve their design, in this case, the excavator. In order to do the position adjustment, since the design is altogether, thus grouping the component is necessary before adjusting its position. Grouping both sides armrest as shown in Fig. 20 by selecting the necessary component and (right click > Group > name the group).

After grouping both sides' armrests, the next step is to add the degree of freedom to the object. This could be proceeding under (Geometry > Kinematics > Degree of Freedom > Create > Add Object > Select the armrest group > Create). The input value is shown in Fig. 21 and Fig. 22.

After adding the degree of freedom to the object, the next step is to analyze the gesture of the manikins. Under Analysis on the top screen menu scroll down and select Comfort Feeling, the comfort value of the current gesture will be displayed in Fig. 23. Any values over 3.5 are considered as uncomfortable. In order to adjust the position and improve the design, (Select the grouped armrest > Right click > Object Properties > Double click the DOF value > Change the DOF value). For the second iteration set the DOF value to 50mm. Then do the Comfort Feeling test again, set the first iteration as the reference, and start the Posture Calculation. The result of the data is shown in Fig. 24.

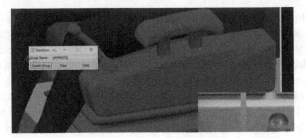

Fig. 20. The grouped armrest.

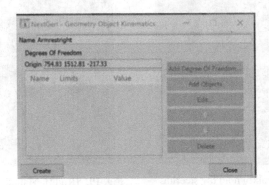

Fig. 21. (Left): The pop-up screen and value input for adding object kinematics

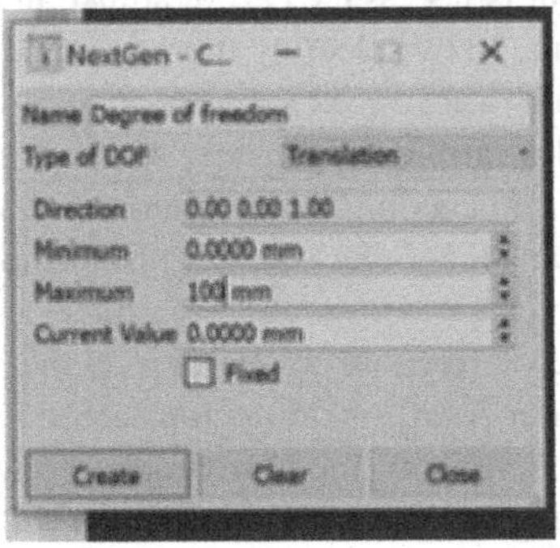

Fig. 22. (Right): The pop-up screen and value input for adding object's degree of freedom

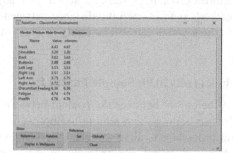

Fig. 23. (Left): the discomfort assessment of the first iteration

Fig. 24. (Right): the discomfort assessment of the second iteration

4 Discussion

4.1 Analysis Result

Table 1. The comfort feeling iteration result for different heights of the armrest

Name	Reference (0 mm)	50 mm	100 mm	Comfort? (3.50)
Neck	4.47	4.26	4.02	Discomfort
Shoulders	3.20	3.07	2.96	Comfort
Back	3.62	3.44	3.22	Comfort
Buttocks	2.88	2.75	2.52	Comfort
Left Leg	3.53	3.34	3.12	Comfort
Right Leg	3.51	3.37	3.22	Comfort
Left Arm	3.75	3.70	3.67	Discomfort
Right Arm	3.72	3.47	3.14	Comfort
Discomfort Feeling	6.36	6.08	5.72	Discomfort
Fatigue	4.74	4.54	4.31	Discomfort
Health	4.76	4.73	4.73	Discomfort

As shown in Table 1, by moving the right armrest up, most of the discomfort position was relieved by raising the right handrail. Moreover, the discomfort value gradually decreases as the right armrest progressively elevated. This shows that raising the armrest allows the elbow to make contact with the armrest does help to alleviate the discomfort when driving. After the armrest was raised to 100 mm, only the neck and left arm felt discomfort. For the left arm, perhaps the problem can be solved by raising the left armrest. However, since the actual operation is not currently feasible, the proposed improvement method is only conjecture. For the neck, the main discomfort is likely to come from the joystick is located too far away, so the manikin needs to lean forward to reach the joystick. However, at the same time, there is a need to look straight ahead, so it leads to neck discomfort. For this reason, there are two methods to improve the discomfort of the neck. The first is to adjust the whole armrest group backward, the second is to adjust the seat forward. The purpose of both methods is to shorten the distance between the person and the joystick, thus ensuring that the joystick can still be easily reached while leaning on the seat.

4.2   Compare and Contrast with Sinchuk et al. (2020) Sample Paper [4]

Comparing with Sinchuk's sample paper, the author believes the content between the sample paper and Project 1 is similar because both of them aiming to improve a kind of working space. Therefore, the general procedure is alike to each other. However, the approach to the same procedure is slightly different. For example, in project one, in order to make the manikin's eye look to the front, Project 1's approach is to add a directional restriction. However, the approach that Sinchuk used is the Move Eye button in the menu. Also, project 1 used Comfort Feeling analysis to determine whether the gesture is comfortable or not, while Sinchuk's project used Joint Analysis.

In addition, the chair of Sinchuk's project was ignored. Thus, the freedom of the body position is higher than in Project 1. Since in Project 1, the designer set the constrain that the manikin has to sit straight on the surface of the chair, if the chair is not moving then the distance between the steering wheel and the body is about the same. On the other hand, Sinchuk's project allows the manikin to sit at distance to the table. This difference would lead slight difference in the ergonomics analysis.

4.3   Author's Experience and Challenge

The author's experience with ergonomics that is similar to the Project 1 is the author's driving experience. This is because both driving and Project 1 has the joystick and steering wheel. When driving, it is particularly important to pay attention to whether the posture is comfortable and correct, otherwise, it will probably lead to accidents. The difference in height and weight of population makes it almost impossible to design a seat that can precisely meet the requirements of each person. Thus, almost all cars have buttons on the side of the seat that can adjust the seat, and most cars can also adjust the position of the steering wheel. The author believes by reference to car driving, it is possible to find a better solution for Project 1.

The greatest challenge that the author mainly overcome during the project is the locational problem. First, since the author's current location has a time lag with America, thus, sometimes it is hard to get immediate help. In addition, due to RAMSIS couldn't provide the license to the author's current location, therefore, the author need to talk to Professor and find an alternative way to complete the project.

5   Future Work

In all, four points that could be further ameliorated if there is a chance to continue this project in the future. First, because of the author's current location, RAMSIS does not work properly after download due to the absence of a license. Therefore, all data is currently derived from Andre's demonstration video. This is an objective factor that leads to incomplete data. Therefore, it is not possible to extrapolate the most suitable angle and posture for a manikin. Nevertheless, the available data do provide a certain degree of direction for improvement, but they cannot provide an optimal solution.

Secondly, the simulation only simulates a medium male figure, so the insufficient types of sample imply that a certain degree of generalizability is lacking. In order to better simulate the effects of various people in the excavator environment, more models should be built and more optimum solutions should be found for each manikin. Finally, the simulation results of all manikins should be integrated to find the most universal design parameters.

Third, since the purpose of Andre's video is more for demonstrating the steps and providing ideas than finding the optimal solution. Therefore, many of the restrictions are not exactly perfect. For example, the manikins' feet and pedals are crossed and the manikins' hands do not fit perfectly on the joystick. Therefore, these details may have some influence on the final results. If the project is pursued, adding more restrictions to make the manikins and objects more compatible is one way to improve the accuracy.

In the fourth place, although the computer's calculation is quite close to reality, it is still based on a relatively idealized state. For instance, all manikins have the same sitting gesture and with perfect body shape, but there is a gap between this and reality. For example, someone will hunch over, or someone will lean against the chair when operating, etc. Although it is not possible to simulate each person's situation completely and perfectly with a computer, these errors caused by the inability to perform calculations can also have an impact on the final results. Therefore, if there are ways to enhance this situation, these improvements will make the simulation results more realistic and reliable.

References

1. Roberta, E.: Universal Design: Principles and Models, 2. CRC Press, Boca Raton, FL (2014)
2. Salvendy, G., Karwowski, W., Duffy, V.: Chapter 35: human digital modeling in design. Essay. In: Handbook of Human Factors and Ergonomics, pp. 1033–35. John Wiley & Sons Inc., Hoboken (2021)
3. Sinchuk, K., Hancock, A.L., Hayford, A., Kuebler, T., Duffy, V.G.: A 3-Step Approach for Introducing Computer-Aided Ergonomics Analysis Methodologies. In: Duffy, V.G. (ed.) HCII 2020. LNCS, vol. 12198, pp. 243–263. Springer, Cham (2020). https://doi.org/10.1007/978-3-030-49904-4_18
4. Zandt, T.: Chapter 1: historical foundation of human factors. Essay. In: Human Factors in Simple and Complex Systems, Third Edition, p. 9. Ohio State University, Apple Academic Press Inc., Columbus (2017)

Grasp Intent Detection Using Multi Sensorial Data

P. Balaji[✉][iD], Debadutta Subudhi[iD], and Manivannan Muniyandi

Touch Lab, Department of Applied Mechanics, Indian Institute of Technology
Madras, Chennai 600036, India
balu960p@gmail.com, dev.subudhi49@gmail.com, mani@iitm.ac.in

Abstract. Upper Limbs are expected to have precise functionality to do normal activities and perform a specific occupation. The functionality loss will impair the performance accuracy of the tasks. The amputation of a limb can lead to a great reduction in the standard of life and daily activities. Each activity follows a particular intent pattern. The grasp is one of the primary activities to interact with the real or virtual worlds. The grasp intent incorporation in the development of an advanced prosthetic hand needs grasp intent detection using multimodal sensorial data. Multimodal sensorial data is expected to detect precise movements and reduce motion artifacts by using modern Tech innovations. We develop a great classification algorithm to predict the specific grasp intent depending on the type of object through continuous feedback during the approach towards the object using multisensorial data from IMU sensors, EMG and cameras. The deep learning (DL) approach has been developed to increase the accuracy of the grasp intent by continuously predicting the intent class while moving the hand towards the object. The deep learning network archives an accuracy of 92.3% over 89% as in literature using hybrid network Convolutional Neural Network (CNN) and Long Short-term Memory (LSTM) networks on visual feed, inertial measurement unit (IMU) and electromyography (EMG) data.

Keywords: IMU · EMG · Eye and hand-view images · CNN · LSTM

1 Introduction

The individuals with the loss of upper limb require innovative research in the field of the robotic prosthesis to enhance quality in life [12]. The developments in electromyography based human intent solutions demonstrated promising results in the literature for the patients with loss of upper limbs at the point of wrist or elbow [2,10,11]. However, artefacts in EMG significantly reduce the prediction accuracy. Some studies also investigate the deep possibility of using EMG with EEG to improve the accuracy [2,4,11,17]. However, the added information from EEG does not provide significant information to boost the prediction

---

Supported by organization IITM.

© The Author(s), under exclusive license to Springer Nature Switzerland AG 2022
V. G. Duffy (Ed.): HCII 2022, LNCS 13319, pp. 112–122, 2022.
https://doi.org/10.1007/978-3-031-05890-5_9

accuracy, as both EEG and EMG models need frequency calibration to nullify the nonstationarity [5]. Also, the EEG and EMG models suffer from variability from electrode placement on the scalp and conductance of the scalp [12]. Moreover, the intent detection models using the EMG and EEG is challenging due to the possibility of amputations at different locations. The grasp intent detection in prosthetics [18,22] is mainly concerned with having a directional approach, directional angles, the position of the object, and kinematics of the motion [8,9] . Also, individuals with prosthetic hands don't have the freedom to choose the approach trajectory towards an object [12]. Hence, the primary focus is to evaluate the intent of grasp from environmental and physiological measurements. The environmental and physiological measurements are extracted from the object recognition of images using convolutional neural net-work models and time series models [4,15]. Prosthetic hand researchers started exploring the use of CNNs as visual evidence processing solution. We used the Open Access HANDS dataset to train the model and compare the results over the classification results from the paper [12].

1.1 Convolution Neural Network (CNN)

Convolutional Neural Network (CNN or ConvNet) is a major category under Neural networks. The inspiration for CNN came from the human eye. In occipetal lobe while processing the visual data, brain takes information generated by the receptive fields and feed forwards to the cortex forming a kernel. The working of visual data processing was observed by Hubel and Wiesel first under animals and CNN's imagination is formed [6,13,21]. This network practically inspired in the creation of LeNet-5. After training with the back propagation, the LeNet-5 was able to distinguish visual patterns from raw pixels without the use of any independent feature engineering method. CNN also made model training easier because it has fewer connections and parameters than conventional Feed forward neural networks with equivalent network sizes. However, despite these advantages, CNN's accuracy in complex issues like deep classification of a high-resolution videos was limited at the time because of non availability of substantial training data, non inclusiveness of regularisation, augmentation, and insufficient computational power [16].

1.2 Long Short-Term Memory Network (LSTM)

LSTMs are a form of Recurrent Neural Network (RNN) that are used to express inter-relationships within sequential data. An RNN is a Feed-Forward Neural Network (FFNN) with loops in the hidden layers that is an extension of an FFNN [19]. This enables the model to take a set of samples as input and detect time correlations between them. They have, however, been discovered to have difficulties learning long-term partnerships. LSTM networks address this problem by incorporating parameters into the hidden node loops, allowing them to acquire and release states based on the input sequence [1]. As a result, states are triggered in response to short-term events, but the network can maintain those states active indefinitely, giving the network long-term memory. The LSTM has been found to be more effective than the traditional RNN at learning sequences [7].

1.3 Data Augmentation

Data augmentation techniques are primarily used in the Deep Learning to create synthetic data which can generalize the model. The models trained over vast variety of transformations can anticipate the outputs in better manner [23]. The commonly used techniques to augment the data are blocking, segmentation, noise insertion, Rotation changing the background blur, focal point changes, inversion, and intersections of data points. But, while working with video feed, segmentation is prohibited [14, 18].

1.4 EMG and EEG Based Grasp Intent Detection Models

Despite the shortcomings in the prediction, many studies are conducted to detect the grasp intent based on human physiological signals e.g., Electroencephalography (EEG) and EMG signals [24]. Even the models achieved good accuracy with small classification label set, they are prone to artifacts. When the label set increases the model's accuracy becomes not reliable as the model lacks stabilization and context. Hence accuracy will be reduced to classify the objects which is hazardous in amputees' crucial life tasks [20]. The modern models depend on human input such as biomedical signals from the subject which includes EMG. As the EMG has many setbacks like artifacts, frequency calibration and localization, can reduce the accuracy of prediction during daily activities [8,9]. Hence, there is a requirement for innovative models to detect grasp intent to control the prosthetic hands.

1.5 Gaps in the Literature and Present Research

The literature models explored the possibility of having individual feed as input and suggested the possibility of fusing the data and giving the context also as input [1,2,8,11]. The accuracy of intent detection models with EEG and EMG can be improved by visual feedback from various positions along with IMU. As the video data available we got an opportunity to process the data and create context top the data and evolve the model while processing the context during individual timesteps. By considering multimodal dataset and single shot Hybrid Neural Network we can eliminate the issues associated with EMG and Image data.

2 Methodology

2.1 Dataset

HANDS dataset contains 413 trails' data over 102 different objects. Every individual trail consists of Hand-View video, Eye-View Video, EMG and IMU data tracked during the trial. Hand-View data is captured by GoPro Hero session Camera of resolution (3648×2736 pixels). Eye-View data is captured by Logitech Webcam C600 of resolution (1600×1200 pixels). EMG and IMU data is acquired from the arm using MYO armband.

2.2 Data Augmentation

We created synthetic data for the training by applying three techniques as shown in Fig. 1a. For Eye-view video we apply random blur to the individual frames in random. Next, we added Gaussian Noise with zero mean and random variance to all three RGB channels. The final transformation is by rotating the Eye-View video randomly within the range of $-15° - 15°$ to generalize the model. The Hand-view video is added with Random Background Blur followed by Noise addition to individual RGB channels with zero noise and random variance. We didn't do rotation of the video as it is interdependent on IMU. This augmentation provides more synthetic data and take into consideration of practical issues. At the end every datapoint consists of two videos and measurements from IMU and EMG.

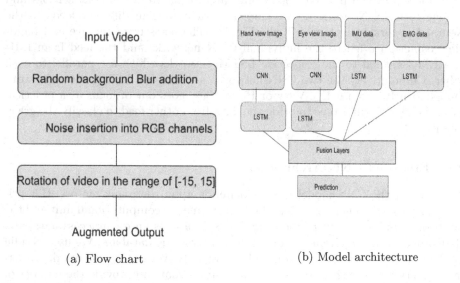

(a) Flow chart   (b) Model architecture

Fig. 1. a. Steps involved in Augmentation of video Data from eye-view and hand-view. Flow chart showing the data feed setup from subsequent sensors such as camera, IMU and EMG

2.3 Need for Continuous Data

A neural Network model's accuracy depends upon the inference time and availability of data. The classification depends upon the position of the object and viewing angle. The classification accuracy can be boosted by using object data from multiple angles. Literature show that the image data in the field of prosthetic hand development mainly using eye-level cameras held at the eye level of the user, typically located on the head. Robotics hands can be developed using the cameras attached to the hand level along with eye level to provide multi directional view positions [3,12]. Similarly the approach will also create challenges as object that we want to grasp may be moving or our view may be moving while grasping the object. Thus having an extra view angle provides context to the main view position and the model learns efficiently. This modelling also stabilizes the artifacts formed during occlusion. If the artifacts are formed during movement or occlusion, The correction happens when we fuse the data from past inference steps to the present step and use the past prediction as an input to the network to give the context. The con-text will be modulated while the data feed is being observed by the model. The accuracy from the context-based models is proven to be having higher accuracy [14].

2.4   Overview of Proposed Model

The novelty in the paper comes from data fusion from different sensors and change in CNN Network. The set-up of data flow from different feeds to the Neural Network is explained in the Fig. 1b. The feeds from the eye and hand-view camera are fed to the individual CNN networks and the feed from IMU and EMG are fed to the respective LSTM networks which are parallel to each other. Cumulatively the two CNN networks and the two LSTM networks work independently. Even if Eye-View or Hand-View goes out of focus as a practical case, the model will evolve to bring the data from other feed to classify the grasp intent.

2.5   Proposed CNN Architecture

Accuracy of the CNN model heavily depends upon the many factors. But primary factors are: generalized data, high-performance computational unit and the network complexity. Out of these, HANDS dataset is an open access database, that provides the requirement of a large-scale training database. We used Nvidia GTX 1080 GPU to train the proposed Network. However, the network depth has uncertainty because there is no such calculation that can provide the number of layers required. Deep networks extract more complex and robust features [17]. We used VGG19 network as basis and added 2 extra dense layers over it to prepare a custom network as shown in Fig. 2. In the literature VGG16 network is used to train the model. Compared to VGG16, VGG19 network has access to deep layers along with extra Relu layers. But, this small change in the network boosts the accuracy of the model for the object detection task [18].

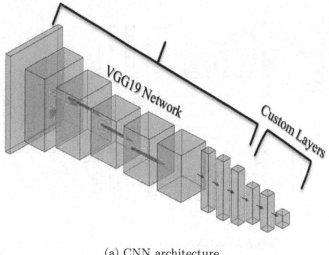

(a) CNN architecture

Fig. 2. Proposed CNN architecture constituting of VGG19 network with custom layers

Before incorporating all the data feed into consideration, as inference takes incremental time we developed different types of models and trained them using the augmented data. The models are created using the VGG19 neural network added with 2 output dense layers to construct a customised model. We incorporated softmax layer with 5 output parameters as number of classes are 5. The hybrid models are created with dense layers at the end. We freezed the model weights of the initial layers of VGG19 network and trained over final dense layers and LSTM parameters. The models that we developed are explained below.

Hybrid Model 1: We trained the first hybrid model which consists of single VGG19 network with feeding Eye-view data only. As explained in the Dataset, The model's performance is expected to have nominal improvement with out using the video data instead of image based classification.

Hybrid Model 2: The hand-view data is incorporated into the model to add another view point for the image data, we used the Conv-net individually over both the views of the images and Fused them at the ending with a dense layer by appending one over another as shown in Fig. 3. The model will be simultaneously using the feed and provide inference.

In this model we used the individual images from eye-view and hand-view instead of video data to train the model. Hence we didn't involved LSTM networks. By using the hybrid model which contains two individual networks with

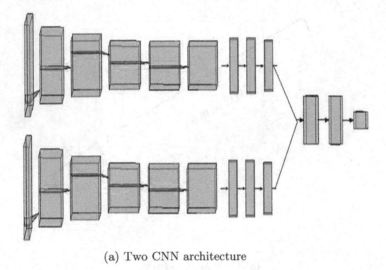

(a) Two CNN architecture

Fig. 3. Architecture of parallel CNN model using data from hand and eye views

different datafeeds we are expected to have invariability while classification even with higher noise in one feed. To provide this functionality we augmented the data with insertion of the noise into individual RGB channels. Thus in the presence of higher noise the model is expected to stabilize after initial frames and classification be robust. But this model only depends upon the visual information, some challenges are posed when tackling transparent and translucent objects.

Hybrid Model 3: Even though IMU produces artifacts and drift, It contains rotational and positional data. The data becomes crucial when the eye view goes out of focus. To incorporate the IMU feed, we use the Conv-net individually over both the views of the images and LSTM over the IMU data as shown in Fig. 4. We fused the outputs at the ending with a dense layer by appending one over another. The model will be simultaneously using the feed and provides inference taking a feed from IMU and Camera views. When dealing with the transparent and translucent objects, the IMU data is expected to stabilize the classification and converges easily.

Hybrid Model 4: Our final Model takes into consideration of data feed from all 4 channels of eye-view and hand-view cameras and IMU and EMG data feed. We built the new model over the hybrid model - 3 used in the previous section. The final model consists of two parallel CNN and LSTM networks respectively for eye view and hand view, and two LSTM networks respectively for IMU feed and

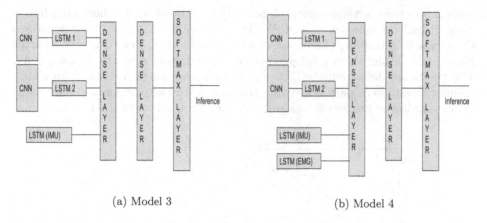

(a) Model 3   (b) Model 4

Fig. 4. Architecture of two parallel CNN and LSTM networks using data from eye-view and hand-view along with a. one LSTM network for IMU b. two LSTM networks for IMU and EMG

EMG. The fusion happened with a dense layer, and we used the combined model for training as shown in following Fig. 4. The accuracies for different models are shown in following Table 1.

Table 1. Model comparison

Models	Accuracy
Original network	89%
Hybrid model 1	89.4%
Hybrid model 2	91.3%
Hybrid model 3	91.5%
Hybrid model 4	92.3%

3 Results and Discussion

The efficiency of the Proposed hybrid model is evaluated using changes in loss occurred and accuracy in grasp type classification. Both Accuracy and loss are convergent and after reaching value of 92.3% accuracy and 0.032 loss there was no significant improvement at epoch 18. After the epoch 18, we observed over-fitting as training accuracy getting improved and validation accuracy was reducing. The plots for loss and accuracy are shown in the Fig. 5. We used different train data and test data splits with randomized distributions and achieved the same accuracy. The proposed CNN model works better with a single view as shown in the table. The model accuracies are dependent on noise, so data augmentation played a key role while generalizing the model. Prosthetic hands wont be having control over the positional approach possibly because of off-the-shelf robot hands without built-in cameras in hand. While it is possible that in future innovations there may be possibility of having extra view so that the model can have a better image data. From a networks' perspective. The dataset contains 2 view-points, The positional data from the IMU and human physiological signal from EMG. Human grasp intent path is heavily correlated with the position and movement of the hand. The prediction loss and accuracies are shown in the Fig. 5.

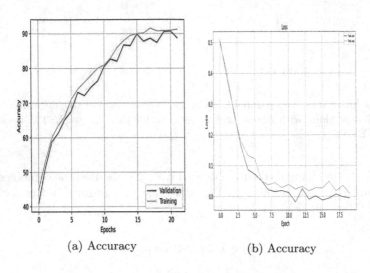

(a) Accuracy   (b) Accuracy

Fig. 5. a. Accuracy of the model b. Loss of the model

4   Conclusion and Future Scope

Using image, EMG, and positional data, this paper proposes a method for multisensory classification of human grasp intent. The use of combined eye-view and hand-view visual data of an object, with context correction, is a novel aspect of the approach. Instead of predicting the label at the end, the model predicts it at each timestamp and corrects it sequentially with the next sample data without relying for the data feed to finish. As a result, the model can handle data feeds of varying durations. This also accounts for artefacts caused by EMG and IMU. The intent recognition uses EMG and other signals to evolve previous estimates based on image data.

The intent of grasp can be useful to predict the grasp task in Virtual environment. Moreover, the error in depth prediction in transparent objects in real or virtual worlds can cause issue in grasping the object, wherein the IMU and EMG data feed can aid in correcting the grasp.

References

1. Bao, T., Zaidi, S.A.R., Xie, S., Yang, P., Zhang, Z.Q.: A CNN-LSTM hybrid model for wrist kinematics estimation using surface electromyography. IEEE Trans. Instrum. Meas. **70**, 1–9 (2020)
2. Bitzer, S., Smagt, P.V.D.: Learning EMG control of a robotic hand: towards active prostheses, pp. 2819–2823. IEEE (2006)
3. DeGol, J., Akhtar, A., Manja, B., Bretl, T.: Automatic grasp selection using a camera in a hand prosthesis. In: 2016 38th Annual International Conference of the IEEE Engineering in Medicine and Biology Society (EMBC), pp. 431–434. IEEE (2016)
4. Deng, J., Dong, W., Socher, R., Li, L.J., Li, K., Fei-Fei, L.: ImageNet: a large-scale hierarchical image database, pp. 248–255. IEEE (2009)
5. Farina, D., Merletti, R.: Comparison of algorithms for estimation of EMG variables during voluntary isometric contractions. J. Electromyogr. Kinesiol. **10**(5), 337–349 (2000)
6. Fu, X., Wang, J., Hu, Z., Guo, Y., Wang, R.: Automated segmentation for whole human eye OCT image using RM multistage mask R-CNN. Appl. Opt. **60**(9), 2518–2529 (2021)
7. Gers, F.A., Schmidhuber, E.: LSTM recurrent networks learn simple context-free and context-sensitive languages. IEEE Trans. Neural Netw. **12**(6), 1333–1340 (2001)
8. Ghazaei, G., Alameer, A., Degenaar, P., Morgan, G., Nazarpour, K.: Deep learning-based artificial vision for grasp classification in myoelectric hands. J. Neural Eng. **14**, 036025 (2017)
9. Gigli, A., Gregori, V., Cognolato, M., Atzori, M., Gijsberts, A.: Visual cues to improve myoelectric control of upper limb prostheses, pp. 783–788. IEEE (2018)
10. Günay, S.Y., Quivira, F., Erdoğmuş, D.: Muscle synergy-based grasp classification for robotic hand prosthetics, pp. 335–338 (2017)
11. Günay, S.Y., Yarossi, M., Brooks, D.H., Tunik, E., Erdoğmuş, D.: Transfer learning using low-dimensional subspaces for EMG-based classification of hand posture, pp. 1097–1100. IEEE (2019)
12. Han, M., Günay, S.Y., Schirner, G., Padır, T., Erdoğmuş, D.: HANDS: a multimodal dataset for modeling toward human grasp intent inference in prosthetic hands. Intell. Serv. Robot. **13**(1), 179–185 (2019). https://doi.org/10.1007/s11370-019-00293-8
13. Jogin, M., Madhulika, M., Divya, G., Meghana, R., Apoorva, S., et al.: Feature extraction using convolution neural networks (CNN) and deep learning. In: 2018 3rd IEEE International Conference on Recent Trends in Electronics, Information & Communication Technology (RTEICT), pp. 2319–2323. IEEE (2018)
14. Karsch, K., Liu, C., Kang, S.B.: Depth extraction from video using non-parametric sampling. In: Fitzgibbon, A., Lazebnik, S., Perona, P., Sato, Y., Schmid, C. (eds.) ECCV 2012. LNCS, vol. 7576, pp. 775–788. Springer, Heidelberg (2012). https://doi.org/10.1007/978-3-642-33715-4_56
15. Krizhevsky, A., Sutskever, I., Hinton, G.E.: ImageNet classification with deep convolutional neural networks. In: Advances in Neural Information Processing Systems 25 (2012)
16. LeCun, Y., Bottou, L., Bengio, Y., Haffner, P.: Gradient-based learning applied to document recognition. Proc. IEEE **86**(11), 2278–2324 (1998)

17. Leeb, R., Sagha, H., Chavarriaga, R., del R Millán, J.: A hybrid brain-computer interface based on the fusion of electroencephalographic and electromyographic activities. J. Neural Eng. **8**, 025011 (2011)
18. Levine, S., Pastor, P., Krizhevsky, A., Ibarz, J., Quillen, D.: Learning hand-eye coordination for robotic grasping with deep learning and large-scale data collection. Int. J. Robot. Res. **37**, 421–436 (2018)
19. Manaswi, N.K.: RNN and LSTM. In: Manaswi, N.K. (ed.) Deep Learning with Applications Using Python, pp. 115–126. Apress, Berkeley (2018). https://doi. org/10.1007/978-1-4842-3516-4_9
20. Maufroy, C., Bargmann, D.: CNN-based detection and classification of grasps relevant for worker support scenarios using SEMG signals of forearm muscles. In: 2018 IEEE International Conference on Systems, Man, and Cybernetics (SMC), pp. 141–146. IEEE (2018)
21. Mopuri, K.R., Garg, U., Babu, R.V.: CNN fixations: an unraveling approach to visualize the discriminative image regions. IEEE Trans. Image Process. **28**(5), 2116–2125 (2018)
22. Redmon, J., Angelova, A.: Real-time grasp detection using convolutional neural networks, pp. 1316–1322. IEEE (2015)
23. Wong, S.C., Gatt, A., Stamatescu, V., McDonnell, M.D.: Understanding data augmentation for classification: when to warp? In: 2016 international conference on digital image computing: techniques and applications (DICTA), pp. 1–6. IEEE (2016)
24. Yap, H.K., Ang, B.W., Lim, J.H., Goh, J.C., Yeow, C.H.: A fabric-regulated soft robotic glove with user intent detection using EMG and RFID for hand assistive application. In: 2016 IEEE International Conference on Robotics and Automation (ICRA), pp. 3537–3542. IEEE (2016)

Research on Adjustable Classroom Desks and Chairs Based on the Human Dimensions of Chinese Minors

Tianyu Shi and Wei Yu[✉]

School of Art Design and Media, East China University of Science and Technology, No. 130, Meilong Road, Xuhui District, Shanghai, People's Republic of China
1774916583@qq.com

Abstract. Chinese minors spend a lot of time in school and spend a lot of time in classroom desks and chairs for learning activities. Many studies have shown that minors are in a period of growth and development, but the existing classroom desks and chairs do not match the size of minors' bodies. This has a negative impact on the physical health of minors and their learning efficiency. The aim of this study is to investigate the height adjustability of classroom desks and chairs for the most affected age group of underage students. This paper ensures that the height of the classroom desks and chairs match the students' body dimensions by determining a reasonable range of adjustment and adjustment scale. The methodology used in this study is based on Chinese minors' body size data to determine the most influential age group. The age range and adjustment scale of the desk and chair were then calculated by substituting the body size data of the age group into the size formula. The results of the study show that the three most affected age groups are 7 to 10 years, 11 to 12 years and 13 to 15 years. Finally, three sets of classroom desk and chair height adjustment ranges and scales were calculated to match each of these three age groups.

Keywords: Chinese minors · Body size · Classroom desks and chairs · Adjustable

1 Introduction

Primary, secondary and tertiary students spend a significant proportion of their day in classroom desks and chairs. Many studies at home and abroad have shown that in both developed and developing countries, the mismatch between the size of classroom desks and chairs and the size of students' bodies is very common. [1, 2] Mismatched classroom desks and chairs can easily cause physical and psychological fatigue, reduce learning efficiency and lead to musculoskeletal disorders in the long term. In China, underage students are under heavy pressure to study and spend a considerable amount of time (8 to 10 h) in the classroom. On the one hand, underage students are at their peak of growth

© The Author(s), under exclusive license to Springer Nature Switzerland AG 2022
V. G. Duffy (Ed.): HCII 2022, LNCS 13319, pp. 123–134, 2022.
https://doi.org/10.1007/978-3-031-05890-5_10

and development, and at the same time there are significant differences in physical development between students and between genders. As a result, it is difficult to match the size of desks and chairs in the same classroom to the body size of each student. On the other hand, underage students who study on mismatched desks and chairs for a long time may develop poor sitting habits, which may lead to poor muscle and bone development. In order to ensure the health of young people and their learning efficiency, the community should pay great attention to the design of desks and chairs for underage students, especially the ergonomic design of desks and chairs.

Many experts and academics have also now proposed options for improvement. One is to provide classroom furniture manufacturers with student body sizes so that they can make different sizes of tables and chairs to suit different students. Another is to design and manufacture classroom desks and chairs with adjustable heights to suit different students. Both of these options are theoretically feasible, but neither has been implemented well in reality. In this paper, a more scientific and feasible solution for adjustable desks and chairs based on the human body dimensions of Chinese minors will be developed in order to more reasonably adapt to the human dimensions of underage students.

2   Current Status of Classroom Desks and Chairs in China

According to research, there are various categories of desks and chairs for primary and secondary school classrooms in China. Classified by variable height, desks and chairs can be divided into fixed height desks and chairs and adjustable height desks and chairs.

2.1   Fixed Height Desks and Chairs

Fig. 1. Fixed height desks and chairs

Currently, most of the desks and chairs used in primary and secondary schools in China are fixed height desks and chairs, as shown in Fig. 1. Schools tend to purchase multiple sets of classroom desks and chairs in certain size increments. However, differences in the size of these desks and chairs exist only between different grades; the size of desks and chairs in the same grade and class is consistent. In fact, there is a very large variation in the body size of underage students in the same grade and in the same class. The use of desks and chairs of the same fixed size in schools often results in a mismatch for some students. Furthermore, in primary and secondary schools, the physical development of pupils varies greatly from one pupil to another throughout the year, with some pupils developing rapidly and others developing slowly. Therefore the incremental sizing method with grade level still does not meet the needs of many students.

2.2 Height-Adjustable Desks and Chairs

In order to meet market demand, height-adjustable classroom desks and chairs began to appear on the market, as shown in Fig. 2. Height-adjustable desks and chairs have started to become popular in many primary and secondary schools in China, especially in developed regions. However, the actual effect is not obvious.

Fig. 2. Height-adjustable desks and chairs

Firstly, some adjustable tables and chairs are not easy to adjust. The user needs to use a tool to unscrew the screws in order to adjust the height. At the same time, this design hides the adjustability of the tables and chairs, and the final result is no different from that of a fixed height desk and chair. Secondly, the range and scale of adjustment of these desks and chairs are not marked with instructions, but only uniformly perforated as the level of adjustment, lacking a scientific basis. Students also have to rely on their senses and make adjustments as they are appropriate at the time. They are not adjusted according to a scientific scale relationship, which can still have a negative effect after a period of time.

As a result, desks and chairs in primary and secondary schools in China currently do not match well with students' body sizes. Although some ways are used to compensate for this, their effectiveness is not obvious.

3 A Study of Adjustable Classroom Desks and Chairs

At present, the problem of mismatch between classroom desks and chairs and the body size of underage students is common. The use of adjustable desks and chairs to improve the mismatch has been mentioned in relevant studies. However, they do not give specific research and solutions for adjustability, and commercially available adjustable desks and chairs do not improve this problem. Therefore, this paper investigates adjustable classroom desks and chairs based on ergonomic principles and data on the human body size of Chinese minors. The paper finally arrives at an adjustable height range and scale for classroom desks and chairs suitable for the body size of underage students.

3.1 Target Groups

The target population for this study is a group of Chinese underage students, mainly in primary and secondary schools, whose age range is from 7 to 17 years old. This age range has a relatively large age span. This study firstly grouped the primary and secondary school students into age groups and secondly selected the age groups with relatively significant differences in body size as the target population. This was to ensure the accuracy and relevance of the study results. This is because, the greater the difference in body size in the same age group, the lower the match with classroom desks and chairs.

According to *the General Requirements for the Establishment of Anthropometric Databases* and *the age grouping methodology of the Chinese Minors*, the 7 to 17 years age group is divided into four age groups: 7 to 10 years, 11 to 12 years, 13 to 15 years and 16 to 17 years.

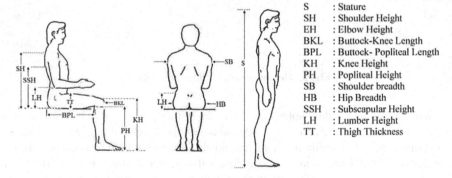

S	: Stature
SH	: Shoulder Height
EH	: Elbow Height
BKL	: Buttock-Knee Length
BPL	: Buttock- Popliteal Length
KH	: Knee Height
PH	: Popliteal Height
SB	: Shoulder breadth
HB	: Hip Breadth
SSH	: Subscapular Height
LH	: Lumber Height
TT	: Thigh Thickness

Fig. 3. Anthropometric charts

The adjustment parameters for adjustable tables and chairs are table height (vertical distance from table top to floor) and chair height (vertical distance from chair surface to floor). According to ergonomic principles, the chair height is related to the human popliteal height (PH) and the table height is related to the human popliteal height, elbow height (EH) and shoulder height (SH), as shown in Fig. 3. Human popliteal height, elbow height and shoulder height are all positively correlated with human body height. In order to more visually compare the variability of body dimensions among the age groups of underage students, human body height was chosen as the parameter for comparison of variability, as shown in Tables 1 and 2.

Table 1. Standard deviation of height of underage males in six regions of China

Age groups	North East China Height Standard Deviation	Midwest China Height Standard Deviation	Lower Yangtze River Region China Height Standard Deviation	Middle Yangtze River Region China Height Standard Deviation	South China Height Standard Deviation	South West China Height Standard Deviation
7–10	86	90	83	84	79	76
11–12	86	75	85	78	69	79
13–15	91	89	83	90	93	86
16–17	59	62	59	59	63	59

Unit: mm.

Table 2. Standard deviation of height of underage females in six regions of China

Age groups	North East China Height Standard Deviation	Midwest China Height Standard Deviation	Lower Yangtze River Region China Height Standard Deviation	Middle Yangtze River Region China Height Standard Deviation	South China Height Standard Deviation	South West China Height Standard Deviation
7–10	88	91	86	95	92	83
11–12	77	81	75	69	71	71
13–15	61	56	60	53	59	60
16–17	54	55	52	52	52	55

Unit: mm.

Table 1 shows that the most significant difference in height was found between the ages of 13 and 15 for minor males, followed by the ages of 7 to 10 and 11 to 12. The difference in height for minor males between the ages of 16 and 17 was relatively flat compared to the other age groups. Table 2 shows that the most significant difference in height was found in the age group 7 to 10 years for minor females, followed by 11 to 12 years and 13 to 15 years. 16 to 17 years for minor females showed a flat difference in height compared to the other age groups.

In summary, height differences among Chinese preteens are most pronounced during the six years of primary school and the three years of junior high school, levelling off at the senior high school level. Due to physiological differences between male and female students, male students show the greatest variability during middle school and female students show the greatest variability during primary school. Based on the differences in body size between age groups and between the male and female genders of underage students, adjustable desks and chairs are more suitable for the primary and junior high school student groups. Therefore, this study is based on considerations such as differences in body size between the age groups of underage students and the adjustment limits and costs of adjustable tables and chairs. The target groups were identified: 7 to 10 years old, 11 to 12 years old and 13 to 15 years old.

3.2 Adjustment Method

Fig. 4. Adjustment method

Most of the adjustable desks and chairs currently used in schools in China use the adjustment method shown in Fig. 4. Their shortcomings have been presented above.

Based on the existing deficiencies, this study uses a knob adjustment method. This type of adjustment is already used in some children's desks and chairs in the home, but is rarely used in school classrooms. The use of knobs not only makes it easier to adjust the height of the desk and chair, but also provides a visual reminder to students or teachers that the desk and chair are adjustable. In addition, the body size of students of different ages varies, corresponding to the range of adjustment of each age group and the scale is also different. In this paper, the adjustment range and scale are calculated according to the body size of each age group. The scale is labelled with the height of the human popliteal fossa on the left and the height of the desk and chair matching the human body size on the right. This allows students to measure their popliteal fossa height and quickly adjust the height of the desk and chair to their own size with relative accuracy. The matching principle is described in more detail below.

3.3 Adjustable Range and Scale

From the above study on the target population, it is concluded that the final target population for this study is the age groups of 7 to 10 years old, 11 to 12 years old and 13 to 15 years old. The body size of each age group was used to determine the adjustment range and scale for each of the three types. This allows for a more scientific and effective way of adjusting the height of the table and chair to suit the needs of different students' sizes. In this study, human body data is substituted into the standard formula to obtain the height adjustment range and scale.

Body Size Data. According to ergonomic principles, the height of a desk and chair is determined based on the popliteal height (PH), elbow height (EH) and shoulder height (SH) of the human body. In order to make the results more general and realistic, this study uses the data counted in GB/T 26158–2010 *Human Body Dimensions of Chinese Minors* and divides the human body dimensions into 11 percentile for each age group. As shown in Tables 3, 4 and 5.

Table 3. Body size percentile for minors aged 7 to 10 years

	Measurement items	P1	P2.5	P5	P10	P25	P50	P75	P90	P95	P97.5	P99
Man	Popliteal height	263	272	280	288	302	324	342	360	371	378	389
	Elbow height	137	147	152	159	173	188	202	217	227	235	249
	Shoulder height	354	367	379	390	419	448	476	502	520	535	559

(continued)

Table 3. (*continued*)

	Measurement items	P1	P2.5	P5	P10	P25	P50	P75	P90	P95	P97.5	P99
Female	Popliteal height	263	269	277	285	300	320	339	357	368	380	387
	Elbow height	137	145	152	159	170	184	199	213	224	235	246
	Shoulder height	346	362	376	387	412	437	470	495	517	535	553

Unit: mm.

Table 4. Body size percentile for minors aged 11 to 12 years

	Measurement items	P1	P2.5	P5	P10	P25	P50	P75	P90	P95	P97.5	P99
Man	Popliteal height	310	318	324	335	349	367	382	399	409	421	430
	Elbow height	155	163	170	177	188	206	224	238	253	264	271
	Shoulder height	404	419	434	444	466	498	531	556	578	596	611
Female	Popliteal height	316	324	331	339	355	371	382	397	404	414	424
	Elbow height	162	166	173	181	195	213	228	246	256	264	271
	Shoulder height	411	422	437	448	477	509	535	567	585	596	611

Unit: mm.

Table 5. Body size percentile for minors aged 13 to 15 years

	Measurement items	P1	P2.5	P5	P10	P25	P50	P75	P90	P95	P97.5	P99
Man	Popliteal height	342	356	363	371	386	403	421	439	447	454	465
	Elbow height	173	181	191	199	217	235	253	271	285	293	310
	Shoulder height	444	463	480	495	528	560	593	620	646	661	706
Female	Popliteal height	333	342	346	356	370	382	396	407	417	424	429
	Elbow height	180	188	195	202	217	235	253	267	278	285	296
	Shoulder height	454	466	480	494	520	549	578	603	617	632	650

Unit: mm.

Based on ergonomic principles, an adjustable range model is used in order to obtain an adjustable range that matches the majority of the group. The concept was to match 5% of the females and 95% of the males in the population, thus matching 90% of the user population. However, in this study, the study group was minors, and the rate of development as well as the cycle of development is not consistent between the underage males and females. Therefore, the 5% and 95% figures are no longer fixed by gender. The lower value of the 5th percentile and the higher value of the 95th percentile were used as the basis for body size for both males and females.

Standard Formulas. Standard formulas is used to obtain the range and scale of height adjustment for desks and chairs corresponding to human dimensions. The standard formulas used in this study are the most commonly used and have been experimentally validated by other researchers.

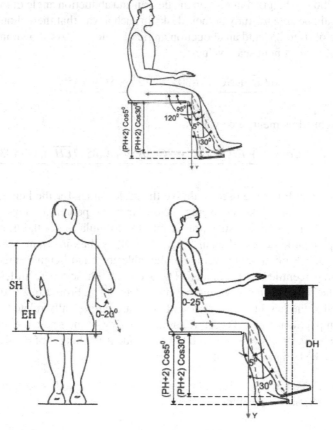

Fig. 5. Correlation between anthropometric dimensions and desk and chair dimensions

Seat height range formula:

$$(PH5\% + SC)Cos30° \leq Seat\,height \leq (PH95\% + SC)Cos5° \tag{1}$$

In Eq. 1, PH refers to the height of the popliteal fossa. SC refers to the height of the shoe, usually taken as 2 cm. 30° and 5° refer to the seat height that allows the knee to bend so that the lower leg forms an angle of 5° to 30° relative to the vertical. This ensures that the student's foot is adequately supported under normal contact with the floor, while avoiding increased pressure on the tissues of the lower thigh area. As shown in Fig. 5.

Desk height range formula:

$$(PH5\% + SC)Cos30° + EH5\% \leq Desk\,height \leq (PH95\% + SC95\%)Cos5°$$
$$+\,0.8517EH95\% + 0.1483SH95\% \tag{2}$$

In Eq. 2, EH refers to elbow height. SH refers to shoulder height. Desk height depends not only on elbow to height, but also on the flexion and abduction angle of the shoulders. Students should be able to study at their desks in such a way that their shoulders meet a flexion angle of 0° to 25° and an abduction angle of 0° to 20°. As shown in Fig. 5.

Seat height adjustment scale values:

$$\frac{(\overline{PH} + SC)Cos30° + (\overline{PH} + SC)Cos5°}{2} \tag{3}$$

Desk height adjustment scale values:

$$\frac{\overline{PH} + SCCos30° + \overline{EH} + \overline{PH} + SCCos5° + 0.8517\overline{EH} + 0.1483\overline{SH}}{2} \tag{4}$$

Equation 3 and Eq. 4 are used to derive the scale values for the height adjustment of the desks and chairs. Take the average size of the 10th percentile boys' size and the 10th percentile girls' size and substitute it into the formula to get the minimum value of the 10th percentile desk and chair height as well as the maximum value, and take the average value. Similarly, the average of the table and chair heights at the 25th, 50th, 75th and 90th percentiles are calculated. The average of these 5 percentiles is used as a reference value for the 5 scales within the adjustment range. From Eq. 2 and Eq. 3, it can be obtained that the height of the desk and chair are numerically related to the height of the human popliteal fossa. Therefore, in the marking of the scale, the left side is the height of the human popliteal fossa and the right side is the height of the desk and chair matched with the human body size.

Final Results. The final result is obtained by substituting the body size data into Eqs. (1) (2) (3) (4). See Table 6 as well as Fig. 6.

Table 6. Height adjustment range and reference scale for desks and chairs for underage students by age group

Age groups	Seat height adjustment range	Scale					Desk height adjustment range	Scale				
7–10	241–372	269	282	301	319	336	393 ~ 643	445	472	507	540	571
11–12	282–410	316	330	345	358	372	452 ~ 715	514	542	577	606	638
13–15	301–448	340	354	367	382	396	492 ~ 786	563	594	626	660	690

Unit: mm.

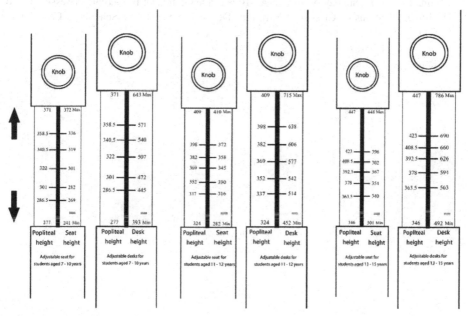

Fig. 6. Model of height adjustment range and reference scale for desks and chairs for underage students by age group

4   Conclusions

In view of the mismatch between the body size of Chinese minors and the size of classroom desks and chairs, this paper conducts a study on the adjustability of desks and chairs based on the body size of Chinese minors. The study identifies the target population of the study by comparing the variability of height data for each age group of minors: 7 to 10 years old, 11 to 12 years old and 13 to 15 years old. The popliteal height, elbow height and shoulder height of the minors in these three age groups were then substituted into a standard formula at the corresponding percentile. Ultimately, the range and scale of adjustment of the desks and chairs were obtained. The results of the study show that there are differences between the adjustable ranges and scales of the desks and chairs for the three age groups, especially in the marking of the scales, reflecting the differences in the body dimensions of the minors in each age group. This reflects the need to derive adjustable ranges and scales based on body size. This study is therefore a reference for the design of adjustable desks and chairs for underage students, and provides a scientific improvement to commercially available adjustable desks and chairs.

References

1. Fidelis, O.P., Ogunlade, B., Adelakun, MSc., S.A.: Incidence of School Furniture Mismatch and Health Implications in Primary School Children in Akure, South-West Nigeria (2021)
2. Obinna Fidelis, P., Sunday Adelakun, A.: Babatunde Ogunlade: Ergonomic Assessment and Health Implications of Classroom Furniture Designs in Secondary Schools: a Case Study (2021)

A Bed Design Model Research for the Self-care Elderly

Xiaoqing Su and RongRong Fu[✉]

College of Art Design and Media, East China University of Science and Technology, Shanghai,
China
1518264747@qq.com

Abstract. With the coming of population aging, the number of the elderly in
China has continued to increase. The demand for the age-appropriate furniture has
also continued to expand. Bed especially occupies a vital position in all varieties
of age-appropriate furniture. In China, the demands of the self-care elderly who
is the largest group compared to nursing elderly and assisted elderly are always
ignored by furniture designers. Therefore, this paper has conducted a research in
order to explore a design method which is more suitable for the self-care elderly
so that they can accept this kind of deign more easily. This paper firstly uses literature analysis to define the self-care elderly and clarify their physiological and
psychological changes. Secondly, the Jack simulation experiment technology was
used to determine the size of the bedding. Thirdly, based on data of the questionnaire survey to construct a KANO model, the kinds of function and structure of
the bedding are confirmed. On the basis of these researches, the design scheme
can be completed. And finally finish the evaluation and the selection of the design
schemes.

Keywords: Self-care elderly · Bed · Design model

1 Introduction

A country or region has entered aging society when the population aged over 65 accounts
for more than 7% according to the classification criteria determined by the United Nations
"The Influence of Population Aging and Its Socio-Economic". The results of China's
seventh census show that the number of people over the age of 65 has reached 13.5%,
which has been constantly increasing. This trend indicates a huge market potential of
age-appropriate furniture. However, the furniture for the elderly in the Chinese market
cannot perfectly meet the needs of the old people, and there are few enterprises engaged
in the production and design of age-appropriate furniture. The elderly are divided into
three types: self-care elderly, assisted elderly and nursing elderly based on the "Basic
Norms of Social Welfare Institutions for the Elderly". The elderly group studied in this
paper is the self-care elderly, who is "the elderly who can basically carry out their living
behaviors independently and can take care of themselves" according to the "Code for
Architectural Design of Elderly Facilities". The furniture designed for self-care elderly

© The Author(s), under exclusive license to Springer Nature Switzerland AG 2022
V. G. Duffy (Ed.): HCII 2022, LNCS 13319, pp. 135–147, 2022.
https://doi.org/10.1007/978-3-031-05890-5_11

has large potential because most of the furniture for the elderly in China is for assisted elderly and nursing elderly and the self-care elderly accounts for the majority of elderly in China [2].

2   Classification of Nursing Beds

There are some health problems with self-care elderly whose self-care ability is relatively better than the other two types of elderly. The nursing beds with suitable functions are essential to both improve the well-being of the elderly and reduce the workload of caregivers. Because with the age increasing, the time spent on bedding by the self-care elderly will increase, and the bed is the bedding that the elderly spend the longest time. And it is inevitable that some facilities are needed for assistance on the bed as the self-care ability declines. By analyzing the existing nursing beds in the Chinese market, it can be roughly divided into two categories: one is medical nursing beds, which are mostly multifunctional and low in price, and can basically meet all the needs of the elderly who are bedridden for a long time. However, the color of this type of bedding is mainly blue and white, and the material is mainly plastic and metal, which is difficult to be favored by the elderly; the second type is household nursing beds, whose appearance are similar to normal furniture. And the price is high, but the function is less. So it is difficult to meet the needs of the elderly. And most importantly, these nursing beds are generally designed for assisted elderly and nursing elderly, so they cannot well meet the needs of self-care elderly, and self-care elderly generally express that they are psychologically unacceptable.

3   Determination of Bed Dimensions

The dimensions of bedding should be adjusted compared to ordinary bedding due to the changes of body dimensions of self-care elderly people. Meanwhile, it is necessary to determine the size of the auxiliary facilities because the self-care elderly with strong self-care skills also need the assistance of them. This paper based on the Jack software to test and analyze digital humans of the elderly and bedding models to determine the specific size of the nursing bed. Jack is a human body modeling and simulation system platform developed by the University of Pennsylvania. As the software that can verify and evaluate efficacy, it has been widely used in industrial fields for many years. The main superiorities of Jack software are the flexible, realistic 3D human simulation behavior and 3D digital humans, especially the simulations of the hands, spine and shoulders[3, 4]. This experiment used Jack software to establish a mannequin that corresponds to the size of the self-care elderly in purpose of obtaining the bedding size which suit the self-care elderly. And on the basis of the accurate simulations of the actions of the human, it can more intuitively verify and determine the size of the bed.

3.1 Establish the Models of Bedding and Humans

First, the bedding model is established based on the size of nursing beds on the market, whose size is 2000 mm × 1000 mm × 450 mm (the mattress is 50 mm thick). Secondly, according to the body size data of the elderly over 60 in Haitao Hu's paper "Anthropometric Measurements of the Elderly", three digital humans, P5, P50 and P95, which conform to the dimension of the self-care elderly's body, are established [5] (as shown in Fig. 1).

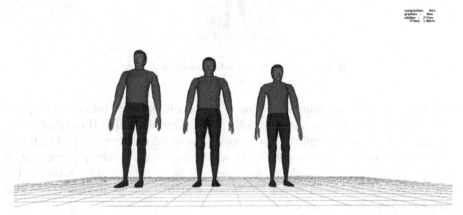

Fig. 1. From left to right are P95 digital human, P50 digital human and P5 digital human.

3.2 Experimental Process/Conclusion

In this paper, the two main purpose of this experiment using Jack software is to test whether the size of the bed is appropriate and determine the dimensions of the component of the bedding based on the simulation of the digital humans.

To check whether the size of the bed model established in this paper is suitable for the elderly, import the bed model and three digital humans P5, P50 and P95 into the Jack system. Then adjust the three models according to the postures of the elderly lying flat and sitting on the bed (as shown in Fig. 2).

To determine the length and height adjustment range of the bed railings, first, adjust the three mannequins P5, P50 and P95 to lie flat on the bed and use the Jack software system to simulate the movement of the palms. Then take the distance from the junction between the range of motion and the edge of the bed to the head of the bed as L1 [1]. After that, turn the mannequins to from lying down to getting out of bed (as shown in Fig. 3), taking the length from them to the bedside as L2. Finally, calculate the height of the old man's upper arm to the bed surface as H. The height adjustment range is obtained by comparing the H of three digital humans (as shown in Table 1).

L1 reflects the reachable range of the elderly's arm, which means that the railing can be installed within this range. Because the existence of the railing cannot hinder the movement of the elderly to get out of bed, L2 represents the maximum length of

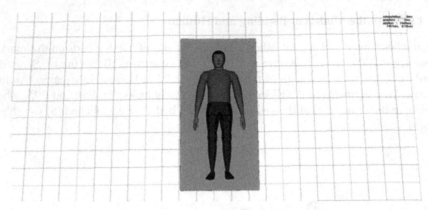

Fig. 2. Adjust the mannequin to a lying position.

the railing. Therefore, the minimum value of L2 should be taken within the range of L1, thereby exporting the length of the railing. The determination of H is based on the maximum and minimum lengths from the upper arm of the elderly to the bed surface.

In this way, under conditions that avoid interfering with the elderly getting out of bed, make convenience for the elderly to get up with the assistance of the railing to the greatest extent. The adjustable railing height enables elderly people of different heights to receive appropriate assistance.

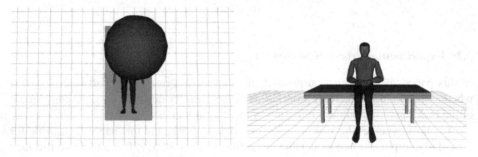

Fig. 3. Measurement process of L1 and L2.

Table 1. Final dimensions of railing height and length (unit: cm)

Number	P5	P50	P95	Final dimension
L1	98.6	103.2	106.1	80
L2	82.7	87.1	90.8	
H	20.5	25.5	30.1	20–30

4 Determination of Bedding Functions

This paper uses questionnaire survey and establishing KANO model to determine the function of the nursing bed. Questionnaires are sent to the elderly and their adult children. On the one hand, their adult children are also one of the buyers, and they pay more attention to functions and are more likely to express the needs of their parents directly. Therefore, the questionnaire for them focuses on the functions of bedding. And the KANO model based on the results is a main reference for functions. On the other hand, the questionnaire for the elderly focuses on the feelings of their daily life and the current nursing bed which is in the form of a scale. Then according to the results, adjust the above functions and appearance designs to make the elderly more easily accept the bedding. A total of 203 questionnaires were returned finally.

4.1 The Investigation for the Adult Children

First, identify the KANO attributes of 11 questions from the questionnaire for the adult children individually based on the survey results (as shown in Table 2). Then establish a Better-Worse coefficient graph based on the results to prioritize problem resolution (as shown in Fig. 4).

Table 2. The numbers and contents of questions

Number	Content
Q1	The appearance is similar to the ordinary furniture's
Q2	Better security (such as rounded corners, set up guardrails, etc.)
Q3	Assist the elderly to complete some daily actions (such as turning over, getting up, etc.)
Q4	Universal wheels for easy movement
Q5	Meet the needs of the elderly to eat in bed
Q6	Assist the elderly to carry out some small-scale recreational activities (such as watching mobile phones, watching TV, reading, writing)
Q7	Assist the elderly in some medical care projects (such as acupuncture, cupping, etc.)
Q8	Assist with some medical items (such as intravenous injections, etc.)
Q9	The function can be added by purchasing accessories and installed without overall replacement
Q10	Conversion from ordinary bed to nursing bed without overall replacement
Q11	Basic sleep functions and ensure comfort

From the Better-Worse coefficient graph, what should be prioritized are the requirements in the fourth quadrant (Basic Quality): Q2-requirement for security, Q3-requirements for some auxiliary facilities and Q8-assistance for the need of medical items (such as intravenous injection). Secondly, the needs in the first quadrant (Performance Quality) should be realized: Q4-demand for universal wheels, Q5-demand for bed tables and Q11-demand for sleep. Finally, it is the turn of the demands in the second quadrant (Attractive Quality): Q6-need for recreational activities, Q7-need for medical care programs, Q9 and Q10-extended use of nursing beds. Q1-demand for the appearance is an Indifferent Quality/Neutral Quality. It is indicated the respondents are not very concerned about the appearance of nursing beds. The respondents are more willing to focus on the function of the nursing bed though most of them indicated that they prefer nursing beds with a similar appearance to ordinary furniture. The survey results are of great reference value for the determination of the function and structure of the nursing bed.

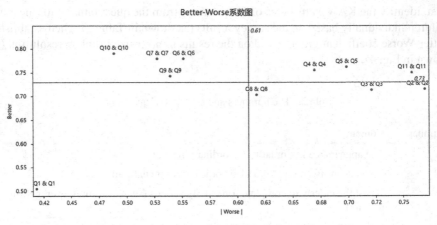

Fig. 4. Better-Worse coefficient graph.

4.2   The Investigation for the Elderly

The questionnaire for the elderly which is in the form of a scale is aimed at investigating the elderly's views on nursing bedding and current living habits. The questionnaire is set up to let the elderly make judgments on the degree of compliance with the questions according to their own circumstances (agreement-disagreement is recorded as 1–5 points). The survey results are shown in Table 3 below.

Table 3. Investigation results for the elderly

Content	Average score
1. You prefer nursing beds that look similar to normal furniture	2.71
2. You will care about the security when using the nursing bed (such as the handling of corners, the setting of guardrails)	1.58
3. Some of your daily activities (e.g. rolling over, getting up)need assistance	4.2
4. You will find it easier with facilities to assist you with daily activities	3.03
5. Some of your recreational activities (such as using your phone, watching TV, reading, writing) are done in bed	3.39
6. You eat in bed sometimes	4.85
7. You spend a long time in bed each day	4.44
8. You don't mind changing your bed frequently	4.39

Through the analysis of Table 4, it is indicated that most of the elderly prefer to nursing beds similar to ordinary furniture, and show a little dissatisfied with the appearance of the current nursing beds. And almost all the elderly pay much attention to the safety facilities of nursing beds, who believe that safety should be the priority. As can be seen from the third and fourth questions, most of them think that they do not need facility assistance at present, but they think this will be helpful to them if such facilities exist. There is not a long time the elderly spend in bed at present, but some of them tend to have recreational activities in bed from the 5th, 6th, and 7th questions. And most elderly people are reluctant to change their bedding which can be seen from the eighth question.

4.3 Investigation Findings

1) The security facilities should be the top priority, because both the elderly and their adult children concerned about the safety issues.
2) The guardrails and the facilities to assist getting up are very necessary, and it is best to assist in some medical projects because of the influence of the existing nursing beds.
3) Recreational facilities should be added to bedding, because the elderly have demands for entertainment.
4) Take care of the feelings of elderly who have strong self-esteem while facilitating their lives.
5) Extending the use period should be considered in the design because respondents are unwilling to replace bedding.

5 Design Process

This part summarizes the principles of nursing bed design for the self-care elderly according to the determination of the bed size using the Jack software and the questionnaire survey for users. And the scheme is formed on the basis of these principles, including the explanation of function and structure of it.

5.1 Principles

1) Security: The principle that should be put first according to the research results, such as rounding the corners, installing guardrails, etc.
2) Humanization: People-oriented. It makes the bedding bring convenience to the elderly just right.
3) Versatility: It is easier for the self-care elderly to accept the universal design due to the strong self-esteem of them. For example, the induction lamp is needed for all age groups at night, which can reduce the discomfort of the elderly.
4) Sustainability: The length of using period of nursing beds is generally short, and it should be extended through reasonable design.

5.2 The Dimensions of the Design Scheme

Using the Jack software to conduct the experiment is able to establish digital humans according to the current body size of the elderly over 60. And it tests the size rationality of the model established with reference to the existing nursing beds on the market. Based on the determined size of bed and guardrails, the bed size drawing is as follows (as shown in Fig. 5).

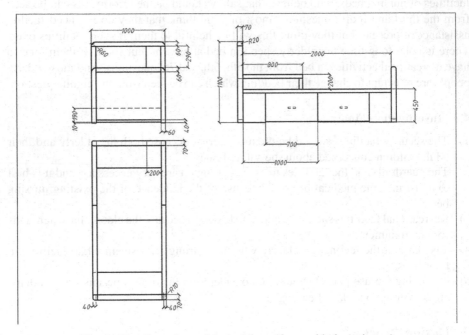

Fig. 5. The dimensions of the bed for self-care elderly (unit:mm).

The overall size of the bed was set to 2000 mm × 1000 mm × 450 mm (the mattress is 50 mm thick) in accordance with the dimensional reasonableness inspection results. According to the L1 and L2 obtained in the experiment, the length of the railing is set to 800 mm, and the adjustment range of the height is set to 200–300 mm. The remaining dimensions are determined based on the results of product research on the market.

5.3   The Functions of the Design Scheme

The functions are determined based on the results of the questionnaire survey and principles. First, the priority of needs is defined according to the survey results of the questionnaires for the adult children. The functions of bedding are as follows:

Table 4. Correspondence between research results and functions

KANO quality	Content and number	Function	Principle
Basic Quality	Q2- Security requirement	Rounded corners, bedside rails, sensor lights	Security, versatility
	Q3- Requirement for ancillary facilities	Bedside rails, adjustable mattress	Humanization
	Q8- Requirement for medical programs	A place for IV pole	Humanization, versatility
Performance Quality	Q4- Requirement for universal wheels	Detachable universal wheel	Humanization
	Q5- Requirement for table on bed	Table on bed	Humanization
	Q11- Requirements for comfortable sleep	The suitable dimensions and mattress	Humanization, versatility
Attractive Quality	Q6- Requirement for entertainment	Bed table, bedside lamp	Humanization, versatility
	Q7- Requirement for health care programs	Auxiliary therapy facilities	Humanization
	Q9 and Q10- Requirement for extended usage time	Accessories, removable adjustable bed frame	Sustainability
Indifferent Quality	Q1- Requirement for the appearance	According to the survey results of the elderly	Humanization

Second, design the appearance of the bedding, and adjust the functions according to the survey results of the questionnaires for the elderly. Since the elderly prefer nursing bedding that is similar in appearance to ordinary furniture, the bedding is made of wood, and the appearance is similar to the style of normal home decoration. In addition, the majority of the elderly have no such needs for some functions of the table on bed, such as dining needs, so the table on bed is designed as an accessory.

5.4 Design Scheme

The reasonable dimensions and functions with the highest user preference obtained by questionnaire survey are integrated into the design scheme (as shown in Fig. 6). This scheme is in warm color, and the style is simple and elegant, which is integrated with most decoration style. The bedding is of reasonable size which conforms to the principle of ergonomics. In addition, according to the security principle, the corners of the bedding are rounded to avoid accidents.

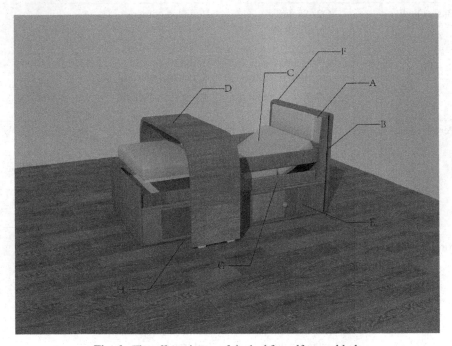

Fig. 6. The effect picture of the bed for self-care elderly

A. Bedside
     To make the elderly more comfortable, the bedside installs a sponge. And a touch-type lamp is installed, which is convenient for the elderly to read and use mobile phones at night.

B. A place for the crutches

This structure facilitates older people who use crutches to place them at the bedside more securely. Some elderly people choose to use crutches to assist their daily life. But ordinary flat corners cannot place crutches firmly, and not all elderly people will choose crutches which can keep standing.

C. Adjustable mattress

Long-term sitting or standing will lead to edema of the legs, because blood circulation slows down with the increasing age. A folding bed frame can adjust the angle freely, and the edema can be relieved by raising the legs. Some elderly also engage in daily activities such as having meals. Adjustments of the angle make the elderly more comfortable when eating.

D. Table on bed

This installation is in the form of accessories, which can be used for activities such as dining in bed and entertainment. To avoid the cervical spine problem caused by incorrect posture, the table can be raised, lowered and rotated 360 degrees to adjust the angle to adapt to the different needs of the elderly. And the bottom is equipped with a universal wheel, which can be easily moved.

E. Storage space

This bedding increases storage space, which can store more personal items, because most of the elderly have requirements for the storage of items. When the elderly need to stay in bed for a long time, it is very useful.

F. A hole for IV pole

The hole is mainly designed for the elderly who need infusion medical care. The device is located at the bedside. When the elderly need to receive medical care such as infusion, an IV pole can be placed in the hole.

G. Guardrails

The guardrails can provide assistance for daily activities of the elderly's, protecting the lumbar spine and knees. And it can be disassembled and is designed to an accessory, which will save resources and avoid unnecessary waste.

H. Infrared sensor lamp

It is located under the bed and induces the elderly's movements through infrared rays. Most of the elderly have the habit of night time urination. The induction-type lamp saves the trouble of finding a switch and avoids accidents in the dark.

6 Design Evaluation

To verify whether the design scheme is in line with the preferences of the target users, the design scheme is compared with two nursing bed on the market. This scheme is verified through user interviews. First, the functions of the design scheme and the other two nursing bed beddings were introduced to the interviewed participants in detail, and the participants were asked the views of the three beddings (as shown in Fig. 7).

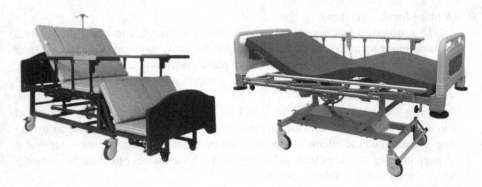

Fig. 7. Two main kinds of nursing beds on the market

There are 6 participants, including self-care elderly and their adult children. And some of them have experience in caring for the disabled. The procedure of this interview are shown in Table 5 below.

Table 5. Process of interview

Number	Procedure
1	Show the three pictures shown in Fig. 6
2	Introduce each type of bedding to participants briefly
3	"Which bedding do you prefer for you/your parents?"
4	"What is your reason for choosing/not choosing this bedding?"

During the interview, 5 out of 6 people chose the design scheme. The reasons given by them include "I prefer nursing beds that look similar to ordinary furniture", "I think that the existence of accessories can reduce the trouble of changing bed", "The existence of storage space can accommodate more personal belongings" and "I think that the presence of infrared sensor lights is convenient for me". However, there were also participants who prefer the other two nursing beds, thinking that these nursing beds have more functions and are more useful to take care of the elderly. And most of the participants indicated that they prefer to control the nursing bed electrically, and the adjustable guardrails.

7 Conclusion

The design of a bed for the self-care elderly, firstly, is based on the results of literature research for the physical and psychological conditions of the elderly, and the results of market research for nursing beds on the market. Secondly, use Jack software to determine the dimensions of the bed. Thirdly, the functions and structure of the bedding are determined based on the results of questionnaire survey and the establishment of the KANO model. Finally, produce and evaluate the design scheme. This paper mainly proposes a framework for designing the multifunctional bedding for the self-care elderly, which aims to attract more attention to them and further enhance their happiness. In addition, it also aims to reduce the frequency of bedding replacement so that resources can be saved, and utilized effectively.

References

1. Zhao, F., Sun, H., Guan, Y.: Ergonomic design of elderly nursing bed based on JACK virtual simulation analysis. Packag. Eng. **41**(24), 30–39 (2020)
2. Zhang, Y., Zhou, C., Zhou, T.: Functional adaptation design of self-care elderly apartment furniture. Furniture **41**(05), 41–45 (2020)
3. Su, S., Wang, H.: The main points of ergonomic simulation analysis based on JACK software. Indus. Design **11**, 115–116 (2017)
4. Zhang, L., Huang, K., Song, J.: Research on virtual maintainability verification of aviation equipment based on jack. Ordnance Indus. Automat. **35**(03), 66–69 (2016)
5. Hu, H.: Anthropometric Measurements of the Elderly. Tsinghua University (2005)

Grasp Synthesis for the Hands of Elderly People with Reduced Muscular Force, Slippery Skin, and Limitation in Range of Motion

Reiko Takahashi[1]($\boxtimes$), Yuta Nakanishi[1], Natsuki Miyata[2], and Yusuke Maeda[1]

[1] Yokohama National University, 79-5 Tokiwadai, Hodogaya-ku, Yokohama, Japan
`takahashi-reiko-cf@ynu.jp`
[2] National Institute of Advanced Industrial Science and Technology, 2-3-26 Aomi, Koto-ku, Tokyo, Japan

Abstract. In this paper, we propose a synthesis method for grasping postures by using a digital hand for the elderly. For the virtual evaluation of inclusive design products, it is necessary to synthesize natural grasps for non-healthy hands, including those of the elderly. In modeling the hand of the elderly, we focused on the following three features: (1) narrowed range of motion (ROM), (2) decline in muscle strength, and (3) decline in friction coefficient. The modeling was based on existing studies of physical characteristics of the elderly, and it is possible to create hand models of any age from 20 to 100 years old. We improved our previous method for synthesizing grasps, which was developed for hands with limited thumb ROM, and synthesized grasping postures for elderly people. We found that the grasping posture of the 60-year-old hand was slightly different from that of the healthy hand and that the 100-year-old hand experienced great difficulty in grasping objects.

Keywords: Grasp synthesis · Digital hand · Inclusive designing

1 Introduction

Virtual evaluation of product usability using a digital hand and a computer-aided design (CAD) model of the product is a human-centered design approach. Virtual evaluation has two major advantages: (1) it reduces the cost of making prototypes and recruiting subjects for usability tests, and (2) ensures the comprehensiveness of the subjects because by preparing comprehensive hand models, evaluation of product usability using various people is possible.

The latter is essential for inclusive designs because it facilitates assessing product usability by various people without real experiments. In inclusive designs [1], product usability by various people who have been excluded from traditional design processes, such as elderly people or people with disabilities, is considered from the early stages of the design process.

For virtual evaluation using a digital hand, it is necessary to synthesize natural grasps for arbitrary product models. [2] investigated the literature on data-

© The Author(s), under exclusive license to Springer Nature Switzerland AG 2022
V. G. Duffy (Ed.): HCII 2022, LNCS 13319, pp. 148–159, 2022.
https://doi.org/10.1007/978-3-031-05890-5_12

driven grasp synthesis such as [3–7]. Data-driven approaches use the database of real human grasps, and the necessary data are identified based on known grasp classification (e.g., [8–12]). Therefore, it is possible to synthesize natural grasps that are similar to real human grasps. Previous studies on grasp synthesis have mainly focused on healthy hands. However, in inclusive designs, non-healthy hands are also considered. Non-healthy hand grasps differ from healthy hand grasps. In the virtual evaluation of inclusive design, it is important to synthesize natural grasps using various hands, including non-healthy ones.

In this study, we have succeeded in synthesizing the grasp of a hand whose thumb range of motion (ROM) is limited, which is typically observed in patients with carpal tunnel syndrome [13]. In this study, we considered the hand of the elderly as representative of non-healthy hands. Moreover, in an aging society, it is important to design products that can be easily grasped by elderly people. Therefore, we propose a method of creating the elderly hand model incorporating the reduction of the muscle force, the lower coefficient of friction, and the limited ROM due to aging. We also propose a method for synthesizing grasping postures using the created hand model of elderly people.

2   Algorithm of Grasp Synthesis

2.1   Grasp Synthesis Method

This section provides an overview of the grasp synthesis algorithm. We extend the method for grasp synthesis of hands whose thumb ROM is limited, which we previously proposed in [13] for the grasp synthesis of elderly hands.

The main feature of this method is the use of a grasp database based on "contact regions." The contact regions are the areas on the hand surface that touch an object while grasping it. An outline of the grasp synthesis method is shown in Fig. 1. The input information for grasp synthesis is (1) target grasping points on a given object, (2) contact regions, and (3) the correspondence between the target grasping points and contact regions. The grasp database contains 814 postures, including 801 typical postures of healthy hands and 13 postures that are observed in hands whose thumb ROM is limited. The postures of the healthy hands were determined by classifying the basic human grasping postures observed in [8] from the viewpoint of the contact regions and changing the distance between the fingertips and the number of fingers used. The grasp database is searched for primitive postures that use the same contact regions as the input contact regions. Next, the primitive grasp postures were interpolated such that the distance between the contact regions matched the distance between the grasping target points, and an interpolated posture was synthesized. Then, the interpolated posture was aligned with the object, and an initial posture was synthesized. Finally, the initial posture was optimized by considering the following four items:

– formation of contacts with an appropriate position and orientation;
– margin from the ROM boundaries;

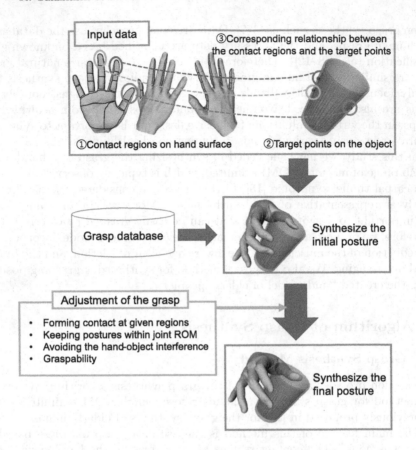

Fig. 1. Outline of grasp synthesis algorithm [13]

- amount of interference between the hand model and the object model; and
- judgement of graspability considering the musculoskeletal model.

Here, the judgement of graspability is checked under these two conditions: (1) the arrangement of the contact points satisfies the force of the closure, and (2) the grasp is balanced against gravity considering the musculoskeletal model [14]. The final grasp posture was then synthesized.

To synthesize grasps by elderly hands, the following points have been mainly changed from our previous method [13].

- Modification of evaluation items for optimization calculation.
- Retrying by changing the initial posture when grasp synthesis fails. (If the synthesis fails after recalculation, it is regarded as an ungraspable condition.)

2.2   Modification of Evaluation Items for Optimization Calculation

In our previous grasp synthesis algorithm, the formation of contacts with an appropriate position and orientation was one of the evaluation items for the optimization calculation. Specifically, the following two items were used:

- The distance between the input grasping target points and the contact regions of the hand model.
- The difference in normal directions between input grasping target points and the contact regions of the hand model.

However, because of the first evaluation item, the posture in which the distance from the target point is close without touching the object is preferred over that where the distance from the target point is far but touching the object. Moreover, owing to the second evaluation item, the posture in which the surface of the fingers is in line with the surface of the object is preferred, even if the hand surface is floating away from the object. For these reasons, the hand tends to move away from the object unless the grasping target points are carefully input.

If the hand is not in contact with the object, it is impossible to compute the distance and normal direction of the contact point. The problem is that the distance and normal vector are calculated forcibly, even when there is no contact. Therefore, we modified the evaluation value design so that the evaluation value would be much worse when the hand was not in contact with the object.

2.3   Retrying by Changing the Initial Posture When Grasp Synthesis Fails

When the finger completely penetrates the object in the synthesized initial posture, it is difficult to escape from the penetration by the optimization calculation. Thereby, the posture synthesis fails because the amount of interference does not change when the joint angle is slightly changed.

Therefore, when the evaluation value of the final synthesized posture is above the ungraspability threshold defined in advance and the posture synthesis is judged to fail, the joints of the initial grasp posture are randomly modified to open the hand, and the optimization calculation is repeated from the new initial posture. This process was repeated up to three times until a graspable posture was obtained. If the graspable posture is still not synthesized after this process, it is judged that the grasping condition is ungraspable.

3   Hand Model of Elderly People

The hands of the elderly were modeled as having a narrower range of motion (ROM), lower muscle strength, and a lower friction coefficient compared to young hands.

3.1   Narrower ROM

It is known that the ROM of the upper extremities of the elderly decreases with age [15]. In this study, the ROM of the wrist, elbow, shoulder, lumbar spine, and cervical spine were measured, and it was found that all ROMs decreased with age, although the degree of decrease varied.

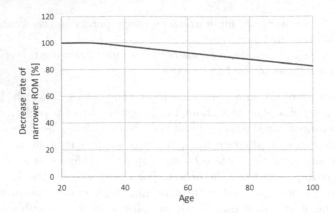

Fig. 2. Decrease rate of narrower ROM due to aging

In our study, we aimed to model the decrease in ROM of the hand joints. Therefore, we focused on the reduction of ROM in the shoulder, elbow, and wrist, which are considered to be relatively similar to hand joints. The ROM of these three joints in the older age group (mean age, 70 years) was on average 93% of that in the younger age group (mean age, 27 years). Therefore, we simplified the results. ROM limitation was applied from 30 years of age, and the ROM was determined to decrease linearly to 90% at 70 years of age. The decrease rate $r_{ROM}[\%]$ is expressed by the following equation.

$$r_{ROM} = \begin{cases} 100 & \text{if } age \leq 30, \\ 100 - 10 \times \frac{age-30}{40} & \text{otherwise.} \end{cases} \tag{1}$$

where age is the age of the hand model to be created. The decrease rate is shown graphically in Fig. 2.

In this study, two methods of ROM expression were considered: one-dimensional ROM for independently controllable finger joints and two-dimensional ROM for joints coordinated with other joints. For one-dimensional ROM, the maximum and minimum relative joint angles from the median are limited according to age. For two-dimensional ROM, the polygonal ROM shrunk similarly based on the centroid of its bounding box. However, when the centroid is located outside of the ROM, a part of the ROM after restriction may be outside the ROM before restriction. This indicates that ROM partially expanded with age. Since such a phenomenon is unlikely to occur in real life, we must avoid a situation in which the ROM after the restriction is larger than that before restriction. Therefore, in this case, the intersection of the original ROM and the shrunk ROM was defined as the final limited ROM due to aging.

3.2   Lower Muscle Strength

According to [16], who studied the changes in muscle innervation that occur during the aging process, the number of muscle fibers decreases with age, and muscle strength declines. The study shows that people aged 70–80 years have 20–40% lower muscle strength than young adults, and people older than 70–80 years of age have more than 50% lower muscle strength. The degree of muscle weakness differs between concentric, eccentric, and isometric muscles. Because these three types of hand muscles are crucial to grasp, it is necessary to apply an appropriate restriction ratio to each muscle to strictly express muscle weakness due to aging. However, in this study, the isometric limiting ratio was applied to all muscles for simplicity. The decline in muscle strength was modeled as a gradual decline in muscle strength until 60 years of age and a sharp decline thereafter, referring to the results of [16]. Because it was difficult to express the decease rate in mathematical formulas, we specified the rate for each age from 20 to 90. The rate was assumed to be constant above 90-years-old. The decrease rate is shown in Fig. 3.

3.3   Lower Friction Coefficient

According to [17], who clarified the effect of aging on changes in the friction coefficient of fingertips, age and friction coefficient are negatively correlated. Some studies suggest that the coefficient of friction does not change with age, but in these studies, the coefficient of friction was measured under conditions in which the moisture content of the hand surface was the same for all age groups. In contrast, the moisture content of the hand surface is natural in [17]. It has also been pointed out by [18] that the moisture content of the skin decreases with aging. In this study, we use the measurement results of [17] because we believe that it is more realistic to use the data measured without modifying the moisture content of the hand surface. Because the friction coefficient depends on the object to be grasped, in this study, the decrease in the friction coefficient with aging was calculated from the friction coefficient values measured in [17]. The decrease in friction on the hand surface indicates that the friction coefficient should decrease linearly from 20 years of age, according to [17]. In [17], the friction coefficient of 20-years-old is approximately 0.55 and that of 80 years old is approximately 0.15. Therefore, the decrease rate $r_{\text{friction}}[\%]$ is expressed by the following equation. The rate was assumed to be constant above 80-years-old.

$$r_{\text{friction}} = \begin{cases} 100\left\{1 - \frac{age-20}{60}\left(1 - \frac{0.15}{0.55}\right)\right\} & \text{if } age \le 80, \\ 100 \times \frac{0.15}{0.55} & \text{otherwise.} \end{cases} \tag{2}$$

where age is the age of the hand model to be created. The decrease rate is shown graphically in Fig. 4.

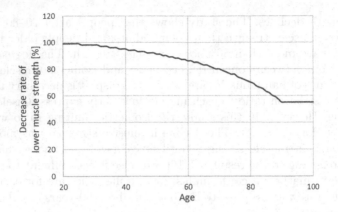

Fig. 3. Decrease rate of lower muscle strength due to aging

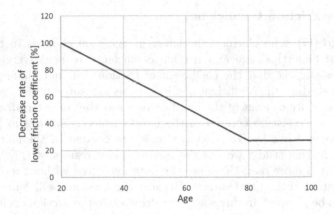

Fig. 4. Decrease rate of lower friction coefficient due to aging

4   Grasp Synthesis Results and Discussion

4.1   Confirmation of Simulated Elderly Hand

First, we confirmed that the features of the hands of the elderly, such as narrow ROM, muscle weakness, and reduced frictional coefficient, can be expressed by comparing the grasping postures of young adults with those of the elderly.

We prepared three conditions of the hand model: (1) a healthy hand of a 20-year-old, (2) an elderly hand of an 80-year-old. The subject for ROM and muscle strength studies for a 20-year-old healthy hand was a female in her twenties. The hand models of the 60-year-old and 100-year-old were created with the aforementioned restrictions applied to the data of the 20-year-old. The shapes of these hand models were reproduced from that of the female subject. The coefficient of friction for a healthy hand was defined as 0.5.

The input contact regions are shown in (1) in Fig. 5 as the colored regions. The target points on the object are empirically input. The posture of picking

(1)	(2)	(3)
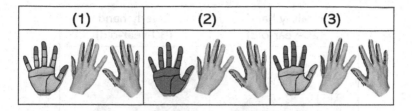		

Fig. 5. Input contact regions

Healthy hand (20-year-old)	Elderly hand (80-year-old)
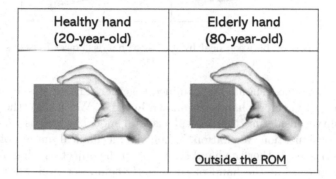	
	Outside the ROM

Fig. 6. Comparison between healthy and aged hands: narrow ROM

up a cuboid using fingertips was compared between the healthy hand and the elderly hand.

Narrower ROM. The object to be grasped was a 60 [mm] × 60 [mm] × 150 [mm] cuboid with a weight of 800 [gf]. The direction of gravity is assumed to be perpendicular to the paper surface. A large grasping object relative to the hand size was employed to increase the effect of ROM narrowing. The grasp synthesis results for the healthy and elderly hands are shown in Fig. 6. We checked the margin from the ROM boundaries which is an evaluation item for the optimization calculation. The synthesized postures were within the ROM for the hand of young adults, while they were outside the ROM for the hands of the elderly, and the elderly grasp was judged to be ungraspable even after modifying the initial posture three times at random. It can be concluded that the input condition is ungraspable for elderly people.

Lower Muscle Strength and Lower Friction Coefficient. The object to be grasped was a 30 [mm] × 30 [mm] × 150 [mm] cuboid with a weight of 5000 [gf]. The direction of gravity is assumed to be perpendicular to the paper surface. The weight of the object to be grasped is set to be heavy so that the effect of muscle weakness and the decline in the friction coefficient is greatly reflected. In this study, the contact was modeled as a simple point contact with friction, and it was difficult to separate the effects of muscle force and friction. Therefore, muscle weakness

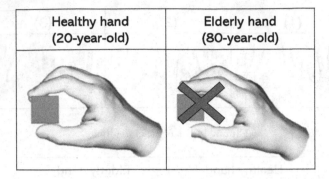

Fig. 7. Comparison between healthy and aged hands: Lower muscle strength

and frictional weakness should be examined together. The grasp synthesis results for the healthy and elderly hands are shown in Fig. 7. We checked the judgement of graspability considering the musculoskeletal model, which is an evaluation item of the optimization calculation. When the mechanical margin of grasp was used to determine whether the hand could grasp the object, the hand of a young adult could grasp, but the hand of the elderly could not even after modifying the initial posture three times at random. It can be concluded that the input condition is ungraspable for elderly people.

4.2   Some Examples of Grasp Synthesis

We prepared three conditions of the hand model: (1) a healthy hand of a 20-year-old, (2) an elderly hand of a 60-year-old, and (3) an elderly hand of a 100-year-old. The subject for ROM and muscle strength of 20-year-old healthy hand studies was a female in her twenties. The hand models of the 60-year-old and 100-year-old were created with the aforementioned restrictions applied to the data of the 20-year-old. The shapes of these hand models were reproduced from that of the 20-year-old female subject.

The object to be grasped was a 40 [mm] × 40 [mm] × 150 [mm] cuboid with a weight of 600 [gf] and a cylinder with a diameter of 40 [mm], height of 150 [mm], and weight of 800 [gf]. The direction of gravity is assumed to be perpendicular to the paper surface. The input contact regions for each grasp are illustrated in Fig. 5 as the colored regions. The cuboid is grasped with the fingertips of five fingers ((1) in Fig. 5), and the cylinder is grasped with the whole fingers ((2) and (3) in Fig. 5). The target points on the object are empirically input. Some examples of the grasp synthesis results are shown in Fig. 8. These objects were judged to be mechanically ungraspable by the elderly hand of a 100-year-old person. In the case of the healthy hand, the palmar surface of the thumb was in contact with the object, while the radial side of the thumb was in contact with the object in the case of the elderly hand of a 60-year-old person in (1) and (2). In (3), the used side of the thumb does not change between the healthy and the 60-year-old hand. The inability of the hands of a 100-year-old person to grasp

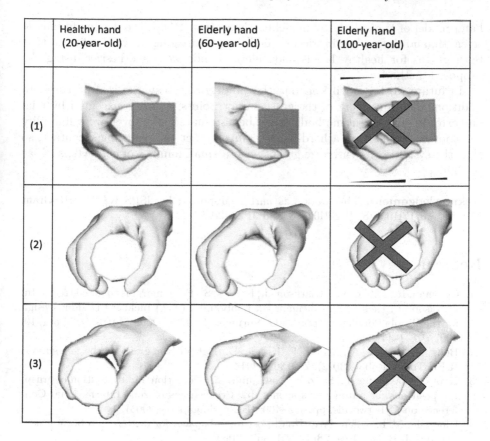

Fig. 8. Some examples of the grasp synthesis

was due to a decrease in muscle strength and friction coefficient. In particular, muscle strength is reduced to approximately 50% of that of a healthy hand, so it is extremely difficult to grasp objects. The use of the radial side of the thumb in the hand of a 60-year-old person is due to the narrowing of the ROM of the thumb and the difficulty of contacting the palmar side. In (3), the ulnar side of the thumb is used explicitly even in the healthy hand. A grasping posture similar to that of the healthy hand can be reproduced by the 60-year-old hand. Therefore, in this input condition, grasping posture did not change significantly between the healthy hand and the 60-year-old hand.

5   Conclusion

In this study, we synthesized grasps for an elderly hand, which can be used to virtually evaluate inclusive design products. The grasp synthesis method for the thumb ROM-limited hand [13] was extended. Based on previous studies on the decline in physical functions in the elderly, we proposed a method to create a hand model of the elderly by modeling the narrow ROM, the decline in muscle strength, and the decline in friction coefficient with aging. It was confirmed that both grasps for healthy hands and elderly hands were synthesized using the proposed method.

In future work, we will evaluate the validity of the synthesized postures. In addition, the adjustment of the grasp target points, which is executed by trial and error in our current method, should be automated. Moreover, we will modify the contact model from a hard-finger point contact to a soft-finger contact, so that the system can synthesize grasps with a small number of contacts, such as pinching.

Acknowledgement. This work was partly supported by JSPS KAKENHI Grant Numbers JP17H05918, JP20H04268, and JP20J20651.

References

1. Coleman, R., Lebbon, C., Clarkson, J., Keates, S.: From margins to mainstream. In: Clarkson, J., Keates, S., Coleman, R., Lebbon, C. (eds.) Inclusive Design: Design for the Whole Population, pp. 10–12. Springer, London (2003). https://doi.org/10. 1007/978-1-4471-0001-0

2. Bohg, J., Morales, A., Asfour, T., Kragic, D.: Data-driven grasp synthesis-a survey. IEEE Trans. Robot. **30**(2), 289–309 (2014)

3. Kyota, F., Watabe, T., Saito, S., Nakajima, M.: Detection and evaluation of grasping positions for autonomous agents. In: Proceedings of 2005 International Conference on Cyberworlds, pp. 453–460. IEEE, Singapore (2005)

4. Ciocarlie, M.T., Allen, P.K.: Hand posture subspaces for dexterous robotic grasping. Int. J. Robot. Res. **28**(7), 851–867 (2009)

5. Goldfeder, C., Allen, P.K.: Data-driven grasping. Auton. Robots **31**(1), 1–20 (2011)

6. Miyata, N., Hirono, T., Maeda, Y.: Grasp database that covers variation of contact region usage. In: Proceedings of 2013 IEEE International Conference on Systems, Man, and Cybernetics, pp. 2635–2040. IEEE, UK (2013)

7. Hirono, T., Miyata, N., Maeda, Y.: Grasp synthesis for variously-sized hands using a grasp database that covers variation of contact region. In: Proceedings of the 3rd International Digital Human Modeling Symposium, #11, Japan (2014)

8. Feix, T., Pawlik, R., Schmiedmayer, H-B., Romero, J., Kragic, D.: A comprehensive grasp taxonomy. In: Robotics, Science and Systems Conference: Workshop on Understand the Human Hand for Advanced Robotic Manipulation, Switzerland (2009)

9. Feix, T., Romero, J., Schmiedmayer, H.-B., Dollar, A.M., Kragic, D.: The GRASP taxonomy of human grasp types. IEEE Trans. Hum.-Mach. Syst. **46**(1), 66–77 (2016)

10. Napier, J.R.: The prehensile movements of the human hand. J. Bone Joint Surg. **38**(4), 902–913 (1956)

11. Kamakura, N., Ohmura, M., Ishii, H., Mitsuboshi, F., Miura, Y.: Positional patterns for prehension in normal hands. J. Rehabil. Med. **15**(2), 65–82 (1978). (in Japanese)

12. Lee, K.-S., Jung, M.-C.: Common patterns of voluntary grasp types according to object shape, size, and direction. Int. J. Ind. Ergon. **44**, 761–68 (2014)
13. Takahashi, R., Miyata, N., Maeda, Y., Nakanishi, Y.: Grasp synthesis considering graspability for a digital hand with limited thumb range of motion. Adv. Robot. **36**(4), 192–204 (2022)
14. Asami, Y., Tada, M., Endo, Y., Ogiwara, N.: Estimation of grasping posture by minimizing internal mechanical load during power grip task using a three-dimensional musculoskeletal model of the human hand. In: Proceedings of the 2017 JSME Conference on Robotics and Mechatronics, 2P2-J01, Japan (2017). (in Japanese)
15. Doriot, N., Wang, X.: Effects of age and gender on maximum voluntary range of motion of the upper body joints. Ergonomics **49**(3), 269–281 (2016)
16. Vandervoort, A.A.: Aging of the human neuromascular system. Muscle Nerve **25**(1), 17–25 (2002)
17. Mabuchi, K., Sakai, R., Yoshida, K., Ujihira, M.: Effect of ageing on friction of human fingers. Biosurf. Biotribol. **4**(4), 117–121 (2018)
18. Potts, R.O., Buras, E.M., Jr., Chrisman, D.A., Jr.: Changes with age in the moisture content of human skin. J. Investig. Dermatol. **82**(1), 97–100 (1984)

Design and Application of Skirt Fit Software for Human Body Ontology Knowledge

Zhengtang Tan[1], Tian Yan[2(✉)], Yufan Zhou[2], and Yi Zhu[3]

[1] Experiment Teaching Center of Fashion Design and Engineering, Hunan Normal University, Changsha 410006, Hunan Province, China
[2] College of Engineering and Design, Hunan Normal University, Changsha 410006, Hunan Province, China
1479453376@qq.com
[3] School of Art and Design, Guangdong University of Technology, Guangzhou 510006, Guangdong Province, China

Abstract. The study used 3D body scanning technology to collect 3D body models and body size data of female college students aged 18–23 years old from Hunan Province, China. The study aims to optimize the fit of clothing, and divides the knowledge of human body shape into top-level ontologies, domain-task ontologies and application ontologies based on the basic level of knowledge ontologies, and develops software to evaluate the fit of skirts. The software was developed to evaluate the fit of skirts. The main functions of the software are 3D body shape knowledge module, body shape classification module and clothing fit evaluation module. Through this software, the current design problem that knowledge of human body shape ontologies and clothing fit evaluation knowledge system is fragmented can be improved to a certain extent, which will help designers to better understand the knowledge of human body size and body shape, provide designers with auxiliary tools for clothing design, and enhance the fit of innovative clothing design.

Keywords: 3D body measurement · Knowledge of shape classification · Fit design

1 Introduction

Knowledge of the human shape directly influences the design and construction of clothing and its size, and determines the fit of clothing. A well-fitting clothing adapts to the user's body shape, meets the requirements of wearing aesthetics and improve the comfort experience, while an ill-fitting clothing can be too tight, too loose or make users difficult to move [1]. With clothing design and its production becoming more and more personalized and customized, body size analysis has become a fundamental key knowledge in the field of clothing and wearable product design. At present, there is still a lack of complete human body size data. For example, in China, the current national standard for adult human body size in China is still in the national standard document

© The Author(s), under exclusive license to Springer Nature Switzerland AG 2022
V. G. Duffy (Ed.): HCII 2022, LNCS 13319, pp. 160–171, 2022.
https://doi.org/10.1007/978-3-031-05890-5_13

issued by the China National Institute of Standardization in 2008. The standard number is GB/T 1335.2–2008 [2]. The data is outdated and the geographical and age span of the subjects is large, resulting in a low reference value of the data in practical design applications. Therefore, the analysis of regional and group body shape subdivisions in China, the formation of a correlative knowledge system based on regional human body shape classification and fitness evaluation, the construction of a computer-aided system for the application and sharing of large sample body model data, and the realization of data-driven innovative design of clothing [3] are the fundamental research issues of great urgency in the design field.

2 Construction of a Mapping Model of Clothing Fit and Knowledge of Human Shape

Knowledge of body measurements is a prerequisite for the design of clothing and wearable products [4]. The Oxford Dictionary defines clothing fit as an ability to shape body and create fit size. Current assessment methods include 3D anthropometry, mathematical and statistical methods and virtual try-on methods [5]. Clothing fit includes both psychological fit and physical fit. Among them, the psychological fit means that the wearing effect meets the subjective expectations of the user, to show the advantages of the wearer's body shape and to cover up the body shape defects as much as possible, that is, the posture, proportion and curve characteristics of the user body shape need to be analyzed in the research. The physiological fit places more emphasis on wearing comfort and meeting the demands of movement. This part requires the researcher to analyze body shape data and generalize body shape types in order to be able to meet the psychological expectations of most users in mass production. Therefore, research on fitness in clothing design is the process of collating, analyzing, integrating discrete body size and shape data to form a complete body shape knowledge system by using appropriate knowledge organization models, to optimize the innovative design of clothing.

Clothing design and fit assessment is an important part of the process of translating creative thinking into a physical presentation of the clothing, involving the process of measurement, structural drawing and fit evaluating. This shows that knowledge of the human shape has a direct impact on the styling outcome of the clothing design. Combining clothing design and production process, this study divides the knowledge of human body shape into top-level ontologies, domain-task ontologies and application ontologies based on Guarino's basic level of knowledge ontologies [6]. The three levels of ontologies are proposed to further clarify the association between clothing fit and ontological knowledge of human shape, and to serve to extract ontological knowledge of human shape accurately in the rapid iterative clothing design.

As shown in Fig. 1, the top-level ontology is the human body model in the initial position of the mapping model, which is the basic and objective knowledge of the study of the human shape, consisting of two parts: human size data and body shape classifying, that is, the objective knowledge generated by the form of the human body model, which is also the factual basis for design research. The domain-task ontologies is the second layer and concerns the knowledge required for the field of clothing design. On the one hand, it contains the size knowledge acquired in different body shape classification models, which is still a part of the domain knowledge of the human shape. On the other hand, it is driven more by the task of clothing design and contains the designer's skills in two-dimensional clothing patterning based on body size data. The application ontologies, on the right side of Fig. 1, is directly related to the styling outcome of the design knowledge, and it requires not only an objective evaluation of the fitting effect on the 3D body from the designer's viewpoint, but also to analyze the psychological expectations of the fitting effect from the user's perspective. As shown in Fig. 1, according to the clothing design process, the whole process of knowledge structure includes the retrieval of body knowledge, and also covers the application process of design products that are visualized by design techniques, forming a knowledge mapping model and mapping relationship from seeking truth to usability.

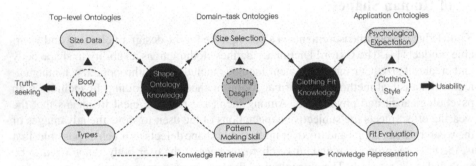

Fig. 1. Mapping model of clothing fit and knowledge of human shape

3   Clothing Fit Evaluation Software Design

The application purpose of the research is to build application and sharing of a large sample of human body model data classification, and to build a computer-aided system to analyze clothing fit. On the base of the mapping model of garment fit and body shape knowledge, this study builds a dress fit evaluation software. The software is divided into three modules: The first module is the 3D body shape knowledge module. The second module is the body shape classification knowledge module and the third module is the clothing fit evaluation module. The specific analysis and design are as follows.

3.1   3D Body Shape Knowledge Module

The 3D body shape knowledge module focuses on providing a reasonable factual basis for research [7], understanding body size measurement methods, key human body size, types of body shape, clarifying the relationship between shape ontology knowledge and clothing pattern design, and initially building a reliable and reusable knowledge system of body size [5].

The human body shape objects of this study are 18–23 years old female college students in Hunan Province, who are also the native people in Hunan Province. Its purpose is to explore the body shape characteristics of this group of human body and the knowledge of body size for the needs of clothing design. In this study, 220 3D body models and 62 size data on parts of the body relevant to clothing design, such as height, bust and hipline and so on, were collected from female college students of Hunan Province from 2019 to 2020, by using a German 3D scanner VITUS SMART LC3. With the consent of the subjects, the body data was blurred and processed into the dress fit evaluation software to build a 3D body database.

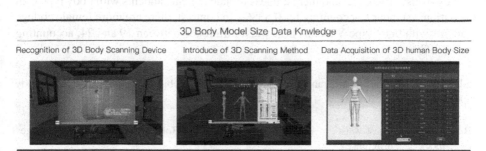

Fig. 2. Key interfaces of 3D body model size data knowledge

Figure 2 is the 3D body model size data knowledge. We try to restore the real scene of the 3D body scanning steps in this module, so the designer can embodied experience the whole process from 3D body measurement to clothing design and production. Firstly, in the virtual environment, the designer walks into the 3D body scanning lab and clicks on the computer on the table to start scanning the body, and the system introduces the 3D scanning method and points for attention. Afterwards, the 3D body model and the size data of the corresponding body parts are obtained, with a total of 22 items, such as height, bust and waistline. The designer can form a system of ontological knowledge of the human body shape in terms of measurement methods, measurement means, measurement steps and data characteristics.

The second part of this module is based on the body shape classification of 220 female college students in Hunan Province of China. The aim of the part is to classify and assist the computer in identifying the specific physical characteristics of this group so that the clothing designer can develop a structured perception of the body shape characteristics of this group [8]. In this part, the study focuses on two questions: 1. What kind of body types can be classified for female students in Hunan Province; 2. what are the data and shape differences in various body part for different body types.

The first step is to extract the main components of body shape from the part size data using factor analysis, and to extract the variables and indicators of body shape characteristics from the main components of body shape using correlation analysis or other methods. In the second step, K means clustering and hierarchical clustering analysis were used to classify human body shape in detail. In this step, the size measurement data of 186 female college students were randomly extracted, and the chest-waist difference, hip-waist difference and body-to-waist (circumference) ratio were extracted as the shape characteristic indicator variables of human subjects. K means clustering of variables was made to explore the body shape types and prototypes of different body types of female university students in Hunan Province [9].

Based on the final clustering centers of the subject's shape characteristics indicator variables, the results of four types of clustering were obtained, as shown in Table 1. Comparing the national standard sizing system for garments GB/T1335–2008 (Table 2) [2], it is found that female college students in Hunan Province have a larger difference in chest-waist difference, and there are less female college students with body type C in the national standard, accounting for 0.538%. In contrast, there are more female college students with body type Y and a chest-waist difference between 19 and 24, accounting for 41.398%.

Table 1. The mean value and range of the variables of the subject characteristic of each body type

Body type code/index of subject characteristics	Chest-waist difference		Hip-waist difference		Body-to-waist ratio		Percentage of sample/%
	Average value	Range	Average value	Range	Average value	Range	
Body Type1	12.879	6.4–19.7	18.096	9.6–22.4	2.334	1.97–2.77	13.369%
Body Type2	15.342	10.2–18.7	26.136	23.1–31.7	2.542	2.21–3.01	18.717%
Body Type3	17.645	14.2–21.9	22.034	15.8–24.2	2.455	1.80–2.86	34.759%
Body Type4	21.991	18.9–32.0	26.535	21.2–34.2	2.642	2.27–3.10	33.155%

Table 2. GB/T1335–2008 Classification of adult female body types

Body type classification code	Chest-waist difference/cm	Number of samples	Percentage of sample/%
Other	>25	12	6.452
Y	19–24	77	41.398
A	14–18	66	35.484
B	9–13	30	16.129
C	4–8	1	0.538

Study found that, as shown in the Table 2, the body type of the sample was concentrated in type Y and type A, with 41.4% and 35.5% respectively, while fewer subjects with body type C, at 0.5%. The finding confirms that the majority of female college students in Hunan Province have a standard body shape, with fewer having an obese body shape [10]. Based on Question 1, the study uses three main morphological characteristic indicators, chest-waist difference, hip-waist difference, and body-to-waist ratio, and found that the body shape clustering of female college students in Hunan Province can be divided into four types, which were shown in Table 1, and the mean and ranges of the subject characteristic index variables for each type are presented. Based on Question 2, this study further explains the shape characteristics of female college students in Hunan Province. The first type is fat H-shaped figure or apple shape. The main body curve is not obvious, and the waist is thick, accounting for 13.369%; the second type is pear-shaped figure, which accounts for 18.717%. The chest-to-waist curve is not obvious, the waist-to-hip curve is obvious, and the waist is flat and thin; the third type is V-shape figure, the chest-to-waist curve is more obvious, the waist-to-hip curve is not obvious, and the waist is well-proportioned. It accounts for 34.759%; the fourth type is hourglass-shaped figure that accounts for 33.155%, with obvious chest-to-waist curves, obvious waist-to-hip curves, and flat and thin waist.

Study constructed a knowledge module based on the 3D body model types, which contains three parts of knowledge, as shown in the Fig. 3. The diagram on the left shows a comparison table of the data of body shape types in Hunan Province, China, and the detailed data are shown in Table 1. The study defines different body shape types from three perspectives, namely chest-waist difference, hip-waist difference and body-to-waist ratio. The middle diagram shows the body shape characteristics based on the body type, that is, the prototype visual features of the fat H-shaped figure, the pear-shaped figure, the standard V-shaped figure, and the skinny hourglass-shaped figure. The rightmost diagram shows the refined 3D human body shape type model in different body shape types. As an example, the model that is enlarged in the diagram is the selected human model that belongs to the third type—standard V body, which has the moderate waistline, moderate relative height, and is well proportioned. The model on the right side of the figure is a fat V-shaped figure, which is fat as a whole. This module provides the designer with visual recommendations from the body size data to the 3D body model.

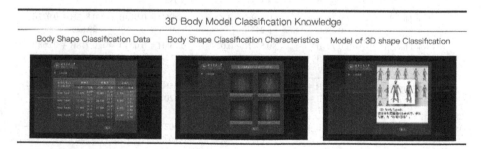

Fig. 3. Key interface to the knowledge of the typology categories of the 3D body shape knowledge module

3.2   Body Shape Classification Module

The body classification module is a mainly part of the domain-task ontologies level. Research on clothing size selection and pattern making skills are made in the study. In this module, a size recommendation table for designers to fit female students in Hunan

Province was constructed, and 15 sets of dress structural drawings were placed in the system to aid design from both domain and task perspective.

This module firstly constructed a size recommendation table that fits the female university students in Hunan Province. Research combined Size System and Designation for Costume to define height and bust as the basic parts of the grading, so the values of other control parts are binary linear functions of the values of the two basic parts (height and bust), calculated using the following binary linear regression equation:

$$y = b_0 + b_1 x_1 + b_2 x_2 \tag{1}$$

x_1, x_2 are the values of height (H) and bust (B), which are the two basic parts of Size System and Designation for Costume, y is the estimated value of other control parts calculated by using x_1, x_2. b_0, b_1, b_2 are constants and regression coefficients. The data of each part from each body type is imported into SPSS for regression analysis to obtain the partial regression coefficient values of each control part from different body shapes with respect to height and bust, appropriate adjustments was made in combination with the actual design and production applications and the current Size System and Designation for Costume, and the corresponding linear regression equations are summarized (Table 3).

Table 3. The regression equation of control parts of each body type

Control part/Body Type		Body Type1 H-shaped figure	Body Type2 Pear-shaped figure	Body Type3 Standard V-shaped figure	Body Type4 Hourglass-shaped figure
Height	Body height	H (Body height)			
	Neck height	0.865H + 0.004B − 3.949	0.812H − 0.04B + 8.125	0.865H − 0.004B − 3.037	0.842H − 0.002B + 0.419
	Chest height	0.776H − 0.086B − 3.637	0.779H − 0.026B − 8.244	0.806H − 0.013B − 13.017	0.807H + 0.077B − 20.826
	Waist height	0.734H − 0.019B − 17.089	0.696H − 0.029B − 10.252	0.734H + 0.026B − 20.158	0.718H + 0.068B − 21.87
	Hip height	0.697H + 0.089B − 39.197	0.595H + 0.012B − 17.847	0.65H − 0.042B − 21.207	0.632H − 0.003B − 22.462
Length	Arm length	0.473H + 0.011B − 23.132	0.389H + 0.049B − 14.128	0.402H − 0.025B − 9.469	0.336H + 0.028B − 3.552
	Leg length	0.675H + 0.006B − 36.491	0.62H − 0.094B − 20.473	0.65H − 0.144B − 20.411	0.612H − 0.081B − 20.059

(*continued*)

Table 3. (*continued*)

Control part/Body Type		Body Type1 H-shaped figure	Body Type2 Pear-shaped figure	Body Type3 Standard V-shaped figure	Body Type4 Hourglass-shaped figure
Girth	Bust girth	B (Bust girth)			
	Neck circumference	$-0.04H + 0.212B + 19.551$	$-0.035H + 0.215B + 18.382$	$0.037H + 0.238B + 4.71$	$0.023H + 0.144B + 14.199$
	Waistline	$0.074H + 0.866B - 13.742$	$-0.034H + 0.938B - 4.835$	$-0.027H + 0.875B - 2.918$	$-0.008H + 0.654B + 8.845$
	Hipline	$0.12H + 0.671B + 12.895$	$0.057H + 0.856B + 13.057$	$-0.023H + 0.763B + 27.828$	$0.128H + 0.469B + 28.545$
	Leg circumference	$0.265H + 0.508B - 35.205$	$0.023H + 0.657B - 5.355$	$0.008H + 0.51B + 5.626$	$-0.001H + 0.569B + 2.605$
Breadth	Neck breadth	$0.000009H + 0.077B + 3.981$	$0.015H + 0.032B + 5.087$	$0.008H + 0.061B + 3.838$	$0.007H + 0.025B + 6.932$
	Shoulder breadth	$-0.006H + 0.103B + 29.978$	$0.044H + 0.231B + 11.731$	$0.063H + 0.211B + 9.88$	$0.079H + 0.245B + 4.044$
	Chest breadth	$0.042H + 0.248B - 0.329$	$-0.075H + 0.142B + 26.689$	$-0.019H + 0.25B + 8.937$	$-0.007H + 0.28B + 3.938$
	Waist breadth	$0.071H + 0.285B - 9.407$	$0.014H + 0.305B - 2.775$	$-0.044H + 0.261B + 9.03$	$0.011H + 0.207B + 3.712$
	Hip breadth	$0.093H + 0.271B - 5.679$	$0.006H + 0.234B + 14.025$	$0.004H + 0.206B + 14.472$	$0.109H + 0.113B + 5.271$
	Thigh breadth	$0.023H + 0.132B + 1.081$	$-0.05H + 0.172B + 10.141$	$0.001H + 0.145B + 3.307$	$-0.02H + 0.137B + 7.56$
	Knee breadth	$0.013H + 0.083B + 2.056$	$-0.019H + 0.076B + 7.999$	$0.011H + 0.135B + 1.419$	$-0.005H + 0.045B + 8.002$
	Calf breadth	$0.005H + 0.074B + 3.445$	$-0.018H + 0.124B + 3.436$	$-0.012H + 0.111B + 3.127$	$0.004H + 0.089B + 2.233$
Depth	Neck depth	$-0.017H + 0.148B + 0.02$	$0.007H + 0.09B + 0.801$	$-0.004H + 0.078B + 3.738$	$0.021H + 0.044B + 2.392$
	Chest depth	$0.003H + 0.344B - 7.054$	$0.018H + 0.264B - 3.456$	$-0.007H + 0.283B - 0.507$	$-0.004H + 0.264B + 0.203$
	Waist depth	$-0.025H + 0.229B + 3.315$	$-0.002H + 0.272B - 4.409$	$-0.04H + 0.304B - 0.935$	$-0.014H + 0.208B + 1.076$
	Hip depth	$0.032H + 0.223B - 1.788$	$0.006H + 0.243B + 1.11$	$-0.02H + 0.276B + 1.355$	$-0.012H + 0.195B + 6.353$
	Thigh depth	$0.06H + 0.135B - 5.299$	$-0.002H + 0.192B + 0.501$	$-0.01H + 0.165B + 3.069$	$0.004H + 0.182B - 0.359$
	Knee depth	$0.041H + 0.062B - 0.287$	$0.003H + 0.071B + 5.365$	$0.017H + 0.103B - 0.166$	$0.035H + 0.1B - 2.623$
	Calf depth	$0.014H + 0.051B + 4.029$	$0.007H + 0.102B + 1.416$	$0.007H + 0.106B + 0.737$	$0.014H + 0.059B + 3.403$

The grading counts of the control part is still a binary linear function of the grading counts of the basic part, the formula is as follows:

$$
\begin{aligned}
\text{grading counts of control parts} &= b_0(\text{constant term}) + b_1 \times \text{grading counts of basic part 1} \\
&+ b_2 \times \text{grading counts of basic part 2}
\end{aligned}
\tag{2}
$$

Height and bust are chosen as basic parts 1 and basic parts 2 respectively, according to the regression equation in Table 3, the grading counts (grading difference) of other key control parts from various shapes can be calculated by importing the grading counts (grading difference) of the basic parts. Based on the binary linear regression equation, a body shape classification module was built in the system (Fig. 4). In this module, users can input two basic parts of the body (height and bust), and the system will push out 28 data on the body in relation to the size of the clothing design, the body shape type, the size table (Table 4), and provide a 2D body prototype plane template closest to the height and bust. The plan template of prototype can be printed or downloaded to assist in the drawing of clothing and wearable products that conform to the body shape characteristics, enhancing design efficiency.

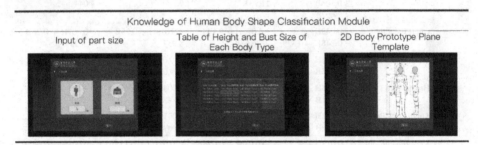

Fig. 4. Key interface for size selection knowledge of the body classification module

Table 4. Height and bust size of female college students in Hunan Province

Body Type1 H-shaped figure	Body Type2 Pear-shaped figure	Body Type3 Standard V-shaped figure	Body Type4 Hourglass-shaped figure
154/77Body Type1	157/75Body Type2	156/79Body Type3	157/77Body Type4
159/81Body Type1	162/79Body Type2	161/83Body Type3	162/81Body Type4
164/85Body Type1	167/83Body Type2	166/87Body Type3	167/85Body Type4
169/89Body Type1	172/87Body Type2	171/91Body Type3	172/89Body Type4
174/93Body Type1	177/91Body Type2	176/96Body Type3	177/93Body Type4

The second part of the module explores the designer's pattern making skills, which are a structural knowledge in clothing design. In this module, researcher set up two different push modes of knowledge based on the cognitive model and the clothing design process. In mode one, 15 sets of common clothing and skirts are placed in the system. Designers can roam in the clothing studio and click on the corresponding skirts. The system provides the pattern and structural drawing of the skirt for the designer to learn about knowledge of pattern making. In Mode 2, the designer will obtain the corresponding one-step skirt structure drawing based on the user's waist and hip size data entered in the previous module and appropriate size was also took into consideration, as shown in the Fig. 5.

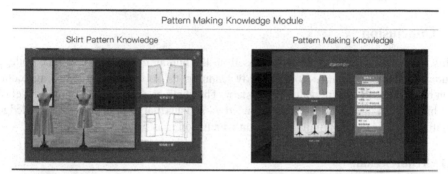

Fig. 5. Key interface for pattern making skills knowledge of body classification module

3.3 Clothing Fit Evaluation Module

It is the application module of 3D body shape knowledge. This module focuses on the visual effect of the fit. The user's psychological expectations, as well as the rational evaluation of the structure and size of the clothing after trying on. Knowledges in this part is interrelated and influences each other, and in the design of system, we have placed the knowledge in a holistic interface, as shown in the Fig. 6. On the right side of each interface is the visual effect of the model after trying on the skirt, which can be rotated 360 degrees in the system to observe the virtual dressing effect of the skirt designed after pattern making. Comparing the virtual dressing effect of the skirt after two plate-making on the left and right sides of Fig. 6, we can see that there are design issues that skirt is too tight or too loose in the fitting evaluation. Designer will observe the virtual dressing effect of the design. According to the design evaluation given by the system, designer can adjust the amount of relaxation for unfit parts such as waist and hips, and until the design is reasonable and aesthetically pleasing.

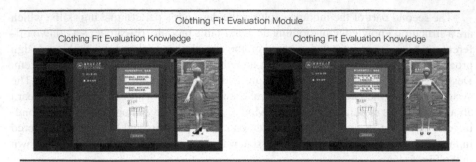

Fig. 6. Key interfaces for knowledge of clothing fit evaluation module

4 Conclusion

This paper created skirt fit software based on the human body data of female college students in Hunan Province from 3D body scanning, for solving the issue of fragmentation of clothing fit and fit evaluation system. The study constructs a mapping model of clothing fit and human body shape knowledge, and auxiliary application of knowledge digitization is realized initially. The main conclusion is as follows:

4.1 Truth-Seeking

Truth-seeking is to explore the body shape characteristics of female college students in Hunan Province. The study corresponded to the classification in Size System and Designation for Costume, and found the shape of sample was concentrated in type Y and type A, accounting for 41.4% and 35.5%. The presence of type C shapes was few, accounting for only 0.5%. This finding confirms that the majority of female college students in Hunan Province have standard body shape, with thinness shapes and fewer fat shapes. The study used three main shape characteristic indicators: chest-waist difference, hip-waist difference and body-to-waist ratio, and concluded that the main body types of female college students in Hunan Province were H-shaped figure, pear-shaped figure, standard V-shaped figure and skinny hourglass-shaped figure. Study finally constructed a binary regression equation for each control parts of each body shapes. The method is reproducible and suitable for further research on human body shape types in different age ranges and innovative applications of computer-aided design.

4.2 Usability

Usability is to achieve the sharing of large sample body size data and the reuse of body size knowledge. Unity was used to develop auxiliary 3D body data classification software. a human body shape ontology knowledge system and auxiliary system was built for clothing design according to the human 3D body shape knowledge module, body shape classification module and clothing fit evaluation module. The software can assist designers to recognize the link of body shape ontology knowledge and clothing fit knowledge. By identifying the body shape characteristics of different human body shapes, the fitness and adaptability of clothing design are improved.

4.3 Shortcomings of the Study

The study focuses on the software design of skirt fit according to the ontological knowledge of human body shape. It emphasizes the designer's learning and overall knowledge of the ontological knowledge of human body shape. There is still a lack of refinement in truth-seeking and usability.

1. From perspective of truth-seeking, the study only considers a single group of university students in Hunan Province. The future research should expand the occupational, age and geographical range of the surveyed subjects to serve more needs in design activities.
2. From perspective of usability, system in this study is still at the stage of prototype design and there are some aspects which can be improved in terms of usability and experience. Less consideration has been given to the innovative design of the clothing design.

Acknowledgments. This paper is a part of MOE (Ministry of Education in China) Project of Humanities and Social Sciences entitled Research on Scenario Service Design of Personal Data in Mobile Internet (17YJCZH275) and one of the phases fruits of project of Hunan Provincial Department of Education, which title is Research and Application of Aging Design of Intelligent Wearable Clothing Based on 3D Human Body Data Acquisition (20K077).

References

1. Alexander, M., Connell, L.J., Presley, A.B.: Clothing fit preferences of young female adult consumers. Int. J. Cloth. Sci. Technol. **17**(1), 52–64 (2005). https://doi.org/10.1108/095562 20510577961
2. Standardization Administration of the People's Republic of China: Standard sizing systems for garments-Women. General Administration of Quality Supervision. GB/T, Inspection and Quarantine of the People's Republic of China 1335.2–2008(2008)
3. Verwulgen, S., Lacko, D., Vleugels, J., Vaes, K., Danckaers, F., Bruyne, D.G., Huysmans, T.: A new data structure and workflow for using 3D anthropometry in the design of wearable products. Int. J. Ind. Ergon. **64**, 108–117 (2018). https://doi.org/10.1016/j.ergon.2018.01.002
4. Chin-Man, C.: Fit evaluation within the made-to-measure process. Int. J. Cloth. Sci. Technol. **19**(2), 131–144 (2007). https://doi.org/10.1108/09556220710725720
5. Renke, H., Wenxiu, Y., Haining, W.: 3D anthropometry of Chinese head. Packag. Eng. **40**(8), 103–110 (2019). https://doi.org/10.19554/j.cnki.1001-3563.2019.08.018
6. Fang, G., Cungen, C.: Ontology research and existing problems in knowledge engineering. Comput. Sci. **31**(10), 1–14 (2004)
7. Woojin, P., Sungjoon, P.: Body shape analyses of large persons in South Korea. Ergonomics **56**(4), 692–706 (2013)
8. Han, M., Mo, L.: Prototype and exemplar view in category research. Psychol. Explor. **2**, 12–16 (2000)
9. Zhongjuan, D., Jinsong, D.: Review of female somatotype research. Melliand China **12**, 57–61 (2016)
10. Haixian, W., Xiaomei, S.: A summary of research on classification methods of human body types. Modern Silk Sci. Technol. **34**(3), 37–40 (2019)

Improvement of Chair in Ladder Classroom Based on Human Data and Behavior Investigation of College Students

Wen-qiang Wang(✉), Jie Zhang(✉), and Yu-chao Cai(✉)

East China University of Science and Technology, Shanghai, Xuhui 200237,
People's Republic of China
616332476@qq.com, 339550316@qq.com, caiyuchao_007@163.com

Abstract. Classroom seats are very important for college students. Students have to sit on the seats for a long time in class. When designing classroom seats, it is very important to consider the matching degree between the ergonomic data of the seats and the human body of college students and the relationship between students' behavior.

Taking East China University of science and technology as an example, this paper collects the comfort evaluation of folding seats in the ladder classroom of students from the school of art design and media through interview and questionnaire, and finally determines the factors that have the highest impact on students' human comfort in the size of classroom seats, which are seat height, seat depth and seat surface angle.

The seat data related to the three influencing factors were measured by using the range finder and standard tape, and then 23 students from the school of art and design of East China University of technology were selected as samples to measure their body data related to the folding seat. Then the measured student body data were brought into the matching standard equation for verification, and the seat height except the seat surface angle was proved. The data of seat depth is reasonable. Therefore, the second questionnaire survey was conducted to study the seat angle, which proved that students felt uncomfortable because the seat angle did not match the relationship between College Students' behavior in class, and put forward some suggestions on the design of classroom folding seats.

Keywords: Ladder classroom seat · Matching standard equation · Student behavior

1 Introduction

1.1 Research Background

College students spend a large part of their daily life in school (5–8 h a day). When they are in school, most of their activities (such as reading and writing) are carried out in school seats. Because they sit in their seats for a long time, students are particularly

© The Author(s), under exclusive license to Springer Nature Switzerland AG 2022
V. G. Duffy (Ed.): HCII 2022, LNCS 13319, pp. 172–184, 2022.
https://doi.org/10.1007/978-3-031-05890-5_14

vulnerable to the negative impact of problematic classroom seats. These problematic seats have various ergonomic problems, which may increase the risk of musculoskeletal diseases. Good classroom seat design can match with students' human body structure, make students feel comfortable physically and mentally, and reduce the occurrence of musculoskeletal diseases. At the same time, the design of classroom seats should consider students' behavior habits. There are two main behaviors of college students sitting in classroom seats: one is listening with their upper body upright, and the other is sitting at the desk and taking notes. This requires that the size of classroom seats should also be considered to match students' behavior, so as to reduce fatigue and improve learning efficiency. If there are ergonomic problems in classroom seats, which can not correctly match the body size and behavior of college students, sedentary students will lead to musculoskeletal pain and discomfort, damage eyes, affect classroom efficiency, and even suffer from musculoskeletal diseases. This paper studies and discusses this background.

1.2 Research Purposes and Significance

At present, many university classroom seats are foldable. The seat height, seat width and seat depth of this kind of seats are fixed values. In order to verify whether the size of classroom seats conforms to the human body data of college students and explore the relationship between seat design and college students' behavior in class, a study was carried out.

Firstly, a questionnaire survey was conducted on the possible problems of seats, the factors that have the strongest impact on College Students' human comfort were extracted, and the classroom seat data related to the impact factors were accurately measured. Then, according to the proportion of male and female students in East China University of science and technology, 23 samples were selected, including 13 boys and 10 girls, The human body data related to the influencing factors are measured by using the standard measurement tools. According to the relevant body data of the subjects, the seat data is checked whether it conforms to the human body of college students by matching the standard equation. Finally, the design suggestions to solve the problem are put forward according to the result analysis.

1.3 Literature Review

In the past decades, more and more scholars began to pay attention to the impact of classroom seats on students' human body, and measured classroom furniture and human body data to compare whether they match.

Samuel A. Oyewole et al. Proposed that children spend more than 30% of their time in school. Most classroom activities require long periods of sitting, and every effort should be made to ensure that young children do not experience back pain and other musculoskeletal disorders from sitting on improperly designed classroom furniture for long periods of time. The author puts forward methods and guidelines for designing ergonomic oriented classroom furniture for first grade students in primary school. Based on meeting the needs of at least 90% of the first grader population in the United States, several suitable classroom furniture data are proposed [1].

Parcels et al. (1999) measured the mismatch between school furniture and students by measuring the human body data of American children. They suggest that less than 20% of students can find an acceptable combination of tables and chairs. Goufali and boudolos (2006) focused on the suitability of school furniture for anthropometry of Greek children, using a combined equation modified according to the principles proposed in the literature [2].

Castellucci et al. Proposed that children spend about five hours sitting in their seats in work class every day. Considering this and the possible shortcomings of school furniture, the author compared the furniture sizes of three different schools with the human characteristics of Chilean students in Valparaiso to assess the potential mismatch between them. 195 volunteer students (94 males and 101 females) from three different schools were selected as samples, ranging in age from 12.5 to 14.5. Six anthropometric indexes (height, popliteal height, hip popliteal length, sitting elbow height, hip width, thigh thickness and subscapular height) and eight sizes of school furniture were collected. The matching standard equation of classroom furniture evaluation is defined. After considering the size of existing classroom furniture in each matching standard equation, the anthropometric characteristics of the considered population are compared to determine the mismatch between the two [3].

The results showed that among the three schools, the seat height of two schools was suitable for the popliteal height of students, and the seat height of three schools was suitable for the popliteal height of students, 14% in two schools and 28% in three schools. The height from the seat to the desk is too high.

99% of the students in one school do not match 100% of the students in another school. Therefore, it is concluded that in almost all cases analyzed, the furniture of the classroom is insufficient. The high mismatch between furniture and student anthropometry may be related to the fact that the acquisition and selection of furniture are not based on any ergonomic problems or relevant standards [4].

Castellucci et al. Proposed that the mismatch between students and school furniture is likely to cause some negative effects [4], such as uncomfortable posture and pain, which may eventually affect the learning process. The main purpose is to review the literature on the standard equations that define the mismatch between students and school furniture, apply these equations to specific samples, and put forward the methods to evaluate the appropriate school furniture according to the results. 2261 volunteers from 14 schools were selected as samples, and 21 equations were determined to test 6 furniture sizes.

Iman dianat et al. Conducted a study to prove that the body size of Iranian high school students did not match the existing classroom furniture, and assessed the potential mismatch between the classroom furniture size and anthropometric characteristics of 978 Iranian high school students (498 girls and 480 boys). The sample students were aged between 15 and 18 years. Nine anthropometric measurements (height, sitting height, sitting shoulder height, popliteal height, hip width, elbow seat height, hip popliteal length, measuring hip knee length and thigh gap) and five dimensions of existing classroom furniture were measured, and then compared using the matching standard equation to determine any potential mismatch between them [1].

The results show that the students' body size does not match the existing classroom furniture, among which the seat height (60.9%), seat width (54.7%) and desktop height (51.7%) are the furniture sizes with a high degree of mismatch. The degree of mismatch between high school grades and gender varies, indicating their special requirements and possible problems. The size of classroom furniture more suitable for students is put forward. These additional information about student anthropometry can be used by the local furniture industry as a starting point for school children to design more suitable furniture, or by schools to help choose furniture [5].

Yanto et al. Conducted a study to evaluate the possible mismatch between the Indonesian national standard school furniture size and the latest anthropometric size of Indonesian primary school children [6]. The results show that in the Indonesian national standard issued by the Indonesian National Bureau of standardization in 1989, the anthropometry of students does not match the size of school furniture, and the percentage of mismatch shows that the current standard size is not suitable for most primary school students. Based on these findings, the current Indonesian national standard for seat size of primary school students (SNI 12-1015-1989) and the national standard for desk size (SNI 12-1016-1989) issued by the Indonesian National Bureau of standardization need to be updated. Four different sizes of school furniture are recommended to cover anthropometric related changes in grades 1 to 6.

This paper studies the possible mismatch between classroom folding seats and college students' body data, focuses on the relationship between seat angle and college students' behavior, proves the existence of the problem through the combination of qualitative and quantitative methods, and puts forward design suggestions for the problem [7].

2 Research Methods

2.1 Investigation on the Comfort of Folding Seats in the Classroom

In view of the problems existing in classroom folding seats, the questionnaire is designed from the two aspects of user background and seat comfort. Finally, the evaluation questionnaire of classroom folding seat comfort is collected from 69 students, 39 boys and 30 girls (the proportion of men and women is calculated according to the overall proportion of the school) from four departments of art design and media School of East China University of science and technology (Figs. 1 and 2).

2.2 Questionnaire Data Analysis

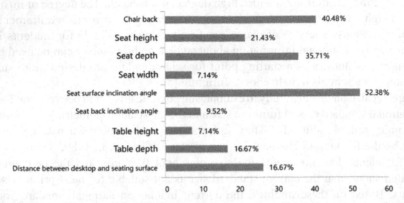

Fig. 1. The folding seats and desks in the classroom make college students uncomfortable

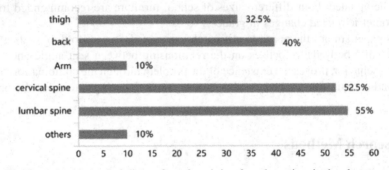

Fig. 2. Parts of physical discomfort after sitting for a long time in the classroom

The survey results show that the uncomfortable seat parts of college students include seat back, seat depth and seat surface inclination. Among them, the angle of classroom folding seat is the most prominent, while the most uncomfortable parts are cervical spine and lumbar spine, 52.5% and 55% respectively, and the back and thigh also account for a large proportion, 40% and 32.5% respectively.

2.3 User Interview

According to the conclusion of the first questionnaire. Ten students were selected from the students who had previously sent out the questionnaire to interview the seat back, seat depth, seat height and seat surface inclination that had the highest impact on comfort. The interview concluded that the seat back is uncomfortable because the backrest material is too hard, and the thigh is uncomfortable because the legs feel uncomfortable due to the pressure of body weight. The discomfort of cervical spine and lumbar spine is caused by looking up at the blackboard or bending down to take notes. The seat depth and height have not been effectively interviewed, which will be verified by experiments later.

The problem with the seat angle with the highest proportion of discomfort is that when leaning against the back of the seat, the seat surface close to the popliteal fossa will compress the thighs, which will lead to discomfort over time. When bend on the desk, the ass will sit at the front of the seat surface, and the seat angle close to the popliteal fossa will tilt downward, so the body will slide downward, It is necessary to exert slight force on the leg muscles to overcome the force of the body sliding from the seat surface, so it will feel tired and affect the learning efficiency. Therefore, the influence of materials on the human body is excluded. Only the aspects that may be related to ergonomic data are discussed, and the seat depth, seat height and seat angle are selected as the research directions. Experiments are carried out on this.

3 Experimental Method

3.1 Define Relevant Data

Extract the elements of human body data related to seat depth and height, as shown in Table 1.

Table 1. Human body data elements related to seat depth and seat height

Seat data to be tested	Human data related to the experiment
Seat height	Popliteal height
Seating depth	Hip popliteal height

3.2 Dimension Measurement of Classroom Furniture

Measure the folding seats in the classroom according to the required data. The measuring tools are laser rangefinder and standard tape. Samples are randomly taken during measurement. In order to avoid seat deformation caused by mismeasurement and external damage, at least 20 seats and desks are measured and averaged. The final measured data is Table 2.

Table 2. Relevant folding seat dimensions

Seating depth	39.3 cm
Seat height	43.5 cm
Seat inclination angle	4°

According to the latest ratio of male to female students in East China University of science and technology, random sample screening was carried out. Finally, 23 students were selected, including 13 boys and 10 girls. They were measured by laser rangefinder and standard tape measure. During the measurement, the students wore light clothes and flat soled shoes to remove the interference of clothing and sole thickness on the data. The measured data are shown in Table 3.

Table 3. Maximum, minimum and average values of popliteal height and hip popliteal height of boys and girls

	Maximum popliteal height	Minimum popliteal height	Average popliteal height	Maximum hip popliteal height	Minimum hip and popliteal height	Average hip popliteal height
Girl student	44.3 cm	42.4 cm	43.7 cm	46.3 cm	43.5 cm	45.18 cm
Schoolboy	47 cm	44.7 cm	45.9 cm	49.5 cm	46.5 cm	47.34 cm

3.3 Application of Matching Standard Equation

Seat height: most researchers have concluded that the popliteal height (PH) should be higher than the seat height (SH) (Parcels et al., 1999; mukdad and Ansari, 2009; Dianat et al., 2013); Otherwise, most students will not be able to rest their feet properly on the floor, increasing tissue pressure on the posterior surface of the knee (Castellucci et al., 2015).

The seat height shall be lower than the popliteal height, so that the lower limbs form an angle of 5–30° relative to the vertical axis, and the angle of the lower legs and thighs is between 95° and 120°. The literature shows that in order to ensure that the angle of the lower legs relative to the vertical axis does not exceed 30° and that the thighs have sufficient support so that students can sit comfortably, the seat height must be greater than

$$[(Ph + 2) \times \cos(30°)] \tag{1}$$

In order to ensure proper contact between students' feet and the floor and avoid increasing the tissue pressure in the lower thigh area, the seat height must be less than

$$[(Ph + 2) \times \cos(5°)] \tag{2}$$

Therefore, the matching standard equation is obtained:

$$(Ph + SC) \cos 30° \leq SH \leq (Ph + SC) \cos 5° \tag{3}$$

(where SC is the sole correction, but SC can be ignored because it is measured with shoes on).

The measured human body value is substituted into the matching equation. Compared with the seat height of the folding seat in the classroom, it is found that the value is matched.

Seat depth: hip popliteal length (length from hip to popliteal fossa) is anthropometric data used to specify the size of seat depth (SD) (Castellucci et al., 2015). Goufali and boudolos (2006) pointed out that SD is at least 5 cm shorter than hip popliteal length (PBL). Other researchers explained that the depth of the seat should be designed to the 5th percentile of the PBL distribution so that the seat back can support the lumbar spine without compressing the popliteal surface.

Parcels et al. (1999) defined that when SD is greater than 95% of the hip popliteal length or less than 80% of the hip popliteal length, it does not match the human body of college students. Therefore, the matching standard equation is:

$$0.80 \text{ PBL} \leq SD \leq 0.95 \text{ PBL} \tag{4}$$

The measured human body value is substituted into the matching equation, and the seat depth of the classroom folding seat is found to be matched. Therefore, it is concluded that the ergonomic data of the height and depth of classroom folding seats are reasonable, and the causes of College Students' physical discomfort may be related to the seat material, seat surface angle, or seat surface shape.

Seat angle: the data are obtained through experiments and the standard equation proves that the data of seat height and seat depth are within a reasonable range. However, the standard equation of seat angle has not been proposed in the literature. Therefore, the research goal is to focus on the seat angle.

It is mentioned in the literature that when students are in class and self-study, their bodies keep leaning forward reading and writing posture for a long time. If the front edge of the seat surface is convex, great body pressure will be generated at the thigh close to the popliteal fossa, and their abdomen will also be badly squeezed. In the forward leaning posture, when the angle between the thigh and the upper body is greater than or equal to a right angle, the body pressure distribution on the seat surface will be more reasonable. According to the needs of students in the forward leaning posture and the national standard, the seat surface inclination of the folding seat is usually 3–6°.

4 Relationship Between Seat Tilt Angle and Students' Behavior

4.1 Use Interviews to Make Assumptions

According to the previous measurement, the average angle of the folding seat in the classroom is 4°, which meets this standard, but the students still feel uncomfortable. Through the interview, it is learned that students not only need to rest on the back of the seat, but also need a lot of time to bend on the desk to take notes and write. Because of the 4° inclination of the seat surface, the thigh and popliteal fossa will be compressed by the seat when writing on the desk. After a long time, you will feel tired and cause musculoskeletal damage. Therefore, it is assumed that the reason for college students' discomfort is the mismatch between the seat angle and students' behavior. If it can not be proved that students lean on the back of the chair for much longer than the time of bend on the desk, the 4° inclination of the folding seat in the ladder classroom is unreasonable.

4.2 The Second Questionnaire Survey

In order to explore the relationship between College Students' behavior and the angle of classroom folding seat, the second round of questionnaire design and investigation were carried out for college students' behavior in class. The results are shown in Figs. 3, 4, 5, 6.

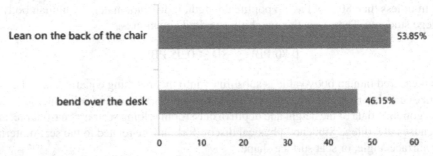

Fig. 3. Time ratio between leaning on the back of the chair and bend over the

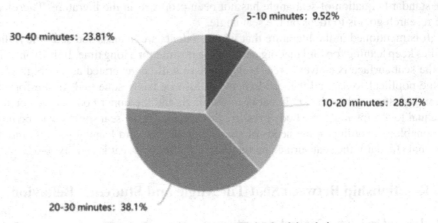

Fig. 4. Time of leaning on the back of the chair

According to the data, the number of college students leaning on the back of the chair is similar to that of sitting at the desk in class, and the time of leaning on the back of the chair and bend over the desk is the most in 20–30 min, accounting for about half of the time of each class. Therefore, the two situations of college students leaning on the back of the chair and bend over the desk in class exist and have similar rates, and the frequency of bend over the desk is mostly 5–6 times or more, There are few students who never bend over the desk. Therefore, it is concluded that the inclination of the seat surface of the classroom at 4° only meets the needs of students to lean on the back of the chair, but can not meet the needs of college students to bend over the desk.

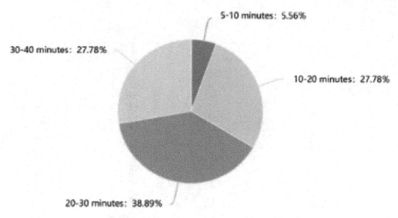

Fig. 5. The time of bend over the desk

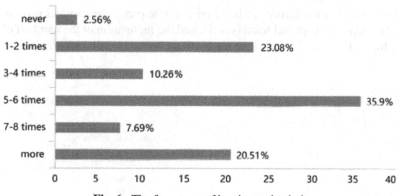

Fig. 6. The frequency of bend over the desk

5 Design Suggestions

In view of the mismatch between the surface inclination of classroom folding seat and students' behavior, this paper puts forward some suggestions for improvement.

(1) The inclination angle of the rear seat surface of the seat can be adjusted. When the students lean forward, the seat angle can be automatically adjusted by the students' own gravity to meet the forward leaning needs of students. When students rest on the back of the chair, the seat angle will be automatically adjusted to meet the needs of students' rest (Figs. 7, 8 and 9).

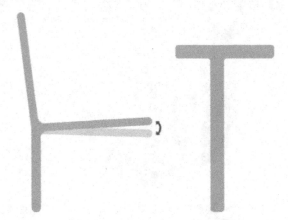

Fig. 7. Seat surface of the seat can be adjusted

(2) The seat surface can be divided into front and rear parts. The inclination of the front half close to the popliteal fossa is − 4°, and the inclination of the rear half close to the hip is 4°, which can meet the needs of backrest rest and desk writing.

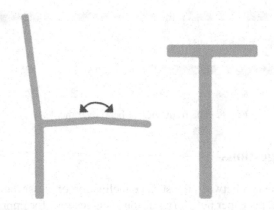

Fig. 8. The seat surface is divided into front and rear parts

(3) The inclination angle of the desktop can be adjusted to 3–5° or more to meet the inclination angle of the seat surface (but the inclination angle should not be too large to cause the computer and notebook to slide and cannot be placed on the desktop), so that students will not have to bend down to write, which is more comfortable.

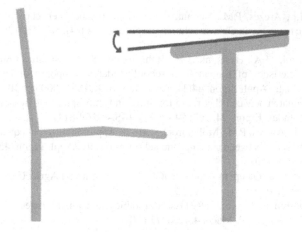

Fig. 9. Desktop adjustable angle

6 Conclusion

(1) The finding of this study is that the matching degree between classroom folding seats and college students' human body is generally acceptable, but there are still problems. This paper aims at the problems of the inclination angle of the seat surface, which may lead to students' inability to rest properly and skeletal muscle discomfort. According to the data obtained, it can be concluded that there are still problems to be solved in classroom folding seats. The irrationality of classroom furniture design should be avoided by considering the relationship between ergonomics and students' behavior.

(2) In addition to the seat angle, the size of folding seats in other classrooms is within a reasonable range, which is suitable for students. In order to solve the problem of folding seat angle, the design thinking is carried out in combination with the literature, hoping to meet the different needs of college students or graduate students when using classroom furniture. When using appropriate classroom furniture, students will study in a comfortable environment, and their physical and mental health will be adversely affected.

(3) There are also deficiencies in this paper. Due to the limitation of the number of samples, the results may be biased. In the future, the sample size can be expanded to obtain more accurate data, because the horizontal distance between the seat and the desk is also the reason that affects the comfort of classroom seats. This paper ignores this aspect because it focuses on the influence of research angle, and will make up for it in the future.

References

1. Oyewole, S.A., Haight, J.M., Freivalds, A.: The ergonomic design of classroom furniture/computer work station for first graders in the elementary school. Int. J. Ind. Ergon. **40**(4), 437–447 (2010). ISSN 0169-8141

2. Castellucci, H.I., Arezes, P.M., Viviani, C.A.: Mismatch between classroom furniture and anthropometric measures in Chilean schools. Appl. Ergon. **41**(4), 563–568 (2010). ISSN 0003-6870
3. Dianat, I., Karimi, M.A., Hashemi, A.A., Bahrampour, S.: Classroom furniture and anthropometric characteristics of Iranian high school students: Proposed dimensions based on anthropometric data. Appl. Ergon. **44**(1), 101–108 (2013). ISSN 0003-6870
4. Kahya, E.: Mismatch between classroom furniture and anthropometric measures of university students. Int. J. Indus. Ergon. **74**, 102864 (2019). ISSN 0169-8141
5. Castellucci, H.I., Arezes, P.M., Molenbroek, J.F.M.: Applying different equations to evaluate the level of mismatch between students and school furniture. Appl. Ergon. **45**(4), 1123–1132 (2014). ISSN 0003-6870
6. Deyu, L.: Ergonomic concept in student seat design. J. Southwest Agric. Univ. (Soc. Sci. Edn.) **10**(01), 185–186 (2012)
7. Zhang, Q.: Design and layout of classroom tables and chairs based on human factors engineering. Times Agricul. Mach. **43**(08), 77 (2016)

Development and Verification of Measurement Tools for Human Dynamic Development

Yulin Zhao(✉) ⓘ, Dingbang Luh, and Yue Sun

Guangdong University of Technology, Guangzhou 510090, China
512080653@qq.com

Abstract. Adolescence is a critical period for female breast development, and young girls' breasts show dynamic changes at different stages of growth and development. Nearly half a century of research shows that 80–85% of girls do not know how to choose the right underwear. The reason for this is mainly caused by the uncritical measurement base and technical methods.

In this study, we propose a new sternal measurement standard in accordance with anthropometry and develop a sternal measurement tool with a stable standard, which can be self-operated and repeatedly measured to improve the accuracy of sternal measurement while accumulating and analyzing sternal measurement data. In this paper, the design process of the measurement tool is first demonstrated, and then the accuracy and precision of the new measurement tool are verified, and the subjective feelings of the users in using the tool are evaluated. The results show that the new measurement tool has good accuracy and precision, and that it is stable, objectivity, comfortable, learnability, and popularity for the users to operate.

Keywords: Chest measurement · Measurement technology · Data accumulation · Ergonomics · Developmental stage

1 Introduction

Adolescence is a critical period for female breast development and appropriate bra products play a key role in their physical health for cardiorespiratory activity [1], mental health for peer interaction play a key role [2].

From the beginning of breast development to maturity, adolescent girls need five stages in ten years, and each stage will show dynamic changes with psychological and behavioral changes, with different needs for bras [3]. Nearly half a century of relevant literature points out that more than 85% of adolescent girls choose inappropriate underwear [4], and actual interviews and analysis of the current status of patents and products for adolescent girls' underwear reveal that the main reason for this is the uncritical measurement base (easily The main reason for the lack of rigorous measurement bases (easily displaced breast points, blurred breast boundaries) and technical methods (using simple upper and lower bust sizes, with little consideration of the dynamically developing breast size). As the human body is a dynamic body, the change of female breast is about 10%–20% every month, which requires regular measurement of the breast [5].

© The Author(s), under exclusive license to Springer Nature Switzerland AG 2022
V. G. Duffy (Ed.): HCII 2022, LNCS 13319, pp. 185–198, 2022.
https://doi.org/10.1007/978-3-031-05890-5_15

In order to obtain the correct body dimensions, the necessary measurement reference points are marked on the body before measurement to indicate the correct measurement location (site), and the measurement reference points are usually at the bones such as bone protrusions, joint ends, cut marks and sutures, which do not change shape even under physical pressure, especially for physiological changes [6]. If the location of the measurement point is not correct, the data of the sample is suspicious or even wrong, and if the measurement point is not stable, it is impossible to accumulate and compare the breast data under dynamic body changes. Depending on the measurement technique, there are currently two types of measurement reference points: contact and non-contact [7].

Contact measurement uses manual touch of skeletal points to identify the marker points, which can be measured in any posture of the body, and the results are highly accurate; contact measurement of the base point also has its drawbacks, such as time-consuming measurement (depending on the measurement sample), plus the skeletal endpoints occupy a considerable area, which is difficult to find from the "surface". "In addition to being covered by the body surface, it takes a long period of training and practice to be able to clearly identify the location of the marker points. The most serious problem in non-contact anthropometry is the datum [8]. Many landmarks on bones used in traditional methods cannot be accurately determined from surface shapes; therefore, they must be determined by palpation by the anthropometrist. Researchers have developed algorithms to automatically calculate the location of landmarks or to automatically detect and calculate the 3D coordinates of marker stickers affixed to landmarks determined by the anthropometrist, but these methods are subject to significant errors, such as the darker areas of the body surface that are affected by their measurement principles In addition to the fact that the sensor sometimes does not capture the corresponding data, for example, it is very difficult to determine the extraction of anterior abdominal protrusion points, greater trochanteric points, cervical points [9], and has the disadvantage of high computational overhead and few acquired body dimensions.

Therefore contact measurements are more accurate than non-contact measurements to obtain a measurement base. However, according to the anatomical description of the human body, the breast is the only organ on the female body without skeletal support, and the interior is mainly composed of glandular breast lobules and fatty tissue [10]. Because of the special characteristics of breast tissue, the reference point for existing breast measurement techniques is extracted from the breast point or the surface features of the body rather than the skeletal points of the body.

The traditional and now mostly used technique of breast size measurement involves the use of a physical method represented by a tape measure to measure the circumference of the bust (around the nipple) and the lower bust (around the bottom of the chest) [11]. This method has limitations, including being prone to error (breast compression deformation) and psychological embarrassment for the subject (Asian women are shy about exposing their bodies, and this method has cultural limitations to its use), and relies heavily on the judgment of the measureer. When using the traditional measurement technique, the reference points for measurement are the breast point and lower bust, which in addition to low accuracy (the data based on only two parts of the bust and lower bust cannot reflect the complex picture of breast shape), the breast point and the lower end of the breast will shift with the growth of the breast and are not stable. These limitations can lead to inaccurate measurement of breast size and consequently, inappropriate bra recommendations, but it has not been completely replaced due to its simplicity and low cost [12].

The introduction of 3D anthropometric scanner measurement systems has revolutionized the way anthropometric data is collected, evaluated and updated [13]. This technology can provide very detailed and accurate anthropometric data to be stored and reused in the future [14]. However, the technology is not yet as readily available as a simple tape measure for chest-type measurements because the system generally has a complex basic structural design, is bulky and expensive, and thus, it is very time-consuming, requires expensive equipment and trained experts to acquire and analyze scans, frequent breast changes need to be measured periodically, and thus directly affects commercial applications and promotion to end-store use, and more importantly, the The precise location of the measurement reference and how to measure these marks can be subjective, resulting in low repeatability of the measurement operation and unstable measurement data [15–17].

In summary, this study proposes a new sternal measurement benchmark in accordance with anthropometry and develops a new sternal measurement tool that can be self-operated and repeatedly measured to improve the accuracy of sternal measurement and to accumulate and analyze sternal measurement data at the same time. In this paper, we first demonstrate the design process of the measurement tool, and then verify the accuracy and precision of the new measurement tool.

2   Design Process of Chest-Type Measurement Tool

2.1   Definition of New Measurement Reference

A reasonable, accurate, and ergonomic base point for measurement should be a human skeletal point with stability characteristics. The skeleton is composed of bone links that form the body's scaffold, which supports weight, protects internal organs, participates in movement, and acts as a lever [18]. The breast measurement sites required for bra production are the chest, shoulders and back and, according to human skeletal anatomy, involve the sternum, ribs and vertebrae in the trunk bone area and the upper limb girdle in the extremity bones of the acromioclavicular joint [19, 20].

The breast is a three-dimensional morphological organ of the hemisphere, one on the left and one on the right, and in addition to the length and width dimensions, the height dimension is included in the measurement, so the parameters of the three-dimensional morphology need to be measured. We chose the suprasternal point and the saber point as potential measurement reference points (see Fig. 1). The saber point is the origin of the plane right-angle coordinate system, with the left and right side as the x-axis and the upward connection to the suprasternal point as the y-axis, and the coordinate system can record the value and displacement changes of the left and right breast in the width and height dimensions. The saber point is the 0 point of the coordinate system, and its vertical mapping to the vertebrae behind forms the z axis, which eventually forms a stable coordinate system with the saber point as the common 0 point and positive intersection of the x, y and z axes.

2.2   Design of Chest Measurement Tools

Human body measurement technology is prone to measurement errors and lack of reliability. Unreliability can be divided into two parts: 1) inaccuracy refers to the measurement error variance caused by the variability within and between observers; And 2) unreliability, a function of physiological changes, such as biological factors, may affect the repeatability of measurement. Inaccuracies may result from inadequate or improper personnel training, difficulties in measuring certain anthropometric features (such as skin folds), and instrumental or technical errors. It is still a more concerned issue in anthropometry.

It has been shown that anthropometric measurements are very difficult even under controlled conditions and after extensive training of the observer, and this is compounded by the fact that measurements are influenced by the water content of human muscles, thermal expansion of the skin, body movements, and breathing patterns, making it even more difficult to obtain accurate anthropometric data, which, according to the study, is unique The study points out that anthropometric data is unique because it is almost impossible to measure the accuracy because there is no "true value" of the measurement with which it can be compared. In addition, breast measurements fail to account for cultural differences because Asian women are shy about exposing their bodies. Although several studies have been conducted to find the best structure of measurement tools, they have focused on the assistance of others rather than on the subjective comfort of self-measurement. Since the human body is dynamic and needs to be measured continuously, there is often inaccuracy and instead of providing them with accurate measurements, users should measure their own breast values to know the degree of change.

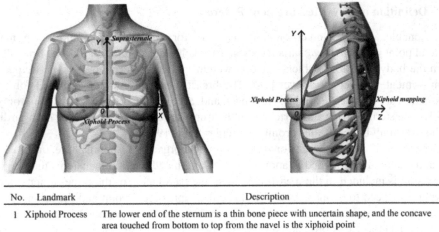

No.	Landmark	Description
1	Xiphoid Process	The lower end of the sternum is a thin bone piece with uncertain shape, and the concave area touched from bottom to top from the navel is the xiphoid point
2	Suprasternale	The deepest point in the hollow of the suprasternal notch lying at the middle of the anterior-superior border of the sternal manubrium
3	Xiphoid mapping	Vertical mapping of xiphoid point to spine

Fig. 1. The new measurement datum and coordinate system

Based on the new reference coordinate system, we developed a wearable self-service breast measurement tool (see Fig. 2), which includes a measuring tape (including two horizontal and two vertical measuring tapes) to measure the detailed dimensions of the breast, which can record the X and Y coordinate dimensions of the transverse breast diameter, vertical breast diameter and breast spacing of breast shape characteristics; and a height tape to record the height of the breast, which can measure the breast height and breast depth. The circumference ruler for measuring the body circumference size can measure the lower bust size.

In the measurement operation procedure, the measuring tool is front-opening type, first of all, the measuring tool is put on, the circumference ruler is close to the lower edge of the breast, and adjusted to its own comfortable state by the adjustment buckle on the side and rear of the tool, according to the human body size instructions, the range of human lower bust is 63–92 cm, also for the reference of the measurement tool lower bust adjustment; secondly, according to the new In order to ensure the level of X-axis in the measurement coordinate system and the vertical state of Z-axis, a level meter is placed at the connection of the ruler and the two horizontal rulers to adjust the balance of the ruler, and the ruler is pulled out to fit the skin to read the lower bust size; again, the height measuring device is installed and placed at the level of the breast point, and finally, by operating the height The height measuring device is installed again and placed at the level of the breast point, and finally the left and right breast dimensions are read by manipulating the height ruler.

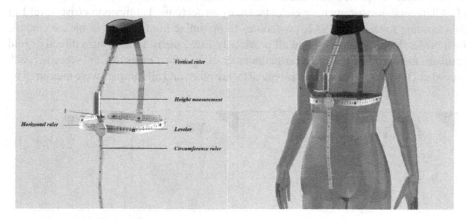

Fig. 2. Wearable self-service chest measurement tool

3   Methodology

3.1   Participants

Thirty healthy women (age 26.40 ± 3.92 years; height 162.60 ± 0.04 cm; weight 56.07 ± 8.36 kg) were recruited and screened according to the BMI of the participants in Guangzhou, China. Participants were classified into three body size groups according to their BMI: standard, obese and thin, and three BMI categories (under-weight: <18.5 kg/m^2, normal: 18.5–24.9 kg/m^2, overweight: 25–29.9 kg/m^2) based on the World Health Organization's international BMI classification (World Health Organization 2006). To determine BMI, each participant's height was measured using a Seca 214 portable rangefinder (Seca Corporation, Hanover, MD, USA), and weight was measured according to standard procedures (Stewart and Marfell-Jones 2011) using a Tanita body composition analyzer (model: TISC24OMA, Tanita, Ill. USA). Based on these data, BMI was calculated as weight (kg)/height2 (m). The protocol of the study was approved by the University Ethics Committee of the Guangdong University of Technology (RNN/100/18/KE). Written informed consent was obtained from all subjects.

3.2 Experimental Materials and Procedures

Breast measurements were performed at different times of the day and under random lighting conditions. Participants were required to be topless, and for comfort, the experiments were done in a laboratory with a room temperature of $(25 \pm 2)°C$, relative humidity of $(65 \pm 5)\%$, and wind speed less than 0.1 m/s. The measurement sites were selected to reflect the five dimensions of breast morphology, which are: breast transverse diameter, breast spacing, lower breast drape distance, breast height and lower breast circumference, representing the circumference factor and morphological factor of breast shape. In order to obtain reference data, measurements were taken for each subject in three steps: (1) All manual measurements were obtained by an accredited anthropometrist (level 1 or 2) according to standard ISAK procedures to minimize human error in measurements, by a professional who performed all previously listed measurement sites directly (gold standard method), measured linear parameters using a tape measure, and recorded each recorded The duration of the measurements were taken and all samples were measured by

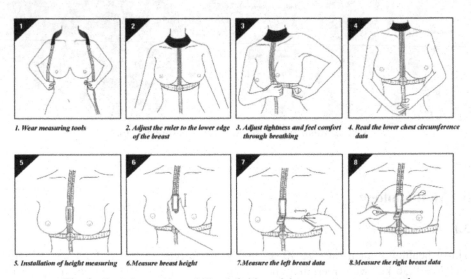

1. Wear measuring tools   2. Adjust the ruler to the lower edge   3. Adjust tightness and feel comfort   4. Read the lower chest circumference
                               of the breast   through breathing   data

5. Installation of height measuring   6.Measure breast height   7.Measure the left breast data   8.Measure the right breast data

Fig. 3. Experimental operability definition of the new measurement tool

one person (plastic surgeon); (2) participants self-measured using the new measurement tool; and (3) a questionnaire was completed to assess comfort of use and learnability of the new tool. In order to be able to measure objectively and accurately, the measurements were taken after practicing once with the new tool according to the operational definition (see Fig. 3).

3.3 Measurement Result

Accuracy is the degree of relationship between the true reference value of an established physical measurement and the corresponding numerical measurement. In all cases of manual measurements, accuracy depends on operator expertise and the average of multiple measurements performed by multiple operators, and the accuracy of the new chest-type measurement tool is assessed by comparing the measurements of the new measurement tool with manual measurements performed by a professional surveyor. Precision assessment was determined by performing three repeated measurements on the subject using the new measurement tool. The new measurement tool was tested for differences in measurement results due to postural differences, respiratory movements and skin compression factors. Subjective evaluation was done by assessing the stability, objectivity, comfort, learnability, and popularity of the new measurement tool by the semantic difference method among users.

3.4 Data Statistics

All statistical analyses were performed using SPSS 24.0 (SPSS for Windows, Chicago, IL, USA). Accuracy was performed as a t-test to compare the mean of all sites in the professional chest measurement with the self-breast measurement, and as an F-test to compare the standard deviation. Precision was determined for three chest measurements performed by the subject using the new measurement instrument, using the intraclass correlation coefficient (ICC) to determine the measurement accuracy (variability or relative reliability of measurements performed by the same observer) for each variable, i.e., the summary statistic describing unit similarity between groups and its 95% confidence interval (95% CI).Hopkins (2000) and Atkinson and Nevill (1998) strongly recommend providing more than one reliability measure. The most common interpretation of ICC values follows Cicchetti's guidelines: values in the range 0.00–0.39 are considered poorly correlated, 0.40–0.59-average correlation, 0.60–0.75-good correlation and 0.75–1.00-very good correlation. The acceptable level of measurement deviation in the thoracic region is less than 1 cm. therefore, such a range would be categorized as good accuracy. The subjective evaluation of the new measurement tool used the semantic difference method to establish 5 levels of semantic difference (Kuijt Evers et al., 2007) to quantitatively evaluate the chest volume measurement tool in five aspects: stable, objectivity, comfortable, learnability, and popularity. The following evaluation model was constructed to facilitate later data processing.

$$F = \Sigma sign(Xi - X), \quad i \in (1, 2, 3...30) \tag{1}$$

where X takes the middle value of the scoring interval 0, Xi indicates the score scored by each user for the same evaluation index, sign is the directional function, and the value interval of F can be calculated as $[-1, 1]$. If $F > 0$, it means that the user is satisfied with the chest volume measurement tool, if $F = 0$, it means that the user is generally satisfied with the evaluation index, and if $F < 0$, it means that the user is less satisfied with the evaluation index.

4 Results

4.1 Accuracy

The accuracy results of subjects measured by professionals and self measured with the new tool are listed in Tables 1 and 2.

Table 1. Descriptive statistics of self measurement and professional measurement

	Group	Group A subjects		Group B subjects		Group C subjects	
		Mean	SD	Mean	SD	Mean	SD
Lower chest circumference		n = 10		n = 10		n = 10	
	Professional measurement	68.020	1.8510	75.080	3.1365	82.360	2.5308
	Self measurement	68.240	2.1956	74.920	2.9578	81.270	1.8756
Left breast height		n = 10		n = 10		n = 10	
	Professional measurement	1.390	0.7564	2.040	1.0200	4.180	1.3357
	Self measurement	1.600	0.3944	2.300	0.9487	4.500	1.4142
Right breast height		n = 10		n = 10		n = 10	
	Professional measurement	1.830	0.6800	2.460	1.0824	4.550	1.3168
	Self measurement	1.600	0.5164	2.450	0.9846	4.650	1.4347
Left breast transverse diameter		n = 10		n = 10		n = 10	
	Professional measurement	15.350	0.9009	16.520	0.8066	17.880	1.2908
	Self measurement	15.660	0.7457	16.850	1.0352	17.120	1.0789
Right breast transverse diameter		n = 10		n = 10		n = 10	
	Professional measurement	15.810	0.7608	16.880	.7815	18.550	1.5587

(*continued*)

Table 1. (*continued*)

Group		Group A subjects		Group B subjects		Group C subjects	
		Mean	SD	Mean	SD	Mean	SD
	Self measurement	15.820	0.7885	16.960	1.0543	17.180	1.1849
Inframammary Distance		n = 10		n = 10		n = 10	
	Professional measurement	17.680	0.3736	17.090	0.5021	17.680	0.8904
	Self measurement	17.400	0.4690	17.140	0.6004	17.580	0.7700
Vertical distance of left lower breast		n = 10		n = 10		n = 10	
	Professional measurement	5.420	0.4872	5.710	0.7564	5.260	1.7258
	Self measurement	5.170	0.5964	5.600	0.9274	4.910	1.4279
Vertical distance of right lower breast		n = 10		n = 10		n = 10	
	Professional measurement	5.190	0.5507	5.870	0.7617	5.230	1.7683
	Self measurement	5.090	0.6244	5.640	0.9021	4.980	1.5859

Table 2. Difference test between self measurement and professional measurement

	Group A subjects				Group B subjects				Group C subjects			
	F	Sig.	t	Sig.	F	Sig.	t	Sig.	F	Sig.	t	Sig.
Lower circumference	0.265	0.613	0.117	0.908	0.265	0.613	0.117	0.908	10.803	0.196	10.094	0.288
Left height	0.022	0.883	−0.590	0.562	0.022	0.883	0.590	0.562	0.050	0.826	0.520	0.609
Right height	0.006	0.941	0.022	0.983	0.006	0.941	0.022	0.983	0.129	0.724	0.162	0.873
Left transverse diameter	0.103	0.752	0.795	0.437	0.103	0.752	0.795	0.437	10.080	0.313	10.429	0.170
Right transverse diameter	0.162	0.692	0.193	0.849	0.162	0.692	0.193	0.849	0.708	0.411	20.213	0.040
Inframammary Distance	0.000	0.989	0.202	0.842	0.000	0.989	0.202	0.842	0.054	0.820	0.269	0.791
Vertical distance of left lower	0.072	0.792	0.291	0.775	0.072	0.792	0.291	0.775	0.813	0.379	0.494	0.627
Vertical distance of right lower	0.020	0.890	0.616	0.546	0.020	0.890	0.616	0.546	0.373	0.549	0.333	0.743

Based on the above output, the F statistics and their sig. values for specific variables such as chest circumference in the F test (i.e., chi-square test) can be obtained. It can be seen that in all three groups, group A, group B and group C, the sig. value (significance) of the F statistic is greater than 0.05 under the condition that equal variances are used, and it can be concluded that there is no difference between the variance of the data measured by professionals and self-measured in all variables in this group.

The same t-test values were obtained for the equality of means, and the sig. values (significance) of the t-statistics were greater than 0.05 in all three groups, group A, group B and group C, under the condition of equal variances, thus concluding that there was no difference between the professional and self-measured data.

4.2 Precision

The precision results of the subjects' three self-measures using the new instrument are presented in Table 3.

Table 3. Descriptive statistics of self measurement and professional measurement

	Group A subjects			Group B subjects			Group C subjects		
	Icc	95% CI	SEM (cm)	Icc	95% CI	SEM (cm)	Icc	95% CI	SEM (cm)
Lower circumference	0.99	0.91–0.99	0.71	0.99	0.97–0.99	0.94	0.95	0.88–0.98	0.59
Left height	0.85	0.64–0.95	0.11	0.98	0.94–0.99	0.28	0.98	0.96–0.99	0.44
Right height	0.93	0.82–0.98	0.17	0.98	0.94–0.99	0.31	0.98	0.95–0.99	0.45
Left transverse diameter	0.89	0.72–0.97	0.21	0.98	0.96–0.99	0.33	0.95	0.87–0.98	0.33
Right transverse diameter	0.92	0.79–0.97	0.23	0.99	0.97–0.99	0.33	0.97	0.91–0.99	0.38
Inframammary Distance	0.87	0.69–0.96	0.14	0.96	0.89–0.99	0.19	0.94	0.85–0.98	0.23
Vertical distance of left lower	0.96	0.88–0.98	0.18	0.97	0.93–0.99	0.30	0.99	0.98–0.99	0.44
Vertical distance of right lower	0.96	0.89–0.98	0.19	0.99	0.97–0.99	0.28	0.99	0.98–0.99	0.49

It can be seen that the ICC value of each variable of Group A is greater than 0.85 and close to 1, so we can judge that the three measurements are highly consistent; the ICC values of each variable of Group B and Group C are greater than 0.9 and close to 1, so we can judge that the three measurements are highly consistent. the absolute reliability

ICC values of Group B and Group C are greater than that of The ICC values of Group B and Group C are greater than those of Group A.

4.3 Subjective Evaluation

The subjective evaluation results of subjects using the new tool are listed in Table 4.

Table 4. Subjective evaluation results of new tools

F_1 (stability)	F_2 (Objectivity)	F_3 (Comfort)	F_4 (Learnability)	F_5 (Popularity)
0.892	0.761	0.616	0.875	0.529

The evaluation results show that the new measurement tool is stable and easy to learn, which proves that the advantages of the new measurement tool are recognized for its simple structure, economy and low learning cost; Popularity needs to be further optimized, which is also where this design scheme needs to be further improved.

5 Discussion

Considering the existing dynamic characteristics of breast and anthropometry, a new chest measurement benchmark in line with anthropometry is proposed, and a chest measurement tool with stable benchmark is developed to improve the accuracy of measurement and realize the accumulation of dynamic data. In this study, we also verified our new measurement tool design by comparing with the "gold standard" direct measurement conducted by professionals and self repeating three measurements. The high consistency of the results shows that the high repeatability of the measurement is independent of the experience of the measurer.

As demonstrated by Odo et al. direct anthropometric measurements are the most reliable method for describing differences between breasts. Reliability has two components: precision and reliability. Precision is the consistency between repeated measurements over time, and reliability is the physiological fluctuations within an individual. Accuracy is the degree to which the "true" value of a measurement is achieved. While random error can affect the reliability of measurements, inaccuracy is caused by systematic bias. Reliability is affected by observer-related problems (e.g., inconsistencies in positioning landmarks or in applying pressure to the instrument) and subject-related problems (e.g., due to breathing or postural changes). In contrast, in indirect anthropometry, the subject is usually wearing well-fitting clothing. Although the measurer does not need to touch the participant's body, there are still some privacy issues. On the one hand there is more privacy because the body is not touched, but on the other hand, the capture of identifiable images of the semi-naked body leads to sensitive personal images and data that may be stored in an insecure environment and potentially available on the Internet.

None of the existing measurement methods are suitable for personal operation; contact measurement techniques will result in large measurement errors compared to professionals, while non-contact measurement techniques, although they can measure more parts and have greatly improved in terms of accuracy, are expensive and have a high technical threshold, requiring the use of high-end computers or external cloud services (not recommended for sensitive data) for lengthy calculations; more importantly, since breasts are soft tissue organs without skeletal support, existing measurement techniques, whether direct or indirect, cannot guarantee repeatability of breast measurements, accumulate personal breast shape data, and predict breast shape changes due to frequent changes and displacements of the reference base.

In this paper, we defined three new chest measurement bases located above the stable bone disc and developed a new chest measurement tool based on this, which can be operated by users themselves and well protects their personal privacy, and it does not require much time for users to feel confident about using it. Because of the natural differences between different BMI chests, it is crucial to validate the tool in different BMI groups. We found that the higher the BMI index, the variance of individual measurement is instead smaller than the variance of professional measurement, and we believe that the measurement error due to skin press and breathing is unavoidable in professional measurement only with the experience of the measurement personnel, while in self-measurement is more The subjective comfort of breathing and skin compressions can be better felt during self-measurement.

The ICC values of each variable in Group A were greater than 0.85 and close to 1, and the ICC values of each variable in Group B and Group C were greater than 0.9 and close to 1, all of which were highly consistent, but in the lower bust circumference measurement, the ICC of Group C was 0.959, but it was lower than that of Group A and Group B. This may be because in this experiment, the Group C had subjects with sagging breasts, which affected the accuracy of the measurement to some extent; the ICC of Group A in breast height, transverse breast diameter, breast spacing, and breast pendulous distance were lower than those of Group B and Group C, respectively, because the sample of subjects in the low BMI group, breast edge identification was more difficult than the other two groups, and according to scholarly research, the inaccuracy of the measurement results may be due to instrument error or The accuracy results of the new tool and the gold standard showed no difference between the data measured by professionals and self-measurement, which is due to the fact that the measurement technique of the gold standard is also through the subjective judgment of professionals, while the measurement tool developed in this study can also achieve the equivalent effect, and it can be known that the new tool based on the new measurement base is stable.

Last but not least, in order to perform an aesthetic breast assessment, it is necessary to measure the degree of asymmetry of the breast, which can be time-consuming when performing direct measurements, whereas in the new measurement tool, the user can use the most natural way to measure in sequence, saving some time.

There are several features and limitations of this study that need to be noted. One of the first limitations is the number of participants; we believe that 10 subjects per group, depending on the BMI grouping, is sufficient to validate the measurement procedure, especially when taking into account the prescribed data quality procedures. This issue was addressed by randomly selecting subjects, resulting in a wide variety of different breast shapes and sizes. However, this may also lead to data bias and therefore further studies should be conducted on a larger sample of women. Separate validation of the different breast deformations should probably be performed. On the other hand, there is the issue of data recording, and in the successive work, the app that the measurement tool is equipped with will be developed to facilitate the storage of measurement data.

6 Conclusion

The new measurement tool we have developed may be a useful tool in breast measurement practice. It offers an objective method of breast measurement that provides high accuracy and precision without processing 3D data and without drawing points and lines on the user's body. Users can accurately assess asymmetries regardless of the measurement environment and time constraints. The new breast measurement tool proposed by this research will enable users who are still in the stage of dynamic breast shape change to accurately measure and purchase suitable bras to protect their own healthy development and subsequently reduce their dependence on "change, disease, medical treatment, orthopedic care", which will help improve the overall national health and social competitiveness and promote the construction of a healthy society.

Acknowledgement. The work described in this paper was substantially supported by Design Science and Art Research Center, Guangdong University of Technology.

References

1. Mcghee, D., Steele, J.R., Munro, B.J.: Female adolescent breast support during physical activity: can an educational intervention improve knowledge and behaviour. J. Sci. Med. Sport **12**, S7–S8 (2009). https://doi.org/10.1007/s003940070019
2. Atefeh, O., Joanna, W.-S., Jenny, S., Ross, W., Nicola, B.: Breast education improves adolescent girls' breast knowledge, attitudes to breasts and engagement with positive breast habits. Front. Public Health **8**, 591927 (2020). https://doi.org/10.3389/fpubh.2020.591927
3. Horlick, M., Thornton, J., Wang, J., Levine, L.S., Fedun, B., Pierson, R.N.: Body composition changes during tanner stage 5. Ann. N Y Acad. **904**(1), 410–415 (2010). https://doi.org/10.1111/j.1749-6632.2000.tb06491.x
4. Wood, K., Cameron, M., Fitzgerald, K.: Breast size, bra fit and thoracic pain in young women: a correlational study. Chiropr. Osteopathy **16**(1), 1–7 (2008). https://doi.org/10.1186/1746-1340-16-1
5. Bitar, A., Vernet, J., Coudert, J., Vermorel, M.: Longitudinal changes in body composition, physical capacities and energy expenditure in boys and girls during the onset of puberty. Eur. J. Nutr. **39**(4), 157–163 (2000). https://doi.org/10.1007/s003940070019
6. Olds, T., Daniell, N., Petkov, J., Stewart, A.D.: Somatotyping using 3D anthropometry: a cluster analysis. J. Sports Sci. **31**(9), 936–944 (2013). https://doi.org/10.1080/02640414.2012.759660
7. Zakaria, N., Gupta, D.: Anthropometry, Apparel Sizing and Design. Woodhead Publishing (2019)
8. Qi, J., Zhang, X., Ying, B., Lv, F.: Comparison of human body sizing measurement data by using manual and 3D scanning measuring techniques. J. Fiber Bioeng. Inform. **4**(1), 83–95 (2011)

9. Istook, C.L., Lim, H.-S., Chun, J.-S.: Comparative analysis of body measurement and fit evaluation between 2D direct body measuring and 3D body scan measuring. The Res. J. Costume Cult. **19**(6), 1347–1358 (2011)
10. Gouvali, M.K., Boudolos, K.: Match between school furniture dimensions and children's anthropometry. Appl. Ergon. **37**(6), 765–773 (2006)
11. Lescay, R.N., Becerra, A.A., González, A.H.: Anthropometry Comparative analysis of technologies for the capture of anthropometric dimensions. Revista EIA/English version **13**(26), 47–59 (2016)
12. Bougourd, J.P., Dekker, L., Grant Ross, P., Ward, J.P.: A comparison of women's sizing by 3D electronic scanning and traditional anthropometry. J. Text. Inst. **91**(2), 163–173 (2000). https://doi.org/10.1080/00405000008659536
13. Vergara, M., Agost, M.J., Gracia-Ibáñez, V.: Dorsal and palmar aspect dimensions of hand anthropometry for designing hand tools and protections. Hum. Factors Ergon. Manuf. Serv. Indus. **28**(1), 17–28 (2018). https://doi.org/10.1002/hfm.20714
14. Farahani, R.M., Nooranipour, M.: Anatomy and anthropometry of human stapes. Am. J. Otolaryngol. **29**(1), 42–47 (2008). https://doi.org/10.1016/j.amjoto.2007.01.004
15. Lescay, R.N., Becerra, A.A., González, A.H.: Antropometría. Análisis comparativo de las tecnologías para la captación de las dimensiones antropométricas. Revista EIA **13**(26), 47–59 (2017). https://doi.org/10.24050/reia.v13i26.799
16. Veitch, D., Burford, K., Dench, P., Dean, N., Griffin, P.: Measurement of breast volume using body scan technology (computer-aided anthropometry). Work **41**, 4038–4045 (2012)
17. Lee, H.-Y., Hong, K.: Optimal brassiere wire based on the 3D anthropometric measurements of under breast curve. Appl. Ergon. **38**(3), 377–384 (2007). https://doi.org/10.1016/j.apergo.2006.03.014
18. Currey, J.D.: Bones: Structure and Mechanics. Princeton University Press (2006)
19. Greggianin, M., Tonetto, L.M., Brust-Renck, P.: Aesthetic and functional bra attributes as emotional triggers. Fash. Text. **5**(1), 1–12 (2018). https://doi.org/10.1186/s40691-018-0150-4
20. Pei, J., Fan, J., Ashdown, S.P.: Detection and comparison of breast shape variation among different three-dimensional body scan conditions: nude, with a structured bra, and with a soft bra. Textile Res. J. **89**(21–22), 4595–4606 (2019)

Collaboration, Communication, and Human Behavior

AI-Driven Human Motion Classification and Analysis Using Laban Movement System

Wenbin Guo[1]([✉]), Osubi Craig[2], Timothy Difato[1], James Oliverio[1], Markus Santoso[1], Jill Sonke[3], and Angelos Barmpoutis[1]

[1] Digital Worlds Institute, University of Florida, Gainesville, FL 32611, USA
{wenbin,tim,james,markus,angelos}@digitalworlds.ufl.edu
[2] Center for the Arts, Migration, and Entrepreneurship, University of Florida, Gainesville, FL 32611, USA
ocraig@arts.ufl.edu
[3] Center for the Arts in Medicine and Assist, University of Florida, Gainesville, FL 32611, USA
jsonke@arts.ufl.edu

Abstract. Human movement classification and analysis are important in the research of health sciences and the arts. Laban movement analysis is an effective method to annotate human movement in dance that describes communication and expression. Technology-supported human movement analysis employs motion sensors, infrared cameras, and other wearable devices to capture critical joints of the human skeleton and facial key points. However, the aforementioned technologies are not mainstream, and the most popular form of motion capture is conventional video recording, usually from a single stationary camera. Such video recordings can be used to evaluate human movement or dance performance. Any methods that can systematically analyze and annotate these raw video footage would be of great importance to this field. Therefore, this research offers an analysis and comparison of AI-based computer vision methods that can annotate the human movement automatically. This study trained and compared four different machine learning algorithms (random forest, K neighbors, neural network, and decision tree) through supervised learning on existing video datasets of dance performances. The developed system was able to automatically produce annotation in the four dimensions (effort, space, shape, body) of Laban movement analysis. The results demonstrate accurately produced annotations in comparison to manually entered ground truth Laban annotation.

Keywords: Artificial intelligence · Human motion classification · Laban movement analysis

1 Introduction

Human movement has been studied in multiple disciplines, including health sciences and the Arts, resulting in a large but disparate assortment of multi-modal datasets, including video, skeletal motion capture, manual annotations, and clinical metadata. Laban

© The Author(s), under exclusive license to Springer Nature Switzerland AG 2022
V. G. Duffy (Ed.): HCII 2022, LNCS 13319, pp. 201–210, 2022.
https://doi.org/10.1007/978-3-031-05890-5_16

notation is a standardized form of kinetograph annotation [1, 2]. Although it was originally proposed for vector-based choreographic transcription [3], it has been successfully applied to several fields that study human motion [4], such as neuroscience [5], kinesiology [6], human-computer interaction [7], as well as theater and dance [8]. Traditional data collection processes often include Laban movement analysis and annotation that parameterizes observed changes in pre-defined 4-dimensional feature space (effort, space, shape, body). Such analysis requires lengthy manual input from professionals who annotate the recorded data through a time-consuming "watch and pause" process, which is also prone to human errors. The majority of automated Laban analysis focuses on processing 3D point sets (skeletal sequences) captured by specialized motion tracking equipment that may require the installation of markers on the user's body and calibration of the devices [6, 8]. However, these technologies are not mainstream, and until today the most commonly used form of observation and documentation of human motion is conventional video recording, typically done from a single stationary camera discretely placed within the professional setting.

In this project, we proposed using Artificial Intelligence (AI) methods to fully automate the annotation process involved in Laban analysis by training and testing different machine learning algorithms on existing video datasets of human motion, focusing on performative movement. First, we trained four different machine learning algorithms through supervised learning on existing dance video datasets in this study. Second, this study tested feature extraction methods (within and across frames) to improve the annotation accuracy. The trained model was then tested in Laban-annotating existing video sequences and validated using manually produced Laban annotation, which was considered our ground truth. Finally, a software application was developed that can be used by researchers to input raw videos and export automatically produced Laban annotation.

2 Related Works

Laban movement analysis was originally developed by Rudolf Laban [2]. Laban system has been widely used for human movement analysis and annotation, and its reliability has been extensively studied and evaluated [9]. Figure 1 shows the detailed hierarchy of the Laban movement analysis in four dimensions. Shape quality has six elements: opening, enclosing, rising, sinking, advancing, and retreating. Shape quality can be described by observing the positioning of the body along the vertical, horizontal, and sagittal axes. Effort quality has eight elements: light, strong, free, bound, sustained, quick, indirect, and direct. The majority of the elements in effort quality can be related to motion features such as velocity and acceleration. The space zone has six elements: side-open, side-across, up, down, forward, and backward. These elements describe the trajectory of human motions. Body phrasing has three elements: impulsive, swing, and impactive. These elements explain the kinematic chains and global locomotion.

With the use of motion tracking technologies, there have been numerous applications of Laban movement analysis in dance emotion recognition [10], folk dance evaluation [8], parameterizing interpersonal behavior [6], and signal interpretation [11], among others. Several of these examples were focused on behavior patterns recognition and human-computer interaction using Laban movement analysis, and the majority of them have been restricted to the effort and shape dimensions of the 4-dimensional Laban annotation space.

More recently, Microsoft Kinect sensors have been employed for Laban-based motion tracking and analysis [12–14]. More specifically, Ajili [13] compared the effectiveness of machine learning methods to classify human actions using Kinect sensors. The results indicated robust classification across the Laban dimensions. Similarly, Kim [14] extracted motion features such as velocity and acceleration of joints to analyze the Laban movement. Although motion sensors such as Kinect have been consistently becoming more affordable, they are still not in mainstream use by consumers. On the contrary, the popularity of video sharing and streaming platforms, ranging from teleconferencing tools to social media, have established conventional video recording (without additional sensors) as the dominant form of recording and documenting the human activity. In professional settings (such as clinical, performative, etc.), the use of a single stationary video camera has been the current standard for observing and recording human movement.

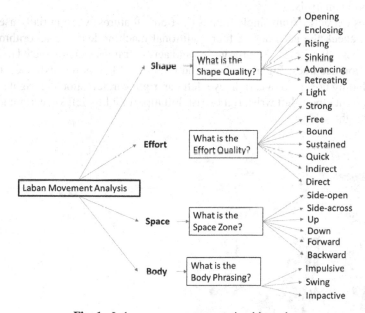

Fig. 1. Laban movement annotation hierarchy

Our method involved the processing of raw video footage of human movement using a sequence of artificial intelligence algorithms. First, human skeleton detection algorithms extracted key skeletal features from the input videos. Then feature vectors were calculated from in-frame and across-frames values and were used to train and test the effectiveness of four machine learning algorithms (random forest, K neighbors, neural network, and decision tree) in automatic Laban classification across the four dimensions of the Laban analysis space. Random forest is an estimator that fits many decision tree classifiers on various sub-samples of the dataset and uses averaging to improve the predictive accuracy and control over-fitting. K neighbors is a classifier that captures the similarity, such as calculating the distance between points on a graph. The neural network is a multi-layer perceptron classifier to optimize the log-loss function. The feedforward network generates a set of outputs from a set of inputs in the neurons.

3 Methods

As in the majority of AI-based methods, our process included the following four milestones: 1) Data preparation, 2) Feature extraction, 3) Training and testing, 4) Automated annotation.

In this pilot study, we used performative video datasets from the Digital Worlds Institute at the University of Florida and videos from the Dance Motion Capture Database of the University of Cyprus [15]. A selection of four videos was manually annotated using Laban movement analysis. In order to identify the skeleton and body joints in the raw input videos, we used Facebook Detectron2 [16], which is an open-source platform for human motion analysis.

Features extracted from single frames (in-frame features) were initially used as the baseline to check the accuracy of four traditional machine learning algorithms. After finding the best algorithms, features within and across frames were extracted to improve the annotation accuracy. Figure 2 shows the total of 17 key points extracted from the video, including nose, left eye, right eye, left ear, right ear, left shoulder, right shoulder, left elbow, right elbow, left wrist, right wrist, left hip, right hip, left knee, right knee, left ankle, and right ankle.

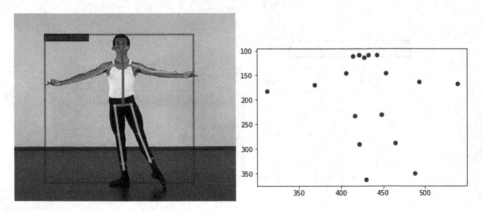

Fig. 2. Skeleton detection from input video (left), Extracted body key points (right)

The x, y coordinates of each key point were estimated for each frame of the video, generating 34 time-series/signals for our analysis. Figure 3 shows the x and y coordinates as signals in the left and right plots, respectively. By visually inspecting these plots, it is evident that patterns can be observed from the corresponding motion activity. Subsequently, these features and other quantities derived from these features, such as

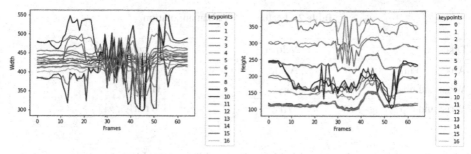

Fig. 3. Plots of the human joint movements. Left: x-coordinate, right: y-coordinate.

distance, velocity, and acceleration, can be correlated with the four dimensions of the Laban analysis system.

After the feature extraction step, we trained four machine learning models to receive a video sequence as input and recognize the body motion changes across the 4-dimensional domain used in Laban annotation, including effort, space, shape, and body. Table 1 shows an example of Laban movement annotation in four dimensions. Each dimension has two elements, and this study created four binary classifiers to annotate the human movement.

Table 1. Laban movement annotation

#	Shape	Effort	Space	Body
1	Enclosing	Light	Side-open	Impulsive
2	Opening	Strong	Side-across	Swing

For our training dataset, we used dance videos from the Graphics Lab at the University of Cyprus. Additional video datasets from the University of Florida Digital Worlds Institute were used for evaluation and testing. We randomly selected 70% of the compiled dataset for supervised training, and the remaining 30% was used for testing. The annotation system was implemented in Python using existing libraries (Scikit-learn) to expedite the project's prototyping phase. The system was developed and tested in UF High-Performance Computing Facility (HiPerGator). Facebook Detectron2 was used to detect the human key points, estimating a total of seventeen key points for each human skeleton. The feature vector that we used to detect the Laban annotation consisted of the velocity and acceleration of each detected key point as well as distances between specific key points, as listed in Table 2.

More specifically, for the experiments in this pilot study, we calculated the distance, velocity, and acceleration between ankle and hip, velocity and acceleration of ankle, hip, and wrist [8]. Each dimension in Laban movement analysis contained multiple elements, and not all the videos covered every element of four dimensions. Therefore, two elements in each dimension were used in this study, and multilabel classification was generated.

In our experiments, we also compared distances between adjacent joints in order to study the suitability of each feature in our feature vector (such as the distance from hip to

Table 2. Features for Laban annotation

Distance	Velocity	Acceleration
Ankle and hip	Ankle	Ankle
Wrist and nose	Hip	Hip
Wrist and hip	Wrist	Wrist

knee, elbow to wrist, elbow to shoulder, and shoulder to shoulder). Hip to knee distance had a minimum standard deviation, and it was regarded as a normalization factor. Based on the average thigh length of humans, this study normalized the data based on the hip to knee distance.

Performance evaluation was based on the precision, recall, and F1 scores. Precision is the ability of the classifier not to label as positive a sample that is negative. The recall is the ability of the classifier to find all the positive samples, and its value ranges from 0–1, with 1 being the best. F1 can be interpreted as a harmonic mean of the precision and recall, and its value also ranges from 0–1. The relative contribution of precision and recall to the F1 score are equal. The formula for the F1 score is:

$$F1 = 2 * (precision * recall)/(precision + recall) \tag{1}$$

Finally, the automated annotation was visualized by Matplotlib, which was a comprehensive library for creating animated and interactive visualization.

4 Results

Multilabel classification treats each label independently whereas multilabel classifiers treat the multiple classes simultaneously. The multilabel approach taken in this pilot study is to break the Laban movement analysis problem into four binary classification tasks and one for each Laban dimension. Each binary classifier decides body (impulsive or swing), shape (enclosing or opening), effort (light or strong), and space (side-open or side-across), respectively. Table 3 shows the results of Laban annotation using four machine learning algorithms, including random forest, K neighbors, neural network, and decision tree. It should be noted that all four algorithms were used in the multilabel classification framework.

The data indicated that Random forest had the best performance compared to the other machine learning algorithms. Additional experiments were performed with larger feature vectors that were generated by adding cross-frame features. The added features were the average, maximum, minimum, and standard deviation of the original frames for a duration of two seconds. These additional features increased the accuracy of Laban annotation, especially the space dimension, side-across, and side-open, which are highly related to the content of the previous frames, as reported in Table 4.

This pilot study also explored the accuracy based on different frame intervals. The frame interval experiments were varied with increments of 10 frames at a time because the manually produced labels were based on ten frames interval. Cumulative mean, standard deviation, maximum, minimum for 10–60 frames interval were calculated as the input data for training. Based on the results, the frame interval that produces the best results was 60 frames.

Table 3. Laban annotation using four machine learning algorithms

	Random Forest			K neighbors			Neural Network			Decision Tree		
	P	R	F1	P	R	F1	P	R	F1	P	R	F1
Enclosing	1.00	0.97	0.98	0.93	0.93	0.93	0.85	0.97	0.90	0.80	0.97	0.88
Impulsive	1.00	0.45	0.62	0.50	0.09	0.15	0.56	0.43	0.49	0.38	0.35	0.36
Light	0.98	1.00	0.99	0.97	0.99	0.98	0.97	0.98	0.98	0.97	0.97	0.97
Opening	1.00	1.00	1.00	1.00	1.00	1.00	1.00	0.99	0.99	1.00	0.98	0.99
Side-across	0.81	0.76	0.79	0.79	0.67	0.72	0.79	0.79	0.79	0.69	0.73	0.71
Side-open	0.80	0.84	0.82	0.81	0.73	0.77	0.81	0.81	0.81	0.74	0.70	0.72
Strong	1.00	0.45	0.62	0.50	0.10	0.17	0.50	0.40	0.44	0.40	0.40	0.40
Swing	0.98	1.00	0.99	0.96	0.99	0.98	0.97	0.98	0.98	0.97	0.97	0.97

Table 4. Laban annotation using cumulative frames

	Random Forest (Single frame)			Random Forest (Cross frame)		
	P	R	F1	P	R	F1
Enclosing	1.00	0.97	0.98	0.88	0.78	0.82
Impulsive	1.00	0.45	0.62	0.94	0.61	0.74
Light	0.98	1.00	0.99	0.98	1.00	0.99
Opening	1.00	1.00	1.00	0.99	0.99	0.99
Side-across	0.81	0.76	0.79	0.95	0.91	0.93
Side-open	0.80	0.84	0.82	0.92	0.96	0.94
Strong	1.00	0.45	0.62	0.94	0.61	0.74
Swing	0.97	1.00	0.99	0.98	1.00	0.99

Figure 4 describes the confusion matrix of Laban annotation using random forest (Cross frame). The results showed the high accuracy of the detection in Laban movement four dimensions including eight elements.

Figure 5 shows an example of our results from a single frame of one of the input videos. The automatically detected human skeleton and the corresponding key points are superimposed on the image. For this frame, the automated Laban annotation in four dimensions was: Shape = opening, Effort = light, Space = side-open, Body = swing. Our developed software was able to successfully produce Laban annotation for each frame of an input video. Our classifier had two elements for each Laban dimension:

effort (light, strong), shape (enclosing, opening), space (side-open, side-across), and body (swing, impulsive). The multilabel binary classifier could produce the annotation such as "light, opening, side-open, swing" for each frame of the input video. The labels reflected the human movement in each frame.

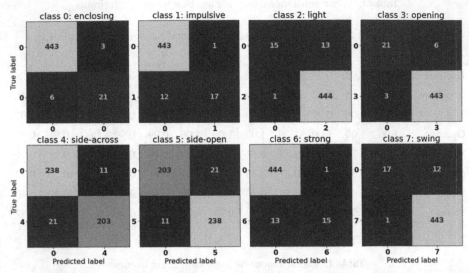

Fig. 4. Confusion matrix of each Laban movement dimension

Fig. 5. Sample demonstration of our results. Detected skeletal features are shown in the frame. Automated Laban classification result for this frame: Effort = light, Shape = opening, Space = side-open, Body = swing.

5   Conclusion

In this pilot study, we developed a method for recognizing Laban movement dimensions from input videos using machine learning algorithms. The study trained and compared four different machine learning algorithms (random forest, K neighbors, neural network, and decision tree) through supervised learning on existing human motion video datasets. Our results obtained high accuracy in three dimensions: shape (enclosing, opening), effort (light, strong), and body (swing, impulsive) for the single-frame analysis. The annotation accuracy was increased in space (side-open, side-across) when cross-frame features were included in our feature vector. These results demonstrated that Laban movement analysis could be fully automated using machine learning algorithms that operate on raw input videos and that AI-driven standardized human motion evaluation systems can be developed.

Our results indicated that such AI-driven movement classification could enable fully automated reporting in commonly used Laban annotation using only a single stationary camera. Furthermore, an AI-based solution to this problem may lead to standardization of data processing and optimize professionals' time and decrease human errors. In the future, this can significantly impact the health science and art areas that use Laban analysis, by bringing AI to new domains and applications such as atlas construction of choreographic data and clinical assessment in dance therapy.

6   Limitations and Future Work

Although AI-based Laban annotation has already shown the improvement of efficiency, this study only trained a limited number of four videos, and more datasets need to be trained in the future. Only a specific genre of dances was included in the dataset; inclusion of more genres may lead to larger variability of cross frames features based on the rhythms and motion patterns. Our binary classifier only detected two elements in each Laban dimension, and all the elements in the four dimensions need to be tested in the Laban annotation in the future.

Facebook Detectron2 only contains x, y coordinates which may bias the annotation to patterns that are visible in the 2-dimensional plane of the video frame. Newer pose estimation models with 3D coordinate detection need to be tested in the future. The inclusion of the z-dimension (depth) of the joints may help us detect more elements in the Laban movement analysis.

In the future, more algorithms can be tested using Tensorflow, such as Convolutional Neural Network (CNN), through supervised learning on the time-series of the features extracted from the video datasets.

Acknowledgment. This project was supported by the 2020 UF AI Catalyst grant from the UF Office of Research. The authors acknowledge the University of Florida Research Computing for providing computational resources and support that have contributed to the research results reported in this publication.

References

1. Hutchinson, A., Guest, A.H., Hutchinson, W.A.: Labanotation: or, kinetography Laban: the system of analyzing and recording movement. Taylor & Francis (1977)
2. Laban, R.: Choreutics: Annotated and Ed. Macdonald & Evans, London (1966)
3. Longstaff, J.S.: Translating "vector symbols" from Laban's choreographie. In: Twenty-Second Biennial Conference of the International Council of Kinetography Laban, ICKL, 26 July-2 August. Ohio State University, Columbus, Ohio. USA 4(1926), 70–86 (2001). Retrieved from http://www.ickl.org/conf01_proceedings/ICKL01_070_086.pdf
4. Davies, E. Beyond dance: Laban's legacy of movement analysis (2007)
5. Foroud, A., Whishaw, I.Q.: Changes in the kinematic structure and non-kinematic features of movements during skilled reaching after stroke: a laban movement analysis in two case studies. J. Neurosci. Methods 158(1), 137–149 (2006). https://doi.org/10.1016/j.jneumeth. 2006.05.007
6. Roudposhti, K.K., Santos, L., Aliakbarpour, H., Dias, J.: Parameterizing interpersonal behaviour with Laban movement analysis - A Bayesian approach. In: IEEE Computer Society Conference on Computer Vision and Pattern Recognition Workshops, pp. 7–13 (2012). https://doi.org/10.1109/CVPRW.2012.6239349
7. Rett, J., Dias, J., Ahuactzin, J.M.: Bayesian reasoning for Laban Movement Analysis used in human-machine interaction. Int. J. Reasoning-based Intell. Sys. 2(1), 13–35 (2010). https://doi.org/10.1504/IJRIS.2010.029812
8. Aristidou, A., Stavrakis, E., Charalambous, P., Chrysanthou, Y., Himona, S.L.: Folk dance evaluation using laban movement analysis. J. Comp. Cul. Heritage 8(4), 1–19 (2015). https://doi.org/10.1145/2755566
9. Bernardet, U., Alaoui, S.F., Studd, K., Bradley, K., Pasquier, P., Schiphorst, T.: Assessing the reliability of the Laban Movement Analysis system. PLoS ONE 14(6), 1–23 (2019). https://doi.org/10.1371/journal.pone.0218179
10. Wang, S., Li, J., Cao, T., Wang, H., Tu, P., Li, Y.: Dance emotion recognition based on laban motion analysis using convolutional neural network and long short-term memory. IEEE Access 8, 124928–124938 (2020). https://doi.org/10.1109/ACCESS.2020.3007956
11. Santos, L., Dias, J.: Motion Patterns: Signal Interpretation towards the Laban Movement Analysis Semantics. In: Camarinha-Matos, L.M. (ed.) DoCEIS 2011. IAICT, vol. 349, pp. 333–340. Springer, Heidelberg (2011). https://doi.org/10.1007/978-3-642-19170-1_36
12. Bernstein, R., Shafir, T., Tsachor, R., Studd, K., Schuster, A.: Laban Movement Analysis using kinect. Int. J. Comp. Elec. Auto. Contr. Info. Eng. 9(6), 1574–1578 (2015)
13. Ajili, I., Mallem, M., Didier, J.Y.: Robust human action recognition system using Laban Movement Analysis. Procedia Comp. Sci. 112, 554–563 (2017). https://doi.org/10.1016/j.procs.2017.08.168
14. Kim, W.H., Park, J.W., Lee, W.H., Chung, M.J., Lee, H.S.: LMA based emotional motion representation using RGB-D camera. In: ACM/IEEE International Conference on Human-Robot Interaction, pp. 163–164 (2013). https://doi.org/10.1109/HRI.2013.6483552
15. University of Cyprus: Dance Motion Capture Database (2018). Retrieved 18 Dec 2021, from http://dancedb.cs.ucy.ac.cy/main/performances
16. Wu, Y., Kirillov, A., Massa, F., Lo, W.-Y., Girshick, R.: Detectron2 (2019). Retrieved 20 Dec 2021, from https://github.com/facebookresearch/detectron2

A Bibliometric Analysis of Robot Collaborative Service During 2011–2021

Xiangjun Hu, Yaqin Cao(✉), Yi Ding, and Yu Liu

School of Economics and Management, Anhui Polytechnic
University, Wuhu, People's Republic of China
caoyaqin.2007@163.com

Abstract. This article aims to conduct a bibliometric analysis of robot collaborative service from 2011 to 2021 based on VOS viewer. 5141 articles have 162,358 cited references were analyzed. Publication source, publication organization, authors, country and citation of articles were recorded and analyzed. Bibliometric maps of authorship, citation, co-citation and network of co-occurrence of keywords are drawn. The China and USA dominates the publications (1279,24.87% or 895, 16.71%) and citations (15960 times or 22017 times). Chinese Academy of Science is the most productive organization. Bu jiajun is the most productive author. The top 5 highly cited journals are "Intelligent Service Robotics", "IEEE Access", "Sensors", "International Journal of Advanced Robotic Systems", "Robotics and Computer-integrated Manufacturing". The 215 minimum number of occurrences of a keyword was set 35, of the 18681 keywords, 97 keywords were divided into four clusters. Cluster 1 mainly about design of robot. Cluster 2 mainly design about task of robot collaborative service. Cluster 3 mainly technology of robot collaborative service. Cluster 4 mainly about fields of application of robot collaborative service. The latest keyword analysis shows that "task", "robot sensing system", "robot kinematics", "deep learning" and "manipulators" have burst end time of 2021.

Keywords: Robot collaborative service · Service robot · Bibliometric · Vos viewer

1 Introduction

Service robot provides necessary services in an unstructured environment, mainly including home service robot, medical robot and public service robot. The research of service robot is making progress and different definitions are proposed to describe service robot. For example, The International Federation of Robotics [1] defines service robots as those "that perform useful tasks for humans or equipment excluding industrial automation applications." Wirtz et al. [2] define them as "system-based autonomous and adaptable interfaces that interact, communicate and deliver service to an organization's customers." A service robot has not only technological features for services but also the ability to engage in human interactions [3]. With the development of computer vision, visual recognition, sensors and artificial intelligence, service robots have also made great progress.

© The Author(s), under exclusive license to Springer Nature Switzerland AG 2022
V. G. Duffy (Ed.): HCII 2022, LNCS 13319, pp. 211–219, 2022.
https://doi.org/10.1007/978-3-031-05890-5_17

Innovations in sensors, navigation systems, and machine learning have made robots smarter, more mobile, and offer fewer service arrangements in dynamic environments, requiring the ability to navigate dense and sometimes restricted areas [4]. Service robots have many potential benefits, such as increased productivity, consistent service quality, and reduced personnel costs. Service Robot enable quickly collects data from the environment, dynamically analyzes it, and meets customers' changing needs. For example, intelligent robot wheelchair, monitoring robot, education robot, therapy robot, entertainment robot and self-driving car [5]. According to the "Gartner Hype Cycle 2019" on ARTIFICIAL intelligence, intelligent robots are rising rapidly and the technology is expected to be widely available within 5 to 10 years. Some of the cost savings in the adoption of service robots can be achieved through automation and human substitution [6].

The growth prospects for the robotics market are very strong. According to MarketsandMarkets [7], the service robotics market is expected to grow from USD 37.0 billion in 2020 to USD 102.5 billion by 2025 at a compound annual growth rate of 22.6%. According to a Brookings Institution survey [8], 52 percent of 2021 adult Internet users feel robots will perform most human activities and 94% of those who have adopted robots say that robots increased productivity in their business.Industrial robots have been widely used in a variety of manufacturing tasks, including hazardous material handling, hazardous handling, and machine monitoring and operation. Service robots, on the other hand, are deployed for specific service functions. Service robots show great opportunities to improve productivity and reduce costs. As COVID-19 is a major threat to public health, consumers are more frequently faced with the choice of human and robotic services in the hospitality industry and have a more positive attitude toward robot-equipped hotels. With the widespread use of robots and artificial intelligence, researchers and practitioners have been discussing the impact of robots on the labor market and economy, as robots have the potential to replace human jobs and labor [9].

Service robots have a mature category [7]. They are widely accepted and requested in a growing number of fields of activity, and the future trend is clear: as long as technical and financial issues allow, a kind of service robot will be available in specific areas of human activity to help and do things faster and better (in most cases, anyway) [10]. With the rapid increase in the variety of service robots, potential users are becoming more and more aware of technological progress. Therefore, it is necessary to take into account users' requirements for such robots: safe and reliable operation, simple programming, easy to learn, low cost and energy saving, friendly and independent, strong adaptability, strong cooperation ability, smart and flexible [11].

Since robot collaborative service has attracted the attention of many disciplines, this field has accumulated numerous research outcomes. Therefore, it is important and timely to make a systematic and comprehensive evaluation of the research output of robot collaborative service over the last decades. Therefore, we use the bibliometric analysis method to achieve this objective. The bibliometric analysis method can be used to investigate the quantity and quality of a research discipline [12] and to indicate the frontiers of scientific research [13], and has advantages on handling a large number of articles compared to traditional literature review method. Hence, it serves as an ideal method in comprehending the status quo of a research discipline. Albeit one study have bibliometrically evaluated the discipline of robot collaborative service, these studies have some limitations, such as with limited publications and out of date (i.e., published 10 years ago). Thus, this article aims to delve into providing a comprehensive and objective analysis of robot collaborative service under different perspectives in the past decades. This paper consists of five sections: (1) introduction, (2) methodology, (3) result, (4) discussion, (5) conclusion.

2   Methodology

This paper aimed to conduct a quantitative and visualized analysis of representative papers related to robot collaboration service through bibliometric methods. Web of Science (WoS) is an online subscription-based scientific citation indexing service that provides a comprehensive citation search, enabling users to acquire and analyze relevant scientific literature including journal articles, conference proceedings, etc. Therefore, WoS was selected as a source database to obtain the initial data to be analyzed. To obtain the maximum number of relevant documents related to robot collaborative service, data were collected and stored for the defined search terms using the "Topic" search in Web of Science Core Collection. And the field tag "Topic" in WoS means that a record will be sorted out if the search terms are included in Title, Abstract, Author Keywords, or Keywords Plus within the record. The keywords used for the initial data collection included different expressions, such as "robot collaboration service", "service robot".In the period from 2011 to 2021, there were 5141 articles after overlapping records retrieved from both sources that were downloaded and recorded from the databases.

A bibliometric analysis was performed using Vos Viewer 1.6.14. The Vos Viewer, developed by Van Eck and Waltman, is a powerful piece of software for building and visualizing bibliometric networks, with keyword emergence, that can process large amounts of items or data extracted from well-known databases such as Scopus and Web of Science.

3   Results and Discussion

3.1   Co-authorship and Journals Analysis

We then investigated the most productive countries. China (1279), USA (895), France (482), Italy (430), and England (380) are the top 5 productive countries, followed by Germany (370), Spain (329), Japan (273) and Canada (203). China dominant this field. The citation of countries can show the quality of publications of each country. And the results show that the top 5 cited countries are USA (22017 times), China (15960 times), Germany (10069 times), Italy (8828 times), and England (8813 times), which are the sources of high-quality publications.

More than 5000 institutions have done research related to robot collaborative service. The most productive organization is University of Chinese Academic of Sciences with 105 publications, followed by Harbin institute technology (103 publications), University of Zhejiang (93 publications), University of Shanghai jiaotong (69 publications), University of munich (53 publications), etc. University of Zhejiang ranked first with citation frequency of papers for 2114 times, followed by University of Hongkong (1660 times), University of London (1592 times), Harbin institute technology (1318 times), University of Paris (1284 times), etc., which means that high-quality papers were mostly from these organizations.

We have further analyzed the co-authorship at the author level. Figure 1 displays the co-authorship network of productive authors by using VOSviewer. The minimum number of documents of an author was set 5, of the 19092 authors, 312 met the threshold. The 312 points represent the 312 authors. Different colors of points divided the authors into different clusters. The size of a point represents the number of publications. The line between two points represents that there exists co-authorship between each author. The distance between two circles is conversely corresponding to the collaboration between each author (Fig. 1 and Table 1).

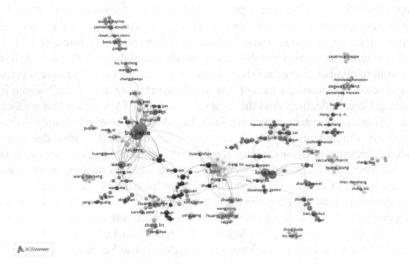

Fig. 1. Co-authorship network of productive authors.

Table 1. The top 10 most productive authors.

Total publications	Author	Total publications	Author
47	Bu, jiajun	14	Dong, W
43	Chen, chun	13	Wang, C
36	Cohen, david	13	Huang, P
23	Ishiguro, H	13	Hagita, N
20	Cavallo, filippo	12	Sterkers, O

The dedication of journals was also analyzed. In Table 2, we can see the top 5 highly cited journals are "Intelligent Service Robotics", "IEEE Access", "Sensors", "International Journal of Advanced Robotic Systems", "Robotics and Computer-integrated Manufacturing".

Table 2. The top 5 most productive journals.

Total publications	Journal
319	Intelligent Service Robotics
234	IEEE Access
136	Sensors
115	International Journal of Advanced Robotic Systems
102	Robotics and Computer-integrated Manufacturing

3.2 Co-citation Network

In a specific scientific activity, co-citations of reference are one of the most significant method to analyse and reflect the evolutionary process. 5141 articles have 162,358 cited references. Figure 2 shows the mapping on co-citation of references. The 40 points represent the 40 cited reference. The identical colour shows that the cited reference is from the same cluster. The point's size represents the citation the paper's frequency. The connection between two points represents that both of articles had been cited in one paper. On the contrary, the distance between two points is corresponding to the closer between each paper. We can see that the top 5 most productive co-cited reference in Table 3.

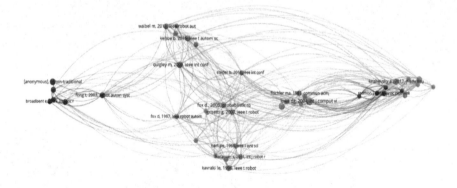

Fig. 2. Mapping on co-citation of references.

Table 3. The top 5 most productive co-cited reference.

Co-cited frequency	Cited article
85	Lowe Dg, 2004, Int j comput vision, V60, P91, https://doi.org/10.1023/b: visi.0000029664.99615.94
68	Dindo D, 2004, Ann surg, V240, P205, https://doi.org/10.1097/01.sla.000 0133083.54934.ae
67	Flores-abad A, 2014, Prog aerosp sci, V68, P1, https://doi.org/10.1016/j. paerosci.2014.03.002
57	Krizhevsky A., 2012, P adv neural inform, V25, P1097, https://doi.org/ 10.1145/3065386
54	Simonyan K., 2014, Arxiv, https://doi.org/10.1109/cvpr.2015.7298594

4   Research Trends Analysis

Figures 3 and 4 show the co-occurrence of author keywords by VOS viewer. The 215 minimum number of occurrences of a keyword was set 35, of the 18681 keywords, 97 keywords were divided into four clusters. Cluster 1 are mainly about design of robot. Cluster 2 are mainly design about task of robot collaborative service. Cluster 3 are mainly technology of robot collaborative service. Cluster 4 are mainly about fields of application of robot collaborative service. The latest burst keyword analysis shows that

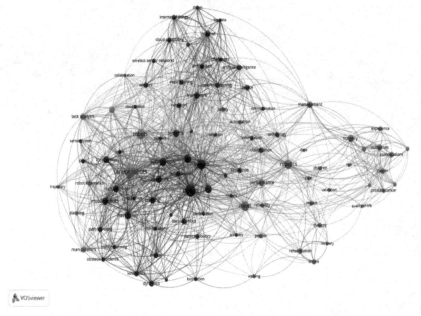

Fig. 3. Network visualization of co-occurrence of keywords.

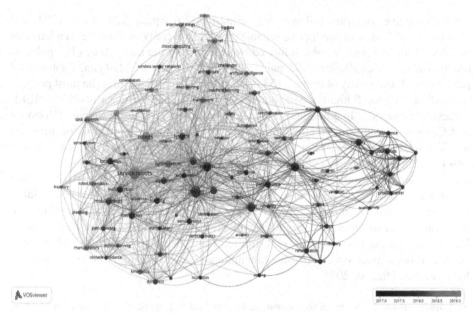

Fig. 4. Overlay visualization of co-occurrence of keywords.

"task", "robot sensing system", "robot kinematics", "deep learning" and "manipulators" have and burst end time of 2021.

5 Discussion

This study uses a quantitative and visual method to evaluate the history, current, and future of publications regarding robot collaborative service. Bibliometric analysis can be applied in an objective manner, eliminating the influence of subjective factors, and in this aspect, it is superior to peer review. However, it cannot take into consideration all special features of the objects to be assessed, that is to say, qualitative knowledge about the scholars involved and the sub-disciplines in which they are active should be combined with bibliometric data. Although relatively objective and comprehensive, there are some limitations in this study. First, extensive databases containing other languages should be considered. Second, predefined terms are used which may make some publications ruled out. Third, bibliometric data are dynamic, but this analysis is based on a static data. Hence, some newly published and outstanding articles may not be cited many times but with a rapid increase. In this condition, a bibliometric analysis may not reflect the truth.

6 Conclusion

This bibliometric analysis showed a visual and systematic review of robot collaborative service in detail by collecting every related paper from Web of science from 2011 to 2021. China (1279), USA (895), France (482), Italy (430), and England (380) are the top 5 productive countries, followed by Germany (370), Spain (329), Japan (273) and Canada (203). The most productive organization is University of Chinese Academic of Sciences with 105 publications, followed by Harbin institute technology (103 publications), University of Zhejiang (93 publications), University of Shanghai jiaotong (69 publications), University of munich (53 publications), etc. Bu jiajun is the most productive author. The top 5 highly cited journals are "Intelligent Service Robotics", "IEEE Access", "Sensors", "International Journal of Advanced Robotic Systems", "Robotics and Computer-integrated Manufacturing". The 215 minimum number of occurrences of a keyword was set 35, of the 18681 keywords, 97 keywords were divided into four clusters. Cluster 1 are mainly about design of robot. Cluster 2 are mainly about robot collaborative service design about task. Cluster 3 are mainly technology of underpins robot collaborative service. Cluster 4 are mainly about fields of application of robot collaborative service. All the summaries of this study mainly depends on databases from Web of science, extensive literature should be collected. Few conclusions may be one-sided. Hence, study should be updated in the future. The latest keyword analysis shows that "task", "robot sensing system", "robot kinematics", "deep learning" and "manipulators" have burst end time of 2021.

Acknowledgments. This work was supported by National Natural Science Foundation of China (grant numbers 71701003, 71801002), the Key Project for Natural Science Fund of Colleges in Anhui Province (grant numbers KJ2021A0502), and the Project for Social Science Innovation and Development in Anhui Province (grant numbers 2021CX075). Further, we thank the editor and anonymous reviewers for their valuable comments and advice.

References

1. Liu, Y., Wang, X.Y., Wang, S.Y.: Research on service robot adoption under different service scenarios. Technol. Soc. 1–2 (2016). https://doi.org/10.1016/j.techsoc.2021.101810
2. Wang, T.Y., Okada, S., Makikawa, M.: Classification of robot service during sit-to-stand through segments coordination. IEEE Photon. Technol. Lett. **29**, 907–31 (2018). https://doi.org/10.1109/LIFETECH52111.2021.9391961
3. Belanche, D., Casalo, L.V., Flavian, C., Schepers, J.: Service robot implementation: a theoretical framework and research agenda. Ser. Indu. J. **40**, 203–225 (2020). https://doi.org/10.1080/02642069.2019.1672666
4. Lai, CJ., Tsai, CP.: Design of introducing service robot into catering services. In: ICSRT '18: Proceedings of the 2018 International Conference on Service Robotics Technologies (2018). https://doi.org/10.1145/3208833.3208837
5. Tschichold-Gurman, N., Vestli, S.J., Schweitzer, G.: The service robot MOPS: first operating experiences. Robo. Autono. Sys. **34**, 165–173 (2001). https://doi.org/10.1016/S0921-8890(00)00120-2
6. Yu, Q.X., Yuan, C., Fu, Z., Zhao, Y.Z.: An autonomous restaurant service robot with high positioning accuracy. Industrial Robot **39**, 271–282 (2012). https://doi.org/10.1108/01439911211217107
7. Choi, Y., Choi, M., Oh, M., Kim, S.: Service robots in hotels: understanding the service quality perceptions of human-robot interaction. J. Hosp. Mark. Manag. **3**, 1–23 (2019). https://doi.org/10.1080/19368623.2020.1703871

8. Lai, C.J., Tang, H.K.: Investigation of human -service robot division and interaction for catering services. In: ICRSA 2019: Proceedings of the 2019 2nd International Conference on Robot Systems and Applications (2019). https://doi.org/10.1145/3378891.3378898

9. Garcia, E., Jimenez, M.A., De Santos, P.G., Armada, M.: The evolution of robotics research - from industrial robotics to field and service robotics. IEEE Rob. Auto. Mag. **14**(1) 90–103 (2007). https://doi.org/10.1109/MRA.2007.339608.2007

10. Yen, H.C., Hsia, T.C., Liao, R.C.: Machine learning in a humanoid intelligent service robot. J. Info. Opt. Sci. **35**, 129–141 (2014). https://doi.org/10.1080/02522667.2013.867737

11. Zhang, T., Yuan, Y., Ueno, H.: A knowledge model-based intelligent coordinative network platform for service robot system. IEEE Int. Conf. Rob. Bio. **12**, 15–18 (2007). https://doi.org/10.1109/ROBIO.2007.4522166

12. Ciupe, V., Maniu, I.: New Trends in Service Robotics. Springer (2014). https://doi.org/10.1007/978-3-319-01592-7_5

13. Pineda, L.A., Rodriguez, A., Fuentes, G., Rascon, C., Meza, I.V.: Concept and functional structure of a service robot. Int. J. Adv. Rob. Sys. **12**, 7 (2015). https://doi.org/10.5772/60026

Subjective Scores and Gaze Distribution in Personality Evaluations: Effect of Subjects' Clothing on Observers' Impressions of Them

Michiko Inoue(✉), Masashi Nishiyama⬤, and Yoshio Iwai

Graduate School of Engineering, Tottori University, 101 Minami 4-chome,
Koyama-cho, Tottori 680-8550, Japan
android63android63@gmail.com, nishiyama@tottori-u.ac.jp

Abstract. The clothing that coworkers and others wear in the workplace affects our evaluations of them, including what personality traits we ascribe to them. In this study, we sought to determine whether observers' subjective impressions of a subject's sincerity and nervousness vary depending on the subject's clothing, and the extent to which observers look at subjects' clothing while making those assessments. We measured subjective scores for sincerity and nervousness as components of personality traits perceived by observers. Specifically, we displayed stimulus images containing subjects wearing several types of clothing and measured observers' subjective scores and gaze distributions. The experimental results indicated that the subjects' clothing strongly affected the observers' subjective assessments of the subjects' sincerity and nervousness. We also confirmed that the observers gazed at both the subjects' clothing and head regions.

Keywords: Clothing · Personality evaluations · Subjective scores · Gaze

1 Introduction

In online-interaction interfaces, observers frequently form positive impressions of subjects in images displayed on screens, and also form unconscious impressions of those subjects. In particular, observers' impressions are strongly affected by the subjects' clothing (e.g., a woman's dress) [7]. Consider a female shopper exploring an apparel shopping website to purchase clothing to wear at the office. Figure 1 shows that she is concerned about what impression her clothing will give to observers; here, we consider that she is imagining herself wearing what the subjects in the images are wearing. In this paper, we report on our study on how observers perceive subjects wearing office-style clothing. We assumed that the observers were unfamiliar with the subjects.

© The Author(s), under exclusive license to Springer Nature Switzerland AG 2022
V. G. Duffy (Ed.): HCII 2022, LNCS 13319, pp. 220–230, 2022.
https://doi.org/10.1007/978-3-031-05890-5_18

Fig. 1. A user buying clothes is concerned about what impression they will give to observers.

We consider that the most important impressions will vary depending on individual contexts; however, many relevant impressions are formed in interpersonal relationships. For example, physical appearance is relevant to the impressions that are formed of employees who interact with the public face-to-face, such as retail clerks or ushers at trade shows. In contrast, personality traits such as sincerity and nervousness are relevant to the impressions that are formed of engineers in IT companies or of human resource personnel. In this study, we considered observers' impressions of others' personality traits in an office workplace. More specifically, we investigated sincerity and nervousness as components of one of the Big Five personality traits, conscientiousness and neuroticism [6]. The Big Five are the most commonly used basic personality traits.

Our aim was to quantitatively measure a subjective sincerity score and a subjective nervousness score from Japanese participants. Perceptions of others' sincerity and nervousness vary depending on various subjective elements, such as their hairstyle, facial expressions, and clothing. In this study, we focus on subjects who are wearing clothing for working in an office. In one study [5], it was reported that work clothing affects perceived personality traits. However, those authors used only a text-based questionnaire for analysis. No researcher has yet examined whether what people are wearing in images affects others' impressions of them. To partially close this research gap, we investigated the following hypothesis in the present study:

Main Hypothesis (H_m): Observers' subjective scores for a subject's sincerity and nervousness will vary depending on what the subject is wearing.

Furthermore, we investigated whether observers viewed subjects' clothes while making their assessments. It is generally well-known that an observer's gaze tends to fixate on the subject's head for a long duration [2]. On the basis of this knowledge, then, we investigated the following hypothesis:

Sub Hypothesis (H_s): Observers will gaze at a subject's clothing as well as their head while making assessments about the subject's sincerity and nervousness.

Experimental results showed that both hypotheses H_m and H_s were supported. We confirmed that the subjects' clothing strongly affected the observers' subjective assessments of the subjects' sincerity and nervousness. We also confirmed

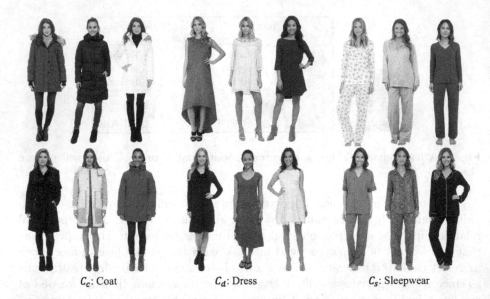

C_c: Coat C_d: Dress C_s: Sleepwear

Fig. 2. The clothing categories of coat C_c, dress C_d, and sleepwear C_s used in our investigation.

that the observers gazed at both the subject's clothing and head regions while making their assessments.

2   Methods for Measuring Subjective Scores and Gaze Distributions During Personality Evaluations

2.1   Stimulus Images

To investigate the hypotheses H_m and H_s, we selected stimulus images from a multiview clothing (MVC) dataset [9]. The MVC dataset consists of 161,260 images comprising 264 clothing category labels, such as button-up shirts, polos, tank tops, swimwear, and sweaters. Each stimulus image contained a person wearing clothing from one of the clothing categories, and was labeled accordingly (e.g., "tops and coats"). We selected only images of women in which the entire body was included. Furthermore, we selected only clothing category labels belonging to whole-body items such as dresses and coats, and eliminated categories containing exclusively upper- or lower-body items (e.g., tops or bottoms). The following labels were assigned to the clothing categories:

Clothing category C_c: Coat,
Clothing category C_d: Dress,
Clothing category C_s: Sleepwear.

Figure 2 shows examples of stimulus images for coat C_c, dress C_d, and sleepwear C_s. The reasons for selecting these clothing categories are described below. We

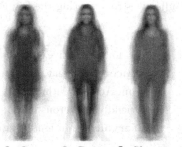

C_c: Coat C_d: Dress C_s: Sleepwear

Fig. 3. Average calculated from the stimulus images for each clothing category.

used coats C_c that are frequently worn when commuting to workplaces such as IT companies and to jobs such as human resources in Japan, where observers' impressions of personality traits are particularly important. We used a dress C_d typical of those worn by sales clerks at workplaces such as retail department stores and trade shows, where a person's appearance is especially salient. We used sleepwear C_s as a simple comparison with the other clothing categories.

We resized the height of all the stimulus images to 960 pixels while maintaining the aspect ratio of the original MVC dataset images. To control the experimental conditions, we used only the frontal orientation of the subject's body. Furthermore, each subject appeared in multiple images and wore different clothes in each. The number of stimulus images for each clothing category was 24 and the total number of stimulus images was 72. We checked the alignment of all the images using the average image computed from all the stimulus images. Figure 3 shows the averaged stimulus images for each clothing category. The positions of the face and torso were deemed to be in rough alignment, while the positions of the wrist and toes were not in alignment.

2.2   Personality Traits

We selected the adjectives to represent personality traits in the present study by referencing existing analytical studies [1,10] that employed the Big Five personality traits. These traits are categorized as [6]: openness to experience, conscientiousness, extraversion, agreeableness, and neuroticism. Table 1 lists the adjectives that represent the factors of each of the Big Five personality traits.

To detect differences in subjective scores, we used the contrasting categories of conscientiousness and neuroticism. Conscientiousness indicates a tendency toward responsibility, diligence, and seriousness, all of which are strongly associated with the workplace and specifically that found in many IT companies and in departments such as human resources. In contrast, neuroticism indicates a tendency toward strong stress tolerance, another feature associated with the workplace.

Table 1. Examples of adjectives representing the Big Five personality traits.

Trait	Adjectives
Openness to experience	Curious, Creative, Imaginative, Smart
Conscientiousness	**Sincere**, Diligent, Conscientious, Cautious
Extraversion	Fun, Active, Enthusiastic, Social
Agreeableness	Friendly, Generous, Kind, Forgiving
Neuroticism	**Nervous**, Emotional, Impulsive, Stressful

Finally, we selected the following adjectives to represent conscientiousness and neuroticism, respectively.

(a) Sincere
(b) Nervous

2.3 Body-Part Attention Probability for Analyzing Gaze Distribution

To investigate the sub hypothesis H_s, we measured the body-part attention probability [8] to validate where the observer's gaze fixated. The body-part attention probability indicated how long an observer viewed which of the subject's body parts in the stimulus image during gaze measurement. This allowed us to directly compare the body-part attention probabilities among all the stimulus images, which contained a variety of subject postures. For example, even though the subjects' hand postures differed among the stimulus images (e.g., the hand is in the pocket or the hand is raised), we could quickly check whether observers' gazes frequently fixated on the hands by viewing the values of the body-part attention probabilities.

To calculate the gaze attention probability, we used the procedure proposed by Kinoshita et al. [8]. Figure 4 shows the body parts used in our gaze analysis. We included 12 body parts: the nose of the face region, the left and right shoulders, the waist of the torso region, the left and right elbows, the left and right wrists, the left and right knees, and the left and right toes. All the body parts except the nose comprised the clothing region. Figure 5 shows examples of 12 body parts automatically detected by OpenPose [4].

2.4 Experimental Conditions

Twenty-four observers (13 men, 11 women; average age 21.9 years) participated in our experiment. We fully explained the limitations of gaze measurement to the participants and obtained their written consent. Figure 6 shows the experimental setting. The observer was seated at 65 cm from the display, and then adjusted the chair height so that their eye level was 110–120 cm above the ground while seated. The display size was 24 in. (resolution: 1920 × 1080 pixels, size: 53 cm × 30 cm).

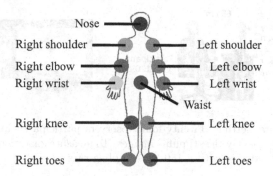

Fig. 4. The 12 body parts included in our gaze analysis. We used the nose of the face region, the left and right shoulders, the waist of the torso region, the left and right elbows, the left and right wrists, the left and right knees, and the left and right toes.

C_c: Coat C_d: Dress C_s: Sleepwear

Fig. 5. Examples of 12 body parts detected in the stimulus images for each subject's clothing category C_c, C_d, and C_s.

We used a Gazepoint GP3 HD eye tracker device to measure eye movement. The sampling rate 150 Hz, and the angular resolution was between 0.5 and 1.0°. We displayed the stimulus image at a random position on the screen to avoid center bias [3]. Each observer viewed 24 stimulus images, selected randomly from the repository of 72 stimulus images.

2.5   Procedure for Measuring Observers' Subjective Scores

The observers were asked the following questions for each stimulus image:

Q_s: How sincere do you perceive the subject to be?
Q_n: How nervous do you perceive the subject to be?

The observers gave their subjective rating for each image on a 4-point scale, ranging from 0 to 3. The higher the score, the more sincere or nervous the observer perceived the subject to be. We used the following procedure to measure observers' scores for the questions.

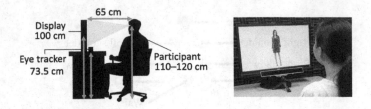

Fig. 6. Experimental setting. Twenty-four observers participated in our experiment. We used a screen to display the stimulus images. To measure gaze distribution, we used a gaze measurement device with a 150-Hz sampling rate.

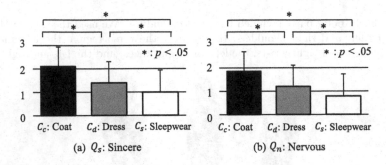

(a) Q_s: Sincere   (b) Q_n: Nervous

Fig. 7. Subjective scores relating to the main hypothesis H_m. In (a), we asked the question Q_s to measure perceived sincerity. In (b), we asked the question Q_n to measure perceived nervousness. We confirmed that the subjects' clothing (C_c, C_d, and C_s) strongly affected the observers' subjective assessments of their sincerity and nervousness.

P_1: We randomly selected one observer.
P_2: We set the question as either Q_s or Q_n.
P_3: We randomly selected one stimulus image.
P_4: We displayed a gray image presented on the screen for 2 s.
P_5: We displayed the stimulus image for 8 s while measuring the gaze movement.
P_6: We displayed a black image for 3 s, and the observer answered the question verbally.
P_7: We repeated the procedure P_3 to P_6 for 24 stimulus images.
P_8: We repeated the procedure P_2 to P_7 for the total number of observers.

3 Experimental Results

3.1 Results for the Main Hypothesis H_m

Figure 7 shows the subjective scores for the main hypothesis H_m. In this figure, (a) shows the results for sincere Q_s and (b) shows the results for nervous Q_n. It is clear that the subjective scores for coat C_c were highest and those for sleepwear C_s were lowest for both questions Q_s and Q_n. Furthermore, the subjective scores for coat C_c in (a) and (b) were higher than the neutral score of 1.5. Additionally,

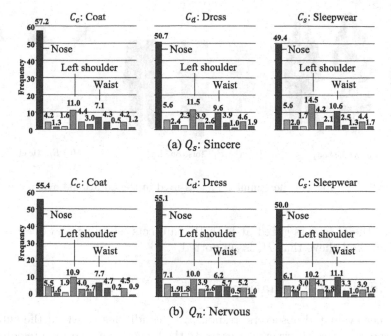

(a) Q_s: Sincere

(b) Q_n: Nervous

Fig. 8. Body-part attention probability (%) for clothing categories C_c, C_d, and C_s. In (a), we asked the question Q_s to measure perceived sincerity; in (b), we asked the question Q_n to measure perceived nervousness. All the body parts except for the nose corresponded to the clothing region. Observers viewed both the subjects' head regions and clothing regions.

the subjective scores for dress C_d and sleepwear C_s were lower than the neutral score of 1.5.

Next, we checked for significant differences in the subjective scores between the clothing categories, C_c, C_d, and C_s, using the Steel-Dwass test for multiple comparisons. Results showed significant differences ($p < .05$) in subjective scores among all the clothing categories for both questions Q_s and Q_n. We confirmed that the subjects' clothing strongly affected the observers' subjective assessments of their sincerity and nervousness. The results indicated that the observers perceived the subjects as more sincere and nervous when the subjects wore coats rather than dresses and sleepwear.

3.2   Results for the Sub Hypothesis H_s

Figure 8 shows the results of the body-part attention probability analysis. As described in Sect. 2.3, the region containing all the body parts except for the nose corresponds to the clothing region. The observers' gazes were fixed on the subjects' head region (i.e., containing the nose) for the most prolonged time duration, and on the subjects' clothing regions for the remaining time. We observed this same tendency for all clothing categories. From these results, we can con-

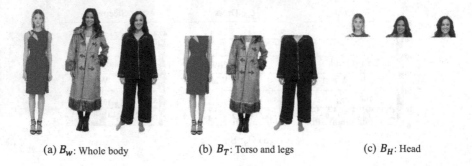

(a) B_W: Whole body   (b) B_T: Torso and legs   (c) B_H: Head

Fig. 9. Examples of the stimulus images used in the additional evaluation.

firm that the observers gazed at both the subjects' clothing and head regions. Therefore, we believe that H_s is supported.

4   Additional Evaluation

We further evaluated observers' responses to conditions in which the subjects' head regions (where observers' gazes fixate the longest) and clothing regions were alternately either visible or not visible. We set the stimulus image conditions as

B_W: Whole body,
B_T: Torso and legs,
B_H: Head.

Figure 9 shows the examples of the stimulus images. In condition B_W of (a) in this figure, the subject's whole body is visible, the same condition as that shown in Fig. 2. In condition B_T of (b), the top 20% of the stimulus image is obscured with the background color. In condition B_H of (c), the lower 80% of the stimulus image is obscured with the background color. The experimental conditions, except for the stimulus images, were the same as those described in Sect. 2.

Figure 10 shows the results for the subjective assessments of the whole body B_W, the torso and legs B_T, and the head B_H for both questions (i.e., regarding perceived sincerity Q_s and perceived nervousness Q_n). Note that the results for B_W shown in this figure are the same as those shown in Fig. 7. A comparison of whole body B_W and torso and legs B_T showed that the ranking order of the subjective scores for coat C_c, dress C_d, and sleepwear C_s was the same. By contrast, a comparison of whole body B_W and head B_H showed that the ranking order of the subjective scores for clothing categories C_c, C_d, and C_s differed. For questions about perceptions of sincerity Q_s when torso and legs B_T was displayed, the subjective score for coat C_c exceeded the neutral score of 1.5. For questions about perceptions of nervousness Q_n when torso and legs B_T was displayed, the subjective scores for C_c, C_d, and C_s did not exceed the neutral score of 1.5. For questions about perceptions of sincerity Q_s when head B_H was

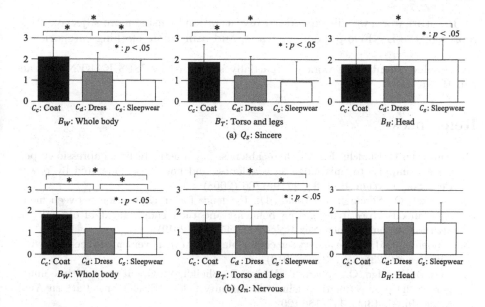

(a) Q_s: Sincere

(b) Q_n: Nervous

Fig. 10. Subjective scores for the stimulus image conditions of whole body B_W, torso and legs B_T, and head B_H used in the additional evaluation. In (a), we asked the question Q_s to measure perceived sincerity. In (b), we asked the question Q_n to measure perceived nervousness. All three clothing categories, C_c, C_d, and C_s, were used. By comparing this figure with Fig. 10, we could conclude that the stimulus images containing the subject's torso and legs, which represent the clothing region, significantly affected the observer's subjective scores compared with those containing only the subject's head region.

displayed, the subjective scores for C_c, C_d, and C_s were higher than the neutral score of 1.5. For questions about perceptions of nervousness Q_n when head B_H was displayed, the subjective scores frf C_c, C_d, and C_s were close to the neutral score. These results illustrate that the stimulus images containing the subject's torso and legs, which represented the clothing region, significantly affected the observers' subjective scores compared with those containing only the subject's head region.

5   Conclusions

In this study, we investigated the influence on observers of the type of clothing being worn by subjects in digitally presented stimulus images. More specifically, observers rated their subjective impressions of the subjects' personality traits in response to images showing subjects wearing a coat, a dress, or sleepwear. Both the main hypothesis H_m and the sub hypothesis H_s, respectively, were supported: observers' perceptions of a subject's sincerity and nervousness varied depending on what the subject was wearing, and observers gazed at both the clothing and the face of the subjects while making their assessments.

In future work, we will expand our investigation by using more adjectives that represent the Big Five personality traits, and using more clothing categories.

Acknowledgment. This work was partially supported by JSPS KAKENHI Grant No. JP20K11864.

References

1. Ames, D.R., Bianchi, E.: The agreeableness asymmetry in first impressions: perceivers' impulse to (mis)judge agreeableness and how it is moderated by power. Pers. Soc. Psychol. Bull. **34**, 1719–1736 (2008)
2. Bareket, O., Shnabel, N., Abeles, D.: Evidence for an association between men's spontaneous objectifying gazing behavior and their endorsement of objectifying attitudes toward women. Sex Roles **81**, 245–256 (2019)
3. Bindemann, M.: Scene and screen center bias early eye movements in scene viewing. Vis. Res. **50**(23), 2577–2587 (2010)
4. Cao, Z., Hidalgo, G., Simon, T., Wei, S.E., Sheikh, Y.: OpenPose: realtime multiperson 2D pose estimation using part affinity fields. IEEE Trans. Pattern Anal. Mach. Intell. **43**(1), 172–186 (2021)
5. Gillani, B.S., Haider, S.K., Jan, F.A.: The relationship of clothing with personal identity of different clothing style personalities among working women. J. Manag. Inf. **3**, 1–4 (2016)
6. Goldberg, L.R.: The development of markers for the big-five factor structure. Psychol. Assess. **4**(1), 26–42 (1992)
7. Johnson, K., Lennon, S.J., Rudd, N.: Dress, body and self: research in the social psychology of dress. Fashion Textiles **1**(1), 1–24 (2014). https://doi.org/10.1186/s40691-014-0020-7
8. Kinoshita, K., Inoue, M., Nishiyama, M., Iwai, Y.: Body-part attention probability for measuring gaze during impression word evaluation. In: Proceedings of 23rd International Conference on Human-Computer Interaction, pp. 105–112 (2021)
9. Liu, K.H., Chen, T.Y., Chen, C.S.: MVC: a dataset for view-invariant clothing retrieval and attribute prediction. In: Proceedings of the ACM International Conference on Multimedia Retrieval, pp. 313–316 (2016)
10. Nandi, A., Nicoletti, C.: Explaining personality pay gaps in the UK. Appl. Econ. **46**(26), 3131–3150 (2014)

A Dynamic Semantics for Multimodal Communication

Jeremy Kuhn$^{(\boxtimes)}$![ORCID]

Institut Jean Nicod, ENS, EHESS, CNRS, Département d'Etudes Cognitives,
PSL University, Paris, France
jeremy.d.kuhn@gmail.com
http://www.jeremykuhn.net/

Abstract. Dynamic semantics provides a mechanism by which information and discourse referents are introduced gradually into context as a discourse unfolds. Dynamic semantics involves left-to-right evaluation: discourse referents must be introduced before they can be accessed. (E.g. *John$_i$ entered the room. He$_i$ began to sing.* vs. **He$_i$ began to sing. John$_i$ entered the room.*) Anaphoric relations also depend on the local contexts introduced by logical operators; for example, pronominal reference is possible within the local context of *nobody* but not outside of it. (E.g. *Nobody received [a prize]$_i$ and bragged about it$_i$.* vs. **Nobody recieved [a prize]$_i$. It$_i$ was made of gold.*) Here, I argue that a similar dynamic system governs the iconic use of space in sign language. Intuitively, one must create a picture before one can point to it. This dynamic iconic system runs parallel to the grammatical system, but interfaces with it, with interpretation similarly modulated by local contexts. I discuss the interaction of 'dynamic iconicity' with sign language examples involving cataphora and embedded indefinites.

Keywords: Iconicity · Dynamic semantics · Sign language · Cataphora · Multimodality

1 Introduction

Human communication expresses meaning both through description ('grammar') and depiction ('iconicity') [7]. An English speaker may describe a scene with words and sentences at the same time as depicting it through co-speech gesture. In sign languages, description and depiction are arguably even more intertwined, with the signing space being used to iconically organize and depict referents that have been introduced in the discourse [8]. In this paper, focusing on data from

The research leading to these results received funding from ERC H2020 Grant Agreement No. 788077—Orisem (PI: P. Schlenker). Research was conducted at the Département d'Etudes Cognitives (ENS), which is supported by ANR-17-EURE-0017 FrontCog.

© The Author(s), under exclusive license to Springer Nature Switzerland AG 2022
V. G. Duffy (Ed.): HCII 2022, LNCS 13319, pp. 231–242, 2022.
https://doi.org/10.1007/978-3-031-05890-5_19

French Sign Language (LSF), I argue that both descriptive and depictive meaning should be represented using dynamic semantics, in parallel but interacting systems.

Dynamic semantics provides a mechanism by which information and discourse referents are introduced gradually into context as a discourse unfolds [10]. Dynamic semantics involves left-to-right evaluation: discourse referents must be introduced before they can be accessed, as shown in (1). Anaphoric relations also depend on the local contexts introduced by logical operators; in (2), for example, pronominal reference is possible only within the local context under *nobody*.

(1) Left-to-right evaluation

  a.   [A man]^i entered the room. He$_i$ began to sing.

  b.   * He$_i$ began to sing. [A man]^i entered the room.

(2) Sensitivity to local contexts

  a.   Nobody received [a prize]^i and bragged about it$_i$.

  b.   * Nobody recieved [a prize]^i. It$_i$ was made of gold.

Here, I argue that a similar dynamic system governs the iconic use of space in sign language. Intuitively, one must create a picture before one can point to it. This dynamic iconic system runs parallel to the grammatical system, but interfaces with it. I motivate this by looking at a number of linguistic phenomena. First, I look at cases of cataphora, or 'backwards anaphora,' which have been claimed to be more restricted in sign language than in spoken language. Second, I look at indefinites appearing in embedded contexts, where iconic inferences are interpreted relative to the local context.

2   Depictive Meaning

2.1   Descriptive and Depictive Representations over Time

Consider how a series of linguistic utterances, unfolding over time, change a discourse representation. In (3), we start out with an empty context; (3a) introduces John into the discourse context; (3b) introduces Mary; (3c) introduces Susan. Linguistic expressions that predicate about these discourse referents establish semantic relations between them (*see, call over*). As the discourse develops, these discourse referents can be referred to by pronouns.

(3) a. John entered.

  b.   Mary saw him.

  c.   She called Susan over.

Now consider how a pictorial production, unfolding over time, changes a discourse representation. In (4), we start out with an empty context; (4a) introduces A into the discourse context; (4b) introduces B; (4c) introduces x. Here, semantic relations are not introduced by linguistic expressions, but rather by holistic iconic mappings acting on the structural, configurational properties of the forms themselves: B is interpreted as a subset of A and x is interpreted as an element of A that is not in B. As the discourse develops, these discourse referents can be referred to, by the labels 'A,' 'B,' and 'x' that name the objects once they have been introduced, or by gestural pointing (in a multimodal setting).

(4)   a.   b.   c.

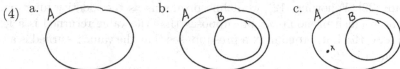

In either case, there is a mechanism to introduce discourse referents. There is a mechanism of predication (although descriptive relations and iconic relations are qualitatively different in nature). And there is a mechanism of indexicality or anaphoricity that allows the retrieval of discourse referents (but only those that have been introduced by that point in the discourse).

In multimodal utterances these two systems may interact. A speaker may point to a depicted object, and refer to it with linguistic anaphora, such as *this*, *that* or *it*. Iconic inferences may be generated about linguistically introduced discourse referents, via depictive elements (gestures, drawings, etc.) that co-occur with an utterance.

In what follows, I will show that sign language provides a rich case study to investigate the interaction of descriptive and depictive meaning. I will argue that the two different kinds of meaning can be productively seen as acting on two separate tiers of representation, with grammatical mechanisms that mediate between them. I will propose a model of the iconic level of meaning that draws heavily on recent theories of dynamic semantics, thus extending the theories that have been built for (3) to the representations manipulated in (4).

2.2 Spatial Features in Sign Language

Sign languages are well known to use space to index discourse referents. A noun phrase may be established at a locus—a point in the horizontal space in front of the signer. Later, the signer may direct a pronoun to this locus to retrieve the relevant discourse referent. This use of space in sign language mirrors the use of logical variables, motivating some researchers to posit that loci are in fact a syntactic realization of variable names [17,21].

On the other hand, [14,16] argue that loci are not themselves variables; rather, they act as morphological features that constrain the value of a pronoun. Specifically, [14] observes that two pronouns may appear at the same locus but nevertheless receive different interpretations. For example, the LSF sentence in (5a) may receive a reading in which one pronoun co-varies under ONLY but the other does not. Loci are thus closer in behavior to the gender features in (5b) than to the variable names in the logical form in (5c).

(5)   a.   ONLY JEAN-a QUESTION POSS-a MOTHER POSS-a FAVORITE COLOR.
             'Only Jean quizzed his mother about his favorite color.'

b. Only Jean quizzed his[masc] mother about his[masc] favorite color.

c. [only Jean^j] $\lambda x.x$ [quizzed j's mother about x's favorite color]

[16, p. 116]

One implementation of this insight is as a presupposition on the value of the pronoun [22]. Following [12], we define pronouns as the identity function. The feminine English pronoun *she* presupposes that the value returned is a female; by analogy, the LSF pronoun IX-a presupposes that the value returned is at locus a, as shown in (6).

(6)   a. $[\![\text{she}]\!] = \lambda x : \text{fem}(x) . x$

b. $[\![\text{IX-a}]\!] = \lambda x : \text{at}(a)(x) . x$

What remains defined, of course, is what the meaning of a locus is and what it means for a value to be 'at' this locus. Below, I will argue that loci like 'a' are referents in a iconic, pictorial representation that grows as discourse develops. Like in standard theories of dynamic semantics, a pictorial discourse referent must be introduced before it can be retrieved. Additionally, the pictorial representation generates iconic inferences arising from a mapping that preserves structural properties of loci. Depending on context, these inferences may include rich geometric structure, such as the geometric configuration of individuals in a three dimensional space, schematic properties such as set relations, or very minimal structure, approximating a simple list of referents. For present purposes, we will assume only a single iconic constraint on loci: namely, a single individual cannot be at two different loci at the same time.[1] This entails that (a) a pronoun at one locus may not be bound by an antecedent at a different locus and, (b) the use of two loci entails the existence of two distinct discourse referents.

3   Cataphora and Order Sensitivity

As mentioned in the introduction, dynamic systems show order sensitivity: discourse referents must be introduced before they can be accessed, as in (7).

(7)   a.   [A man]^i entered the room. He$_i$ began to sing.

b.   * He$_i$ began to sing. [A man]^i entered the room.

If iconic representations are also governed by a dynamic system, then we should expect to see similar order sensitivity. Here, I argue that evidence in favor of such order sensitivity comes from examples involving cataphora, in which a pronoun precedes its binder. Notably, on the definition in (6b), there are two values to be bound—the value of the pronoun (x), and the value of the locus (a). Even when a pronoun is subject to quantificational, in-scope binding, the locus

---

[1] We leave it open whether this is an entirely iconic constraint that can be weakened in appropriate contexts, or whether there is also a stricter constraint that requires morphosyntactic feature matching; of relevance, see [22] on bound iconic loci.

still requires dynamic binding of the iconic variable. I will argue that certain cases of cataphora allow a dissociation of these two levels. In these examples, quantificational binding of the pronoun proceeds as normal, but dynamic binding of the locus is no longer possible.

3.1 Cataphora as In-Scope Binding

Cataphora describes a phenomenon in which a pronoun precedes its binder, as shown in (8b).

(8) a.   Before Jean^i left the office, he$_i$ turned out the lights.

     b.   Before he$_i$ left the office, Jean^i turned out the lights.

Exactly what is going on in cases of cataphora has been the subject of some discussion [2,6]. One particular point of note regards the nature of binding in these examples: is it quantificational binding or dynamic binding? I think that a reasonable case can be made that at least some of these examples are cases of quantificational, in-scope binding. First, cataphora is becomes extremely degraded across sentence boundaries, as (9). This suggests that the binding relation in (8b) arises from sentence-internal mechanisms.

(9) a.   Jean^i left the office. He$_i$ forgot to turn out the lights.

     b.   * He$_i$ left the office. Jean^i forgot to turn out the lights.

Second, at least some cases of cataphora allow binding by quantificational expressions, including negative quantifiers, as in (10). These facts suggest that the subordinate clause in these examples is interpreted at a lower position (possibly adjoined to the verb phrase), where the pronoun is in the scope of the quantificational expression.

(10) a. When his$_i$ child throws a tantrum, [no father]^i can sit idly by.

      b. Unless they$_i$ bought it$_j$ in the last year, [none of my relatives]^i own [a gun]^j.

3.2 Iconic Constraints on Cataphora in Sign Language

Interestingly, it has been remarked occasionally that cataphora (or 'backwards anaphora') is significantly *less* available in sign language than it is in a spoken language like English [11,13,19]. An example from LSF is provided in (11). The syntactic structure is equivalent to the grammatical English example in (8); however, the LSF sentence becomes ungrammatical when an overt pronoun points to a locus where the antecedent will later be introduced, in (11b).

(11) a.   JEAN-a LEAVE OFFICE BEFORE, IX-a LIGHT-OFF
            'Before Jean left the office, he turned out the lights.'

    b.   * IX-a LEAVE OFFICE BEFORE, JEAN-a LIGHT-OFF
         Intended: 'Before he left the office, Jean turned out the lights.'

Koulidobrova and Lillo-Martin (2016) offer an informal explanation of this observation: one can't point to something (an object or a demonstration) until it has been introduced. This is exactly the constraint on iconcity that we aim to spell out in dynamic terms.

Expressing this as a constraint on space and iconicity makes a further prediction. Specifically, cataphora should sometimes be possible in LSF, but only in cases in which a non-iconic pronominal form is used. This prediction seems to be borne out. First, LSF (like a number of other sign languages) allows the use of null pronouns in certain positions. As observed by [21], since null pronouns have no overt form, they generate no iconic inferences and cannot be subject to iconic constraints. As seen in (12), null pronouns also *do* allow cataphora. Second, some relational nouns have been argued to involve implicit anaphora (*neighbor* = 'neighbor of x') [1,18]. Unlike pronouns, these nouns allow a neutral form that does not invoke any iconic use of space; for example, the sign NEIGHBOR in (13) is signed in the neutral space in front of the signer. As seen in (13), the interpretation of the sentence allows a cataphoric relation, in which the implicit argument is bound by the later noun phrase.[2]

(12)   __ LEAVE OFFICE BEFORE, JEAN-a LIGHT-OFF
      'Before he left the office, Jean turned out the lights.'

(13)   WHEN NEIGHBOR NOISE, MARIE-a CALL POLICE
      'When (her) neighbor makes noise, Marie calls the police.'

These examples provide further evidence that the unavailability of cataphora in examples like (11) arises from the use of space and iconicity.

3.3 Analysis: Cataphora with Iconicity

Based on the evidence in Sect. 3.1, we analyze our examples of cataphora as in-scope, quantificational binding. Specifically, we assume that a sentence with an adverbial phrase has an underlying structure in which the antecedent c-commands the pronoun that it binds. A syntactic operation dislocates the temporal phrase to the left, but a mechanism of reconstruction allows the pronoun to be interpreted in its lower position, bound by its antecedent.

To this static analysis, we add a dynamic component that manages the pictorial representation. That this representation is pictorial, and not just a list of discourse referents, will be seen in the fact that iconic inferences can be drawn the geometric relations between the locations in space. In the example below, though, only a single discourse referent is established in the dynamic picture, so no iconic inferences appear. The present system is thus for the moment highly similar to a standard dynamic semantics that manages discourse referents.

---

[2] In some cases, this interpretation may compete with an interpretation in which the implicit argument is interpreted as the signer—for example SISTER = 'my sister.'

Building on [3,4] meaning is modeled as a tuple which pairs the basic static meaning of an expression with its dynamic effect on the pictorial representation that is being constructed in context. For linguistic expressions that make no reference to this representation, their static meaning x can be converted to a dynamic type via the unit operator η in (14), which passes along a pictorial representation unchanged.

(14) $\eta(x) = \lambda \mathcal{P}.\langle x, \mathcal{P} \rangle$

We note that one formal difference between this model and standard dynamic models is that there is no nondeterminism. In linguistic utterances, indefinites like *somebody* can introduce discourse referents whose value varies across a set of assignment functions. In contrast, pictures are always definite, so only a single pictorial representation is needed at any given stage of the computation.

In iconic constructions, when noun phrases and pronouns are indexed in space, they manipulate or make reference to the pictorial representation. Noun phrases at loci introduce a new pictorial discourse referent, then presuppose that the relevant individual is at this pictorial referent, as shown in (15). Pronouns do not change the pictorial representation, but presuppose that the value that they return is at the indicated pictorial referent, as shown in (16).

(15) $[\![\text{JEAN-a}]\!] = \lambda \mathcal{P}. \left\langle \begin{cases} j & \text{if at}(a)(j) \text{ in } \mathcal{P}+a \\ \# & \text{otherwise} \end{cases} , \quad \mathcal{P} + a \right\rangle$

(16) $[\![\text{IX-a}]\!] = \lambda \mathcal{P}. \left\langle \begin{cases} \lambda x.x & \text{if at}(a)(x) \text{ in } \mathcal{P} \\ \# & \text{otherwise} \end{cases} , \quad \mathcal{P} \right\rangle$

The rules of composition are defined to pass dynamic information from left to right. Following [3], we define these rules directly, but see [5] for discussion about how to define them in terms of an applicative functor. Critically, in these definitions, regardless of whether a function appears to the left or the right of its argument, the pictorial information is updated first by the element on the left and then by the element on the right.

(17)   a.   A/B   B   →   A
               m n $\lambda \mathcal{P}.\langle f(x), \mathcal{P}'' \rangle$ where $\langle x, \mathcal{P}'' \rangle = n(\mathcal{P}')$
                                                                                                                        $\langle f, \mathcal{P}' \rangle = m(\mathcal{P})$

          b.   B   B\A   →   A
               m n $\lambda \mathcal{P}.\langle f(x), \mathcal{P}'' \rangle$ where $\langle f, \mathcal{P}'' \rangle = n(\mathcal{P}')$
                                                                                                                        $\langle x, \mathcal{P}' \rangle = m(\mathcal{P})$

As an example, consider an LSF sentence with an overt cataphoric pronoun. Since the subordinate clause appears linearly first, it updates the iconic representation first, via the definitions in (17). The resulting meaning is provided in (18). Of note, because the pronoun is evaluated before locus a has been introduced, the meaning presupposes that the value of the pronoun (Jean) is at a in the input context $\mathcal{P}$. This presupposition is not satisfied, so the sentence is infelicitous.

(18)   ⟦IX-a LEAVE OFFICE BEFORE, JEAN-a LIGHT-OFF⟧

$$= \lambda \mathcal{P}. \left\langle \begin{array}{ll} \text{light-off}(j) \text{ before leave}(j) & \text{if at(a)}(j) \text{ in } \mathcal{P} \\ & \text{and at(a)}(j) \text{ in } \mathcal{P}\text{+a} \quad, \quad \mathcal{P} + \text{a} \\ \# & \text{otherwise} \end{array} \right\rangle$$

4   Iconicity and Local Contexts

4.1   The Problem with Presuppositions on the Global Context

[14] evaluates a hypothesis, very similar to the one proposed here, on which loci introduce a presupposition that constrains the full range of values that can be taken by a pronoun. The hypothesis is stated in (19).

(19)   **Referential locus hypothesis:** In a context c, the value of a locus is provided by the assignment function g_c, where $g_c(i)$ is the set of type $\langle e, t \rangle$ that corresponds to the noun indexed at locus i in c.

  a. $\forall$ assignment functions s, $\llbracket \text{IX-}i_k \rrbracket = s(k)$ if $s(k) \in g_c(i)$; $\#$ otherwise

[14, p. 455]

[14] ultimately rejects this hypothesis, however, based on examples in ASL in which two quantified expressions range over the same set of individuals. Empirically, [14] observes that the two quantifiers in (20)–(21) may both range over the same set of individuals; in (20), for example, John may be either the helper or the person helped. If loci introduce a global presupposition on the values that a pronoun can take, this means that the presupposition introduced by locus a and locus b will be identical, since $g_c(a) = g_c(b)$. And, if IX-a and IX-b carry exactly the same presupposition, then a pronoun at either locus is predicted to be ambiguous. But this prediction is not borne out: pointing to locus a or locus b *does* disambiguate the sentence.

(20)   WHEN SOMEONE-a HELP SOMEONE-b, IX-b HAPPY
     'When someone helps someone, he [=the latter] is happy.'

(21)   [ALL BOY]-a TELL [ALL OTHER BOY]-b IX-a WILL WIN
     'Every boy told every other boy that he [=the former] would win.'

(ASL; [14, p. 456])

I contest that the source of this problem is that the presupposition in (19) is taken to be a constraint on the *global context*. A related presupposition, such as the one I have proposed in (6b), can avoid these pathological predictions if we relativize the presupposition to the *local context* of the locus.

4.2   Local Contexts in Dynamic Semantics

A local context describes the immediate scope in which an expression is interpreted. This includes information from the global context (roughly, the common ground), but also incorporates information about the syntactic environment in which the expression appears [20].

For non-iconic phenomena, constraints related to discourse reference have been shown to be sensitive to the local context. The simplest such constraint is that a pronoun can only be used in a context in which it has a non-empty value. For example, as foreshadowed in the introduction, the pronoun in (22a) cannot be anaphoric to the indefinite *a prize*, since the context in which it appears entails that there is no such object. This, however, does not mean that no such discourse referent is introduced—indeed, a pronoun within the scope of *nobody* can refer back to it felicitously, as in (22b). In its local context, this pronoun has a non-empty value.

(22) a.   * Nobody recieved [a prize]^i. It$_i$ was made of gold.

         b.   Nobody received [a prize]^i and bragged about it$_i$.

Similarly, the adjectives *other* and *else* presuppose the existence of another individual—but once again, this is evaluated with respect to the local context. Examples (23)–(25) illustrate the point. In (23), the two indefinites are unembedded, so the local context and the global context are the same; the sentence entails that there are two boys, one who coughed and one who laughed. In examples with embedding, though, the local context and global context differ, generating different judgments. In (24a), for example, *another American* is interpreted in the scope of the *when* clause; in this local context, the existence of another American has been entailed, so the presupposition of *another* is satisfied. In contrast, in (24b), *another American* appears in the following sentence, in a global context which does not entail the existence a first American; the sentence is thus degraded. Similarly, in (25a), *every other boy* is interpreted in the distributive scope of *every boy*, a local context which entails the existence of another boy. In the global context, the two quantified expressions can thus range over the same set of individuals. But in (25b), when *every other boy* appears in the following sentence, *other* must be interpreted with respect to the global context, so the only interpretation is one in which the there are two distinct groups of boys, one which coughed and one which laughed.

(23) One boy coughed. Another boy laughed.

(24) a.   When an American sees another American, they say hi.

         b.   ? When an American goes to Paris, they take a lot of pictures. When another American goes to Paris, they go to the Louvre.

(25) a.   Every boy told every other boy that he would win.

         b.   ? Every boy coughed. Every other boy laughed.

4.3 Local Contexts for Iconicity

Parallels with the English examples in (24a) and (25a) can help us understand the ASL examples in (20) and (21). As discussed in Sect. 2.2, we have been assuming a rather weak iconic inference—namely, that the use of two loci entails that there are two distinct individuals. By analogy with the English examples, it is clear that this is satisfied in the local contexts for both of the ASL sentences.

On the other hand, because this iconic inference is so weak, it is impossible to dissociate it from inferences that already arise from (20) and (21). Specifically, the existence of two distinct individuals is already strongly implicated by (20) and is entailed by the word OTHER in (21), independent of the use of loci.

In order to isolate the contribution of the iconic inference, and its modulation by the local context, we can thus consider new examples in which the use of two indefinites does not independently implicate the existence of two individuals. The sentences in (26) provide one such example, in which the signer is explaining the rules of a card game. In (26a), the same locus is used twice; in (26b), two distinct loci are used. In both (26a) and (26b), the values of SOMEONE range over the set of all individuals; the use of space thus does not introduce any global constraints on the interpretation of these pronouns. However, within the local context introduced by the conditional IF, there is an iconic inference. When two distinct locations in space are used, the two discourse referents must be distinct. In (26a), the person who loses may or may not be the person who drew the card; in contrast, (26b) entails that the person who loses is *not* the person who drew the card. Iconic inferences thus exist, but they, like the presupposition of *other*, are evaluated with respect to the local context.

(26)   *Context:* Explaining the rules of a card game

　　a. IF SOMEONE-a DRAW IX SNAKE, SOMEONE-a LOSE.
　　　　'If someone draws the snake card, someone loses.'

　　b. IF SOMEONE-a DRAW IX SNAKE, SOMEONE-b LOSE
　　　　'If someone draws the snake card, someone else loses.'

Finally, we note that [15] argues that, while it is not obligatory, there is often a *tendency* to interpret iconicity with respect to the global context. Such an inference may have a variety of effects, including a preference to avoid bound pronouns under negative quantifiers when other strategies are available [9], or the preference of some signers to interpret (21) as referring two groups of students, analogous to the interpretation of (25b) [14].

5   Conclusion

Drawing on a number of sign language phenomena in which grammatical operations intersect with iconicity, I have argued that iconic representations are governed by a dynamic system that is order-sensitive and mediated by local contexts. I have provided an explicit proposal in which descriptive and depictive meaning are represented in parallel but interacting systems, which thread a growing iconic representation through the discourse.

References

1. Barker, C.: Possessive Descriptions. CSLI Publications, Stanford (1995)
2. Brasoveanu, A., Dotlačil, J.: Incremental and predictive interpretation: experimental evidence and possible accounts. In: D'Antonio, S., Moroney, M., Little, C.R. (eds.) Proceedings of the 25th Semantics and Linguistic Theory Conference (SALT 25), pp. 57–81. LSA and CLC Publications (2015). https://doi.org/10.3765/salt.v25i0.3047
3. Bumford, D.: Incremental quantification and the dynamics of pair-list phenomena. Semant. Pragmatics **8**(9), 1–70 (2015). https://doi.org/10.3765/sp.8.9
4. Charlow, S.: On the semantics of exceptional scope. Ph.D. thesis, New York University (2014)
5. Charlow, S.: Static and dynamic exceptional scope (2019). Manuscript, Rutgers University. https://ling.auf.net/lingbuzz/004650
6. Chierchia, G.: Dynamics of Meaning: Anaphora, Presupposition, and the Theory of Grammar. University of Chicago Press, Chicago (1995)
7. Clark, H.H.: Depicting as a method of communication. Psychol. Rev. **123**(3), 324–347 (2016). https://doi.org/10.1037/rev0000026
8. Goldin-Meadow, S., Brentari, D.: Gesture, sign and language: the coming of age of sign language and gesture studies. Behav. Brain Sci. (2015). https://doi.org/10.1017/S0140525X15001247
9. Graf, T., Abner, N.: Is syntactic binding rational? In: Proceedings of the 11th International Workshop on Tree Adjoining Grammars and Related Formalisms, Paris, France, pp. 189–197 (2012)
10. Groenendijk, J., Stokhof, M.: Dynamic predicate logic. Linguist. Philos. **14**(1), 39–100 (1991). https://doi.org/10.1007/BF00628304
11. van Hoek, K.: Anaphora and Conceptual Structure. University of Chicago Press, Chicago (1997)
12. Jacobson, P.: Towards a variable free semantics. Linguist. Philos. **22**(2), 117–184 (1999)
13. Koulidobrova, H., Lillo-Martin, D.: A 'point' of inquiry: the case of the (non-) pronominal IX in ASL. In: Grosz, P., Patel-Grosz, P. (eds.) Impact of Pronominal Form on Interpretation. Studies in Generative Grammar. Mouton de Gruyter (2016)
14. Kuhn, J.: ASL loci: variables or features? J. Semant. **33**(3), 449–491 (2016). https://doi.org/10.1093/jos/ffv005
15. Kuhn, J.: Logical meaning in space: iconic biases on quantification in sign languages. Language **96**(4), e320–e343 (2020). https://doi.org/10.1353/lan.2020.0082
16. Kuhn, J.: Disjunctive discourse referents in French sign language. In: Kwon, C., Dreier, N. (eds.) Proceedings of the 31st Semantics and Linguistic Theory Conference (SALT 31) (2021)
17. Lillo-Martin, D., Klima, E.: Pointing out differences: ASL pronouns in syntactic theory. In: Fischer, S., Siple, P. (eds.) Theoretical Issues in Sign Language Research, vol. 1, pp. 191–210. University of Chicago Press, Chicago (1990)
18. Partee, B.H.: Binding implicit variables in quantified contexts. In: Wiltshire, C., Music, B., Graczyk, R. (eds.) Papers from CLS 25, pp. 342–56. Chicago Linguistic Society, Chicago (1989)
19. Sandler, W., Lillo-Martin, D.: Sign Language and Linguistic Universals. Cambridge University Press, Cambridge (2006)

20. Schlenker, P.: Local contexts. Semant. Pragmatics **2**(3), 1–78 (2009)
21. Schlenker, P.: Donkey anaphora: the view from sign language (ASL and LSF). Linguist. Philos. **34**(4), 341–395 (2011). https://doi.org/10.1007/s10988-011-9098-1
22. Schlenker, P.: Featural variables. Nat. Lang. Linguist. Theory **34**(3), 1067–1088 (2015). https://doi.org/10.1007/s11049-015-9323-7

The Interaction Space
Considering Speaker-Hearer Location in Co-speech Gesture Analysis and Annotation

Schuyler Laparle$^{(\boxtimes)}$ (iD)

University of California, Berkeley, Berkeley, CA 94704, USA
schuyler_laparle@berkeley.edu

Abstract. This paper argues for the importance of addressee position in the annotation and analysis of co-speech gesture. In the case of deictic (e.g. Kita 2003) and 'interactive' gestures (e.g. Bavelas et al. 1992), gesture position relative to both interlocutors is recognized as a primary component of the gesture's meaning. I argue that the attention granted to gesture position in these special cases should be extended to gesture description more generally. In order to implement this argument, I introduce the 'interaction space', defined as the physical space between the speaker and their primary addressee. The meaning of a gesture's position, and its contribution to discourse management, is then described relative to this shared interaction space, rather than the speaker-centred 'personal gesture space' used more traditionally in gesture analysis.

Keywords: Co-speech gesture · Discourse structure · Deixis

1 Introduction

When we speak, we move, and as we move, we consider the affordances permitted by the space around us. We know how far we have to extend our arm to grab a glass of water on the table in front of us, the hand shape we would use to pick it up, and how energetically we can gesture without knocking the glass over.

When in a dialogue with a co-present interlocutor, we also consider the affordances granted to them, and how they may align or not with our own spatial perception. This is most clearly demonstrated in "deictic" gestures, such as pointing to an object to incite joint attention [23]. However, speakers are attuned to their interlocutor's affordances throughout co-present communication, not just in moments of overt spatial reference to an object. This paper argues that all

I would like to thank my advisors, Eve Sweetser and Line Mikkelsen, for their support in the evolution of this project. I would also like to thank my research assistants, Annabel Davis, Char Juin Chin, Kahini Achrekar, Kat Huynh, Karsen Paul, Miranda Cheung, Pranav Jayachand, Sarah Roberts, Sanjeev Vinodh and Irene Yi for their help in data collection. Lastly, I would like to thank Andy Lücking, Alexander Mehler, and Cornelia Ebert for providing a supportive and productive interdisciplinary space in which to share my work.

© The Author(s), under exclusive license to Springer Nature Switzerland AG 2022
V. G. Duffy (Ed.): HCII 2022, LNCS 13319, pp. 243–262, 2022.
https://doi.org/10.1007/978-3-031-05890-5_20

communicative gestures are made relative to the position of both the speaker and their addressee(s), where 'communicative gesture' means any movement of the head, face, body or hands that conveys meaning in concert with the accompanying speech. This entails that understanding a gesture's function and meaning requires consideration of both interlocutors' positions. To systematically encode and discuss this spatial information, I introduce the *interaction space*, a space between interlocutors used to organize and manage discourse.

The interaction space is defined in full in Sect. 2. The discussion of how speakers use the interaction space is then divided into two sections. First, I discuss the physical delineation of the interaction space and how speakers use bodily orientation to regulate engagement with different interlocutors (Sect. 3). I then turn to the internal structure of the interaction space, and discuss how it is organized in relation to both interlocutors (Sect. 4). Section 5 concludes with suggestions for implementing the proposed system and directions for future research.

2   Position and Orientation in Gesture Studies

The position of gesture, when it is described at all, is largely described relative to the speaker's body only, as demonstrated by the predominance of McNeill's gesture space [27,29] in the gesture literature. This traditional personal gesture space is roughly a cube in front of the speaker's chest. It is primarily this personal gesture space that is used in proposed annotation schemes, especially those designed for computer modelling [22].

The importance of considering *mutual* space when analyzing gesture is recognized for specific 'types' of gesture, namely 'deictic' gestures (e.g. pointing) used to incite joint attention, and 'interactive' gestures used to manage the social interaction [1,23]. Recognition of the importance of mutual space to gesture more broadly is limited, but includes Sweetser and Sizemore's work on 'interpersonal space' [44] and Kendon's work on 'use space' [21]. However, these discussions have yet to make it into common practice in either gesture analysis or annotation. The increasingly popular view of gesture as fundamentally *multifunctional* makes this even more problematic, as we begin to understand *every* gesture as having deictic and interactive components [25,43]. To remedy this, I argue that an 'interaction space' must be routinely included in gesture analysis.[1]

The interaction space, as defined here, consists of all space in between interlocutors along the 'speaker-hearer line' [44,45], at approximately the width and height of the individual's personal gesture spaces.[2] This is depicted in Fig. 1. Unlike Sweetser & Sizemore's 'interpersonal space', which is only the space

---

[1] The term 'interaction space' is chosen intentionally, as it appears informally in discussions of spatial meaning in gesture, but, to my knowledge, has yet to be formalized.

[2] Just as the size of the personal gesture space varies across individuals and speech communities [8,20,27], so might the size of the interaction space. The interaction space should be considered to scale up or down in accordance with the participants' personal gesture spaces.

in between the interlocutors' personal gesture spaces, the proposed interaction space subsumes both the interpersonal space and the individuals' personal gesture spaces. The dimensions and management of the interaction space are also influenced by the particular affordances of the physical space in which the discourse is taking place. For example, a desk between interlocutors may effectively raise the lower limit of the interaction space.

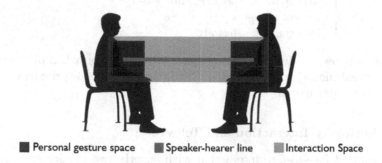

■ Personal gesture space   ■ Speaker-hearer line   ■ Interaction Space

Fig. 1. Gesture space

With this proposal, I do not mean to abandon the more traditional personal gesture space. Instead, I advocate for an understanding of gesture meaning such that the position of a gesture can convey meaning, often simultaneously, in relation to both the speaker's personal space and the shared interaction space. However, the meaning conveyed is different. Under this proposal, only the interaction space is used for discourse management; gesture position relative to a speaker's personal gesture space does not convey interactive meaning, and is not used to manage a discourse's structure. Following from this, I argue that where interactive meaning and discourse structure are the main focus of study, gesture position should be described and analyzed relative to the interaction space.

The interaction space is used to convey interactive meaning and manage discourse structure in two ways. First, speakers can manage their *engagement* with an interaction space. By orienting their heads, gaze, body, and manual gestures *toward* an interlocutor, speakers *engage* with the interaction space, and signal the start or continuation of a discourse. By moving or turning away from an interlocutor, speakers *disengage* from the interaction space, signalling a desire to discontinue the present discourse. This form of management via the interaction space is discussed in Sect. 3. Second, the participants of a given interaction space can perform actions on the contents of an interaction space by introducing, locating, and removing physical and virtual objects that are under discussion. This form of management is discussed in Sect. 4.

Formally, I define the interaction space as a tuple consisting of *participants*, who delineate the physical boundaries of the interaction space, *content*, physical and virtual objects within the interaction which pertain to the discourse, and *management*, the actions participants perform on the content. Every discourse move by a participant (roughly each utterance and distinct gesture sequence) corresponds to a distinct state of the interaction space (IS_t). Each state is specified for participants and their roles (speaker or addressee), contents (active discourse topics and referents), and the action that the speaker performs on the contents via gesture. Below is a proposed formal representation of an interaction space state t.

$$(1) \quad IS_t = \begin{cases} \text{Participants} : \textit{Speaker, Addressee} \\ \text{Content} : \textit{Topics} \\ \text{Management} : \textit{Action} \end{cases}$$

I will only use the full interaction space representation when discussing discourse content management in Sect. 4. Until then, I will focus primarily on interaction space participants.

2.1   Multiparty Interaction and Television

In an idealized face-to-face interaction with exactly two participants, the proposed interaction space is relatively straightforward. However, actual communication rarely occurs under such neat conditions. We are frequently attending to multiple social, physical, and cognitive tasks at once [31]. We shift our attention between friends at dinner, juggle attending to our pet, distracted child, and partner every morning, and never quite finish our phone call by the time we get to the counter or board the bus. In all of these cases, it is not enough to simply say that there is an interaction space between interlocutors which is maintained and managed throughout a discourse. We need systematic ways to account for distractions, digressions, and multitasking. We need clear mechanisms for the creation, activation, and closing of these spaces, and for that we can look to the study of proxemics – how body position and orientation mediates social interaction [11,13,14,19,21]. Following this tradition, I argue that an interaction space is created and maintained when a speaker orients their head and body toward an interlocutor, their primary addressee at the time of speaking. When a speaker turns away from an interlocutor, breaking the speaker-hearer line, they are disengaging from that particular interaction space, either temporarily to attend to another interaction, or permanently to end the interaction.

To account for the complexities of multiparty interaction, I suggest that multiple interaction spaces can be 'open' at any given time, so long as each open interaction space has an existing discourse structure that can be referred to and added to by the interlocutors maintaining the space.

All data in this study comes from interviews between a talk show host and at least one guest on a television set with a live audience.[3] This means that there

---

[3] With the exception of the final example, all data comes from UCLA's television news archive, accessed in collaboration with the Red Hen Lab. For these examples, corpus file names are given. The final example was found serendipitously, and a youtube link is provided.

is always, at least, two open interaction spaces: a space between the interviewer and interviewee, and a space between the speaker and the live audience. Both of these spaces are considered open and active throughout the interview since the behavior of the speaker is observable by all co-present interlocutors. However, in most cases only one interaction space is in *focus*. This is the space in which the speaker is actively managing a discourse, by acting on topics in the interaction space between them and their primary addressee. We will consider interaction spaces to exist only between *pairs* of interlocutors. When it appears that a speaker is dividing their attention across multiple spaces at once, we will consider both spaces to be in focus.[4]

3 Interaction Spaces in Focus

In complex multiparty interactions, such as those discussed in this paper, speakers must navigate a set of distinct, often partially overlapping, interaction spaces. As shown in previous work, this is primarily done through the orientation of the speaker's body, head, and gaze [4,18]. When a speaker is oriented toward an addressee, they are considered engaged in the interaction space between themselves and that particular addressee. It is this interaction space that is in focus, and the discourse encoded in this space that is being managed.

In the remainder of this section I discuss three examples in which communication either succeeds or fails based on the speaker's capacity to orient themselves toward the appropriate interlocutor. In the first example, the speaker switches between interaction spaces of co-present interlocutors – the interviewer and the live audience. In the following two examples, the speaker attempts to *create* an interaction space between themselves and an imagined interlocutor, but only succeeds in doing so when they carefully avoid engaging in another open interaction space.

For each example, I introduce the participants and basic discourse context, including a list of open interaction spaces. I then provide screen shots of relevant gesture sequences and a co-indexed transcript.

3.1 Co-present Participants and Space Shifting

Perhaps the most straightforward navigation of multiple interaction spaces can be seen when a speaker pauses a discourse in order to engage in another interaction. This first example comes from an interview between the American talk show

---

[4] There is a helpful analogy to be made between this navigation of interaction spaces and Mental Spaces theory [9]. Each mental space, roughly the state of a possible world at a particular time, contains distinct information which can be negotiated and added to independently of other spaces. Using this analogy to understand the creation and maintenance of interaction spaces has the added benefit of aligning with a growing body of gesture literature integrating the concept of mental spaces with gesture interpretation [35,39,42].

host Stephen Colbert and American comedian Kathy Griffin.[5] Griffin is telling
Colbert about how she successfully promoted her own show when professional
promoters refused to work with her. The audience cheers for her success, at which
point she turns to address them directly, thanking them for their applause. There
are thus two interaction spaces open to Griffin, one between her and Colbert,
and one between her and the studio audience.

(2)   Spaces available to Griffin in discourse excerpt (3):
      $IS1$ = Participants: $Griffin_S$, $Colbert_A$
      $IS2$ = Participants: $Griffin_S$, $Audience_A$

Now consider Griffin's movements between these spaces, as given in Fig. 2.
From Griffin's head and gaze orientation, we can see that she is engaged in IS1
(Griffin & Colbert) in frames A-B, E, and G; and IS2 (Griffin & audience) in
C-D. In frame F, Griffin appears to not be actively engaged in *any* space, as she
looks up and leans her head away from both open interaction spaces.

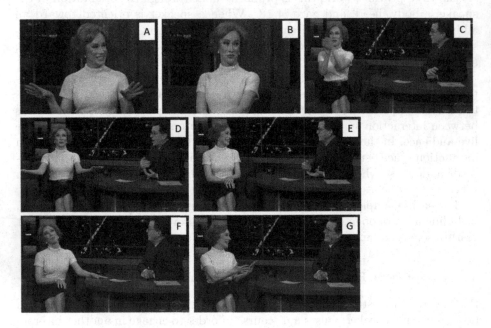

Fig. 2. Frames depicting the interaction between Kathy Griffin and Stephen Colbert,
corresponding to the transcript in (3).

These shifts in orientation align directly with two significant changes in the
discourse structure. A transcript of this discourse excerpt is provided in (3). To
the left of each line is a letter corresponding to the relevant frame in Fig. 2.

---

[5] File name: 2018-12-08_0735_US_KCBS_The_Late_Show_With_Stephen_Colbert.

To the right of each line, the open interaction spaces are given (IS1, IS2), with the focused interaction space underlined.

(3) **A**   GRIFFIN: so um I had everyone in Hollywood saying   [IS1, IS2]
               you can't sell any tickets
     B   GRIFFIN: and I sold out Carnegie Hall in less than 24   [IS1, IS2]
               hours
     C   GRIFFIN: Thank you   [IS1, IS2]
     D   GRIFFIN: Thank you   [IS1, IS2]
     E   GRIFFIN: [*laughs*]   [IS1, IS2]
     (off screen) COLBERT: I never sold out Carnegie hall
     (off screen) GRIFFIN: I sold it out five times
     F   GRIFFIN: Anyway um   [IS1, IS2]
     G   GRIFFIN: so... so then I decided to promote my own   [IS1, IS2]
               shows

Lines A-B are a part of the main discourse, the interview. Each of the two lines expresses a step in the story she is telling about promoting her own shows, and is accompanied by a distinct gesture. First, Griffin performs a two-handed palm down gesture signalling the exhausitivity ("everyone in Hollywood", "any tickets") and negation ("can't sell") that is co-expressed in the aligned speech (ex. 3, line A).[6] Next, Griffin performs a facial gesture consisting of a smirk and eyebrow raise, aligning with the story's 'punch line' (ex. 3, line B).

Griffin's first shift away from the main interaction space between her and Colbert coincides with a digression from the main discourse. Her reorientation toward the audience contributes to maintaining a coherent discourse structure in two ways. First, Griffin's reorientation toward the audience disambiguates the deictic pronoun "you" in lines C-D – because of her orientation, we know which interaction space is in focus and that her primary addressee is the audience, not Colbert. Second, the expressions of gratitude are *not* a part of the story she is telling, this is also disambiguated by her disengagement from the interaction space in which her main storytelling takes place.

Griffin then momentarily returns to the interaction space she shares with Colbert, at which point Colbert begins another digression from the main discourse with an aside about his relative lack of success selling out Carnegie Hall. To recover from this second digression, Griffin disengages from the interaction space once more, while using the discourse marker "anyway" to co-express the end of the digression in speech [34]. When Griffin finally returns to her story, she

---

[6] See discussions of formally and functionally similar gestures in the work of Harrison and Kendon [15, 20].

also fully reengages with the interaction space between her and Colbert by reorienting her head, body and gaze toward Colbert and performing a presentational gesture with open upturned hands, as if to present an object for inspection.[7]

3.2 Imagined Participants and Space Creation

Things get even more interesting when *imagined* participants are introduced. In this section I will discuss two examples of speakers addressing an imagined interlocutor, one which succeeds rhetorically, and one which results in a derailment of the discourse. I show that the relative success or failure of these performances is dependent on the speaker's ability to navigate existing interaction spaces and to create new temporary spaces.[8]

In the first example, American actor Lin-Manuel Miranda is telling his interviewer, Stephen Colbert, about a Twitter habit he has, tweeting "goodnight", and the misunderstandings that have resulted from it.[9] In this humorous clip, Miranda pretends to engage directly with his Twitter followers, trying to explain the confusion (he's not *actually* going to bed when he logs off of Twitter). As in the previous example, there are two open interaction spaces, one between Miranda and Colbert (IS1), and one between him and the audience (IS2). Miranda then creates a third interaction space (IS3) between and above these two, in which he can unambiguously address his imagined interlocutors. This is summarized in (4).

(4)   Spaces available to Miranda in discourse excerpt (5):
      $IS1$ = Participants: *Miranda$_S$, Colbert$_A$*
      $IS2$ = Participants: *Miranda$_S$, Audience$_A$*
      $IS3$ = Participants: *Miranda$_S$, Twitter followers$_A$*

Now consider how Miranda reorients himself to each of these three spaces in Fig. 3. In frames A and B, Miranda is oriented toward Colbert with both his gaze and body (IS1). In frame C, he then widens the two-handed open palm gesture he was holding and turns toward the audience (IS2). Still holding the two-handed gesture, Miranda then looks up to a space that is between and above Colbert and the audience, thus creating a third space in which to interact with his imagined Twitter followers (IS3). Finally, in frame E, Miranda returns to the interaction space between him and Colbert to continue his explanation (IS1).

---

[7] See the work of Müller for extensive discussion of the pervasiveness of so-called 'palm up open hand' presentational gestures in language [30].

[8] Similar imagined space creation has been described in the enactment of quotation in narrative discourse [40,41,44].

[9] File name: 2018-11-23_0735_US_KCBS_The_Late_Show_With_Stephen_Colbert.

Fig. 3. Frames depicting Miranda shifting between real and imagined interaction spaces, corresponding to the transcript in (5).

As before, a transcript of this discourse excerpt is provided in (5). To the left of each line is a letter corresponding to the relevant frame in Fig. 3. To the right of each line, the open interaction spaces are given (IS1, IS2, and sometimes IS3), with the focused interaction space underlined. Because IS3 is a created space delineated by Miranda and an imaginary interlocutor, it is not considered 'open' unless Miranda is actively maintaining the space.

(5) **A** MIRANDA: everyone thinks I'm literally going to bed   [<u>IS1</u>, IS2]
     B MIRANDA: I'm not   [<u>IS1</u>, IS2]
     C MIRANDA: I'm just saying goodnight to you to be polite   [IS1, <u>IS2</u>]
     D MIRANDA: because I like you and I like the time   [IS1, IS2, <u>IS3</u>]
               we've shared on twitter
     E MIRANDA: um anyway   [<u>IS1</u>, IS2]

As in the example with Kathy Griffin, Miranda's reorientation to different interaction spaces helps to disambiguate his use of the deictic pronoun "you". As he shifts from his interaction space with Colbert to the interaction space with the audience, he also shifts his discourse style from one of explanation to a kind of direct appeal. Miranda returns to the interaction space with Colbert only when he is ready to continue the main discourse, co-expressing the end of the digression in the accompanying speech with the discourse marker "anyway" (ex. 5, line E).

To successfully create the third interaction space, Miranda had to first consider the locations of his co-present interlocutors and then reorient toward an unambiguously 'unclaimed' space. The next example clearly demonstrates the misunderstandings that can arise when such considerations are not made.

This example is from an interview between English talk show host James Corden (now living in America) and American politician Hilary Clinton, and her daughter, Chelsea Clinton.[10] In this interaction, we are primarily concerned with Hilary Clinton's attempts to shift between real and imagined interaction spaces. As before, there is an interaction space between Clinton and her interviewer (IS1) and Clinton and the audience (IS2). There is also a space between her and the other interviewee, her daughter (IS3). Corden sets the discourse topic by asking Clinton what it was like to be on stage with Donald Trump during the presidential debates. In this particular excerpt, Hilary Clinton describes how Trump would sometimes hover behind her, and how she wished she had confronted him about this unacceptable behavior. As she enacts this imagined encounter, she attempts to open a fourth interaction space between her and an imaginary Trump (IS4).

(6)   Spaces available to Clinton in discourse excerpt (7):
  $IS1$ = Participants: $Clinton_S$, $Corden_A$
  $IS2$ = Participants: $Clinton_S$, $Audience_A$
  $IS3$ = Participants: $Clinton_S$, $Daughter_A$
  ($IS4$ = Participants: $Clinton_S$, $Trump_A$)

Unlike Miranda, Clinton fails to create the new interaction space. Instead, she unintentionally puts the interaction space between her and her daughter into focus. As depicted in Fig. 4, instead of orienting toward empty space to engage with an imagined interlocutor, she turns her body, head, and gaze toward her daughter. This results in a complete derailment of the discourse as Clinton's utterance is interpreted as an insult to her daughter. Her daughter then takes the floor, as Clinton laughs off her mistake. Clinton remains disengaged from the open interaction spaces as she recovers.

Fig. 4. Frames depicting Clinton shifting between interaction spaces

[10] File name: 2019-11-06_0837_US_KCBS_The_Late_Late_Show_With_James_Corden.

(7) **A** CLINTON: It's a difficult question, because y'know   [IS1, IS2, IS3]
        I thought
     B CLINTON: well maybe I should just turn on   [IS1, IS2, IS3, ~~IS4~~]
        him and say back up you creep
     C CLINTON: umm   [IS1, IS2, IS3]
     C DAUGHTER: why is she looking at me   [IS1, IS2, IS3]
     D DAUGHTER: you coulda done that to James. C'mon   [IS1, IS2, IS3]

Chelsea Clinton's orientation shift in frames C and D are also worth mention. In C, she turns and looks directly at the audience to express her dismay. She had not been active in the discourse, and so perhaps assumes the audience to be most sympathetic. She then turns, looks at James, and reaches toward him with an open upturned hand as she says "you coulda done that to James". This, in a way, is also a failed navigation of the open interaction spaces because the "you" she is referring to is *not* her gestural addressee, but her mother.

These two examples demonstrate that the locations of all participants are relevant to gesture interpretation and management in multiparty interactions, even when a participant is not the primary addressee.

4 Managing Spaces

So far, we have seen how speakers structure discourse by engaging and disengaging with different interaction spaces. However, each individual interaction space is also subject to management. In this section, I discuss the ways in which speakers introduce, organize, and dismiss discourse topics by acting upon physical and virtual objects within the interaction space.

In this work I only consider a small set of possible management actions: PRESENT, REFER, CONTRAST, and REMOVE. The PRESENT action adds a new topic to the interaction space, either in the form of a physical object being discussed, or a metaphoric object located in the space via abstract deixis [28]. The REFER action picks out a topic already present in the interaction space. The CONTRAST action differentiates two topics through physical separation. The REMOVE action ends a discourse topic by removing it from the interaction space.

I'll begin with a relatively simple example in which the discourse topic being managed is represented by an actual physical object in the interaction space. In this example, the two interlocutors, American actor Natalie Portman and American talk show host Stephen Colbert, are discussing a particular tweet that Colbert has printed out on a physical card.[11] Screenshots depicting two types of management actions are given in Fig. 5.

---

[11] File name: 2018-09-04_0635_US_KCBS_The_Late_Show_With_Stephen_Colbert.txt.

Fig. 5. Manipulating physical objects in the interaction space

In frame A, Portman is asking Colbert for more information about the tweet under discussion, in particular whether the author of the tweet wished her happy birthday (8).

(8) **A** PORTMAN: Did he say happy birthday?

Though the utterance *requests* information about the immediate topic under discussion, the manual gesture, a flat handed point toward the tweet, simply *refers* to the topic. This gestural discourse move is formally represented in (9). For this particular discourse move, Portman is indexed as Speaker (S), and Colbert as Addressee (A); the content of the interaction space, for simplicity, consists only of the active discourse topic, represented by a physical object on the desk (the printed tweet); the management performed by Portman on the content of the interaction space is a REFER action.

$$(9) \quad IS_A = \begin{cases} \text{Participants} : Portman_S, \ Colbert_A \\ \text{Content} : Tweet \\ \text{Management} : REFER_{Tweet} \end{cases}$$

In frame B, Colbert decides to close the topic of the tweet and move on with the interview. In speech, the topic dismissal is signalled by the discourse marker "anyway". The topic dismissal is co-expressed gesturally as Colbert physically removes the printed tweet from the interaction space and places it beneath his desk.

(10) **B** COLBERT: Anyway, congrat... happy birthday, happy birthday. Good
          to see you again.

In this discourse move, formally represented in (11), the roles are reversed, Portman is indexed as addressee, and Colbert as speaker. The content of the space being acted upon is still the tweet. The discourse management enacted by Colbert is the physical removal of this content from the interaction space, a REMOVE action. In subsequent states of the interaction space, the tweet would no longer appear in the interaction space's content, unless the topic was reintroduced via a PRESENT action.

(11) $IS_\mathrm{B} = \begin{cases} \text{Participants} : Portman_\mathrm{A}, \ Colbert_\mathrm{S} \\ \text{Content} : Tweet \\ \text{Management} : REMOVE_\mathrm{Tweet} \end{cases}$

4.1 Introducing and Dismissing Virtual Objects

In studies of interactive and discourse management gestures, recurrent gesture patterns have been identified for performing both topic introduction and topic dismissal. In topic introduction, speakers frequently raise an up turned open hand toward their interlocutor, as if to present an object for inspection [1,30]. In topic dismissal, speakers frequently perform so-called 'away' gestures [2,3, 10,46]. Bressem, Müller and colleagues describe this latter family of gestures as motivated by an action schema of moving unwanted objects away from the body. Crucially, when these gestures are used for topic dismissal, I argue that the movement being enacted is not just movement away from the speaker's body, but movement away from the entire interaction space. This is demonstrated with manipulation of a physical object in the previous example, and a virtual object in the following example.

This example comes from an interview between Colbert and Irish actor Andrew Scott in which Scott is excitedly talking about how long he's willing to watch and act in a play.[12] Screenshots of the relevant management gestures are provided in Fig. 6, and the corresponding transcript is given in (12).

Fig. 6. Frames depicting topic introduction and dismissal, corresponding to the transcript given in (12).

The discourse excerpt begins with Scott presenting an "idea" to Colbert. At the point of topic introduction, Scott is fully engaged with the interaction space between him and Colbert, with his body, head, and gaze all oriented toward Colbert. He then continues to gesture about this idea, including with a metaphoric gesture of "cutting" in frame B. Scott then grows self-conscious

---

[12] File name: 2018-10-04_0635_US_KCBS_The_Late_Show_With_Stephen_Colbert.

of his own excitement and stops himself. He stops gesturing (frame C), and then performs an 'away' gesture, moving his right hand in a large arc beginning in the center of the interaction space and moving outward (frame D). Even though the result of the away gesture sequence is Scott's disengagement with the interaction space, the gesture originates from his interaction with Colbert, and is thus assessed relative to that space. After performing this topic dismissal, Scott remains relatively disengaged, looking down (frame E), and then briefly engages with the audience via gaze and head orientation (frame F) before eventually being coaxed back into the interview by Colbert.

(12)	**A**	SCOTT: so the idea is	[IS1, IS2]
	B	SCOTT: don't cut it down just make it four hours of	[IS1, IS2]
		really exciting	
	C	SCOTT: um play...plays	[IS1, IS2]
	D	SCOTT: anyway I'll stop	[IS1, IS2]
	E	SCOTT: talking	[IS1, IS2]
	F	SCOTT: Shakespeare	[IS1, IS2]

The "idea" to be discussed is introduced to the interaction space by Scott on an upturned open hand. Unlike in the previous example where the discourse topic was represented by a physical object, this topic is virtual. The formal representation of the topic presentation, given in (13), is the same as it would be if there were a physical object introduced.

$$(13) \quad IS1_A = \begin{cases} \text{Participants} : Scott_S, \, Colbert_A \\ \text{Content} : Shakespeare \, plays \\ \text{Management} : PRESENT_{\text{Shakespeare plays}} \end{cases}$$

Just like with the physical object, the virtual object introduced into the interaction space by Scott can be subsequently referred to, manipulated, and removed by either participant. Because Scott introduces and dismisses the topic within a single conversational turn, he is the only interlocutor actually performing management actions on this particular topic. The final action he performs on the virtual object is, of course, the removal gesture depicted in frame D, and formally represented in (14).

$$(14) \quad IS1_D = \begin{cases} \text{Participants} : Scott_S, \, Colbert_A \\ \text{Content} : Shakespeare \, plays \\ \text{Management} : REMOVE_{\text{Shakespeare plays}} \end{cases}$$

In both discourse moves formally represented, it is necessary to assess the action relative to the interaction space between Colbert and Scott. Scott introduces the topic to be discussed in his discourse with Colbert, and then decides to end the topic. Analysing these gestures as pertaining to the same discourse, requires that they are analyzed relative to the particular interaction space where the discourse is being managed, rather than Scott's personal gesture space which can be used to interact with distinct interaction spaces and distinct discourses, as discussed in Sect. 3.

4.2   Topic Organization

The final example shows how addressee position is relevant for the interpretation of the spatial organization of multiple discourse topics within an interaction space. Previous literature has shown that virtual topics can be spatially organized according to temporal, causal, and contrastive relations. For example, events are frequently represented along a virtual left-to-right timeline[13] in front of the interlocutor [5], and contrasting topics are frequently presented in different regions of the speaker's gesture space to metaphorically convey conceptual differences [16,17]. However, these discussions rarely consider spatial organization relative to the addressee.

In this discourse excerpt, comedian Trevor Noah (from South Africa, currently residing in the US) is answering a question from an audience member about the possibility of reparations in America.[14] Noah disagrees with the audience member's stance, but must present his argument in such a way as to not alienate the audience member. To accomplish this, Noah spatially separates topics in the interaction space in order to metaphorically differentiate the argument he is making from that of the audience member. The main topic under discussion, *reparations for Black Americans*, and subtopics therein, are intentionally positioned *away* from his addressee, whereas the topics that the addressee is referring to, namely discrimination by class, are located relatively close to the addressee (Fig. 7).

Fig. 7. Frames depicting spatial separation of discourse topics, corresponding to the transcript in (15)

(15)   **A**   NOAH: to your question, I think you have to understand what the word reparations means first so reparations, you are repairing something that you have broken, you are paying for something that you were supposed to pay for.

     B   NOAH: I'm not saying there aren't people living in America today who aren't suffering.

     C   NOAH: But reparations is a specific conversation about a specific time in America, and that is Black people were slaves.

---

[13] The direction of the virtual timeline is subject to contextual and cultural variation. See work by Casasanto & Jasmin for variation within English, and Núñez & Sweetser for cross-linguistic variation [6,32].

[14] Available online: https://www.youtube.com/watch?v=Jpg_o0Gk6wg.

To begin his argumentation, Noah refers in both speech and gesture to the discourse topic the audience member presented. Though the audience member does not have direct physical access to the interaction space due to distance from the stage, Noah cooperates by showing that the topic introduced is within the interaction space. This is done through a two-handed referring gesture in which his right hand delineates a region of space on his desk, and his left hand performs and open-hand point toward the same location (frame A). This management action is formally represented in (16).

$$(16) \quad IS1_A = \begin{cases} \text{Participants}: Noah_S,\ Audience\ Member_A \\ \text{Content}: Reparations \\ \text{Management}: REFER_{\text{Reparations}} \end{cases}$$

However, Noah is now tasked with differentiating class suffering from the racial discrimination for which reparations are actually owed. The first step he takes is to clarify that what the audience member is actually talking about is injustices endured by lower and working classes in America. He does this by acknowledging suffering in America, presenting this reframing of the issue by changing his hand shape, but referring to the same position in the center of the interaction space (frame B).

$$(17) \quad IS1_B = \begin{cases} \text{Participants}: Noah_S,\ Audience\ Member_A \\ \text{Content}: Reparations,\ Class\ Suffering \\ \text{Management}: PRESENT_{\text{Class.Suffering}} \end{cases}$$

Having acknowledged and reframed the point made by the audience member, Noah then moves onto his own argument. For this he introduces the actual intended topic, reparations owed to Black Americans by the US government. For this topic introduction, Noah performs a containment gesture, with open hands facing toward each other as if to place an object on the table (frame C). This gesture sequence performs two management actions, as represented in (18). First, it PRESENTS a topic by indicating a new position in the interaction space. Second, it CONTRASTS this topic with the previous through spatial distancing. Noah reinforces this CONTRAST move by leaning away from the previous topic (frames B-C). Despite leaning and gesturing toward the periphery of the interaction space, Noah maintains engagement by orienting his head and gaze toward the audience member.

$$(18) \quad IS1_C = \begin{cases} \text{Participants}: Noah_S,\ Audience\ Member_A \\ \text{Content}: Reparations,\ Class\ suffering, \\ \qquad\qquad Black\ Americans \\ \text{Management}: PRESENT_{\text{B.Am.}}, \\ \qquad\qquad CONTRAST_{\text{B.Am\&Class.Suff}}, \end{cases}$$

The conceptual contrast signaled by the spatial separations of topics in the interaction space cannot be fully appreciated without also considering the relative distance of each topic from the addressee. Noah's topic of reparations for

Black Americans is located to the far left of the interaction space not only to contrast it with a previously mentioned topic, but to contrast it with the argument made specifically by the addressee.

5   Discussion

In this paper, I have looked at ways in which gesture is used in discourse and interaction management. In particular, I discussed the ways in which physical orientation determines the speaker's primary addressee, and thus the discourse being contributed to. I also explored the ways in which speakers manage the topics of a discourse by manipulating physical and virtual objects. Crucially, however, these discussions centered around a *mutual* interaction space rather than a *personal* gesture space. For all cases, the contribution of the gestural behavior could not be appropriately analysed without considering the positions of both the speaker and their primary addressee. Analysing gesture position in this way helps us better understand the contribution gesture makes to discourse management, and how certain discourse structural moves, such as digressions and distractions, are signalled.

In fields of technology, including virtual reality [33], robotics [38], and human-computer interaction [36,37], acknowledging communication as a fully embodied and multimodal system has gained popularity. However, the results of implementing such theoretical developments will only ever be as good as our understanding of embodied multimodal communication in face-to-face human interaction. The field of linguistics is uniquely positioned to developing formal theories of multimodal communication, and it is to linguistics that we should turn for appropriate models that can then be applied to technological development. The work presented here on the recognition and formalization of the interaction space contributes to this endeavor.

In terms of integrating the interaction space into annotation methodology, I have two specific, straightforward proposals. First, in *all* interactions with more than two participants, every utterance should be encoded for the interaction space in focus. Second, research concerning interactive or discourse structural meaning in particular should consistently describe gesture position relative to the interaction space, rather than the personal gesture space. Both of these can be accomplished by adding annotation tiers to the researcher's annotation scheme, and neither should be particularly onerous.

There are three significant opportunities for further research. The first is in regards to delineation of interaction spaces. In this paper, I have framed the interaction space as always being delineated by two participants, the speaker and primary addressee. However, in multiparty interactions where a single discourse is being actively constructed by more than two participants, speakers can orient themselves toward both addressees, creating, for example, a triangular or circular space. It is unclear in these situations whether this reorientation is a compromise between multiple two-party interaction spaces, or the creation of a single larger interaction space.

Secondly, the relationship between interaction space management and particular gesture forms needs to be further understood. In this paper I have made some initial suggestions based both on existing literature and the data presented. In particular, I have shown that open palm gestures are associated with PRESENT actions, used to introduce a topic to the interaction space, and that 'away' gestures are associated with REMOVE actions, used to dismiss topics from the discourse.

Finally, the use of the interaction space can be used to inform existing and developing models of gesture-speech integration. These models are being developed within many linguistic frameworks, including Cognitive Grammar [7], Functional Discourse Grammar [24], Head-Driven Phrase Structure Grammar [26], and Lexical Functional Grammar [12], all of which contribute to a more complete picture of human communication. Before a truly complete picture can be formed, in any framework, it is important that we have a thorough understanding of both the speech and gestural components of communication. The present work contributes a better understanding of the gestural component, specifically how interactive and discourse structural meaning can be systematically assessed in face-to-face interaction.

References

1. Bavelas, J.B., Chovil, N., Lawrie, D.A., Wade, A.: Interactive gestures. Discourse Process. **15**(4), 469–489 (1992)
2. Bressem, J., Müller, C.: The family of away gestures: Negation, refusal, and negative assessment. In: Müller, C., Cienki, A., Fricke, E., Ladewig, S., McNeill, D., Tessendorf, S. (eds.) Body-Language-Communication: An International Handbook on Multimodality in Human Interaction, vol. 2, pp. 1592–1604. De Gruyter Mouton Berlin & Boston (2014)
3. Bressem, J., Müller, C.: The "negative-assessment-construction"-a multimodal pattern based on a recurrent gesture? Linguist. Vanguard **3**(s1), 1–9 (2017)
4. Brône, G., Oben, B., Jehoul, A., Vranjes, J., Feyaerts, K.: Eye gaze and viewpoint in multimodal interaction management. Cogn. Linguist. **28**(3), 449–483 (2017)
5. Calbris, G.: From left to right...: coverbal gestures and their symbolic use of space. In: Metaphor and Gesture, pp. 27–53. John Benjamins (2008)
6. Casasanto, D., Jasmin, K.: The hands of time: temporal gestures in English speakers. Cogn Linguist. **23**(4), 643–674 (2012)
7. Cienki, A.: Spoken language usage events. Lang. Cogn. **7**(4), 499–514 (2015)
8. Efron, D.: Gesture, Race, and Culture. Mouton, The Hague (1941)
9. Fauconnier, G., Turner, M.: The Way We Think: Conceptual Blending and the Mind's Hidden Complexities. Basic Books (2008)
10. Gawne, L.: 'Away'gestures associated with negative expressions in narrative discourse in Syuba (Kagate, Nepal) speakers. Semiotica **239**, 37–59 (2021)
11. Gill, S.P., Kawamori, M., Katagiri, Y., Shimojima, A.: The role of body moves in dialogue. Int. J. Lang. Commun. **12**, 89–114 (2000)
12. Giorgolo, G., Asudeh, A., Butt, M., King, T.H.: Multimodal communication in LFG: gestures and the correspondence architecture. In: Proceedings of the LFG11 Conference, pp. 257–277 (2011)

13. Hagemann, J.: Proxemics and axial orientation. In: Müller, C., Cienki, A., Fricke, E., Ladewig, S., McNeill, D., Tessendorf, S. (eds.) Body-Language-Communication: An International Handbook on Multimodality in Human Interaction, vol. 2, pp. 1310–1323. De Gruyter Mouton (2014)
14. Hall, E.: Handbook for Proxemic Research. Society for the Anthropology of Visual Communication, Washington, DC (1995)
15. Harrison, S.: Evidence for node and scope of negation in coverbal gesture. Gesture **10**(1), 29–51 (2010)
16. Hinnell, J.: The verbal-kinesic enactment of contrast in North American English. Am. J. Semiotics **35**(1), 55–92 (2019)
17. Jannedy, S., Mendoza-Denton, N.: Structuring information through gesture and intonation. Interdisc. Stud. Inf. Struct. **3**, 199–244 (2005)
18. Jokinen, K., Nishida, M., Yamamoto, S.: Eye-gaze experiments for conversation monitoring. In: Proceedings of the 3rd International Universal Communication Symposium, pp. 303–308 (2009)
19. Kendon, A.: Conducting Interaction: Patterns of Behavior in Focused Encounters, vol. 7. CUP Archive (1990)
20. Kendon, A.: Gesture: Visible Action as Utterance. Cambridge University Press, Cambridge (2004)
21. Kendon, A.: Spacing and orientation in co-present interaction. In: Esposito, A., Campbell, N., Vogel, C., Hussain, A., Nijholt, A. (eds.) Development of Multimodal Interfaces: Active Listening and Synchrony. LNCS, vol. 5967, pp. 1–15. Springer, Heidelberg (2010). https://doi.org/10.1007/978-3-642-12397-9_1
22. Kipp, M., Neff, M., Albrecht, I.: An annotation scheme for conversational gestures: how to economically capture timing and form. Lang. Resour. Eval. **41**(3–4), 325–339 (2007)
23. Kita, S.: Pointing: Where Language, Culture, and Cognition Meet. Psychology Press (2003)
24. Kok, K.: The grammatical potential of co-speech gesture: a functional discourse grammar perspective. Funct. Lang. **23**(2), 149–178 (2016)
25. Kok, K., Bergmann, K., Cienki, A., Kopp, S.: Mapping out the multifunctionality of speakers' gestures. Gesture **15**(1), 37–59 (2016)
26. Lücking, A.: Gesture. In: Müller, S., Abeille, A., Borsley, R.D., Koenig, J.P. (eds.) Head Driven Phrase Structure Grammar: The Handbook, pp. 1201–1250. Language Science Press, Berlin (2021)
27. McNeill, D.: Hand and Mind: What Gestures Reveal About Thought. University of Chicago Press (1992)
28. McNeill, D.: Pointing and Morality in Chicago. Pointing: Where Language, Culture, and Cognition Meet, pp. 293–306 (2003)
29. McNeill, D.: Gesture and Thought. University of Chicago Press (2005)
30. Müller, C.: Forms and uses of the palm up open hand: a case of a gesture family. Semant. Pragmatics Everyday Gestures **9**, 233–256 (2004)
31. Norris, S.: Multiparty interaction: a multimodal perspective on relevance. Discourse Stud. **8**(3), 401–421 (2006)
32. Núñez, R.E., Sweetser, E.: With the future behind them: convergent evidence from Aymara language and gesture in the crosslinguistic comparison of spatial construals of time. Cogn. Sci. **30**(3), 401–450 (2006)
33. O'hara, K., Kjeldskov, J., Paay, J.: Blended interaction spaces for distributed team collaboration. ACM Trans. Comput.-Hum. Interact. (TOCHI) **18**(1), 1–28 (2011)
34. Park, I.: Marking an impasse: the use of anyway as a sequence-closing device. J. Pragmat. **42**(12), 3283–3299 (2010)

35. Parrill, F., Sweetser, E.: What we mean by meaning: conceptual integration in gesture analysis and transcription. Gesture **4**(2), 197–219 (2004)
36. Pustejovsky, J., Krishnaswamy, N.: Situated meaning in multimodal dialogue: human-robot and human-computer interactions. TAL **61**, 17–41 (2020)
37. Pustejovsky, J., Krishnaswamy, N., Draper, B., Narayana, P., Bangar, R.: Creating common ground through multimodal simulations. In: Proceedings of the IWCS Workshop on Foundations of Situated and Multimodal Communication (2017)
38. Saunderson, S., Nejat, G.: How robots influence humans: a survey of nonverbal communication in social human-robot interaction. Int. J. Soc. Robot. **11**(4), 575–608 (2019)
39. Stec, K.: Meaningful shifts: a review of viewpoint markers in co-speech gesture and sign language. Gesture **12**(3), 327–360 (2012)
40. Stec, K., Huiskes, M., Redeker, G.: Multimodal analysis of quotation in oral narratives. Open Linguist. **1**, 531–554 (2015)
41. Stec, K., Huiskes, M., Redeker, G.: Multimodal quotation: role shift practices in spoken narratives. J. Pragmat. **104**, 1–17 (2016)
42. Sweetser, E.: Looking at space to study mental spaces co-speech gesture as. Methods Cogn. Linguist. **18**, 201–224 (2007)
43. Sweetser, E.: Gestural meaning is in the body(-space) as much as in the hands. In: Janzen, T., Scheffer, B. (eds.) Signed Language and Gesture Research in Cognitive Linguistics, pp. 357–366. Mouton de Gruyter, Boston/Berlin (in press)
44. Sweetser, E., Sizemore, M.: Personal and interpersonal gesture spaces: functional contrasts in language and gesture. In: Language in the Context of Use: Discourse and Cognitive Approaches to Language, pp. 25–51 (2008)
45. Sweetser, E., Stec, K.: Maintaining multiple viewpoints with gaze. In: Dancygier, B., Lu, W., Verhagen, A. (eds.) Viewpoint and the Fabric of Meaning: Form and Use of Viewpoint Tools Across Languages and Modalities, pp. 237–258. Walter de Gruyter GmbH & Co KG (2016)
46. Teßendorf, S.: Pragmatic and metaphoric-combining functional with cognitive approaches in the analysis of the "brushing aside gesture." In: Müller, C., Cienki, A., Fricke, E., Ladewig, S., McNeill, D., Tessendorf, S. (eds.) Body-Language-Communication: An International Handbook on Multimodality in Human Interaction, vol. 2, pp. 1540–1557. De Gruyter Mouton, Berlin/Boston (2014)

Safety Issues in Human-Machine Collaboration and Possible Countermeasures

Liang Ma[✉][iD] and Chen Wang[iD]

Lab of Enhanced Human-Machine Collaborative Decision-Making,
Department of Industrial Engineering, Tsinghua University,
Beijing 100084, People's Republic of China
{liangma,chenwang}@tsinghua.edu.cn

Abstract. Autonomous machines are more and more capable of executing complex tasks with the support of intelligent algorithms, and they are deploying rapidly at an unprecedented pace. In the meanwhile human-machine teaming is promising to accomplish more and more challenging tasks by integrating strengths and avoiding weaknesses from both sides. However, due to imperfections from both human and machine sides and their interactions, potential safety issues should be considered in advance so that researchers and engineers could prevent or tackle those issues with preparation and make the human-machine system safer and more successful. In this paper, we proposed a framework under the context of human-machine (algorithm) collaboration, and we addressed possible safety issues within and out of the human-machine system. We classified those safety issues into internal safety issues representing the safety issues within the human-machine system and external safety issues representing safety issues out of the human-machine system to organizational and societal levels. To tackle those safety issues, under this proposed framework, we listed possible countermeasures according to the literature so that we could provide pedals to control the autonomous agents and human-machine teaming and enable safer human- machine collaboration in the future.

Keywords: Human-machine collaboration · Algorithm · Human factors · Human-machine teaming

1 Introduction

Autonomous machines [46], such as robots [64] and autonomous vehicles [5], are more and more capable of executing complex tasks with the support of intelligent algorithms, such as Machine Learning (ML), Deep Learning (DL), Artificial Intelligence (AI), etc. In recent years, those machines have been deployed

This study is supported by the National Natural Science Foundation of China under grant numbers 72192824 & 71942005.

© The Author(s), under exclusive license to Springer Nature Switzerland AG 2022
V. G. Duffy (Ed.): HCII 2022, LNCS 13319, pp. 263–277, 2022.
https://doi.org/10.1007/978-3-031-05890-5_21

in different domains with great success, such as in transportation [4,32], health care [66], manufacturing [23], etc. In the meanwhile, those AI systems are being deployed at an unprecedentedly rapid pace in massive-scale production systems, and they are generating impacts on millions or even billions of people [48].

Together with the machine, human-machine teaming is promising to accomplish more and more challenging tasks by integrating strengths from both sides [63]. Great effort has been contributed and achievements have been done in various fields in human-machine collaboration [11], and the relationship between human and autonomous machine has been evolved with the increasing level of machine autonomy [20]. For example, in industrial application, the human-robot relationship has been shifted from isolation through co-existence and cooperation to collaboration [38]. It is believed human-machine collaboration would be more prevalent in the future [49].

However, due to imperfections from both human and machine sides, recent failures in human-machine collaboration have led to fatal accidents in autonomous driving [9] and airplane autopilot [30]. Concerns and critiques have been raised along with the rapid deployment of those machines as well about the propensity to replicate, reinforce or amplify existing social biases [48]. Therefore, potential safety issues should be considered in advance so that researchers and engineers could prevent or tackle those issues with preparation [25]. The machine element and human element should be systematically considered as a whole for any AI safety plan [51].

In this paper, we are about to analyze potential safety issues in human-machine collaboration, and we are about to propose a framework to analyze potential risks within human-machine collaboration in Sect. 2, and list possible countermeasures according to the literature in Sect. 3 followed by conclusions in Sect. 4.

2   Framework of Safety Issues in Human-Machine Collaboration

In this paper, the machine refers to "an intelligent system that can make decisions in an autonomous and (partially or fully) independent manner, and the machine's autonomy is realized through AI, DL, or other algorithms" [46]. The machine's physical appearance could be in any form, such as a robot, a computer, or some other type. The machine possesses different specialties realized by the algorithm, and it is used to work with a human operator to tackle a/some specific task(s).

In human-machine teaming, the workflow between human and machine could be illustrated as in Fig. 1. For a given task, both human operator and machine complete a mission together to achieve the goal of a task under a certain context in a specific environment. In general, to achieve the goal of the task with the machine, the human operator acts in a sequence composed of sensation, perception, cognition, decision-making, and action [56]. In parallel, the machine

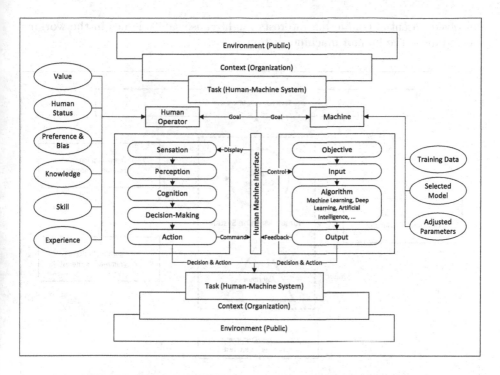

Fig. 1. Illustration of work flow in a human-machine team

collects data from the human operator's input and the task within its belonging organization in its working environment and then autonomously executes its pre-designed functions.

During this autonomous procedure, the machine is designed with a specific objective that represents or partially represents the goal of the task, and it implements embedded algorithm(s) and generates output or actions. Both outputs from human and machine fuse to accomplish the task. The outputs from human and machine are fed back to each side as input for the sequential operations. The interaction between human and machine is realized by the human-machine interface [53] to transfer bilateral input and output.

In this human-machine system, there are different stakeholders involved (see Fig. 2), including the human operator who operates the machine, the owner of the machine (organization), the end-user/customers, and some other potential subjects influenced by the system, and the public in the society [10]. The task goal might represent the purpose of the organization which the human operator and the machine work for, while the human operator has his/her value, attitude, physical/mental status, experience, and preference during the task. In particular, the machine itself is shaped by its objective, its training data, its selected method (algorithm or expressive model), and adjusted parameters [42]. There are potential conflicting interests among those stakeholders, and those conflicts might emerge among their representative parts in the system and the society, and unsolved potential conflicting interests might cause safety issues in the working procedure of the human-machine system.

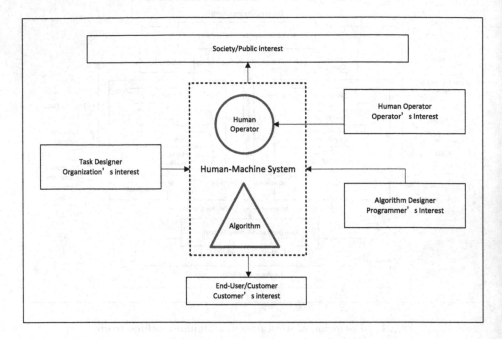

Fig. 2. Different parties involved in the human-machine system

Inspired by the definition of accidents in Amodei et al. (2016) [1], we define safety issues in human-machine collaboration " as unintended and harmful behavior that may emerge from human-machine collaboration when we specify the wrong objective function, are not careful about the learning process, or commit other machine-learning-related and human-related implementation errors in human-machine collaboration".

In this illustrated simplified human-machine system, we have different risk factors which might impair the function of human-machine collaboration, and we classify them into internal safety risks and external safety risks [2]. The internal safety risks are bounded within the human-machine system. They represent the risks that human and machine together could not fulfill the task requirements and might cause malfunctions or task failures even human and machine work close with each other. In addition to that, the internal safety risks might also include harms caused by either side of the system to the other side, and then further result in fatal failures of human-machine collaboration. Internal risk factors might be endogenous (human or machine element itself) or exogenous (interaction with the other system elements) [2]. The external safety risk is regarded as the risk caused by the human-machine system to the other entities out of the human-machine system, and it mainly comes from the rapid spread of the human-machine system.

2.1 Internal Safety Issues

Machine Side Issues: In a human-machine system, internal risks can be caused by the formulation of intelligent algorithms themselves [1]. First, each algorithm has a specific objective pre-defined by its designer. The objective of the algorithm might not be fully aligned with the task goal of the organization. Second, those intelligent algorithms, are mainly developed in rich data-driven approaches, and plenty of data are required to train the algorithm. In this approach, the performance of the algorithm has a strong dependency on the training data. If the training data quality is not good, potential bias and flaws would occur in the output. Furthermore, when this algorithm is used in extrapolation, where the input is out of the scope of the training data, potential error/failure might happen. In addition to that, the trained algorithm depends highly on the training data which have already been limited by the data themselves, since the data are collected under certain conditions. Those conditions might not be further satisfied while handling newly generated data due to the changing context and environment, and the algorithm could not further fit the new context and new environment [21]. The sensitivity of the algorithm is also a vulnerable point in the human-machine system [16].

The outcome (the accuracy) of the algorithm is statistical results and it has a strong dependency on the selection of training data and test data within a limited spatiotemporal scope. Therefore, the evaluation of the algorithm could also be problematic. The algorithm's overall performance depends on multiple cases and only shows statistical results. However, for a single case, it is difficult to judge if the machine (algorithm) functions well or not. Even the conditions could be the same, the algorithm itself might be quite sensitive to noise, which would cause the failure of the algorithm, even in simple classification tasks. However, the human operator has no clue about when and how those errors might happen [16]. The uncertainty of a single case might cause functional errors and further hinder people from working together with the machine.

Human Side Issues: In the human-machine system, human is also a vulnerable part and might cause the failure of the whole human-machine system. Different human operators have different values, and those values might not be the same as the designer of the algorithm or the goal of the task. Those different understanding of the task goal might lead to maloperation of the machine. Even with the same understanding of the task goal, the human operator is prone to subjective preferences and various cognitive biases. Besides that, human operator is also not a stable part in the system, and he/she could be easily influenced by emotion [41], fatigue [36], stress [68], and so on. The instability of the human operator could increase the difficulties within the communication between human and machine, and further, impair the performance of the human-machine system.

Besides that, the human operator's attitude towards the machine could also impact the safety of the whole system. The attitude could be roughly classified into acceptance of the machine [54] and the trust towards the machine [37]. The former determines whether the human operator would like to take the machine as a teammate to work together, while the latter determines whether the human operator could use the output of the machine without a doubt. Both are essential to the safety of the human-machine system. For example, in [39], people who interact with AI can be roughly classified into Skeptics, interactors, and Delegators, and each archetype is formed through long-term interaction with AI and is influenced by personal traits and task traits.

In addition, the human-machine relationship is another determinant factor for the safety of the human-machine system [63]. In general, the machine serves the human operator in a subordinate position and provides recommendations or suggestions to a human operator for further decision-making. However, with the increasing power of AI, the relationship between human and machine could be changed as well. If their positions were wrongly positioned in the organization, potential safety risks might be raised [20].

Human-Machine Interaction Issues: In addition, the trained algorithm itself might have a better performance than traditional machines, but the algorithm itself is difficult to explain due to its "black box" feature. Therefore, unlike traditional machines driven by automation techniques [37] which are mainly analytically designed with high transparency, autonomous agents are prone to unknown underlying causality mechanisms, unanalytical structure, and unexplainable procedure, which increases the risk of the human-machine system dramatically. The algorithm itself lacks transparency and explainability, and that hinders effective collaboration between the human operator and the machine. In general, it would cause loss of situation awareness during the work [40], overtrust or distrust towards the machine [17], and sometimes even resistance to the collaboration [19].

Internal risks could also come from the ineffective communication between human and machine. Productive human-machine collaboration requires effective communication between humans and machine. The first demand is mutual understanding between human and machine, which means human needs to construct appropriate mental model towards the machine, while the machine needs to find proper ways to understand human. Although impressive progress has already been achieved in the state of the art, mutual understanding is still difficult and far to reach. The second demand is effective interaction via different manners. Multimodal methods have been developed to enrich human-machine interaction, but the machine still cannot generalize those findings to provide appropriate feedback under different contexts. Deficiencies in value alignment, intention detection, bi-lateral communication hinder the advancement of human-machine collaboration and meanwhile might result in different safety issues [40].

2.2 External Safety Issues

Since the duplication of "the machine" is easy, the autonomous agent could be rapidly deployed in an organization or even across the world. The human-machine system might gain more unexpected power due to the intelligence possessed by the machine itself, such as autonomous weapons and algorithmic justice. Great potential safety risks might occur at organizational and societal levels [29]. However, it is believed that at the society level "society lacks both clear normative principles regarding how people should collaborate with algorithms as well as empirical evidence about how people do collaborate with algorithms" [18].

Organizational Perspective: Due to the conflicting interests and different values and goals held by different parties within the human-machine system, value misalignment might occur within the human-machine team and the organization. The value misalignment would cause deviations in human-machine teaming in task accomplishment, and then further lead to failures in achieving the goal of the organization. In addition, with the deployment of machines as teammates within the organization, the relationship among people would be changed to the relationship among agents including people and machines. This change brings new connections and strengthens/weakens existing connections among agents, and impacts the conventional working procedure within the organization. New safety issues would emerge within the organization, especially when human does not get used to the new role of the machine in their working life.

Societal Perspective: First, in a massive-scale deployed human-machine system, the objective function of the algorithm usually has a very specific focus on local purpose and neglects that the local optimization might not bring "global optimal" of the whole society. The adverse impact might occur during the deployment of those human-machine teams at the societal level. Second, the machine could be implemented under different situations where the algorithm might not be sufficiently tested, and local implementation could also be risky. For example, different countries and different organizations hold different values towards the same task, such as moral ethics, etc., a largely deployed system might be vulnerable to the changing context and environment. Third, due to the unexplainable nature of the autonomous algorithm and its large deployment, once there were flaws within the system, serious consequences might be brought up world-widely in a higher order of magnitude. Therefore, before implementing intelligent machines on a large scale, their potential safety impact on society should be audited and tested. Last but not least, the societal impact also includes the new relationship between mankind and machine [46]. Those safety issues at the societal level should also be considered before the deployment of AI systems.

3   Possible Countermeasures

As shown in Fig. 3, countermeasures to the safety issues in the human-machine system should be considered systematically. In a down-top approach, those measures could be at the individual machine level, human operator level, interaction level, organizational level, and societal level.

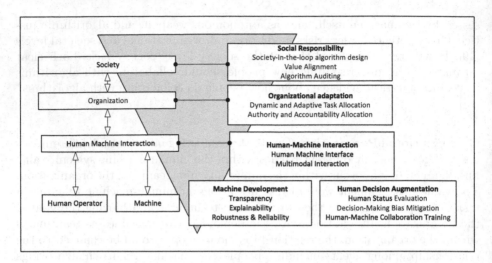

Fig. 3. Possible countermeasures to increase the safety of the human-machine system

3.1 Machine Development

Algorithm Transparency and Explainability: The algorithm's transparency impacts the confidence and perceived reliability of the machine system [62], which is crucial for human-machine teaming. To achieve high transparency, twofold work should be merged. First, increase the explainability of the algorithm itself [58] to support the transparency of the algorithm and to help the human operator understand the underlying mechanism of the algorithm. During algorithm design, the interpretability of the algorithm should be considered and evaluated in advance to suppress the "black box" effect on the human operator. Second, the transparency of the algorithm should be displayed appropriately to enhance its interpretability. For example, Explainable AI (XAI) has already been promoted by DRAPA [61] to support human-AI teaming [35], and Situation Awareness-based Agency Transparency has already been developed and applied in human-machine teaming. Uncertainty quantification would also help understand prediction system structure and defensibly quantify uncertainty, and that could benefit the transparency of the algorithm [3].

Understanding Towards Human Operator - Intention Recognition: Effective and safe human-machine collaboration requires that the machine is capable of recognizing and "understanding" human operator's activity and intention accurately [44]. Machine with intention recognition is capable of being aware of the human operator's intention, which enables pro-activeness, in cooperating or promoting cooperation, and in pre-empting danger [43]. That could reduce the need for classical direct human-machine interface and communication [57]. Intention recognition has already been performed with learning or using past experience from a database of past interactions. Bayesian Network is often employed to generate statistical evidence and tune the machine with new observations [43].

Algorithm Reliability: Reliability (or Robustness) of the algorithm is critical for the collaboration between human and machine. Similar to the security attack to the Machine Learning Algorithm, in the real working environment, data poisoning or wrong input, adversarial cases with noise, and model flaw with incomplete or incorrect knowledge [16] would appear unintentionally, and that might cause serious failures of the machine system. Therefore, to increase the reliability of the algorithm, data sanitization, robust learning, and extensive testing should be implemented [21]. Besides that, sufficient tests might be another way to assess the reliability of the algorithm.

3.2   Human Status Evaluation and Decision Augmentation

Human Status Evaluation: Human-machine collaboration requires real-time evaluation of human status [36] and then predicts the potential influence of changing human status on human-machine system performance. With the development of wearable devices, it is promising to use those devices to capture human status in a real-time manner [59]. Some studies have already integrate human fatigue model [14], acute stress [68], emotion [8] into human-machine system, which enables the system to respond accordingly. Besides that, we should enrich our scientific understanding of humans themselves, since it is the fundamental knowledge of building up reliable computational models about humans.

Decision-Making Bias Mitigation: When working together with an algorithm, human operators struggles to interpret and effectively use algorithms. In addition, the human operator often uses algorithms in unexpected and biased ways [47]. Particularly, in decision-making, human operators are prone to different types of cognitive biases [22], which might harm the collaboration between human and machine. In contrast, a machine normally works in a rigid approach and could make a decision in an analytical approach. Debiasing of human decision-makers would improve the performance of the human-machine system. Various researches have been conducted in the literature in decision-making debiasing [55], however, few studies have been conducted in the human-machine collaboration context. In human-machine teaming, the machine needs to detect and/or recognize the decision-making bias and then select the most appropriate and effective way to persuade the human operator to change his/her biased decision into a rational one [28].

Human-Machine Collaboration Training: Safe human-machine collaboration requires intensive training as well. With a machine as a teammate, perceptual and procedural teaming changes. The way human operators perceive and work with AI agents is fundamentally different from working with a human teammate. Therefore, different from classical human-human team training, the human operator needs to be trained to recognize his/her role, to understand the machine, and to interact with the machine properly [40]. It is worth noting that the human's mental model towards a machine evolves along with the working procedure with the machine [34], and convergent stable human-machine collaboration might achieve after a long-term human's adaptation to the machine.

3.3 Human-Machine Interaction

Human-Machine Interface: human-machine Interface is another key element to ensure the safety of the human-machine system [65], and it evolves from a control interface via a human-assisted interface, to a human-delegated system and human supervised system. As the role of the human operator changes along the level of automation, commands, and controls should be designed to fit the requirements of different roles, as well as the information displayed on the interface.

Multimodal Interaction: In a human-machine system, if the machine has a high autonomous level, the role of the human operator shifts to monitoring the status of the machine and acting intervention when necessary. In this procedure, it is necessary to have multiple modular feedbacks to increase the human operator's presence in the loop, so that the human operator can identify misbehavior by the system and provide an accountable entity in case of the system misbehaves. In the literature on autonomous driving, different warning feedbacks have been studied to enable effective take-over [67]. Those findings could also help the other autonomous systems work together with human operator [60].

3.4 Organization Reconfiguration

It is worth noting that the human-machine system does not exist in a vacuum, but deploys in a concrete organization. From an organizational perspective, it is often unclear how the organization should collaborate with algorithm [18]. "Poor partnership between people and automation will become increasingly costly and catastrophic" [33].

Dynamic and Adaptive Human-Machine Task Allocation: Due to the dynamic nature of work and the increasing capabilities of the machine, human-machine task allocation is essential to the safety of the system as well [24]. Incorrect task allocation would cause deficiencies on both sides and cause more workload and risks to the task. From the organizational perspective, it should be decided when and how human and machine collaborate to accomplish which part of the task. Dynamic adaptive task allocation would consider the strengths and weaknesses of both sides and enable more effective collaboration between human and machine [26].

Authority and Accountability Allocation: The determinant factor of the relationship in the human-machine system is authority and accountability allocation [63]. Currently, due to the limited capabilities of the machine, human and machine often work in a supervisor-subordinate relationship. However, in a broad view, invisible algorithms invade our work and life and govern labor, and human and machine could also work as partners or even people can work for the machine. Those managerial policies in a human-machine relationship would also bring up potential safety risks in human-machine collaboration [20]. To assign decision authority and accountability appropriately, human-machine teaming design should be considered. Team member competencies could be one approach to study the composition of a human-machine team [27].

3.5 Social Responsibility in Algorithm

Society-in-the-Loop: In the case of human-machine system works in a broad function and a larger area, society-in-loop has been introduced by Rahwan into AI algorithm design [45]. This is a shift from "human-in-the-loop", and this shift could embed values of the society into algorithm design and has a broad implication on algorithm governance of societal outcomes.

Value Alignment: Moral value in AI is concerned most in recent studies, and multi-objective reinforcement learning [50] and moral theories, such as utilitarianism [13] have been mathematically formulated to make moral decisions in algorithms. Computational moral decision-making model has also been developed and implemented in application [31]. Those advances indicate that the machine has already become a moral agent with its value from the algorithm designers. As we mentioned previously, different stakeholders involved in the human-machine system hold different values, and value alignment [12] is essential for the proper function of the whole system. Principles for value alignment have been addressed in [15]. Value alignment verification has also been proposed to formalize and theoretically analyze how to efficiently test whether the behavior of another agent is aligned with a human's values [6].

Algorithm Auditing: Before the deployment of the algorithm, algorithm auditing has been recently discussed in the literature to solve concerns regarding the social implications of AI systems [52]. An internal algorithm auditing framework was introduced in [48] to support AI system development from end to end. However, the algorithm auditing has a special focus on the algorithm itself [7], but it does not pay sufficient attention to the combination of human and system. Besides that, it is still challenging for practitioners to identify harmful repercussions before deployment.

4 Conclusions

With the increase of human and intelligent machine cooperation/collaboration in different industrial/domestic settings, we should be aware of potential safety issues raised in those applications. In our proposed framework, conflicting interests from different stakeholders involved in the human-machine collaboration should be considered during human-machine system design and implementation. Within the human-machine system, strategic thinking and tactical advances to enhance mutual understanding between human and machine shall be considered. Out of the human-machine system, organizational/managerial measures and societal participation in technology deployment should be implemented.

References

1. Amodei, D., Olah, C., Steinhardt, J., Christiano, P., Schulman, J., Mané, D.: Concrete problems in AI safety, pp. 1–29 (2016)
2. Baudin, É., Blanquart, J.P., Guiochet, J., Powell, D.: Independent safety systems for autonomy: state of the art and future directions. Ph.D. thesis, LAAS-CNRS (2007)
3. Begoli, E., Bhattacharya, T., Kusnezov, D.: The need for uncertainty quantification in machine-assisted medical decision making. Nat. Mach. Intell. **1**(1), 20–23 (2019). http://dx.doi.org/10.1038/s42256-018-0004-1
4. Biondi, F., Alvarez, I., Jeong, K.A.: Human-vehicle cooperation in automated driving: a multidisciplinary review and appraisal. Int. J. Hum.-Comput. Interact. **35**(11), 932–946 (2019)
5. Bonnefon, J.F., Shariff, A., Rahwan, I.: The social dilemma of autonomous vehicles. Science **352**(6293), 1573–1576 (2016)
6. Brown, D.S., Schneider, J., Dragan, A., Niekum, S.: Value alignment verification. In: International Conference on Machine Learning, pp. 1105–1115. PMLR (2021)
7. Brown, S., Davidovic, J., Hasan, A.: The algorithm audit: scoring the algorithms that score us. Big Data Soc. **8**(1), 2053951720983865 (2021)
8. Chen, M., Zhou, P., Fortino, G.: Emotion communication system. IEEE Access **5**, 326–337 (2016)
9. Claybrook, J., Kildare, S.: Autonomous vehicles: no driver... no regulation? Science **361**(6397), 36–37 (2018)
10. Daugherty, P.R., Wilson, H.J.: Human+ Machine: Reimagining Work in the Age of AI. Harvard Business Press (2018)
11. de Melo, C.M., Marsella, S., Gratch, J.: Human cooperation when acting through autonomous machines. Proc. Natl. Acad. Sci. **116**(9), 3482–3487 (2019)
12. Eckersley, P.: Impossibility and uncertainty theorems in AI value alignment (or why your AGI should not have a utility function). arXiv preprint arXiv:1901.00064 (2018)
13. Faulhaber, A.K., et al.: Human decisions in moral dilemmas are largely described by utilitarianism: virtual car driving study provides guidelines for autonomous driving vehicles. Sci. Eng. Ethics **25**(2), 399–418 (2019)
14. Fu, J., Ma, L.: Long-haul vehicle routing and scheduling with biomathematical fatigue constraints. Transp. Sci. **56**, 404–435 (2021)
15. Gabriel, I.: Artificial intelligence, values, and alignment. Mind. Mach. **30**(3), 411–437 (2020)
16. Gehr, T., Mirman, M., Drachsler-Cohen, D., Tsankov, P., Chaudhuri, S., Vechev, M.: AI2: Safety and robustness certification of neural networks with abstract interpretation. In: 2018 IEEE Symposium on Security and Privacy (SP), pp. 3–18. IEEE (2018)

17. Glikson, E., Woolley, A.W.: Human trust in artificial intelligence: review of empirical research. Acad. Manag. Ann. **14**(2), 627–660 (2020)
18. Green, B., Chen, Y.: The principles and limits of algorithm-in-the-loop decision making. Proc. ACM Hum.-Comput. Interact. **3**(CSCW), 1–24 (2019)
19. Guznov, S., et al.: Robot transparency and team orientation effects on human-robot teaming. Int. J. Hum.-Comput. Interact. **36**, 650–660 (2020)
20. Haesevoets, T., De Cremer, D., Dierckx, K., Van Hiel, A.: Human-machine collaboration in managerial decision making. Comput. Hum. Behav. **119**, 106730 (2021)
21. Hamon, R., Junklewitz, H., Sanchez, I.: Robustness and explainability of artificial intelligence. Publications Office of the European Union (2020)
22. Haselton, M.G., Nettle, D., Murray, D.R.: The evolution of cognitive bias. Handb. Evol. Psychol. 968–987 (2015)
23. Hentout, A., Aouache, M., Maoudj, A., Akli, I.: Human-robot interaction in industrial collaborative robotics: a literature review of the decade 2008–2017. Adv. Robot. **33**(15–16), 764–799 (2019)
24. Hoc, J.M.: From human-machine interaction to human-machine cooperation. Ergonomics **43**(7), 833–843 (2000)
25. Honig, S., Oron-Gilad, T.: Understanding and resolving failures in human-robot interaction: literature review and model development. Front. Psychol. **9**(JUN), 861 (2018)
26. Hu, B., Chen, J.: Optimal task allocation for human-machine collaborative manufacturing systems. IEEE Robot. Autom. Lett. **2**(4), 1933–1940 (2017)
27. Inagaki, T., Sheridan, T.B.: Authority and responsibility in human-machine systems: probability theoretic validation of machine-initiated trading of authority. Cogn. Technol. Work **14**(1), 29–37 (2012)
28. Ishowo-Oloko, F., Bonnefon, J.F., Soroye, Z., Crandall, J., Rahwan, I., Rahwan, T.: Behavioural evidence for a transparency-efficiency tradeoff in human-machine cooperation. Nat. Mach. Intell. **1**(11), 517–521 (2019)
29. Jaume-Palasi, L.: Why we are failing to understand the societal impact of artificial intelligence. Soc. Res.: Int. Q. **86**(2), 477–498 (2019)
30. Johnston, P., Harris, R.: The Boeing 737 MAX saga: lessons for software organizations. Softw. Qual. Prof. **21**(3), 4–12 (2019)
31. Kim, R., et al.: A computational model of commonsense moral decision making. In: Proceedings of the 2018 AAAI/ACM Conference on AI, Ethics, and Society, pp. 197–203 (2018)
32. Klumpp, M.: Automation and artificial intelligence in business logistics systems: human reactions and collaboration requirements. Int. J. Log. Res. Appl. **21**(3), 224–242 (2018)
33. Lee, J.D., See, K.A.: Trust in automation: designing for appropriate reliance. Hum. Factors **46**(1), 50–80 (2004)
34. Lin, R., Ma, L., Zhang, W.: An interview study exploring tesla drivers' behavioural adaptation. Appl. Ergon. **72**, 37–47 (2018)
35. Lyons, J.B., Wynne, K.T., Mahoney, S., Roebke, M.A.: Trust and human-machine teaming: a qualitative study. In: Artificial Intelligence for the Internet of Everything, pp. 101–116. Elsevier (2019)
36. Ma, L., Chablat, D., Bennis, F., Zhang, W., Hu, B., Guillaume, F.: Fatigue evaluation in maintenance and assembly operations by digital human simulation in virtual environment. Virtual Reality **15**(1), 55–68 (2011)
37. Madhavan, P., Wiegmann, D.A.: Similarities and differences between human-human and human-automation trust: an integrative review. Theor. Issues Ergon. Sci. **8**, 277–301 (2007)

38. Matheson, E., Minto, R., Zampieri, E.G., Faccio, M., Rosati, G.: Human-robot collaboration in manufacturing applications: a review. Robotics **8**(4), 1–25 (2019)
39. Meissner, P., Keding, C.: The human factor in AI-based decision-making. MIT Sloan Manag. Rev. **63**(1), 1–5 (2021)
40. National Academies of Sciences Engineering, and Medicine: Human-AI Teaming: State of the Art and Research Needs. National Academies Press (2021)
41. Norman, D.A., Ortony, A., Russell, D.M.: Affect and machine design: lessons for the development of autonomous machines. IBM Syst. J. **42**(1), 38–44 (2003)
42. O'Neill, T., et al.: Human-autonomy teaming: a review and analysis of the empirical literature. Hum. Factors (2020). https://doi.org/10.1177/0018720820960865
43. Pereira, L.M., et al.: State-of-the-art of intention recognition and its use in decision making. AI Commun. **26**(2), 237–246 (2013)
44. Rafferty, J., Nugent, C.D., Liu, J., Chen, L.: From activity recognition to intention recognition for assisted living within smart homes. IEEE Trans. Hum.-Mach. Syst. **47**(3), 368–379 (2017)
45. Rahwan, I.: Society-in-the-loop: programming the algorithmic social contract. Ethics Inf. Technol. **20**(1), 5–14 (2017). https://doi.org/10.1007/s10676-017-9430-8
46. Rahwan, I., et al.: Machine behaviour. Nature **568**, 477–486 (2019)
47. Raisamo, R., Rakkolainen, I., Majaranta, P., Salminen, K., Rantala, J., Farooq, A.: Human augmentation: past, present and future. Int. J. Hum. Comput. Stud. **131**, 131–143 (2019)
48. Raji, I.D., et al.: Closing the AI accountability gap: defining an end-to-end framework for internal algorithmic auditing. In: Proceedings of the 2020 Conference on Fairness, Accountability, and Transparency, pp. 33–44 (2020)
49. Robla-Gomez, S., Becerra, V.M., Llata, J.R., Gonzalez-Sarabia, E., Torre-Ferrero, C., Perez-Oria, J.: Working together: a review on safe human-robot collaboration in industrial environments. IEEE Access **5**, 26754–26773 (2017)
50. Rodriguez-Soto, M., Serramia, M., Lopez-Sanchez, M., Rodriguez-Aguilar, J.A.: Instilling moral value alignment by means of multi-objective reinforcement learning. Ethics Inf. Technol. **24**(1), 1–17 (2022)
51. Saberi, M.: The human factor in AI safety. arXiv preprint arXiv:2201.04263 (2022)
52. Sandvig, C., Hamilton, K., Karahalios, K., Langbort, C.: An algorithm audit. Data and discrimination: collected essays, pp. 6–10. New America Foundation, Washington, DC (2014)
53. Seeber, I., et al.: Machines as teammates: a research agenda on AI in team collaboration. Inf. Manage. **57**(2), 103174 (2020)
54. Sohn, K., Kwon, O.: Technology acceptance theories and factors influencing artificial intelligence-based intelligent products. Telematics Inform. **47**, 101324 (2020)
55. Soll, J.B., Milkman, K.L., Payne, J.W.: A user's guide to debiasing (2014)
56. Solso, R.L., MacLin, M.K., MacLin, O.H.: Cognitive Psychology. Pearson Education, New Zealand (2005)
57. Tahboub, K.A.: Intelligent human-machine interaction based on dynamic Bayesian networks probabilistic intention recognition. J. Intell. Rob. Syst. **45**(1), 31–52 (2006)
58. Tjoa, E., Guan, C.: A survey on explainable artificial intelligence (XAI): toward medical XAI. IEEE Trans. Neural Netw. Learn. Syst. **32**(11), 4793–4813 (2020)
59. Tsao, L., Li, L., Ma, L.: Human work and status evaluation based on wearable sensors in human factors and ergonomics: a review. IEEE Trans. Hum.-Mach. Syst. **49**(1), 72–84 (2019)
60. Turk, M.: Multimodal interaction: a review. Pattern Recogn. Lett. **36**, 189–195 (2014)

61. Warden, T., et al.: The national academies board on human system integration (BOHSI) panel: explainable AI, system transparency, and human machine teaming. In: Proceedings of the Human Factors and Ergonomics Society Annual Meeting, vol. 63, pp. 631–635. SAGE Publications, Los Angeles (2019)

62. Wright, J.L., Chen, J.Y., Lakhmani, S.G.: Agent transparency and reliability in human-robot interaction: the influence on user confidence and perceived reliability. IEEE Trans. Hum.-Mach. Syst. **50**(3), 254–263 (2020)

63. Xiong, W., Fan, H., Ma, L., Wang, C.: Challenges of human-machine collaboration in risky decision-making. Front. Eng. Manage. **9**(1), 1–15 (2022)

64. Yang, C., Zhu, Y., Chen, Y.: A review of human - machine cooperation in the robotics domain. IEEE Trans. Hum.-Mach. Syst. **52**(1), 12–25 (2022)

65. Young, S.N., Peschel, J.M.: Review of human-machine interfaces for small unmanned systems with robotic manipulators. IEEE Trans. Hum.-Mach. Syst. **50**(2), 131–143 (2020)

66. Yu, K.H., Beam, A.L., Kohane, I.S.: Artificial intelligence in healthcare. Nat. Biomed. Eng. **2**(10), 719–731 (2018)

67. Zheng, J., Zhang, T., Ma, L., Wu, Y., Zhang, W.: Vibration warning design for reaction time reduction under the environment of intelligent connected vehicles. Appl. Ergon. **96**, 103490 (2021)

68. Zhou, X., Ma, L., Zhang, W.: Event-related driver stress detection with smartphones among young novice drivers. Ergonomics 1–19 (2022). https://doi.org/10.1080/00140139.2021.2020342

ViCon - Towards Understanding Visual Support Systems in Collaborative Video Conferencing

Kay Schröder[1,2]([✉]) [iD] and Steffi Kohl[2,3] [iD]

[1] Human Data Interaction Lab, Zuyd University of Applied Sciences,
Heerlen, The Netherlands
[2] Human Computer Interaction Center RWTH Aachen, Aachen, Germany
kay.schroder@zuyd.nl
[3] Maastricht University, Maastricht, The Netherlands

Abstract. While meetings take up a significant part of the workday, participants often perceive them as poor and unproductive. With the surge in videoconferencing meetings for work due to the COVID-19 pandemic, many employees experienced that videoconferencing can even aggravate negative experiences in meetings. Past research has shown that the level of engagement during meetings is a crucial aspect of meeting a success. While there have been some attempts towards utilizing post-analysis feedback, there is little effort towards real-time support to improve engagement. This research explores the development of a visual support system for automated, real-time feedback on team communication behavior during online meetings. We present a novel, fully working visual support system that was evaluated with positive results. This study outlines the step-wise development of the method. We collected a range of qualitative feedback measures to understand better how users perceive the visual support system. First, we collected qualitative feedback from participants and eye-tracking data (n = 4) to evaluate four visualization approaches. The second step evaluated the best-performing visualization by a user study with participants (N = 72) working in groups of four on a collaborative problem-solving task. Users give the tool good scores on a seven-point Likert scale: perceived usefulness (4.8), ease of understanding (5.6), and perceived precision (5.1). Our results indicate that our novel system can enhance the quality of video conferencing through real-time visual support.

Keywords: Visual support systems · Feedback · Video-conferencing

1 Introduction

In today's highly collaborative work environments, meetings are often a significant time investment, with up to 23 h per week spent in meetings. Optimizing productivity in these meetings is one of the keys to organizational success. Effective meetings are a medium for communication and collaboration during which

© The Author(s), under exclusive license to Springer Nature Switzerland AG 2022
V. G. Duffy (Ed.): HCII 2022, LNCS 13319, pp. 278–288, 2022.
https://doi.org/10.1007/978-3-031-05890-5_22

ideas are developed and information is shared between team members. However, research shows that between 25% and 50% of all meetings are poor [27], and 71% of surveyed managers considered their meetings unproductive [18].

Past research has shown that the level of engagement during meetings is a crucial aspect of meeting success. Low levels of engagement have been linked to lower perceived meeting effectiveness, diminished decision quality and lower collective intelligence [24,26,27]. Many online platforms such as Zoom, Teams, or Jitsi already provide options for automated meeting scripts, participation analysis and video recordings. While there have been some first attempts towards utilizing these automatically generated data streams for post-analysis [24], there is little effort towards data driving real-time support for meetings to increase meeting engagement.

Research has shown that feedback for skills development is best presented immediately instead of delayed. This presents a particular challenge in the context of online meetings. The relevant information must be understood by all meeting members and conveyed without interrupting the meeting flow.

This paper explores how visualization can be used as automated, real-time feedback on team communication behavior. Specifically, the focus will be on establishing what type of visualization provides the most effective means of intuitively and effectively communicating spoken contributions between the participants.

The rest of this paper is organized into five sections. Section 2 briefly reviews the relevant literature for feedback tool development and the current state of tools developed for this purpose. Section 3 presents an overview of the methodology followed in the project. Section 4 details the user evaluation study. Section 5 discusses the results before the conclusion is presented in Sect. 6.

2   Related Work

2.1   Effective Feedback for Skills Development

Feedback is generally considered to be one of the most critical support strategies for optimal learning [22]. However, the impact of individual forms of feedback has shown to vary considerably [25]. Particularly in dynamic decision-making contexts, the literature generally favors providing immediate feedback over delayed. Two types of feedback are generally considered within the space of immediate feedback: *real-time feedback* and *near real-time feedback*, with near real-time feedback being the more common form of immediate support [6,20,21,24]. In contrast to near real-time feedback, real-time feedback is presented within the context of actual time passing; that is, the feedback does not interrupt or stop the contextual timeline. Near real-time feedback, however, is either delivered upon completion of a task or interrupts the contextual timeline.

Near real-time feedback is often picked over real-time feedback as the challenge with implementing feedback in real-time is that it may disrupt the process and distract people from their primary task. In real-time feedback, two distinct sources of information—the ongoing communication and the feedback—compete for cognitive resources. These competing streams of information may risk cognitive overload and, consequently, cause detrimental effects on learning [11]. Trying to avoid this, a study by O'Neil et al. [17] found that in the case of immediate feedback, the modality of the feedback presented should complement the information modality of the training task. In other words, in a verbal/audio task, providing feedback in a visual mode is more effective, avoiding an overload of the audio channel with additional audio information. These findings are also supported by Fiorella et al. [6].

2.2   Real-Time Feedback Systems in Video Conferencing Meetings

Past research has explored the feasibility of using real-time feedback in computer-mediated communication for skill development. This work has included, among others, text or auditory [6] feedback. Further, researchers have developed multiple tools using data visualization for automated feedback systems. These tools include Breakout [1], an open measurement and intervention tool for distributed peer learning groups, and ReflectLive [5], a system that provides real-time feedback about non-verbal communication behavior to clinicians with the aim of improving their communication behavior. While the approach of using visual support systems in video conferencing meetings seems in line with the idea of complementing the information modality channels, both of these projects appear to have been abandoned. One reason might be the very complex nature of approaches that integrate multiple signals within the visual support system. Mixing these signals might make it hard for participants to learn from the provided feedback as causality could be unclear. Further, some signals such as spoken communication exist only in the moment. Real-time speech can not be searched or analyzed as it exists only in the memories of people. Asking conversation participants to recall what they said often produces distorted, inaccurate representations of the original conversation. Even recorded communications are hard to analyze due to their temporal and multi-channel nature.

2.3   The Impact of Social Signals on Team Meetings

Spoken communication consists of four channels: 1) The semantic verbal channel that contains the meaning of the words which are uttered; 2) The expressive verbal channel that contains the paralingual and prosodic features of language; 3) The nonvocal channel that contains, for example, gestures, eye focus, and body posture; 4) The relational channel that contains the manner in which two more individuals connect and reflect.

Numerous studies in various domains have attempted to explain what makes groups work together effectively. Approaches in the area of human–computer interaction have focused on social signal processing to understand the impact of communication channels 2 and 3 on various team outcomes such as creativity [8] or performance [16]. However, previously published studies on the effect of social signals on team outcomes are not consistent, identifying various signals as potentially relevant. In line with this Kohl et al. demonstrated that during

Early Visualization Concepts

Fig. 1. Early design studies: A) Timeline visualizations below the participants showing historic contribution; B) Changes in participant video feed size proportional to the respective contribution

different stages of collaboration, teams display different social signals [12,13]. A detailed overview of the current state of the literature was compiled by Praharaj et al. [19]. When differentiating between types of meetings, we are able to detect more meaningful patterns. Equal participation seems to be most present in meetings focusing on Ideation [12]–compared to other stages of the design thinking process– and equal participation has shown beneficial in collaborative decision-making discussions [4]. Research investigating how to create equal distribution of communication in team shown, that it is most relevant to reduce the contribution of the over-participator [3].

3   Designing ViCon

3.1   Problem Context Analysis

An equal contribution and balanced collaboration of the participants is vital to the success of collaborative problem-solving (CPS) tasks [4]. While there are many approaches to analyzing individual contributions after a session [20], the field remains mute on how to give efficient real-time feedback. Real-time understanding of speech contribution within a specific task is challenging as the attention is primarily drawn to the task itself, namely the verbal interaction through speech and the visual feedback via facial expressions. Therefore, the feedback method needs to be very simple and easy to understand to not distract from the primary task. As CPSs require a high level of interaction, a high risk of cognitive overload exists [6,11]. Self-perception of communication behavior is limited without external feedback. Prior research has shown that the channel encoding of feedback should complement the perceptual channel of the actual task [17]. As a CPS is based on audio conversation, a visual stimulus seems the most promising approach. Multiple visual encodings for quantitative data exist and can be described as channels and marks [15]. The individual visual encodings influence how they are perceived [10]. Therefore visualization design focuses on aligning the most efficient encoding within a specific task. However, past research focused primarily on the accuracy and understanding of complex phenomena and less on the direct feedback of low-complexity data. Therefore, a careful justification of design choices is needed to validate the efficiency in the given scenario.

3.2   Iterative Visualization Design

We initiated an iterative design process. We started with three fundamentally different approaches within an iterative design process: First, we used a split screen (see Fig. 1 A). Second, we used direct encoding of the individual contribution in the video stream and scaling the respective streams (see Fig. 1 B). Third, we designed a mixed approach where the feedback system is centrally positioned between the streams (see Fig. 2). After evaluating the individual approaches, we ended with four different visualization methods (see Fig. 2). We included a dynamic orb visualization as this is similar to the visualization used in Breakout [1], the most similar tool to ViCon we could find in the literature. As an additional approach, we added a bar chart because this approach is commonly used in post-meeting analysis [2].

Glikson et al. [7] proposed using a horizontal stacked bar chart to overview the individual team contribution. However, this approach was not suitable for our use case as the relationship between area and contributor was not applicable to a video setting without significantly increasing the cognitive load. We also included two types of area encodings: rectangles and triangles. For further validation, we conducted an eye-tracking study (n = 4), during which the participants solved four different tasks, one each per visualization approach (see Fig. 4). We found that users tended to overlook the orbs, which is especially surprising as it is the primary method used in nearly all past research projects. The latter could explain the fact that previous research, which commonly used orbs, was abandoned without evidence of positive results. We also conclude that the bars are difficult to perceive as users need to jump between multiple areas.

Following the tasks, all participants were interviewed in a focus group to reflect on their experience with the different visualizations. All users agreed that triangle and area encodings work better than bar charts and orbs, with orbs being the least preferred visualization method. Based on the focus group feedback and eye tracking, we concluded that triangles and area encodings worked equally well for users. As triangles have a smaller overlap with the streams, we decided to use this method as the final design. Together with users, we found that triangles and area encodings work better than bar charts and orbs.

Final Visualization Design

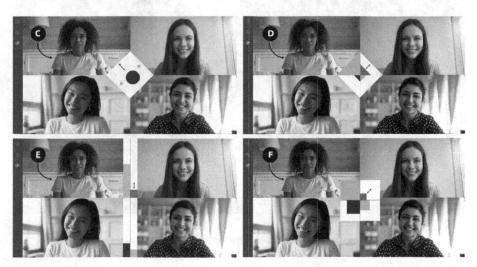

Fig. 2. Visualization methods included in the eye-tracking study: C) dynamic orb visualization; D) triangular area encoding; E) bar chart visualization; F) rectangular area encoding

4   User Evaluation Study

This section describes the user study we conducted to assess ViCon. We elaborate on the study design as well as the variables collected.

4.1   Participants

We recruited 150 participants to take part in a 30-minute study in exchange for course credit. All participants were randomly assigned to a team of five. Only teams with at least four members present were allowed to participate in the study. As participation was voluntary, 10 teams arrived with fewer than four members and were excluded from the study. Two teams were discounted from the participant pool as they experienced technical difficulties, leaving 72 participants (25.9% male; Mage = 18.7 years, SD = 1.21) and 18 teams.

4.2   Questionnaire

The questionnaire was used to assess user evaluation as well as to obtain qualitative feedback from the participants. We used part of the technology acceptance model (TAM) measures to assess user evaluation. The TAM model is the dominant model used to explain users' behavior toward technology, consisting of two variables, Perceived Ease of Use (PEOU) and Perceived Usefulness (PU) [14].

Fig. 3. Final visualization design used in the evaluation study

For this study, we focus on PU, which assesses how a user expects a system to enhance their job performance. We did not assess PEOU as participants only used the application to talk and had no further interaction with the software that could be assessed. Instead, we included questions on Ease of Understanding (EU) the visualization and Perceived Precision (PP) of the visualization. PU was measured through seven questions, and EU and PP were measured through two questions. Each set of questions involved reverse-coded items to assess the internal validity of the answers. Answers were averaged to assess the perceived usefulness of ViCon. In addition, we asked participants to reflect on ViCon in terms of the factors: fun, enjoyable, interesting, absorbing, and boring. Last, participants were asked to give qualitative feedback on the experience with ViCon in the form of a written "think aloud protocol" (Fig. 3).

4.3   Task and Stimuli

For this study, the participating teams were instructed to solve two divergent thinking tasks: an Unusual Uses Task (UUT), a classic and widely used measure of divergent thinking [9] and a consequences task [23]. Each team used ViCon to solve the task during a video conferencing session. For one of the sessions, participants could see the stimuli, whereas for the other, they could not. We randomized the order of showing the stimuli to exclude the possibility of sequencing effects.

4.4   Procedure

Participants arrived at the test site in teams of four. After signing a consent form, each participant was guided to a separate room and set up with a laptop

Fig. 4. Gaze detection for different visualizations in ViCon. The screenshots show the beginning of each session before the visualisation displays each user's speech contribution. From top left to bottom right, the stimuli are: triangle area plot, square area plot, dynamic orb area plot, bar chart.

on which ViCon was already started. All participants were presented with written instructions for the task, and the researchers made sure that all participants had read and understood the task before starting the session. Participants had 3 min to solve each task, after which they were asked to complete the questionnaire before proceeding to the instructions for the next task.

5   Results

The results for the user evaluation measures can be found in Fig. 5. All measures were taken on a 7-point Likert scale. PU, EU and PP were all evaluated above average with scores of 4.8, 5.6 and 5.1, respectively. Users further evaluated ViCon as *fun* (5.1), *interesting* (5.3), and *enjoyable* (5.1) and not *boring* (2.5). However, users did not perceive ViCon as *absorbing*, with an average score of 3.7. The answers to the open-ended feedback questions indicate that ViCon influenced participation in the task and individual attitudes in most cases. Participant feedback included statements like, "After having used the tool, I still tried to be more actively involved in the discussion", "I think the square in the middle is really helpful to see who speaks the most and who the less. I felt the pressure to say something", and "[I was] confused about the different colored triangles in the middle of the screen, not sure what they mean."

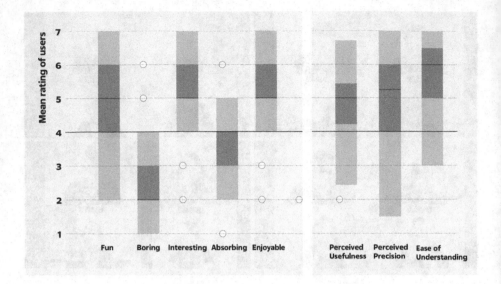

Fig. 5. Boxplots displaying the user experience measures.

6   Conclusion

Our work represents a first step to improving team performance in video conferences through visual support systems. During the visualization design process, we developed several glyph designs to provide immediate visual stimuli requiring a low cognitive load. Surprisingly, user evaluation showed that the most suitable approach is different from the most commonly used approach in the literature. We present a fully working visual support system that enables users to reflect on their speech behavior in real time and, therefore, can directly contribute to the quality of the meeting outcome. Users positively evaluated the resulting application and could intuitively use the application. It appears the visual feedback might have two effects–helping people who don't say anything and putting the brakes on people who say more than everyone else.

However, more research needs to be done to shed light on how the effect of real-time feedback can be measured and quantified. The need for more research applies to understanding the impact the visual support system has on the cognition and speech behavior of the participants and how this impact translates into various outcome variables such as team satisfaction, rapport and performance. First, the visual design space needs to be evaluated more extensively to control whether the evaluated effects persist in larger sample sizes and how design choices affect perception in terms of understanding, attention and cognitive load.

Following an extensive design evaluation, we believe it is important to gain a comprehensive understanding of how real-time visual support in meetings affects teams and their collaboration. This evaluation should go beyond evaluating only direct effects on performance but also aim to understand secondary outcomes such as rapport or satisfaction. Diminishing the negative effects of meetings and building a workplace culture in which everyone is encouraged to and feels free to contribute can hold large financial benefits for companies that go beyond simple performance measures.

References

1. Calacci, D., Lederman, O., Shrier, D., Pentland, A.: Breakout: an open measurement and intervention tool for distributed peer learning groups. arXiv preprint arXiv:1607.01443 (2016)
2. DiMicco, J.M., Hollenbach, K.J., Pandolfo, A., Bender, W.: The impact of increased awareness while face-to-face. Hum.-Comput. Interact. **22**(1–2), 47–96 (2007)
3. DiMicco, J.M., Pandolfo, A., Bender, W.: Influencing group participation with a shared display. In: Proceedings of the 2004 ACM Conference on Computer Supported Cooperative Work, pp. 614–623 (2004)
4. Dong, W., Lepri, B., Kim, T., Pianesi, F., Pentland, A.S.: Modeling conversational dynamics and performance in a social dilemma task. In: 2012 5th International Symposium on Communications, Control and Signal Processing, pp. 1–4. IEEE (2012)
5. Faucett, H.A., Lee, M.L., Carter, S.: I should listen more: real-time sensing and feedback of non-verbal communication in video telehealth. In: Proceedings of the ACM on Human-Computer Interaction, vol. 1(CSCW), pp. 1–19 (2017)
6. Fiorella, L., Vogel-Walcutt, J.J., Schatz, S.: Applying the modality principle to real-time feedback and the acquisition of higher-order cognitive skills. Educ. Technol. Res. Dev. **60**(2), 223–238 (2012)
7. Glikson, E., Woolley, A.W., Gupta, P., Kim, Y.J.: Visualized automatic feedback in virtual teams. Front. Psychol. **10**, 814 (2019)
8. Gloor, P.A., Almozlino, A., Inbar, O., Lo, W., Provost, S.: Measuring team creativity through longitudinal social signals. arXiv preprint arXiv:1407.0440 (2014)
9. Guilford, J.P.: The nature of human intelligence (1967)
10. Heer, J., Bostock, M.: Crowdsourcing graphical perception: using mechanical turk to assess visualization design. In: Proceedings of the SIGCHI Conference on Human Factors in Computing Systems, pp. 203–212 (2010)
11. Kalyuga, S., Chandler, P., Sweller, J.: Managing split-attention and redundancy in multimedia instruction. Appl. Cogn. Psychol.: Off. J. Soc. Appl. Res. Mem. Cogn. **13**(4), 351–371 (1999)
12. Kohl, S., Graus, M.P., Lemmink, J.G.A.M.: Deciphering the code: evidence for a sociometric DNA in design thinking meetings. In: Stephanidis, C., Antona, M., Ntoa, S. (eds.) HCII 2020. CCIS, vol. 1293, pp. 53–61. Springer, Cham (2020). https://doi.org/10.1007/978-3-030-60700-5_7
13. Kohl, S., Graus, M.P., Lemmink, J.G.: Context is key: mining social signals for automatic task detection in design thinking meetings. In: International Conference on Human-Computer Interaction. Springer (2022)
14. Marangunić, N., Granić, A.: Technology acceptance model: a literature review from 1986 to 2013. Univ. Access Inf. Soc. **14**(1), 81–95 (2014). https://doi.org/10.1007/s10209-014-0348-1
15. Munzner, T.: Visualization Analysis and Design. CRC Press, Boca Raton (2014)

16. Olguin, D.O., Gloor, P.A., Pentland, A.S.: Capturing individual and group behavior with wearable sensors. In: Proceedings of the 2009 AAAI Spring Symposium on Human Behavior Modeling, SSS, vol. 9 (2009)

17. O'Neil, H.F., Chuang, Sh.S., Baker, E.L.: Computer-based feedback for computer-based collaborative problem solving. In: Ifenthaler, D., Pirnay-Dummer, P., Seel, N. (eds.) Computer-Based Diagnostics and Systematic Analysis of Knowledge, pp. 261–279. Springer, Boston (2010). https://doi.org/10.1007/978-1-4419-5662-0_14

18. Perlow, L.A., Hadley, C.N., Eun, E.: Stop the meeting madness. Harv. Bus. Rev. 95(4), 62–69 (2017)

19. Praharaj, S., Scheffel, M., Drachsler, H., Specht, M.M.: Literature review on co-located collaboration modeling using multimodal learning analytics can we go the whole nine yards. IEEE Trans. Learn. Technol. 14, 367–385 (2021)

20. Samrose, S., et al.: MeetingCoach: an intelligent dashboard for supporting effective & inclusive meetings. In: Proceedings of the 2021 CHI Conference on Human Factors in Computing Systems, pp. 1–13 (2021)

21. Samrose, S., et al.: CoCo: collaboration coach for understanding team dynamics during video conferencing. Proc. ACM Interact. Mob. Wearable Ubiquit. Technol. 1(4), 1–24 (2018)

22. Shute, V.J.: Focus on formative feedback. Rev. Educ. Res. 78(1), 153–189 (2008)

23. Silvia, P.J., et al.: Assessing creativity with divergent thinking tasks: exploring the reliability and validity of new subjective scoring methods. Psychol. Aesthet. Creat. Arts 2(2), 68 (2008)

24. Wang, T., Keck, M., Vosough, Z.: Discussion flows: an interactive visualization for analyzing engagement in multi-party meetings (2021)

25. Wisniewski, B., Zierer, K., Hattie, J.: The power of feedback revisited: a meta-analysis of educational feedback research. Front. Psychol. 10, 3087 (2020)

26. Woolley, A.W., Aggarwal, I., Malone, T.W.: Collective intelligence and group performance. Curr. Dir. Psychol. Sci. 24(6), 420–424 (2015)

27. Yoerger, M., Crowe, J., Allen, J.A.: Participate or else!: The effect of participation in decision-making in meetings on employee engagement. Consult. Psychol. J.: Pract. Res. 67(1), 65 (2015)

Revolutionizing Ergonomics in Manufacturing Processes Using Collaborative Robots: A Systematic Literature Review

Asra Sheikh[1]([✉]) and Vincent G. Duffy[2]

[1] Purdue University, West Lafayette, IN 47907, USA
sheikh9@purdue.edu
[2] School of Industrial Engineering, Purdue University, West Lafayette, IN 47907, USA
duffy@purdue.edu

Abstract. Manufacturing processes have been a long-standing component of industrialization. Nearly all products used in everyday life are achieved through manufacturing. As rapid modernization occurs, human-robot collaboration should be encouraged to ensure the wellbeing of human workers. Ergonomics of factory working conditions are often discounted until dire injuries are reported. Implementation of collaborative robots will reduce the manual labor load on operators in manufacturing and assembly lines. In this systematic literature review, current and emerging publications on ergonomics, collaborative robots, and manufacturing were evaluated using tools such as Harzing's Publish or Perish, VOS Viewer, CiteSpace, Vicinitas, MAXQDA, and Mendeley. A variety of databases were referenced including Web of Science, Google Scholar, and Scopus to identify emerging trends. Co-citation analysis, cluster analysis, and content analysis supported the literary investigations and provided evidence on areas of greatest interest while also highlighting areas that have potential for growth.

Keywords: Ergonomics · Collaborative Robot · Manufacturing · Human-Robot Collaboration

1 Introduction and Background

Human operators have been the backbone of manufacturing processes for years since industrial development. These workers are constantly on-site performing a variety of manual labor. Due to growing populations leading to rapid urbanization and hence an increased demand for products, manufacturing process workers are often subject to many workplace stressors. These include long shifts, repetitive tasks, or "inflexible, mass customized workspaces" (El Zaatari et al. 2019). As of 2016, almost 30% of European workers in manufacturing industries faced pain in their lower back according to the US Department of Labor (Cherubini et al. 2016). Poor ergonomic work conditions and physically taxing jobs are a leading cause of musculoskeletal disorders (MSDs) among assembly line operators (Maurice et al. 2017). While automation is normalized in manufacturing, conventional industrial robots are incapable of achieving the same

© The Author(s), under exclusive license to Springer Nature Switzerland AG 2022
V. G. Duffy (Ed.): HCII 2022, LNCS 13319, pp. 289–305, 2022.
https://doi.org/10.1007/978-3-031-05890-5_23

delicate control a human operator can in difficult but intricate tasks. In such cases, the answer lies with human-robot collaboration, where a worker and robot work alongside each other to complete tasks efficiently and with reduced load on the human counterpart.

1.1 Ergonomics in Manufacturing Processes

Ergonomics is a fundamental aspect of occupational safety. Regardless of the work type, ergonomics aims to ensure worker well-being is maintained. It is an area of constant concern amongst manufacturing process workers. Assembly line workspaces are often non-adjustable, leading to workers having to re-adjust their positions frequently to reduce the "loading" on body parts that may feel uncomfortable (Mcatamney and Corlett 1993). Limb disorders and back injuries are not uncommon in the manufacturing world. These issues were often addressed after a worker sustained considerable discomfort by conducting an ergonomic intervention. However, this solution is not entirely sustainable in the long run. To achieve complete ergonomic success in manufacturing processes, a well-established 'work design' is crucial. The goal of a work design is to strategize work conditions in a way that certain inevitable stressors on workers are limited to an allowable extent (Spath and Braun 2021). In other words, the manufacturing industry should be optimized to be more "human-centered" where workers' physical, mental, and emotional health is protected (Spath and Braun 2021).

1.2 Collaborative Robots

Automation and robotics have revolutionized multiple industries allowing for increased throughput and efficient production. Industrial robots are used widely in manufacturing to take over many physically demanding tasks. Such robots are designed to perform repetitive tasks and often operate away from humans under strong safety protocols such as cages (Pearce et al. 2018). However, it can prove to be inefficient if programing the "functional sequence" is laborious (Spath and Braun 2021). Collaborative robots, also known as 'cobots' are a rising solution to increase manufacturing flexibility. These robots work alongside humans assisting the operator in their tasks. For example, aiding in laying parts on an assembly line. This means that human skills can be harnessed without risk of injury and can be combined with the benefits of a robot to achieve optimum performance and improved worker ergonomics (Bänziger et al. 2020). As collaborative robots work in close proximity with the operators, increased safety measures are necessary to facilitate secure human-robot interaction.

2 Problem Statement

The purpose of this study is to conduct a systematic literature review of existing publications on the feasibility of using collaborative robots in manufacturing processes to enhance worker ergonomics. This literature review will shed light on the current emergence of the topic and areas for further research. An effective literature analysis can be facilitated using software such as Harzing's Publish or Perish, Vicinitas, VOS Viewer, CiteSpace, BibExcel, MAXQDA, and Mendeley.

3 Procedure

3.1 Data Collection

Data collection serves as a primary step for a literature review. For this research, data was collected from three databases – Web of Science, Google Scholar, and Scopus. Web of Science can be further narrowed to the Web of Science 'Core Collection' or 'All databases'. For this review, the Web of Science Core Collection was selected. Results from Google Scholar were obtained using Harzing's Publish or Perish. Harzing is a valuable bibliometric analysis tool that can retrieve data from numerous databases. Google Scholar was selected as it has a much more extensive scope of articles and can produce a greater number of results. It is important to note that search results in Harzing are limited to 1000 as a default. Lastly, Scopus also has a considerable range of publications, but for the purpose of this research, it was selected due to its variety of statistics and trend analyses generated for any search term(s). The search terms used in all databases were "ergonomics" AND "collaborative robot" AND "manufacturing". Only using the word 'manufacturing' was crucial as it allowed for a more exhaustive search. Adding any other words such as manufacturing 'process' or 'industry' severely limited the number of articles obtained, though both words have similar meaning. The resulting number of articles and their respective publication year range for each database can be seen in Table 1. 2022 was included in the publication time range only for Google Scholar in an effort to collect the latest and upcoming works. Articles in Web of Science and Scopus were limited to 2021.

Table 1. Number of articles obtained from each database using respective keywords

Database	Keywords and Delimiters	Publication Years	Number of Articles
Web of Science	"ergonomics" AND "collaborative robot" AND "manufacturing"	2015–2021	51
Google Scholar (Harzing's Publish or Perish)	"ergonomics" AND "collaborative robot" AND "manufacturing"	1989–2022	980
Scopus	"ergonomics" AND "collaborative robot" AND "manufacturing"	2001–2021	543

4   Research Methodologies

4.1   Trend Analysis

Trend analyses in a literature review offer support in identifying how prevalent an emerging topic is. Web of Science offers a variety of categories with which search term results can be analyzed, such as documents published per year, times cited, authors, research areas, countries, etc. These analyses can be visualized in the form of a bar chart, treemap chart, or table.

The purple bars in Fig. 1 present a trend analysis for publications per year for 51 articles on 'ergonomics' and 'collaborative robot' and 'manufacturing'. A promising growth pattern can be seen over the years with the number of publications increasing in recent times, with 2019 and 2021 having the highest number of documents published. This indicates the topic is rapidly emerging and research is actively being conducted. It is interesting to note that there is a slight drop in the publications in 2020, which could possibly be attributed to the COVID-19 pandemic and its uncertainties.

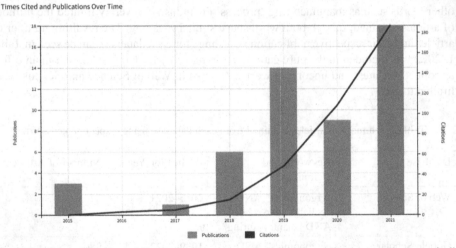

Times Cited and Publications Over Time

Fig. 1. Trend analysis for publication years and number of times publications on "ergonomics" AND "collaborative robot" and "manufacturing" were cited over time (Web of Science, n.d.)

The blue curve in Fig. 1 presents the number of times a publication is cited over time. It can be seen that the curve is steadily increasing from 2015 to 2021, with 18 citations this year. Certain years such as 2015, 2018, and 2019 appear to have relatively low citations when compared to the number of publications. This shows that there is significant attention and exploration given towards using collaborative robots and improving ergonomics in manufacturing processes.

4.2   Relevant Statistics

During a literature evaluation, leading lists are useful for identifying the most prevalent authors, sources, universities, etc. that publish works in a particular area of interest.

The leading tables were obtained using BibExcel. Using the keywords "ergonomics" and "collaborative robot" and "manufacturing", metadata was extracted from Google Scholar via Harzing and imported to BibExcel. BibExcel was used "due to its flexibility to work with large datasets and the compatibility with different computer applications including Excel" (Fahimnia et al. 2015). Its capability to analyze results from Google Scholar allows for a much more expansive database to be analyzed. For this review, leading authors and leading sources were identified.

Leading Authors. The top 14 leading authors for works on ergonomics and collaborative robots in manufacturing were identified and are presented in Table 2 along with the respective number of publications. It can be seen that Raunch E and Gualtieri L have published the greatest number of articles. For further graphical emphasis, the information was imported to Excel and organized in a PivotTable as shown in Fig. 2.

Table 2. Top 14 leading authors for articles about ergonomics and collaborative robots in manufacturing (BibExcel, n.d.)

Author	Number of Publications
Rauch E	20
Gualtieri L	17
Malik AA	10
Vidoni R	9
Colim A	9
Matt DT	9
Lorenzini M	9
Faccio M	8
Liau YY	8
Kim W	8
Zanchettin AM	7
Bilberg A	7
Makrini I El	7
Mark BG	7

Leading Sources. The top 10 leading sources for works on ergonomics and collaborative robots in manufacturing were identified and are presented in Table 3. It can be seen that Procedia CIRP and Robotics and Computer-Integrated Manufacturing have published the most papers, i.e. 35 and 22 respectively. The information was then imported to Excel and organized in a PivotTable as shown in Fig. 3.

Fig. 2. PivotTable for leading authors for number of publications on ergonomics and collaborative robots in manufacturing (BibExcel, n.d.)

Table 3. Top 10 leading sources for articles about ergonomics and collaborative robots in manufacturing (BibExcel, n.d.)

Source	Number of Articles
Procedia CIRP	35
Robotics and Computer-Integrated Manufacturing	22
Procedia Manufacturing	19
IFAC-PapersOnLine	19
Applied Sciences	14
IEEE Robotics and Automation and Letters	12
International Journal of Automation Technology	12
Sensors	11
Proceedings of the Computational Methods in Systems and Software	10
arXiv preprint arXiv	10

4.3 Further Justifications

Applications Justification. The topic of ergonomics and collaborative robots in manufacturing is emerging in numerous fields of study. Evidence of this was shown using the keywords "ergonomics" and "collaborative robot" and "manufacturing" in Scopus. The results were then analyzed. Figure 4 presents a pie chart reflecting different subject areas the scopus results came from and their percent breakdown.

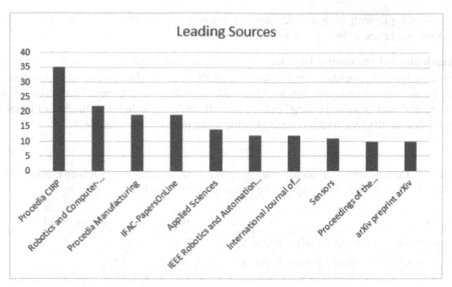

Fig. 3. PivotTable for leading sources for number of publications on ergonomics and collaborative robots in manufacturing (BibExcel, n.d.)

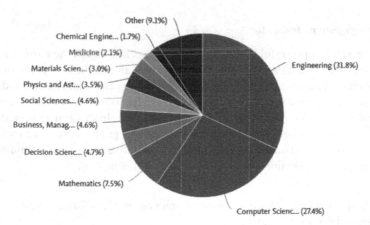

Fig. 4. Breakdown of publications on ergonomics and collaborative robots in manufacturing based on various subject areas (Scopus, n.d.)

It can be seen from Fig. 4 that a diverse set of subject areas are covered ranging from engineering and medicine to social sciences and business. This indicates that the topic of ergonomics and collaborative robots in manufacturing has applications in multiple industries and expanding the research can be advantageous to a large audience. This can be attributed to the fact that human-robot interaction is an interdisciplinary field encompassing "classical robotics, cognitive sciences, and psychology" (Bauer et al.

2008). A topic with such a wide range of research areas allows for more applications variety and hence a stronger justification for emergence.

Academic Justifications. Ergonomics and collaborative robots in manufacturing is a topic of growing popularity in academia as well. This can be confirmed by observing the publications trend over 5 years. Using the keywords "ergonomics" and "collaborative robot" and "manufacturing" in Google Scholar via Harzing, the number of articles published in 2015 vs. in 2020 were identified and presented in Table 4.

Table 4. Comparison of the number of articles published in a span of 5 years related to ergonomics and collaborative robots in manufacturing (Harzing's Publish or Perish, n.d.)

Database	Year	Number of Articles
Google Scholar (Harzing's Publish or Perish)	2020	236
Google Scholar (Harzing's Publish or Perish)	2015	17

It can be seen from Table 4 that there has been an immense increase in the number of articles published, jumping from 17 to 236 in a fairly short timeframe. Thus, this justifies that this topic is quite promising and suitable for conducting a systematic literature review.

4.4   Engagement Indicator

Social media is a powerful tool to share new ideas and assess the current audience for a certain topic. Social media indicators can provide insight into community interest surrounding research areas that may seem limited to academia or niche industries. For this research, Twitter was used as the social media source, and metadata on hashtags was pulled using Vicintas. Due to the concept of the hashtag, it is important to note that keywords must be brief or abbreviated. In this case, the topic search was separated into 'ergonomics and manufacturing' and 'collaborative robot and manufacturing'. The respective metrics obtained from Vicinitas are shown in Table 5.

Table 5. Analytics indicating engagement of ergonomics and collaborative robots in manufacturing on social media (Vicinitas n.d.)

Topic	Users	Posts	Engagement	Influence
Ergonomics and manufacturing	13	15	6	24.7K
Collaborative robot and manufacturing	5	5	16	87.0K

It can be seen from Table 5 that Vicintas provides quantitative information on the 'users', 'posts', 'engagement', and 'influence' for any topic. 'Ergonomics and manufacturing' has a higher number of users and posts, however, the engagement is 6 which is relatively low. This could be due to ergonomics being a well-established study rather than a developing area. 'Collaborative robot and manufacturing' resulted in a lower number of users and posts, but a higher engagement of 16, indicating a stronger social medial presence on the use of collaborative robots in manufacturing industries.

4.5 Emergence Indicator

Emergence indicators are valuable for supporting the need for systematic literature reviews. By proving the emergence of a topic, the potential to expand and investigate it in-depth increases. In this systematic literature review, research funding agencies were explored from Web of Science. It was found that from the 51 articles identified for 'ergonomics', 'collaborative robot', and 'manufacturing', there were 46 funding agencies supporting research on this topic, with 'European Commission' funding the most. A greater number of funding agencies indicates a strong, diverse interest in ergonomics and collaborative robots in manufacturing and a desire for more research, thus indicating emergence of the topic.

5 Results

5.1 Co-citation Analysis

Using the 51 articles from Web of Science, a co-citation analysis was conducted using VOS Viewer software. Publications are said to be co-cited if they are listed simultaneously in the reference lists of other articles (Fahimnia et al. 2015). Web of Science was the database of choice as it allows 'full record and cited references' content to be exported in a plain text file. The text file was then imported to VOS Viewer. The minimum number of citations of a cited reference was defined to 3. This led to 62 meeting the threshold out of a total of 1804 cited references. In an effort to keep the number of citations relevant to the topic of interest, only 30 cited references that had the greatest link strength were selected for this co-citation map which can be seen in Fig. 5.

It can be seen from the co-citation map for 'ergonomics' and 'collaborative robot' and 'manufacturing', that the 30 items are organized into 3 distinct clusters – red, blue, and green. There are 343 links with a link strength of 451. This indicates that there is significant work done in this field, and there is literature connecting 'ergonomics' and 'collaborative robot' and 'manufacturing'. Increasing the minimum number of citations can yield more specific results. However, this review is analyzing the relation between three different topics, thus having a lower number of minimum citations allows for a less restricted search. Additionally, the emergence of this topic can be further ascertained from Fig. 5 by looking at the co-citation dates. Most of the co-citations are fairly recent, within the past 6–7 years.

Co-citation with Cluster Analysis. While VOS Viewer can organize co-citations into clusters and color them to show the distinction, it does not have the capability to extract cluster names. Having a co-citation with cluster names can aid in identifying which group of literary works in the co-citation map are most relevant to the topic of interest, thus making the evaluation process efficient. This type of analysis can be achieved using

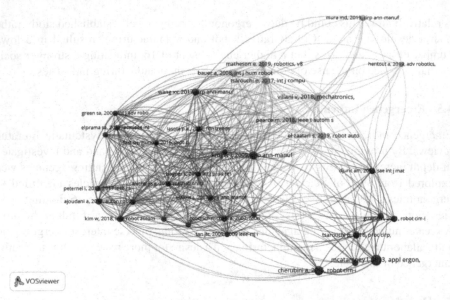

Fig. 5. Co-citation analysis for Web of Science articles on 'ergonomics' and 'collaborative robot' and 'manufacturing' (VOS Viewer, n.d.)

CiteSpace, which is a far more powerful and intensive tool for conducting a cluster analysis.

Using the same 51 articles from Web of Science, the metadata was uploaded to CiteSpace. Based on the findings from the VOS Viewer co-citation analysis that most articles are fairly recent, the time span for the CiteSpace attempt was set to 2017 to 2021. This will limit the analysis to only display the most current publications. The software was run, leading to 47 records being identified. After the basic co-citation map was obtained, cluster labels were extracted using keywords. The resulting cluster analysis can be seen in Fig. 6. The top five clusters included 'artificial intelligence', 'human body posture', 'risk assessment', 'optimization', and 'collaborative robot'. All of these can be related to the topic of this literature review.

Citation Burst. CiteSpace also has a 'citation burst' feature, in which the references with the strongest surge of citations can be discerned. "Citation burst is an indicator of a most active area of research" (CiteSpace, n.d.). Based on the topic of interest, certain parameters of the CiteSpace control panel may need to be adjusted to obtain a citation burst. In this case, the 'betweenness centrality score' was set to 0.1. The resulting citation burst is presented in Fig. 7.

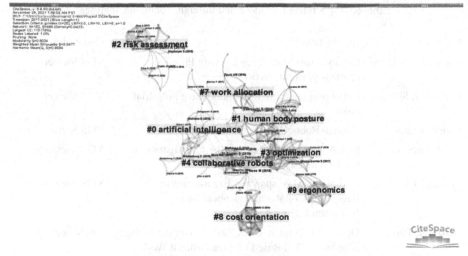

Fig. 6. Co-citation and cluster analysis for Web of Science articles on 'ergonomics' and 'collaborative robot' and 'manufacturing' (CiteSpace, n.d.).

Top 6 References with the Strongest Citation Bursts

References	Year	Strength	Begin	End	2017 - 2021
Boessenkool H, 2013, IEEE T HAPTICS, V6, P2	2013	1.12	**2017**	2018	
Bohlin R, 2014, 3 INT DIG HUM MOD S, V0, P0	2014	1.12	**2017**	2018	
Ajoudani A, 2018, AUTON ROBOT, V42, P957, DOI 10.1007/s10514-017-9677-2, DOI	2018	0.62	**2019**	2021	
Battini D, 2017, INT J PROD RES, V55, P7452, DOI 10.1080/00207543.2017.1363427, DOI	2017	0.62	**2019**	2021	
Battini D, 2016, INT J PROD RES, V54, P824, DOI 10.1080/00207543.2015.1074299, DOI	2016	0.62	**2019**	2021	
Baenziger T, 2020, J INTELL MANUF, V31, P1635, DOI 10.1007/s10845-018-1411-1, DOI	2020	0.62	**2020**	2021	

Fig. 7. Citation burst for Web of Science articles on 'ergonomics' and 'collaborative robot' and 'manufacturing' (CiteSpace, n.d.).

It can be seen that 6 references were identified and sorted based on strength. Boessenkool H and Bohlin R are the top 2 authors with the highest strength of 1.12. "Optimizing human–robot task allocation using a simulation tool based on standardized work descriptions" by Baenziger T is the most recent reference.

Identification of Key Articles. Using the results from both co-citation analysis, the cluster analysis, and citation burst, the top 8 articles were selected based on their popularity and relevance to ergonomics and collaborative robots in manufacturing and presented in Table 6. The articles were then reviewed in-depth to aid in the re-appraisal of the topic of ergonomics and collaborative robots in manufacturing for this paper.

5.2   Content Analysis

A content analysis is beneficial for classifying keywords related to a particular topic. These keywords can then be used for further lexical searches. Using Google Scholar via

Table 6. Top 8 references identified through co-citation analyses

Main Author	Article Title	Co-citation Source
Cherubini, Andrea	Collaborative Manufacturing with Physical Human–robot Interaction	VOS Viewer
El Zaatari, Shirine	Cobot programming for collaborative industrial tasks	VOS Viewer
Bauer, Andrea	Human–Robot Collaboration: a Survey	VOS Viewer
Mcatamney, L	RULA: a survey method for the investigation of work-related upper limb disorders	VOS Viewer
Pearce, Margaret	Optimizing Makespan and Ergonomics in Integrating Collaborative Robots Into Manufacturing Processes	VOS Viewer
Bänziger, Timo	Optimizing Human–robot Task Allocation Using a Simulation Tool Based on Standardized Work Descriptions	CiteSpace
Ranz, Fabian	Capability-based Task Allocation in Human-robot Collaboration	VOS Viewer
Battini, Daria	Preventing Ergonomic Risks with Integrated Planning on Assembly Line Balancing and Parts Feeding	CiteSpace

Harzing, 980 results from the search terms 'ergonomics' AND 'collaborative robot' AND 'manufacturing' were downloaded and imported to VOS Viewer. Google Scholar was the database of choice for this analysis because a large set of results can be investigated, thus allowing for more content.

In VOS Viewer, the total number of terms was 8805. The minimum number of occurrences of a term was set to 24, and 95 terms met the threshold. As a default, only the terms with 60% relevance are selected by the software. In this case, 57 terms were identified. The system also allows word filtration before creating the final content map. Out of the 57 terms, all irrelevant words were removed. The resulting content map can be seen in Fig. 8.

7 clusters can be identified from Fig. 8 – purple, dark blue, yellow, red, green, orange, and light blue. It can be seen that the largest clusters with the highest occurring terms are 'collaborative robot' (purple), 'ergonomic' (dark blue), and 'manufacturing' (yellow). It is interesting to note that 'collaborative robot' and 'human robot collaboration' are separated in different clusters, though they share a similar meaning. This could be due to different authors using the terminology of their choice resulting in the content map considering both terms as independent. This sheds light on the importance of search terms and how a content analysis can help extract them. The similarities between the topic of interest and the main keywords from the content analysis provide further evidence that Google Scholar is a highly suitable resource for identifying relevant publications.

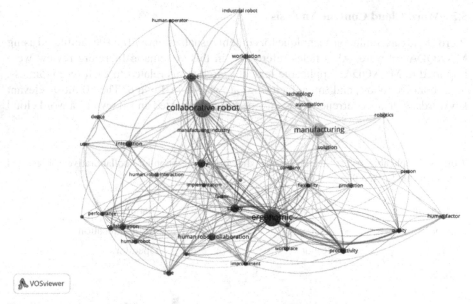

Fig. 8. Content analysis from Google Scholar (via Harzing) articles on 'ergonomics' and 'collaborative robot' and 'manufacturing' (VOS Viewer, n.d.)

Using the content analysis, the keywords with the highest occurrence and their % relevance were collected and presented in Table 7. It can be seen that 'collaborative robot' and 'ergonomic' had the most occurrences, whereas 'human robot collaboration' and 'robotics' had the highest relevance scores.

Table 7. Relevant keywords identified for ergonomics and collaborative robots in manufacturing (VOS Viewer, n.d.)

Keyword	Occurrence	Relevance
Collaborative robot	640	0.41
Ergonomic	574	0.37
Manufacturing	392	0.43
Cobot	159	0.44
Safety	147	0.35
Human robot collaboration	122	0.51
Technology	100	0.33
Robotics	73	0.48

5.3   Word Cloud Content Analysis

Word clouds are a valuable technique for content visualization and can be facilitated using MAXQDA software. All articles referenced in this systematic literature review were imported to MAXQDA. Applicable lexical search terms related to each 'ergonomics', 'collaborative robot', and 'manufacturing' are shown in Table 8. The 50 most relevant keywords with an occurrence frequency of 4 were extracted and shown as a word cloud in Fig. 9.

Table 8. Applicable lexical search terms extracted for ergonomics, collaborative robots, and manufacturing (MAXQDA, n.d.)

Ergonomics	Collaborative Robot	Manufacturing
Safety	Cobot	Work Allocation
Posture	Robot	Operator

Fig. 9. Word cloud content analysis constructed from articles on ergonomics and collaborative robots in manufacturing. 'Human' in the center emphasizes the importance of human-centric designs and solutions (MAXQDA, n.d.)

6   Discussion

It has been well established that worker ergonomics in manufacturing processes is an area of great concern. As the manufacturing demand grows exponentially, expectations on human operators to meet deliverables are also increasing. Assembly lines are proven to be the most demanding of manual human skill, partially due to such productions having frequent re-configurations and design upgrades (Ranz et al. 2017). In an effort to ease worker physical strain and develop better ergonomic work practices, collaborative robots are encouraged in manufacturing processes. This systematic literature review has demonstrated a significant amount of research conducted in this area, many of which reiterate the poor ergonomics of manufacturing that must be addressed, as well as the economic and socio-technical feasibly of adopting human-robot collaborative practices. Lexical keywords that can aid in conducting further research were identified to be 'cobot', 'work allocation', 'safety' etc. Collaborative robots, unlike traditional industrial robots, are far more adaptable due to their advanced programming capabilities (Ranz et al. 2017). This makes them useable in many industries including automobile, fashion, medicine, etc. Interestingly, genetic algorithms are a recent approach to improving human-robot task allocations, in which a "cost function" can be defined based on the cost of manual labor and usage of robots (Bänziger et al. 2020). The use of collaborative robots is also found to be instrumental to Lean Manufacturing where the goal is to eliminate waste, increase productivity, and "achieve sustainable operations improvement" (Quenehen et al. 2019) in the manufacturing industry. This concept of 'lean-automation' where a process should have 'just enough' automation to perform a task while maintaining the human-operator's well-being be could be achieved though 'cobots' (Malik and Bilberg 2017).

Another area of interest is trust and safety. As with all forms of advancement, there is some apprehension and concern when considering robots working closely with humans. While traditional robots operated away from humans, collaborative robots physically interact with workers. This can lead to risks such as fingers trapped in mechanical arms, skin injures due to sharp edges, or unexpected contact with the robot, etc. (Gualtieri et al. 2020). Though these issues are significantly less when compared to hazards surrounding traditional robots, it indicates the need to build trust among workers. Trust can be largely attributed to their own beliefs and experiences. Additionally, their stress and mental states can impact their perception of human-robot collaboration (Chen and Barnes 2021). Research efforts such as "DARPA's eXplainable AI" are being conducted to address these concerns (Chen and Barnes 2021).

7 Future Work

The use of collaborative robots is still in the process of becoming normalized. As technological advancements are made, 'Smart Factories' are the future of manufacturing. In addition to human-robot collaboration, smart factories may be able to utilize 'big data' obtained from machines via sensors to make a multitude of improvements to manufacturing processes (Gao et al. 2020). Additionally, 'cyber-physical systems' (CPS) is an emerging approach to manufacturing processes, where a human operator is simply in charge of operations management, monitoring, system control, etc. controlled by a "computing and communicating core" (Gao et al. 2020), further reducing the need for manual labor. The National Science Foundation (NSF) of the United States publishes outstanding awards and funding to promising research. A recent award titled "Manufacturing USA: Intelligent Human-Robot Collaboration for Smart Factory" was granted to the Research Foundation for The State University Of New York in 2020. This research aims to improve the efficiency of human-robot collaboration by creating a technology-enriched factory. The goal is to use "integrated algorithms and robotic test beds to sense, predict, and control" (NSF Award # 1954548) interactions between workers and robots (NSF Award Search 2020). Lastly, the importance of education is mentioned as the awardees are aspiring to build a robotics and smart factory program for college students. Collaborative robots and their influence on ergonomics in manufacturing is a recent topic, yet it is in no way under-developed. A wealth of publications and opportunities identified for future research reveal favorable expansion of this topic.

References

Bauer, A., Wollherr, D., Buss, M.: Human–robot collaboration: a survey. Int. J. Humanoid Rob. **5**(01), 47–66 (2008)

Bänziger, T., Kunz, A., Wegener, K.: Optimizing human–robot task allocation using a simulation tool based on standardized work descriptions. J. Intell. Manuf. **31**(7), 1635–1648 (2020). https://doi.org/10.1007/s10845-018-1411-1

BibExcel.: (n.d.). https://homepage.univie.ac.at/juan.gorraiz/bibexcel/

Chen, J.Y., Barnes, M.J.: Human–Robot Interaction. In: Salvendy, G., Karwowski, W. (eds.) Handbook of Human Factors and Ergonomics, pp. 1121–1142 (2021). https://doi.org/10.1002/978 1119636113.ch44

Cherubini, A., Passama, R., Crosnier, A., Lasnier, A., Fraisse, P.: Collaborative manufacturing with physical human–robot Interaction. Rob. Comp.-Integ. Manuf. **40**, 1–13 (2016). https://doi.org/10.1016/j.rcim.2015.12.007

CiteSpace.: (n.d.). https://citespace.podia.com/

El Zaatari, S., Marei, M., Li, W., Usman, Z.: Cobot programming for collaborative industrial tasks: An overview. Robotics and Autonomous Systems **116**, 162–180 (2019). https://doi.org/10.1016/j.robot.2019.03.003

Fahimnia, B., Sarkis, J., Davarzani, H.: Green supply chain management: a review and bibliometric analysis. Int. J. Prod. Econ. **162**, 101–114 (2015). https://doi.org/10.1016/j.ijpe.2015.01.003

Gao, R.X., Wang, L., Helu, M., Teti, R.: Big data analytics for smart factories of the future. CIRP Ann. **69**(2), 668–692 (2020)

Gualtieri, L., Palomba, I., Wehrle, E.J., Vidoni, R.: The Opportunities and Challenges of SME Manufacturing Automation: Safety and Ergonomics in Human–Robot Collaboration. In: Matt, D.T., Modrák, V., Zsifkovits, H. (eds.) Industry 4.0 for SMEs, pp. 105–144. Springer, Cham (2020). https://doi.org/10.1007/978-3-030-25425-4_4

Harzing's Publish or Perish.: (n.d.). https://harzing.com/resources/publish-or-perish

Malik, A.A., Bilberg, A.: Framework to implement collaborative robots in manual assembly: a lean automation approach. In: DAAAM Proceedings, DAAAM Proceedings, pp. 1151–60 (2017). https://doi.org/10.2507/28th.daaam.proceedings.160

Maurice, P., Padois, V., Measson, Y., Bidaud, P.: Human-oriented design of collaborative robots. Int. J. Ind. Ergon. **57**, 88–102 (2017). https://doi.org/10.1016/j.ergon.2016.11.011

MAXQDA.: (n.d.). https://www.maxqda.com/

Mcatamney, L., Corlett, E.N.: RULA: a survey method for the investigation of work-related upper limb disorders. Applied ergonomics **24**(2), 91–9 (1993)

NSF Award Search: Award # 1954548 - NRI: INT: COLLAB: Manufacturing USA: Intelligent Human-Robot Collaboration For Smart Factory (2020). https://www.nsf.gov

Pearce, M., Mutlu, B., Shah, J., Radwin, R.: Optimizing makespan and ergonomics in integrating collaborative robots into manufacturing processes. IEEE Trans. Autom. Sci. Eng. **15**(4), 1772–1784 (2018). https://doi.org/10.1109/tase.2018.2789820

Quenehen, A., Pocachard, J., Klement, N.: Process optimisation using collaborative robots - comparative case study. Ifac-papersonline **52**(13), 60–65 (2019). https://doi.org/10.1016/j.ifacol.2019.11.131

Ranz, F., Hummel, V., Sihn, W.: Capability-based task allocation in human-robot collaboration. Procedia Manufacturing **9**, 182–189 (2017). https://doi.org/10.1016/j.promfg.2017.04.011

Scopus.: (n.d.). https://www-scopus-com.ezproxy.lib.purdue.edu/

Spath, D., Braun, M.: Human Factors and Ergonomics in Digital Manufacturing. In: Salvendy, G., Karwowski, W. (eds.) Handbook of Human Factors and Ergonomics, pp. 1438–1459 (2021). https://doi.org/10.1002/9781119636113.ch54

VOS Viewer.: (n.d.). https://www.vosviewer.com/

Web of Science. (n.d.). https://www-webofscience-com.ezproxy.lib.purdue.edu/wos/woscc/summary/a7d66ed0-bc6b-4063-9a0a-0c41216543a7-15ab5f0e/relevance/1

Multimodal Analysis of Interruptions

Liu Yang[⊠], Catherine Achard, and Catherine Pelachaud

Institut des Systèmes Intelligents et de Robotique (CNRS-ISIR),
Sorbonne University, 75005 Paris, France
{yangl,catherine.achard,catherine.pelachaud}@isir.upmc.fr

Abstract. During an interaction, interactants exchange speaking turns. Exchanges can be done smoothly or through interruptions. Listeners can display backchannels, send signals to grab the speaking turn, wait for the speaker to yield the turn, or even interrupt and grab the speaking turn. Interruptions are very frequent in natural interactions. To create believable and engaging interaction between human interactants and embodied conversational agent ECA, it is important to endow virtual agent with the capability to manage interruptions, that is to have the ability to interrupt, but also to react to an interruption. As a first step, we focus on the later one where the agent is able to perceive and interpret the user's multimodal behaviors as either an attempt or not to take the turn. To this aim, we annotate, analyse and characterize interruptions in human-human conversations. In this paper, we describe our annotation schema that embeds different types of interruptions. We then provide an analysis of multimodal features, focusing of prosodic features (F0 and loudness) and body (head and hand) activity, to characterize interruptions.

Keywords: Interruption · Dyadic interaction · Multimodal signals · Turn taking

1 Introduction

Human-computer interfaces are becoming more and more frequent and appreciated in daily life, and the development of Embodied Conversational Agents (ECAs) is booming as they allow very natural interactions, without artifices. However, many difficulties arise since natural interactions are very complex and involve a multitude of research areas going from psychology to signal processing. A lot of work has already been done, both on verbal and non-verbal signals, and several embodied conversational agents have already been developed. However, one important faculty has not yet been sufficiently studied: the interruptions.

They are however very frequent in natural conversations [6] and appear when one interlocutor attempts to grab the turn while the other person is still holding it. Interruptions are an integral part of the turn-taking mechanism. In some early studies, interruptions were described as a symbol of dominance and power [22, 37, 53], since most of the conversations follow the rule of one-person-speaks-at-a-time.

© The Author(s), under exclusive license to Springer Nature Switzerland AG 2022
V. G. Duffy (Ed.): HCII 2022, LNCS 13319, pp. 306–325, 2022.
https://doi.org/10.1007/978-3-031-05890-5_24

However, interruptions are essential in natural interactions, they help to regulate the rhythm of the dialogue, to show an interest, to reinforce the engagement [57].

During natural interactions, speakers exchange turns quickly and naturally. Humans are able to predict the end of their partner's turn in order to smoothly take the floor [15], without any discontinuity in the fluidity of the exchange. In the same way, humans can easily recognize when their partners are displaying a backchannel as a sign of participation in the discussion. When an interruption occurs, the speaker can decide to give or not the speaking turn to the interruptee.

Our aim is to create Embodied Conversational Agent ECA able to engage their human interlocutor in natural interaction. We believe it is important to give ECA the ability to manage interruption [8], either by interruption their human interlocutor or by responding to an interruption. To this aim, the ECA should recognize when its human interlocutor produces multimodal signals if it is a backchannel or an interruption, that is an attempt or not to grab the speaking turn. The ECA should be able to recognize the different types of speaking turn exchanges.

To reach this objective, we study natural speaking turn exchanges in human-human interaction gathered in the dyadic corpus NoXi [9]. We propose a schema of annotate interruption. We also provide an analysis of multimodal features to study the non-verbal behaviors involved during each type of turn switches. Our goal is to define which features are used by humans to understand the situation and endow them to ECA. As multimodal features we consider prosodic features and body (head and hands) activity.

We first start by presenting studies on turn-taking and more particularly on interruption in human-human interaction in the following section. In Sect. 3, we follow by presenting a state of the art on existing works that focused on predicting turn-taking exchange and interruptions. Section 4 presents the NoXi corpus and Sect. 5 the annotation we have conducted. The multimodal features we have extracted automatically are presented in Sect. 6 and their analyses are described in Sect. 7.

2   Background

In this Section, we introduced major works on turn-taking and how they are marked multimodally.

2.1   Modeling Turn Taking

The study of interaction has interested many scholars since long. Emanuel A. Schegloff [47] defined sequencing rules that manage natural conversations. Ten years later, Harvey Sacks [46] proposed the idea of conversation analysis and described its most basic structure as turn-taking. Actually, interlocutors have to coordinate and exchange speaking floor based on rules to maintain the conversation with the hypothesis they cannot speak and listen at the same time. Using this basic structure, the turn taking, Kendon [38] and Duncan [18] introduced a model of conversation that uses three basic signals:

- Turn-yielding signals from the speaker: the listener may take the turn when a turn-yielding signal is displayed; the speaker yields the turn when the listener shows a willingness to take the floor.
- Attempt-suppressing signals from the speaker: the speaker uses attempt-suppressing signals to maintain the turn and prevent the listener to take the turn.
- Backchannel signals from the listener: the listener gives feedback information. It is not attempting to take the turn. It is not considered as a turn.

Sacks, Schegloff and Jefferson [46] proposed a conversation turn-taking model, often referred as the SSJ model, indicating the turn-taking mechanism. It is based on rules such as: (i) The current speaker may select the next speaker, the selected person must speak next. (ii) If the current speaker selects no one, then one of the participants may self-select to speak next. (iii) If no one is self-selected, the current speaker may continue to speak or terminate the conversation.

Sacks and colleagues made the hypothesis that interlocutors predict rather accurately the turn end timing, leading to 'no gap, no overlap' between speaking turns. However, Coates [12] analysed the distribution of timing interval during turn exchanges. He found a high number of overlaps occurrence at the end of a turn in different conversation settings, thus refuting the hypothesis 'no gap, no overlap'.

2.2   Taxonomy of Speaking Turn Exchanges

Schegloff and Sacks [49] proposed to study some specific speaking turn exchanges corresponding to simultaneous speeches, that are classified as either, interruption, overlap or parenthetical comments such as backchannels. Backchannels are actually not tending to disturb the speech flow or to grab the floor, they are short messages to show the listener's attention, or if the listener agrees or not with the speech [1]. Overlap is when the listener takes the floor that the speaker is yielding but has not yet completed her speech; thus an overlap usually arises on the last word(s) or syllable(s) of the current speaker and the first word(s) of the listener (next speaker) [46]. On the contrary, interruption occurs when the listener grabs the floor against the speaker's wishes [49] without letting the speaker finish his/her utterance, and is described as a violation of the current speaker's turn which overlap is not [43].

Beattie [6] proposed another taxonomy of speaking turn exchanges using both simultaneous speech and willingness to yield the floor, as shown in Fig. 1. The three considered classes are overlap, interruption and smooth switches.

Goldberg [24] described a taxonomy based on interruption meaning. He considered two main types: competitive and cooperative interruptions. Competitive interruptions are when the listener interrupts to take the control of the interaction, and disrupt the flow of dialogue between the partners, which can be seen as a conflict:

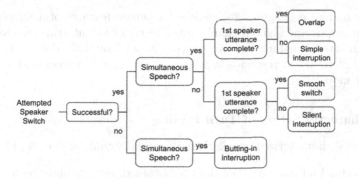

Fig. 1. Classification of interruption and smooth speaking turn exchange [6]

- Disagreement: The listener disagrees with the current speaker and expresses immediately his/her own opinion.
- Floor taking: The listener grabs the floor and expands on the current speaker's topic.
- Topic change: The listener grabs the turn and changes the current topic of conversation.
- Tangentialization: The listener grabs the turn and sums up the information received from the current speaker to prevent listening to more unwanted information.

On the opposite, a cooperative interruption helps to complete the conversation:

- Agreement: The listener shows understanding or support to the speaker.
- Assistance: The listener interrupts to provide the current speaker with a word, a phrase or an idea to help complete the utterance.
- Clarification: The listener expects the current speaker to clarify or explain the information about which the listener is not clear.

2.3   Characterization of Speaking Turn Exchanges

Most of the studies indicate the importance of prosodic features such as fundamental-frequency (F0) or intensity during speaking turn exchanges [23,39, 54]. Studies found that people raise their energy and voice when they attempt to interrupt the current speaker [26,50]. Hammarberg [27] provided similar evidence regarding pitch and amplitude.

Features of the interrupters such as speech rate, cutoffs and repetitions are also analyzed by conversational analysts. For example, Schegloff [48] found that variations in prosodic profiles and repetitions are used by interrupters. He also mentioned that interrupting sentences usually have a faster speaking rate, thus providing evidence about the role of speech rate to deal with speakership conflicts.

Gravano and colleagues [26] analysed acoustic features of a telephonic conversation corpus and showed significant differences for interruptions in intensity and pitch level, speaking rate and Inter-Pausal Unit IPU duration. An Inter-Pausal Unit (IPU) corresponds to a sequence of words surrounded by silences of 50 ms or more.

2.4 Characterization of Turn Ending

Duncan [18] characterized speaker's multimodal signals at the end of the turn:

- phrase-final intonation other than a sustained, intermediate pitch level;
- a drawl on the final syllable of a terminal clause;
- the termination of any hand gesticulation;
- a stereotyped expression;
- a drop-in pitch and/or loudness in conjunction with a stereotyped expression;
- the completion of a grammatical clause.

Duncan also mentioned that the higher the joint frequency of these cues, the greater the probability that the listener take the floor. However, when the speaker is gesturing, the incidence of listener turn-taking attempts falls to zero. The speaker gesticulation is identified as an attempt suppression cue that cancel out the effects of turn-ending cues.

Another turn-taking attempt suppression cue has been proposed by Beattie [5] and Ball [2] that showed that filled pauses reduced the probability of a speaker-switch, at least for a short period after their occurrence.

To estimate the end of a speech turn, Riest *et al.* [45] and De Ruiter *et al.* [15] argued that semantic information is useful while contextual information is employed in [55] or [7].

Stivers et al. [52] mentioned that the intervals between speech turns last on average 200 ms. But psycholinguistic research has shown that it takes at least 600 ms to produce even a single word utterance [31]. Thus, certain cognitive processes by the next speaker must be involved to predict the end of the turn of the current speaker [16,30]. Further results show that predictive processes work with other processing layers that allow simultaneous production planning and comprehension [15]. However the prediction of turn ending timing is sometime not that accurate and thus cause simultaneous speeches.

3 State of Art

In a conversation, the listener (to be the next potential speaker) has to project the exact timing when the current speaker will finish and what will be her words, so the listener can prepare to initiate the next turn at an appropriate timing and start planning what to say [30]. Several computational models are geared to predict turn-taking and to detect interruptions. They rely on models proposed by conversational analysts [15,49].

3.1 Turn-taking Prediction

A lot of studies on turn-taking prediction (turn ending or turn starting timing) have been done to investigate feature sets and prediction models. The majority of investigated feature sets include prosodic features such as fundamental frequency (F0) and energy [25,44]. Linguistic features were also investigated such as syntactic structure, turn-ending markers, and language model [35,36,42]. Moreover, multimodal features, such as eye-gaze [14,32], respiration [29,33], and head-direction [51], were also considered.

Hara et al. [28] took into account the concept of the Transition Relevance Place (TRP) in accordance with prosodic, speech and linguistic features to predict whether to take the turn at each instant by calculating the posterior probability of turn-switch. Each feature is modeled by an individual LSTM and the outputs of those LSTMs are concatenated and fed into a linear layer that outputs the posterior probability of the output label. More precisely, a first sub-model is used, using a single user, to detect TRP at the end of each IPU. Then, a second sub-model predicts whether to take the turn by calculating the posterior probability of turn-switch. An accuracy of 89.5% is obtained as the best result.

Ishii et al. [34,35] proposed to predict the turn management willingness of speaker and listener to help predict the occurrence of turn switch using acoustic, linguistic and visual (gaze, head movement, respiration) cues from both speaker and listener. Results show that turn-management willingness and turn-exchange are predicted most precisely when all modalities from speaker and listener are used.

Coman et al. [13] proposed to build an automated system capable of estimating the dialog state and the appropriate turn-taking point token-by-token (word by word) in an incremental setting by exploiting lexical features. The authors developed two modules: an incremental Dialog State Tracker (iDST) that consists of an encoder-based classifier to track the dialog state change after each token (word); and an incremental Turn-Taking Decider (iTTD) that takes as input the output of iDST, and that decides if a turn switch should happen or not.

3.2 Interruption Prediction

Several works have been dedicated to predicting when an interruption may occur.

Lee and Narayanan [41] use a hidden conditional random field (HCRF model) to predict occurrences of interruption in dyadic conversations. They found the following cues:

- Interrupter: mouth opening distance, eyebrow and head movement
- Interruptee: energy and pitch values of audio

The authors annotated the turn transitions into two classes: smooth transition and interruption. Their model predicts the upcoming turn exchange type with the behavior of the interrupter and interrupted one second before the relevant transition point.

Chýlek et al. [11] presented their study to predict the speaking turn switch timing. Three types of overlaps are defined by the voice activity: internal overlap (INT), overlap resulting in a switch of turns (OSW) and a clean switch of turns (CSW). INT corresponds to the case where speaker B starts speaking during speaker A's utterance, but speaker A continues his turn, OSW to the case where speaker A ends his utterance during the overlapping segment and CSW occurs when there is no overlap during the turn exchange. INT and OSW samples refer to overlaps (OVR), which are considered as interruptions in their work. Prediction of all three types (INT, OSW and OVR) is tested separately. The authors tested different ML models such as support vector machines, decision trees, and neural networks. The deep residual learning networks (ResNet-152) with only acoustic features gave the best performance.

Other works have been more interested in determining the interruption types and more particularly on classifying between cooperative and competitive interruptions. Yang [57] reported that competitive interruptions have higher pitch and intensity levels, while collaborative interruptions have a relatively lower pitch level. Lee and Narayanan [40] proposed a multimodal analysis method to classify the interruption type. They observed that the absence of hand motions signal the occurrence of cooperative interruptions with high probability. Moreover, the number of occurrences of disfluencies in the speech is significantly higher in the case of competitive interruptions. Their best classification results of interruption type combine hand motion with speech intensity. Khiet and colleagues [54] used SVM to classify overlaps with acoustic features, gaze behaviour and head movement annotations. With a delay of 0.6 s after the start of overlap, the model begins to show a good accuracy only using overlapper's acoustic features. They also mentioned that slight improvement was obtained when gaze information during overlap was added, while adding acoustic information from the overlappee did not improve performance. Chowdhury et al. [10] classified competition and cooperative overlapping speech using a Sequential Minimal Optimization (SMO) model with prosody, voice quality, MFCC, energy and spectral features. Egorow et al. [19] considered two emotion dimensions (*control* and *valence*) combined with acoustic features to classify overlaps with SVM model.

4   Corpus

We choose the NoXi corpus [9] for our study. NoXi is composed of multimodal data (video and audio) that contains free dyadic interactions. For each dyad, both interactants have been recorded separately (video and audio) during a screen-mediated interaction, allowing to easily separate the audio sources, as shown in Fig. 2. The video of each interactant shows almost their full body except the feet. Both interactants' audios and videos have been synchronized and transcribed.

In the NoXi database, participants take the role of either 'expert' or 'novice'. An 'expert' shares her knowledge on a subject (among over 45 given topics) with a 'novice' who is interested in that subject. Each interaction is about 20 mn long.

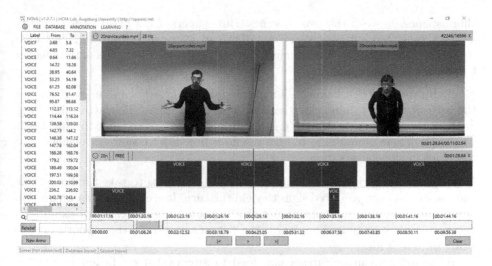

Fig. 2. Example of NoXi dyads

NoXi database has been acquired in seven languages. We chose the French part of NoXi corpus for our study, including 21 dyadic conversations, for about 7 h in total (21 * 20 mn).

5 Annotation

We use this database to study the difference in multimodal signals occurring during different speaking turn exchange types. In a first step, we annotate the database based on voice activity detection VAD. For each of these changes in the vocal track, we annotate if it is a backchannel, a smooth speaking turn exchange or an interruption.

Three taxonomies of speaking turn exchanges have been presented in the background section. Altogether, they cover most of the situations we may encounter in daily conversations; but individually, they lack some details. Schegloff and Sacks [49] focused only on simultaneous speeches and thus, did not consider smooth speaking turn exchanges or interruptions that happened during a silence. Beattie's taxonomy [6] does not include backchannel and Goldberg's one [24] includes only different types of interruption. So, we propose a new annotation schema that merges and completes these three taxonomies.

Before presenting our taxonomy, we introduce some definitions.

5.1 Definition

The three speaking turn exchanges we consider in our study are defined below.

Smooth Turn Exchange: These speaking turn exchanges occur when one person ends speaking and another person takes the floor. Very often there is a short silence between the two speeches. But sometimes, a short overlap exists as the listener has anticipated the end of the speaker's utterance [30]. The main characteristic of smooth turn exchange is that there is a willingness of the speaker to give up her speaking turn.

Backchannel: A backchannel is a multimodal signal, verbal and nonverbal, that the listener displays to indicate that she/he is listening, to show attitudinal (e.g. agreeing or not) and emotional (e.g. happiness) reactions to what the speaker is saying [1]. There is no desire to take the floor but just to show engagement and reactions in the conversation.

Interruption: During an interruption, the listener aims to take the floor while the speaker has not produced signs to yield the turn. It is common that an overlap is present during an interruption but this is not always the case; for example if the speaker is searching for a word, the listener may take this opportunity to bring up a new idea.

Interruptions can be further classified in **successful or failed interruptions**. A successful interruption corresponds when the listener grabs and maintains the speaking turn and the current speaker stops talking.

In a failed interruption, the current speaker does not give up her speaking turn and continues talking. We illustrate this distinction through examples taken from the NoXi database (and translated from French to English).

The following situations can be considered as a successful interruption:

- The interrupter grabs the turn successfully and the current speaker has to quit even she/he has not finished the current utterance.
  Example:
  Person A:... it's like sports, it's not physical, basically not phy[sical but I ...]
  Person B: [I agree with] you for example to train in football...

- The listener speaks over the speaker (e.g. by asking quickly a clarification question). The speaker doesn't stop and keeps her turn, but takes into account what the listener says (e.g. by answering the listener's question).
  Example:
  Person A: ...sometimes you can see the mushrooms, that's why you [have to be care]ful. yeah, especially the optics...
  Person B: [Mushrooms?]

Here are examples of failed interruption:

- The listener abandons the interruption before his utterance is completed and let the current speaker continues her turn; the speaker does not pay extra attention to the listener's attempt.
  Example:
  Person A: ...for competitions, maybe I'm wrong and I see your point of view,

I unders[tand but finally] maybe it's easy ...
Person B: [Ah no no you...]

– The listener begins to speak to get attention from the speaker. He does not respond after completion of his utterance. The speaker continues her speech.
Example:
Person A: ...I didn't pay even one euro for Hearthtone, and I uh I still [have my meta decks] up to now, I can...
Person B: [Ah me neither, it's useless no?]

5.2 Schema

In this section we introduce our annotation schema composed of three levels as presented in Fig. 3.

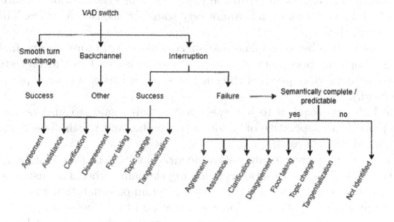

Fig. 3. Interruption annotation schema

At the first level, each VAD switch is classified into *interruption, backchannel* or *smooth turn-exchange* according to the definitions presented above.

The second level deals with the accomplishment of speaking turn exchange. Smooth turn exchanges are always annotated as successful (*success*) and backchannels, which are not aiming to grab the turn, are annotated as *Other*. Interruptions can be annotated as successful (*success*) or as failed (*failure*).

Finally, in the third level, the type of interruptions is annotated based on the speech content using the eight classes proposed by [24]: Agreement, Assistance, Clarification, Disagreement, Floor taking, Topic change and Tangentialization. Successful interruptions can easily be classified into their different classes while failed interruptions can be too short to perform this classification. In such a case they are annotated as *Not identified*. As in [24], we group the classes in "two super-classes" where Agreement, Assistance, Clarification belong to the cooperative interruption class while Disagreement, Floor taking, Topic change and Tangentialization belong to the competitive interruption class. The annotation of interruption class at this level is based on the linguistic analysis of what is being said.

5.3 Annotation Process

We annotate NoXi database using our annotation schema. The annotation is done in three steps, one per level. For each dyad, we use the Nova tool [4] to display and synchronize the visual and audio channels of the video of both interactants. Annotation is done semi-automatically. When it requires semantic analysis, we rely on manual annotation. We now describe the steps we follow.

At first, we apply the automatic Voice Activity Detection (VAD). It gives us points where both interactants speak simultaneously or when there is a change of speaker. The next step consist to classify these points in either backchannel, smooth turn exchange or interruption (level 1). This classification requires analyzing the linguistic terms, and cannot rely solely on acoustic features. This step is done manually.

The distinction between failed and successful interruptions is done manually (level 2). For each occurrence of interruptions annotated in the first step, we listen to the occurring speech of the current speaker and of the other participant of the dyad.

The last step requires to analyse what is being said, to understand if an interruption is a cooperative or a competitive one, and which class among the eight possible it is (level 3).

In order to measure the annotation accuracy, all videos have been annotated three times by the same annotator, following the same process as just described. There was one-month interval between each round of annotation to ensure that the annotator has forgotten the video content and the annotations.

To compute the annotation accuracy, we consider the agreement for annotation on the three levels. After the first two rounds of annotation, we accepted all records with full agreement (for the three levels). For the other records, we applied a third round of annotation. After this third round, we accepted the records for which the three annotation levels (levels 1, 2 and 3) are identical to the first or second round annotations. We disregarded the other records (318 among 4301).

After three rounds of annotation, we have a global annotator self-acceptance of 92.6%. When comparing level 1 annotation value over the three annotation rounds, we have an agreement level of: 84.07% for interruption, 92% for smooth turn exchange and 98.8% for backchannel.

5.4 Annotation Analysis

Following this annotation process, we obtain 3983 VAD switch points for the French part of the NoXi database. Among them, there are 1403 smooth turn exchanges, 1651 backchannels and 929 interruptions. When, removing backchannels that do not correspond to a speaking turn exchange, interruptions represent 33% of turn-taking situations. This reinforces our intuition that they have a fundamental role in natural interactions.

Considering interruption, most of them (81.7%) are successfully performed and thus, the speaker succeeds in taking the floor. Moreover, among the successful interruptions, there are almost as many cooperative interruptions (54.36%) as competitive ones. The probability distribution according to the 8 types of interruption is given in Fig. 4. *Agreement interruptions* are the most frequent ones over all the interruption types. They represent also the majority of the cooperative interruptions. For competitive interruptions, *Floor taking* ones are the most frequent. *Floor taking* interruptions do not involve a change of topic. The distribution of interruption classes may be specific to the NoXi database as it involves dyads chit-chatting on topics that one person wishes to share information about and another person wishes to learn about it. The interaction setting is rather a friendly one. This is congruent with the majority of interruption types that is found in the corpus.

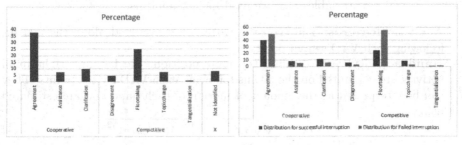

(a) Distribution according to the 8 types of interruption.

(b) Distribution according to the 8 types of interruption for failed and successful interruptions.

Fig. 4. Distribution of interruption.

For 44.71% of failed interruptions, the type cannot be determined because they are too short to understand the meaning of the speech. When the type has been determined, the types distribution of successful and failed interruptions is represented in Fig. 4. We find again that *Agreement* and *Floor taking* interruptions are the two largest types for both competitive and cooperative interruptions, whatever their accomplishment.

6   Features

For every conversation, we extracted separately the acoustic, facial and body features of each participant.

- The acoustic features are extracted using Opensmile [21], including: F0, loudness and 13 features of MFCC. We normalize each acoustic features by subtracting its mean value along the whole sequence.
- The facial expressions are extracted using Openface [3] and encoded with Action Units (coded with Facial Action Coding System (FACS) [20]).
- The facial positions are also estimated using Openface [3]. They include head movement (position & rotation in x-y-z axis) and gaze direction.
- The body features are extracted using Alphapose [56] and are composed of positions of 15 key joints except the feet (position in x-y axis). To standardize the position features, instead of using the absolute positions provided by Alphapose and Openface, we center the position by taking the middle of the two shoulders as the origin of the coordinate system $(0, 0)$. It allows us to avoid the bias caused by the interactant's initial position. This is used to calculate the *scaled joint position*. Moreover, for each video, we pick one frame when the interactant is facing the camera and note the distance between the two shoulders (*scale*). Then, the coordinate system is changed using a normalisation of x and y such as $scale = 1$.

Based on the extracted features and the voice activity detection records, we define several new variables that we used for our analysis.

- **Acoustic features:** The acoustic features are averaged along the 600 ms following each VAD switch points.
- **Hand activity:** After scaling the joint position, the left and right hand activity are computed on the 600ms following each VAD switch points. They can be interpreted as the amount of motion of each hand and are estimated using:

$$v_{Hand}(i) = \sqrt{(x_i - x_{i-1})^2 + (y_i - y_{i-1})^2} \tag{1}$$

and:

$$Hand\_act = \sum_{i}^{i+N} v_{Hand}(i)/N \tag{2}$$

where x_i and y_i are the coordinates of the hand (right or left) at time-step i, N is the number of frame corresponding to 600 ms. i is the instant of a particular VAD switch points.

Hand activities are normalized using z-scores to be invariant to the quantity of behaviors of interactants:

$$(Hand)\_act = \frac{(Hand)\_act - \mu}{\sigma} \tag{3}$$

Where μ and σ are, respectively, the mean and standard deviation of $v_{Hand}(i)$ along the whole sequence. Doing this for both hands leads to the two features $left\_hand\_act$ and $right\_hand\_act$.

- **Head activity:** similar to hand activity, head activity is estimated over the 600 ms following each VAD switch points using:

$$v_{Head}(i) = \sqrt{(x_i - x_{i-1})^2 + (y_i - y_{i-1})^2 + (z_i - z_{i-1})^2} \tag{4}$$

and:

$$Head\_act = \sum_{i}^{i+N} v_{Head}(i)/N \qquad (5)$$

Head activities are then normalized in the same way than hand activities.

- **IPU length:** After annotating all the conversations, we apply a script to split voice activity into Inter-Pausal Unit (IPU). An Inter-Pausal Units is defined as a speech unit of a single speaker without pauses longer than 200ms [17]. The feature *IPU length* corresponds to the length of the IPU following each annotated VAD switch point.

7 Analysis

7.1 IPU Length Analysis

We first analyzed the length of the IPU following each annotated voice activity change in the level 1 annotation as illustrated on the left side of Fig. 5.

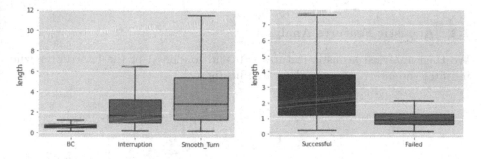

Fig. 5. Average value of IPUs or backchannels length for the level 1 (left) & the level 2 (right) annotation.

The IPU length following smooth turn exchanges are statistically longer than those following interruptions. Moreover, the length of backchannels is smaller than the IPU after an interruption or a smooth turn.

Considering the level 2 annotation, that is the accomplishment (success/failure) of interruptions, we can see on the right side of Fig. 5 that IPUs that follow successful interruptions have longer duration (3.33 s on average) than those that follow failed interruptions (1.04 s on average).

For the level 3 annotation (left figure in Fig. 6), IPUs that follow competitive interruptions are longer than those that follow cooperative ones, but the difference is less significant between the different IPUs considered at the level 2.

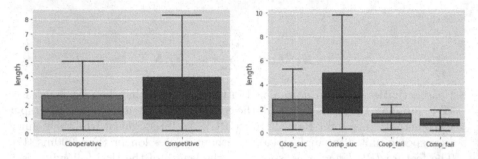

Fig. 6. Average value of IPUs length for the level 3 annotation (left) & combining the level 2 and 3 annotations (right).

When taking into account both accomplishment and interruption types (annotated respectively at level 2 and level 3), IPUs that follow successful competitive interruptions have longer duration than IPUs that follow successful cooperative ones. We do not find significant differences between IPUs that follow cooperative and competitive interruptions for the failed interruptions as illustrated on the right side of Fig. 6.

7.2   Acoustic Features Analysis

We then analysed acoustic features (F0 and loudness) of the interrupter who initiates the interruption as illustrated in Fig. 7.

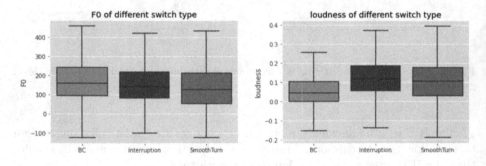

Fig. 7. Average value of F0 (left) & loudness (right) for the level 1 annotation.

No significant differences appear for F0 or loudness between interruptions and smooth turn exchanges. However, we note that backchannels have a lower loudness. We could not draw any conclusions by studying levels 2 and 3 of annotation.

7.3 Head and Hand Activities Analysis

For body motion, we only study the level 1 annotation (left side of Fig. 8). No significant differences appear for head activity, except a small activity for backchannels.

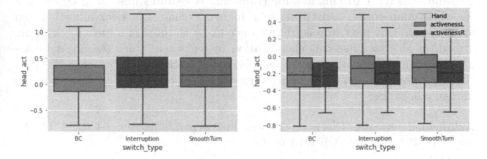

Fig. 8. Average value of head activity (left) & hand activity (right) for the first level of annotation.

When looking at the hands activity, we can see from the right side of Fig. 8 that the left hand has larger spatial extent than the right hand. In contrast, there is no significant difference between backchannel, interruption and smooth turn.

8 Discussion

In our database, we detected 929 interruptions over 3983 VAD switches. Excluding backchannels, interruptions take almost 40% of the turn switches, which is a quite large number and shows the importance of interruptions in natural conversation.

In our corpus, the interruptions are successful most of the time. There are only 18.3% of the cases where the person does not succeed to take the turn.

Considering the acoustic and body features we analysed, some of them seem important to distinguish backchannel, interruption and smooth turn exchange such as the IPU length or loudness. We did not find significant differences for the other features. We could not replicate all the results from previous studies [26,40,48]. Such dissimilarities may come from the scenarios of the corpora used in the different studies. Other, which were supposed to be relevant, such as hand activity, did not show significant differences.

9 Conclusion and Perspectives

Being interested by interruptions, we first propose a three levels schema annotation that allow characterizing each type of VAD switches. We used it to annotated the NoXi corpus and found that interruptions are very frequent in natural interactions. Then, we extracted all the voice activity switches. We conducted analyses on acoustic and body movement features to computationally characterize these switches.

This work is a first step toward the modeling of interruptions for an embodied conversational agent. In the near future, we aim to endow ECA with the possibility to react to human's interruptions. It requires first to recognize if a speech overlap corresponds to a smooth turn exchange, a backchannel, or an interruption. Our next step is to introduce these features in a machine learning algorithm able to make this classification in real time. Once the agent knows if its human interlocutor interrupts, displays a backchannel or takes the turn slightly before the agent's speaking turn, the agent can plan how to respond to human's behavior.

Acknowledgements. This work was performed as part of ANR-JST-CREST TAPAS and ANR-JST-DFG PANORAMA project.

References

1. Allwood, J., Nivre, J., Ahlsén, E.: On the semantics and pragmatics of linguistic feedback. J. Semant. **9**(1), 1–26 (1992)
2. Ball, P.: Listeners' responses to filled pauses in relation to floor apportionment. Br. J. Soc. Clin. Psychol. (1975)
3. Baltrusaitis, T., Zadeh, A., Lim, Y.C., Morency, L.P.: OpenFace 2.0: facial behavior analysis toolkit. In: 2018 13th IEEE International Conference on Automatic Face & Gesture Recognition (FG 2018), pp. 59–66. IEEE (2018)
4. Baur, T., et al.: explainable cooperative machine learning with NOVA. KI - Künstliche Intelligenz (2020)
5. Beattie, G.W.: Floor apportionment and gaze in conversational dyads. Br. J. Soc. Clin. Psychol. **17**(1), 7–15 (1978)
6. Beattie, G.W.: Interruption in Conversational Interaction, and Its Relation to the Sex and Status of the Interactants. Walter de Gruyter, Berlin/New York (1981)
7. Bögels, S., Torreira, F.: Turn-end estimation in conversational turn-taking: the roles of context and prosody. Discour. Process. **58**(10), 903–924 (2021)
8. Cafaro, A., Glas, N., Pelachaud, C.: The effects of interrupting behavior on interpersonal attitude and engagement in dyadic interactions. In: Proceedings of the 2016 International Conference on Autonomous Agents & Multiagent Systems, pp. 911–920 (2016)
9. Cafaro, A., et al.: The NoXi database: multimodal recordings of mediated novice-expert interactions. In: Proceedings of the 19th ACM International Conference on Multimodal Interaction, pp. 350–359 (2017)
10. Chowdhury, S.A., Danieli, M., Riccardi, G.: Annotating and categorizing competition in overlap speech. In: 2015 IEEE International Conference on Acoustics, Speech and Signal Processing (ICASSP), pp. 5316–5320. IEEE (2015)
11. Chýlek, A., Švec, J., Šmídl, L.: Learning to interrupt the user at the right time in incremental dialogue systems. In: Sojka, P., Horák, A., Kopeček, I., Pala, K. (eds.) TSD 2018. LNCS (LNAI), vol. 11107, pp. 500–508. Springer, Cham (2018). https://doi.org/10.1007/978-3-030-00794-2_54

12. Coates, J.: 11 no gap, lots of overlap: turn-taking patterns in. Researching language and literacy in social context: a reader, p. 177 (1994)

13. Coman, A.C., Yoshino, K., Murase, Y., Nakamura, S., Riccardi, G.: An incremental turn-taking model for task-oriented dialog systems. arXiv preprint arXiv:1905.11806 (2019)

14. De Kok, I., Heylen, D.: Multimodal end-of-turn prediction in multi-party meetings. In: Proceedings of the 2009 International Conference on Multimodal Interfaces, pp. 91–98 (2009)

15. De Ruiter, J.P., Mitterer, H., Enfield, N.J.: Projecting the end of a speaker's turn: a cognitive cornerstone of conversation. Language **82**(3), 515–535 (2006)

16. Dediu, D., Levinson, S.C.: On the antiquity of language: the reinterpretation of Neandertal linguistic capacities and its consequences. Front. Psychol. **4**, 397 (2013)

17. Demol, M., Verhelst, W., Verhoeve, P.: The duration of speech pauses in a multilingual environment. In: Eighth Annual Conference of the International Speech Communication Association (2007)

18. Duncan, S.: Some signals and rules for taking speaking turns in conversations. J. Pers. Soc. Psychol. **23**(2), 283 (1972)

19. Egorow, O., Wendemuth, A.: On emotions as features for speech overlaps classification. IEEE Trans. Affect. Comput. (2019)

20. Ekman, P., Friesen, W.V.: Facial action coding system. Environ. Psychol. Nonverbal Behav. (1978)

21. Eyben, F., Wöllmer, M., Schuller, B.: OpenSmile: the Munich versatile and fast open-source audio feature extractor. In: Proceedings of the 18th ACM International Conference on Multimedia, pp. 1459–1462 (2010)

22. Ferguson, N.: Simultaneous speech, interruptions and dominance. Br. J. Soc. Clin. Psychol. **16**(4), 295–302 (1977)

23. French, P., Local, J.: Turn-competitive incomings. J. Pragmat. **7**(1), 17–38 (1983)

24. Goldberg, J.A.: Interrupting the discourse on interruptions: an analysis in terms of relationally neutral, power-and rapport-oriented acts. J. Pragmat. **14**(6), 883–903 (1990)

25. Gravano, A., Brusco, P., Benus, S.: Who do you think will speak next? Perception of turn-taking cues in Slovak and argentine Spanish. In: INTERSPEECH, pp. 1265–1269 (2016)

26. Gravano, A., Hirschberg, J.: A corpus-based study of interruptions in spoken dialogue. In: Thirteenth Annual Conference of the International Speech Communication Association (2012)

27. Hammarberg, B., Fritzell, B., Gaufin, J., Sundberg, J., Wedin, L.: Perceptual and acoustic correlates of abnormal voice qualities. Acta Otolaryngol. **90**(1–6), 441–451 (1980)

28. Hara, K., Inoue, K., Takanashi, K., Kawahara, T.: Turn-taking prediction based on detection of transition relevance place. In: Proceedings of Interspeech 2019, pp. 4170–4174 (2019). https://doi.org/10.21437/Interspeech.2019-1537

29. Heldner, M., Edlund, J.: Pauses, gaps and overlaps in conversations. J. Phon. **38**(4), 555–568 (2010)

30. Holler, J., Kendrick, K.H., Casillas, M., Levinson, S.C.: Turn-taking in human communicative interaction. Front. Media SA (2016)

31. Indefrey, P., Levelt, W.J.: The spatial and temporal signatures of word production components. Cognition **92**(1–2), 101–144 (2004)

32. Ishii, R., Otsuka, K., Kumano, S., Matsuda, M., Yamato, J.: Predicting next speaker and timing from gaze transition patterns in multi-party meetings. In: Pro-

ceedings of the 15th ACM on International conference on multimodal interaction, pp. 79–86 (2013)

33. Ishii, R., Otsuka, K., Kumano, S., Yamato, J.: Using respiration to predict who will speak next and when in multiparty meetings. ACM Trans. Interact. Intell. Syst. (TiiS) **6**(2), 1–20 (2016)

34. Ishii, R., Ren, X., Muszynski, M., Morency, L.P.: Can prediction of turn-management willingness improve turn-changing modeling? In: Proceedings of the 20th ACM International Conference on Intelligent Virtual Agents, pp. 1–8 (2020)

35. Ishii, R., Ren, X., Muszynski, M., Morency, L.P.: Multimodal and multitask approach to listener's backchannel prediction: can prediction of turn-changing and turn-management willingness improve backchannel modeling? In: Proceedings of the 21st ACM International Conference on Intelligent Virtual Agents, pp. 131–138 (2021)

36. Ishimoto, Y., Teraoka, T., Enomoto, M.: End-of-utterance prediction by prosodic features and phrase-dependency structure in spontaneous Japanese speech. In: Interspeech, pp. 1681–1685 (2017)

37. Itakura, H.: Describing conversational dominance. J. Pragmat. **33**(12), 1859–1880 (2001)

38. Kendon, A.: Some functions of gaze-direction in social interaction. Acta Physiol. **26**, 22–63 (1967)

39. Kurtić, E., Brown, G.J., Wells, B.: Resources for turn competition in overlapping talk. Speech Commun. **55**(5), 721–743 (2013)

40. Lee, C.C., Lee, S., Narayanan, S.S.: An analysis of multimodal cues of interruption in dyadic spoken interactions. In: Ninth Annual Conference of the International Speech Communication Association (2008)

41. Lee, C.C., Narayanan, S.: Predicting interruptions in dyadic spoken interactions. In: 2010 IEEE International Conference on Acoustics, Speech and Signal Processing, pp. 5250–5253. IEEE (2010)

42. Maier, A., Hough, J., Schlangen, D., et al.: Towards deep end-of-turn prediction for situated spoken dialogue systems (2017)

43. Moerman, M., Sacks, H.: Appendix B. on "understanding" in the analysis of natural conversation. In: Talking Culture, pp. 180–186. University of Pennsylvania Press (2010)

44. Niebuhr, O., Görs, K., Graupe, E.: Speech reduction, intensity, and F0 shape are cues to turn-taking. In: Proceedings of the SIGDIAL 2013 Conference, pp. 261–269 (2013)

45. Riest, C., Jorschick, A.B., de Ruiter, J.P.: Anticipation in turn-taking: mechanisms and information sources. Front. Psychol. **6**, 89 (2015)

46. Sacks, H., Schegloff, E.A., Jefferson, G.: A simplest systematics for the organization of turn taking for conversation. In: Studies in the Organization of Conversational Interaction, pp. 7–55. Elsevier (1978)

47. Schegloff, E.A.: Sequencing in conversational openings 1. Am. Anthropol. **70**(6), 1075–1095 (1968)

48. Schegloff, E.A.: Overlapping talk and the organization of turn-taking for conversation. Lang. Soc. **29**(1), 1–63 (2000)

49. Schegloff, E.A., Sacks, H.: Opening up Closings. Walter de Gruyter, Berlin/New York (1973)

50. Shriberg, E., Stolcke, A., Baron, D.: Observations on overlap: findings and implications for automatic processing of multi-party conversation. In: Seventh European Conference on Speech Communication and Technology (2001)

51. Skantze, G., Johansson, M., Beskow, J.: Exploring turn-taking cues in multi-party human-robot discussions about objects. In: Proceedings of the 2015 ACM on International Conference on Multimodal Interaction, pp. 67–74 (2015)
52. Stivers, T., et al.: Universals and cultural variation in turn-taking in conversation. Proc. Natl. Acad. Sci. **106**(26), 10587–10592 (2009)
53. Tannen, D., et al.: You Just Don't Understand: Women and Men in Conversation. Virago, London (1991)
54. Truong, K.P.: Classification of cooperative and competitive overlaps in speech using cues from the context, overlapper, and overlappee. In: Interspeech, pp. 1404–1408 (2013)
55. Van Berkum, J.J., Brown, C.M., Zwitserlood, P., Kooijman, V., Hagoort, P.: Anticipating upcoming words in discourse: evidence from ERPs and reading times. J. Exp. Psychol. Learn. Mem. Cogn. **31**(3), 443 (2005)
56. Xiu, Y., Li, J., Wang, H., Fang, Y., Lu, C.: Pose flow: efficient online pose tracking. In: BMVC (2018)
57. Yang, L.C.: Visualizing spoken discourse: prosodic form and discourse functions of interruptions. In: Proceedings of the Second SIGdial Workshop on Discourse and Dialogue (2001)

Correlation Study of Clothing Pressure and Reducing Exercise Fatigue During Exergames

Chang Yao, Ting Han[✉], and Xuewen Sun

School of Design, Shanghai Jiao Tong University, 800 Dongchuan Road, Minhang District, Shanghai 200240, China
hanting@sjtu.edu.cn

Abstract. Background: Exergames are very closely integrated with technological tools such as wearable devices. Sportswear should be functional and comfortable to meet people's pleasurable experiences while exercising. Clothing pressure is one of the factors affecting clothing comfort. This study aimed to investigate the effect of clothing pressure induced by sportswear on people's level of exercise fatigue during exergames.

Methods: A Switch game intervention was performed on five young women aged 22–24 years under different clothing pressure stimuli, and their game score, clothing pressure on the anterior thighs and posterior calves, and electromyographic index during exercise were measured, and a subjective fatigue scale was collected from participants after exercise. Correlation analyses were compiled in conjunction with SPSS software to determine the effect of clothing pressure on muscle fatigue.

Results: Persona Correction showed a statistically significant correlation between clothing pressure and exercise fatigue at $p < 0.01$.

Conclusions: The greater the clothing pressure within a certain range, the less fatigue people experience and the better their athletic performance when playing exergames under the same conditions.

Keywords: Clothing pressure · Exergames · EMG index · Subjective fatigue · Exercise experience

1 Introduction

The prolonged blockade and quarantine measures under the epidemic have harmed people's mental and physical health, leading to significant changes in their lifestyles [1]. Physical activity and exercise can help people to keep healthy and happy [2]. Exergames are video games based on physical movements and are an engaging form of exercise. Regular physical activity is influenced by the structure of the environment, the form of displacement in space, the proximity of the venue, and previous experience of exercise, but exergames present a more fun and at-home approach that motivates users to exercise and are an excellent alternative to regular physical activity [3, 4]. Much of the literature

© The Author(s), under exclusive license to Springer Nature Switzerland AG 2022
V. G. Duffy (Ed.): HCII 2022, LNCS 13319, pp. 326–341, 2022.
https://doi.org/10.1007/978-3-031-05890-5_25

points to the positive effects of exergames on people's improved physical abilities, which include balance, muscle strength, gait, and falls. Compared to regular physical activities, exergames are superior in keeping people fit and happy and in preventing illness.

The demand for smart textile-based health interaction products is also showing a rapid growth in the context of the epidemic. Personal healthcare and well-being are also the fastest growing areas of consumer electronics [5]. Textiles or smart equipment based on sportswear can help protect the body by providing support for muscles and joints and reducing muscle jitters during exercise. High-stretch fabrics and tight shapes put pressure on the muscles and help relieve muscle fatigue and promote recovery [6, 7].

Surface EMG measurements and subjective fatigue scale methods are commonly used when determining muscle fatigue in humans. The use of EMG to detect muscle activity is also commonly used in sports and medicine. In addition to the use of objectively measured data indicators, the subjective feelings people have when participating in the exercise are also important. Postural stability is considered to underpin the ability to control the center of mass. To maintain postural stability, the central nervous system must rapidly integrate sensory information from the visual, vestibular, and somatosensory systems. The CNS must also selectively use this information to generate complex motor responses that balance the interference of the surrounding environment with postural stability [8]. Exercise-induced muscle fatigue can affect some of the sensory information and motor commands required to regulate posture. Therefore, the subjective sensations induced by muscle fatigue can lead to alterations in postural control and affect the motor experience, and such subjective sensations are generally obtained using a subjective fatigue scale.

This study aims to investigate the correlation between clothing pressure and reduced exercise fatigue during exercise, and to provide theoretical and technical support for a more comfortable, functional, and user-centered selection of exercise clothing pressure by establishing a link between exergames and exercise clothing, to improve user comfort and exercise performance during exercise, to increase the frequency and viscosity of users' use of health products and to achieve the desired exercise effect.

2   Literature Review and Research Hypothesis

Databases such as PubMed, Cochrane, Science Direct, and Springer were searched for this study. The literature includes research on the benefits of exergames, the development of major technology platforms and tools, and the development of exergames or textile-based wearable devices during exercise. Finally, two hypotheses were formulated based on a literature search and observational methods, questionnaires, and expert interviews.

2.1   Technological Tools for the Development of Physical Activity or Exergames

Technology has changed the way people live their lives. There are a large number of technological tools, including fixed devices such as computers; wearable devices such as smart textiles, helmets, smart belts, and smart bracelets that help people improve their quality of life, health, and well-being [9].

In 2006, Nintendo released the Wii gaming system. This game used interactive physical movement and pioneered exergames. Physical activity video games or so-called "exergames" have become popular, especially in the context of medical rehabilitation [10]. Exergames are played on video game systems and require the user to move their body to interact with a virtual character in a VR interface that engages in movement activities. In this case, exergames require additional assistive devices such as VR glasses, protective clothing, monitors, etc.

Physical activity is divided into aerobic exercise, which promotes cardiorespiratory fitness, and intensity exercise, which promotes musculoskeletal health. However, this type of physical activity, while improving physical health, requires supervision and prevention to minimize the risk of excessive injury. At the same time, because of technological developments, human-computer interaction (HCI) has helped to focus on the changing needs of people through the adoption of information technology has occurred [11], for which health platforms that can integrate monitoring, protection, feedback, and enhancement of interest of these user needs are now deeply considered by the industry. This health system requires infrastructure such as appropriate hardware and software, the design of algorithms and applications, and finally implementation and evaluation.

Product-oriented production systems have been replaced by human-centered systems and a human-centered design approach has evolved. User-oriented design is an interdisciplinary approach that meets the expectations and needs of the user through the ergonomic characteristics of the product. In user-oriented design, the designer's task is to make the design fit the user's needs or experience, to provide a more humane technological approach when people perform exergames, and to ensure that users can use exergames or perform physical activity as intended with minimal effort [12].

2.2   The Use of Wearables to Support Physical Activity or Exergames

The use of textile-based wearables in exergames is becoming increasingly popular, but in addition to technological advances in system integration, the comfort experience of wearables for exergames during the user's exercise is also one of the influencing factors that affect how people evaluate exergames, and comfortable exercise clothing can also lead to a better exercise experience.

The demand for textile-based wearable health interaction products has been growing rapidly [13], and there are already many textile-based exercise options, with the Lyne UP smart t-shirt being a registered medical device designed to strengthen back muscles by encouraging positive postures [14]. Sensoria is a smart sock that is infused with comfortable textile pressure sensors. They notify people in real-time when they strike with the heel or palm of their foot and visualize a heat map of the foot on the Sensoria Fitness mobile apps [15]. The shirt is a smart shirt made from nylon polyester and knitted with silver thread. It contains a range of sensors for capturing real-time data. For example, an electrocardiogram (ECG) and accelerometer allow users to monitor changes in their heartbeat during a workout. Other sensors can calculate the calories burned throughout a workout [16].

Clothing comfort is determined by a variety of material and design factors. Garment systems can be thought of as a combination of interactions that ultimately affect the overall garment function and wearing comfort. Garment formation can be divided into two main clusters. One is the textile factor, which includes the basic yarns and fibers used for knitting or weaving the fabric itself in terms of different physical parameters such as quality, yarn count, stitch density, etc. The second is the garment factor, which includes, for example, garment design [17]. During sports activities, clothing pressure is a factor that affects both clothing comfort and sports experience. Therefore, this study wanted to investigate reducing people's fatigue during exercise and improving the exercise experience by controlling the variable of clothing pressure.

2.3 Research Hypothesis

This study was conducted to investigate the physiological and psychological changes produced by the stress of clothing on users during exergames and to investigate whether clothing stress can be used as a means of assessing better physical sensation in exergames using wearable interactive products and to alleviate muscle fatigue and improve exercise performance during exergames. Two hypotheses were formulated for this study.

Hypothesis 1: Appropriate clothing pressure has a positive effect on the body, relieves muscle fatigue during exergames, facilitates post-exercise muscle recovery, and improves sports performance.

Hypothesis 2: Clothing pressure indicators of wearable interactive products in exergames can be linked to user physiological indicators.

3   Methods

3.1   Participants

Five young women (22–24 years old) were recruited from students at Shanghai Jiao Tong University and Dong Hua University. Their height, weight, thigh circumference, and calf circumference are shown in Table 1. The experimental procedures were fully explained to the participants verbally and in writing before informed written consent was obtained and a health screening questionnaire was completed.

Table 1. Basic information of participants

Number	Height/cm	Weight/kg	Thigh/cm	Calf/cm
1	164	50	48	30
2	167	54	50	32
3	175	64	56	36
4	169	58	52	33
5	167	58	54	34

3.2 Experimental Stimuli

The experimental stimuli were designed to allow participants to experience different clothing pressure stimuli while playing exergames. The experimental garments consisted of three women's sports tights with the same design. The fabric of the leggings consisted of 80% polyester and 20% spandex. The fabric is comfortable and absorbs sweat. Three sizes (XS, M, and XL) were chosen to create different levels of pressure perception on the participants as the independent variables for this study Table 2. The quadriceps muscle is the muscle on the front side of the thigh and is the most important muscle in protecting our knee joints (Fig. 1).

Table 2. Basic information of clothing

SKU	Size	Waist/cm	Length/cm	Hipline/cm	Thigh/cm	Mouth/cm
AULQ018-1	XS	51	82	64	39.5	9.15
AULQ018-1	M	61	86	74	44.5	9.75
AULQ018-1	XL	71	90	84	49.5	10.35

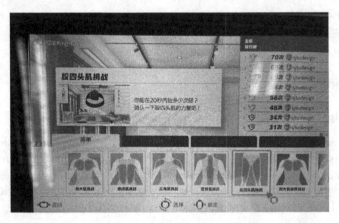

Fig. 1. Switch fitness ring adventure "quadriceps challenge"

3.3 Experimental Equipment

The experimental equipment consisted of a Switch national console. The Switch console included a joystick, fitness ring, leg straps, HDMI cable, power cable, box, and a large screen for casting. The experimental tests were conducted using an airbag contact stress test system and myoelectric equipment. The heart of the airbag contact pressure testing system is the AMI3037-10-II airbag pressure transducer, which consists of an airbag transducer, mainframe, and other accessories (Fig. 2) that display pressure measurement data in real-time. The system utilizes contact to accomplish tiny wearing pressures on flexible materials such as garments, is characterized by high repeatability and accuracy, and allows continuous data collection and analysis as required. It is widely used in the fields of garment engineering, textile materials, fabric take-up testing, ergonomics, and assessment of garment functionality. This study focused on measuring the pressure values of the garment on the participant's thighs and calves. The EMG equipment consisted of a Noraxon MR3 surface EMG instrument, a computer, and adapters. The Noraxon MR3 surface electromyography measures the electromyographic index of the participants before and after playing exergames with the different stresses on the clothing.

Fig. 2. AMI3037-10-II airbag pressure sensor

3.4 Experimental Protocol

Before the experiment began, the five participants were given an overview of the experiment, given instructions, and were guided through a warm-up exercise of about 1 min after obtaining their consent to participate and signatures. Two staff members were responsible for disinfecting the participants' clothing and marking the measurement locations. There were four points of clothing pressure measurement: the anterior thighs and posterior halves of the legs. Electromyography was measured at the same locations as the stress measurement points, and the electromyographic index of the quadriceps muscle and the electromyographic index of the gastrocnemius muscle in the triceps muscle of the lower leg were measured in both legs.

Each of the five participants underwent three sets of clothing stress interventions: a "quadriceps challenge" in which they wore, in turn, specially made sportswear with low, medium and high-stress levels. Each group consisted of three rounds of exergames with a 3-min break each. The participants were measured during the exergames and the results were averaged over the three rounds. Participants had their quadriceps and gastrocnemius EMG measured before and after each set and completed a subjective fatigue scale and a subjective clothing stress scale after the exercise. Participants rested for 30 min after each set of clothing stress level tests and then proceeded to the next clothing stress level test (Fig. 3).

Fig. 3. Photographs of the experiment in progress

At the end of the experiment, three questions were asked of each of the five participants. The first question was "Do you think that appropriate clothing pressure has a positive effect on reducing exercise fatigue?" The second question was "Do you think that appropriate clothing pressure has a positive effect on improving game scores?" The third question was "Does this experiment influence your choice of sportswear when playing sports or exergames?". At the end of the experiment, all scales and questionnaires were collected, the equipment organized and inventoried, and the laboratory environment restored.

4   Results

4.1   Exergames Results

In this experiment, the three exercise performances of each participant at the same clothing pressure level were averaged, with pressures 1–3 corresponding to participants wearing XL, M, and XS clothing respectively, as the score for this level of pressure. As can be seen in Table 3 as the stress level increases, the exergame scores increase. The results of the exergame for the five participants in this study after nine rounds of the exergame intervention for each participant are shown in Fig. 4.

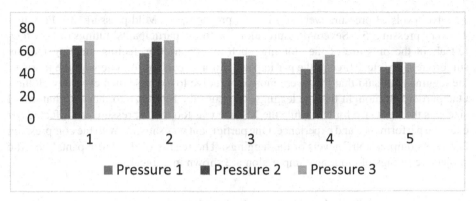

Fig. 4. Exergames results

4.2 Pressure Test Analysis

Garment pressure is a key factor affecting human comfort. Garment pressure is the vertical force exerted on the human skin as a result of the body or external forces being squeezed and stretched and deformed during the static or dynamic process of the fabric. According to the reference literature, the comfort pressure range for general clothing is 1.96 to 3.92 kPa and the comfort range for human calf clothing pressure is less than 2.65 kPa [6]. Five participants were tested using the AMI3037-10-II airbag contact pressure testing system wearing experimental sports tights at different pressure levels. Where position 1, 2, 3, and 4 corresponded to the participants' left anterior thigh, left posterior calf, right posterior calf, and right anterior thigh respectively.

The dynamic pressure of the five participants at the three pressure levels was measured for 20 s per round of play. The airbag type pressure testing system is a real-time measure tool and the measurements are continuous curve changes, for statistical purposes in this study, the instantaneous pressure values of the participants at 5 s, 10 s, 15 s, and 20 s were taken and averaged to obtain the results in Table 3.

Table 3. Clothing pressure results

	Pressure 1 (kPa)				Pressure 2 (kPa)				Pressure 3 (kPa)			
	P1	P2	P3	P4	P1	P2	P3	P4	P1	P2	P3	P4
1	0.045	0.056	0.013	0.02	1.348	1.458	1.398	1.22	2.123	2.456	2.678	2.793
2	0.023	0.013	0.02	0.009	1.3	0.948	1.684	3.726	2.254	2.134	2.45	2.643
3	0.112	0.212	0.045	0.034	2.03	1.23	1.872	1.542	2.356	2.192	2.74	2.045
4	0.023	0.045	0.012	0.045	1.928	1.044	1.594	1.612	2.456	2.732	2.943	2.345
5	0.034	0.002	0.043	0.012	1.238	1.048	1.366	1.422	2.145	2.782	2.463	2.1

Five levels of pressure were set: 1 – No pressure, 2 – Mild pressure, 3 – Pressure, 4 – Very pressure, 5 – Severe pressure, along with the participants' ratings of how they felt about the pressure of the clothing, such as constriction feeling, tickling feeling, smooth feeling, etc. Three of the participants did not feel comfortable with the fabric of the leggings but said that they were more conducive to exercise than everyday clothes. One participant thought that the leggings were not the right size for her and that the M size was the right size for her, while the XS size was too much pressure and affected her exercise performance and experience. One participant was satisfied with the compression 2 versus compression 3 levels of the leggings. The results of the participants' specific subjective ratings of clothing compression are shown in Table 4.

Table 4. Subjective evaluation of clothing pressure

No.	Pressure 1	Pressure 2	Pressure 3
1	1	2	4
2	2	3	5
3	3	4	5
4	1	3	5
5	1	3	5

4.3 Fatigue Test Analysis

Exercise-induced muscle fatigue is most commonly defined as the inability to maintain strength during exercise. The surface electromyographic index (sEMG index) is one of the indicators of the state of physical activity in people. sEMG is effective in determining the degree of muscle fatigue and injury, and the EMG signal can point to significant changes in muscle fatigue before and after exercise [18]. sEMG is an index of muscle fatigue that is analyzed by recording and displaying the frequency changes generated by muscle activity [19]. By analyzing changes in EMG data from the quadriceps and gastrocnemius muscles of the lower leg, data are obtained on the number of motor units involved in the activity of that muscle and the size of the discharge of each motor unit. Hollies' five-interval scale was used as the standard, using a combined time-frequency analysis, where the root mean square (RMS) and the medium frequency (MF) of the time-frequency metrics were used for surface EMG testing [6].

In this study, measurements were made using a Noraxon MR3 surface EMG instrument and the corresponding channel number was matched to the electrodes. The matched EMG sensor was attached to the four points where the pressure of the garment was measured and the direction of the indicated arrow on the sensor was aligned with the direction of the muscle fibers. Participants were asked to do a knee flexion and leg lift, raising the thigh to the horizontal, for a measurement time of 15 s. Each participant took one EMG measurement before and after each test at different pressure levels and the results were recorded as dynamic data at a frequency of 2000 Hz for a total of three rounds of experiments.

The results of the EMG tests are shown in Figs. 5, 6, and 7. It can be seen that the thigh muscle has a smaller EMG peak than the calf muscle, and the pre-exercise EMG peak is smaller and fluctuates relatively more than the post-exercise EMG peak. The higher the stress level the smoother the change in peak value and the less obvious the fatigue. The increase in clothing pressure had a relieving effect on participants' muscle fatigue, and within a certain range, the higher the pressure, the more pronounced the relieving effect.

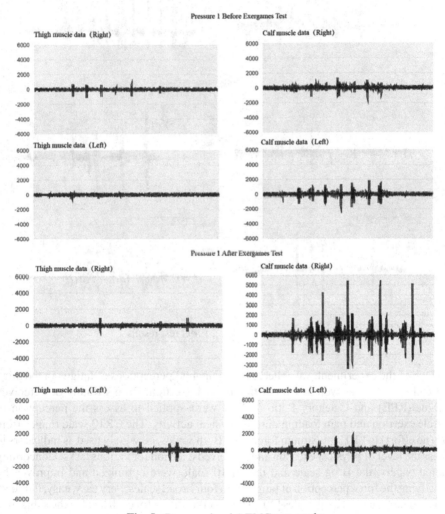

Fig. 5. Pressure level 1 EMG test results

336   C. Yao et al.

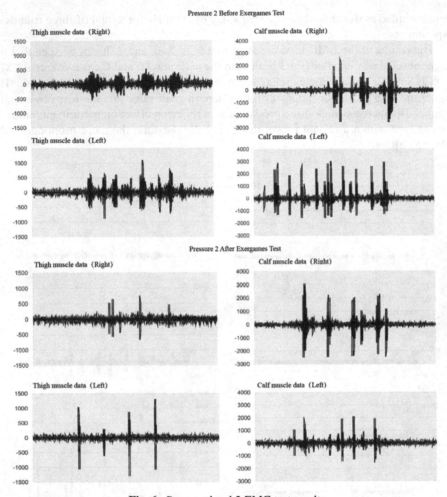

Fig. 6. Pressure level 2 EMG test results

During the experiment, we collected participants' perceptions of fatigue in the thigh and calf segments as well as overall fatigue and exertion. Brog's Rating of Perceived Fatigue (RPE) and Category Ratio (CR10) were applied to assess the perception of muscle exertion and pain loading during physical activity. The CR10 scale ranges from "0" (no effort) to "10" (maximum force) [8]. Both scales are widely used as indicators to assess the level of physical exertion and perceived exertion for various tasks. Concerning related papers, the Brog scale and the CR10 scale were optimized and improved by classifying the force perception of fatigue into four broad scales: very easy, easy, fatigued, very fatigued, and 1–12 subscales [20]. The specific values for each level of the subjective fatigue scale are shown in Table 5. By collecting data from five subjects and taking the average of the fatigue of the five subjects at different levels of the Switch's quadriceps game as an example (see Table 6), it can be seen that the higher the clothing pressure, the

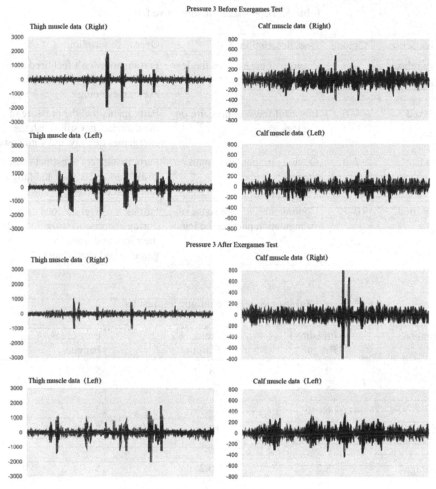

Fig. 7. Pressure level 3 EMG test results

lower the subjective fatigue of the subjects within a certain range for the same exergame content and time.

4.4 Fatigue Test Analysis

Significance analysis of stress change and subjective fatigue was conducted using SPSS Statistics software. Because the analysis was conducted between subjective variable scales, Person Correlation was used. Person Correlation requires the variable type to be a continuous numerical variable. In this study, the correlation between the two bivariate variables, clothing stress and subjective fatigue, was analyzed for 45 rounds of experiments with five participants under three sets of stress levels. If $p < 0.01$, then clothing pressure was considered to be correlated with subjective fatigue and the Person Correlation results are shown in Table 7. As shown in the analysis, $p = 0.001$ between the two

338   C. Yao et al.

Table 5. Brog's scale of subjective fatigue

Force sense	Grade	Legs description	Overall description
Very relaxed	1–3	A sense of pressure on the legs	Participants don't feel tired at all and feel like they can keep the exergames going
Relaxed	4–6	Powerful sense of pressure on the legs	Participants feel the pressure of the exercise, but still finish the exergames quickly and with power
Tired	7–9	Obvious strangulation pain on the legs	Participants feel a distinct sense of strain during exercise and fatigue increased over time
Very tired	10–12	Continuous and sore sense of strangulation pain on the legs	Participants feel obvious pain during exercise to struggle to lift their legs and want the exercise game to end immediately

Table 6. Subjective fatigue test results

Number	Pressure 1 Fatigue	Pressure 2 Fatigue	Pressure 3 Fatigue
1	9	8	5
2	7	3	3
3	6	4	3
4	11	10	8
5	8	6	6
Average	8.2	6.2	5

variables, so $p < 0.01$ and there was a significant correlation between clothing pressure and exercise fatigue.

Table 7. Person correlation results between clothing pressure and fatigue

Correlations			
		Pressure	Fatigue
Pressure	Pearson correlation	1	$-.489^{**}$
	Sig. (2-tailed)		0.001
	N	45	45

(continued)

Table 7. (*continued*)

Correlations			
		Pressure	Fatigue
Fatigue	Pearson correlation	$-.489^{**}$	1
	Sig. (2-tailed)	0.001	
	N	45	45

** Correlation is significant at the 0.01 level (2-tailed).

At the end of the experiment, the results of the three questions collected on the questionnaire were that all five participants felt that appropriate clothing pressure had a positive impact on reducing fatigue; that appropriate clothing pressure had a positive impact on improving exercise performance; and that after this experiment, the choice of exercise clothing for exercise was considered afterwards.

5 Conclusions

The results of the experiment revealed that an increase in clothing pressure reduced participants' exercise fatigue under the same conditions and within a range of clothing pressures. To a certain extent, the higher the clothing pressure the better the reduction in exercise fatigue, the more the number of leg lifts during the game, the higher the score and the better the exercise experience for the participants. The experiment proves that Hypothesis 1 holds true: the right clothing pressure has a positive effect on the body, relieving muscle fatigue during exergames, facilitating post-exercise muscle recovery and improving athletic performance.

The experiment also has shortcomings. The data analysis of the experimental results showed that clothing pressure indicators in exergames showed a positive correlation with users' physiological indicators, but because of the limitations of venue, time and student funding, young women within the campus area were chosen as experimental subjects, and the number and variety of experimental subjects were small, so the magnitude of the correlation could not be calculated quantitatively, so Hypothesis 2 still needs a wider range of experimental subjects to refine the experimental results.

The study explores the correlation between clothing stress and the relief of muscle fatigue from the fields of ergonomics, clothing engineering, interaction design and physiology to provide a theoretical basis and technical support for the design of textile-based sports interaction wearable devices. This study provides fundamental suggestions for a balanced relationship between exergames and textiles, experiences in sportswear selection for young people or special groups who want to keep fit, and design references for developers of sportswear in terms of fabric, fit and pressure control. Based on this study more participants can be sought to take part in the experiment, more in-depth research can be done on the correlation between the pressure of sportswear and the level of muscle fatigue relief, more functional clothing for exergames or sports can be developed and the joint development of the textile and exergames industry can be promoted.

Compliance with Ethical Standards. This experiment complies with the Declaration of Helsinki and informed consent was obtained from participants. All relevant ethical safeguards have been met with regard to subject protection.

References

1. Liu, M.-B., et al.: The impact of the COVID-19 pandemic on the mental health of young people: a comparison between China and the United Kingdom. Chin. J. Traumatol. **24**, 231–236 (2021)
2. Langhammer, B., Bergland, A., Rydwik, E.: The importance of physical activity exercise among older people. BioMed Res. Int. **2018**, 1–3 (2018). https://doi.org/10.1155/2018/785 6823
3. Monteiro-Junior, R.S., Rodrigues, A.C.M.A., Felício, L.F.F., Figueiredo, L.F.S., Xavier-Rocha, T.B.: Chapter 37 – Exergames: what they are and how they can be used to successful aging? In: Martin, C.R., Preedy, V.R., Rajendram, R. (eds.) Assessments Treatments and Modeling in Aging and Neurological Disease, pp. 415–424. Academic Press (2021). https://doi.org/10.1016/B978-0-12-818000-6.00037-8
4. Zhou, W., Zhang, M.: Research on children's personalized sports in the environment of smart wearable devices. Microprocess. Microsyst. **81**, 103758 (2021)
5. Khokhlova, L., Belcastro, M., Torchia, P., O'Flynn, B., Tedesco, S.: Wearable textile-based device for human lower-limbs kinematics and muscle activity sensing. In: Perego, P., Taher-iNejad, N., Caon, M. (eds.) ICWH 2020. LNICSSITE, vol. 376, pp. 70–81. Springer, Cham (2021). https://doi.org/10.1007/978-3-030-76066-3_6
6. Mu, Y., Jin, Z., Jin, J., He, Y., Yan, Y.: Correlation study of football shin guards oppression and muscle fatigue during sports. In: Long, S., Dhillon, B.S. (eds.) MMESE 2019. LNEE, vol. 576, pp. 65–73. Springer, Singapore (2020). https://doi.org/10.1007/978-981-13-8779-1_8
7. Wu, J.H., Jin, Z.M., Jin, J., Yan, Y.X., Tao, J.W.: Study on the tensile modulus of seamless fabric and tight compression finite element modeling. Text. Res. J. **90**, 110–122 (2020)
8. Jo, D., Bilodeau, M.: Rating of perceived exertion (RPE) in studies of fatigue-induced postural control alterations in healthy adults: Scoping review of quantitative evidence. Gait Posture **90**, 167–178 (2021)
9. Lucerón-Lucas-Torres, M.I., Valera-Ortín, J.: Health technology tools used to increase physical activity and improve cardiovascular parameters in older adults: a review. Enferm. Clín. (Engl. Ed.) (2022). https://doi.org/10.1016/j.enfcle.2021.05.004
10. Fernandes, C.S., Magalhães, B., Gomes, J.A., Santos, C.: Exergames to improve rehabilitation after anterior cruciate ligament injury: systematic review and GRADE evidence synthesis. Int. J. Orthop. Trauma Nurs. **44**, 100917 (2022)
11. Varriale, L., Tafuri, D.: Technological trends in the sport field: which application areas and challenges? In: Nóvoa, H., Drăgoicea, M. (eds.) Exploring Services Science, pp. 204–214. Springer International Publishing, Cham (2015). https://doi.org/10.1007/978-3-319-14980-6_16
12. Balkış, M., Koca, E., Ferreira, A.M.: Design for health and wellbeing: innovative medical garment design. In: Raposo, D., Neves, J., Silva, J., Castilho, L.C., Dias, R. (eds.) Advances in Design, Music and Arts: 7th Meeting of Research in Music, Arts and Design, EIMAD 2020, May 14–15, 2020, pp. 343–353. Springer International Publishing, Cham (2021). https://doi.org/10.1007/978-3-030-55700-3_24
13. IDC: Prognose zum Absatz von Wearables weltweit von 2014 bis 2024. Statista. https://de.statista.com/statistik/daten/studie/417580/umfrage/prognose-zum-absatz-von-wearables/

14. Intelligent module analysis of French Percko intelligent posture correction clothing. https://percko.com/gbp/en/shop/lyneup/?gclid=EAIaIQobChMIidmHnfCm9QIVopvCCh2KRwH7EAAYASAAEgK38_D_BwE
15. Smart Running System. https://store.sensoriafitness.com/
16. OMsignal Smart Clothing. https://smartclothinglab.com/brands/omsignal/
17. Raccuglia, M., Sales, B., Heyde, C., Havenith, G., Hodder, S.: Clothing comfort during physical exercise – determining the critical factors. Appl. Ergon. **73**, 33–41 (2018)
18. Hong, L.I.U., Dongsheng, C., Qufu, W.E.I.: Effect of clothing pressure on human physiology and objective testing. J. Text. Res. **31**, 138–142 (2010)
19. Varrecchia, T., et al.: Bipolar versus high-density surface electromyography for evaluating risk in fatiguing frequency-dependent lifting activities. Appl. Ergon. **95**, 103456 (2021)
20. Shen, Y., Li, C., Zou, T.: Study on biomechanical response and subjective fatigue symptoms of human body wearing personal protective equipments. In: Long, S., Dhillon, B.S. (eds.) MMESE 2021. LNEE, vol. 800, pp. 116–121. Springer, Singapore (2022). https://doi.org/10.1007/978-981-16-5963-8_16

Study on the Sailors' Athletic Ability Change Rule of Long-Time Simulated Voyage

Chi Zhang[1]([✉]), Si Li[2], Yulin Zhang[1], Xin Wang[1], Jin Liang[1], Yang Yu[1], Liang Zhang[1], Chao Yang[1], Ziang Chen[1], and Qianfei Chen[1]

[1] China Institute of Marine Technology and Economy, Beijing 100081, China
zc810@126.com
[2] China Institute of Marine Human Factors Engineering, Qingdao 266400, China

Abstract. Due to special task environment, ocean vessel sailors on a long voyage have to face many adverse factors, such as long-time isolation, narrow space, irregular daily schedule and so on. Long-time isolation may affect sailors physically and psychologically which fluctuates over time. Narrow space cannot provide sufficient exercise conditions, and will limit forms of exercise. The situation directly reduces the amount and desire of exercise. Irregular daily schedule may cause biological rhythm disorder, and influence the physical state and exercise desire. Multiple factors will have a compound effect on the sailors' athletic ability, affect related athletic performance and operation ability, and have a profound impact on the maintenance of task capability and performance.

The purpose of this study was to explore the long-time change rule of sailors' athletic ability. The environment of long-time voyage was simulated by isolated lab module. During the experiment, the participants were isolated from outside and conducted the experiment independently following the manual with guidance. The participants took athletic ability test at set intervals to record athletic performance at corresponding time. The indicators included strength, breathing function, body flexibility and body balance. By analyzing the data, the change rule of sailors' athletic ability could be explored.

Through data collection and analysis during the experiment, it was found that in simulated long-time voyage, the athletic ability was affected by multiple factors, which presented different change rule. In conclusion, the change rule of athletic ability indicators is staged, which relates to many factors, including long-time isolation, exercise space restriction, daily schedule and training effect of test items.

Keywords: Long time voyage · Athletic ability · Experimental study · Change rule

1 Introduction

Generally, the working environment of ocean vessel sailors is narrow and isolated, lacking of exercise space and equipment. The living condition is also particular, lacking of supplies for daily life. Because of the above reasons, exercise conditions and opportunities of sailors are limited, and exercise desire may decrease.

© The Author(s), under exclusive license to Springer Nature Switzerland AG 2022
V. G. Duffy (Ed.): HCII 2022, LNCS 13319, pp. 342–353, 2022.
https://doi.org/10.1007/978-3-031-05890-5_26

During a long-time voyage, such factors extremely limit the mode and amount of sailors' exercise. Long-time isolated environment and irregular sleep patterns probably lead to sailors' low desire of exercise. Multifaceted factors may lead to decline in athletic ability of sailors.

Zhang et al. [1] and Fu et al. [2] summarized the effects of ship environment on the physiological functions and biochemical indicators of seamen, and believed that disadvantages of the long-distance navigation environment had great influence on the human body. Le et al. [3] explored the effect of long-distance voyage on cardiopulmonary function and endurance for 60 days. Cardiac and pulmonary functions, physical tolerance and physical work capacity of submariners were influenced to a certain degree during a prolonged navigation of 60 days. Hu et al. [4] discussed the impact of underwater navigation on sailor's physical fitness. The seamen's physical work capacity and maximum oxygen intake were shown decreased significantly after a 60-day under water voyage. Su et al. [5] found that Fatigue caused by a long-term voyage had an impact on the balance function of the crew. Sun et al. [6] summarized that grip strength played an important role in the stability of fine hand movements, and was an important indicator of physical fitness. Shen et al. [7] and Ou et al. [8] investigated the effects of long voyages on the pulmonary ventilation function of sailors. According to previous studies, the time of standing with closed eyes decreases with age, which is related to muscle strength and reaction time [9]. Yu et al. [10] explored the influence of long-term navigation on mental health in warship crews, summarized that ocean-going navigation has influence of the crew's mental health.

According to our literature research, there are relatively few studies on the change rule of athletic ability under such special conditions, but small number of studies on influencing factors mainly about physical and mental health. It is necessary to study the rule of change in ability under such special task conditions, explore the factors affecting the athletic ability of sailors on long voyage, and acquire the variation rule of the long-term athletic ability of sailors, which can provide strategy for ocean vessel sailors' athletic ability maintenance and improvement.

This paper is aimed to explore the long-time change rule of sailors' athletic ability. The environment of long-time voyage was simulated by isolated lab module, which involving several important factors, such as long-time isolation, narrow space dimension and non-24-h task cycle. The participants carried out the experiment in the module. During the experiment, the participants could not get out and the person outside could not get in, in order to achieve physical isolation. The participants conduct the experiment independently following the manual with guidance. The communication with outside was forbidden so as to achieve information isolation. The participants took athletic ability test at set intervals to record athletic performance at corresponding time. The indicators included strength, breathing function, body flexibility and body balance. By analyzing the data, the change rule of sailors' athletic ability during simulated long-time voyage could be explored, and the influence of related factors on the sailors' athletic ability could be obtained. Methods, such as descriptive statistics, difference analysis, curve fitting, were used for in-depth analysis to explore inner relationship between indicators.

2 Method

2.1 Experiment Design

We performed a long time isolated experiment to simulate a long time voyage and verify the hypothesis that long time voyage has significant effect on sailors' athletic ability. The independent variable was the sampling points of time and different groups of participants. There were fourteen sampling points from baseline period to the ending, and there was no grouping in this experiment. The dependent variables were grip strength (left and right hand), number of push-ups in one minute, lung capacity, sit-and-reach, time of standing on one foot with eyes closed (hereafter referred to as eye-closed standing), which respectively reflected the strength of hand grip, the strength of upper limb muscle, body flexibility, body balance.

2.2 Task Design

In the experiment, participants worked in a simulated lab module for a period of time according to the schedule. Participants inside could not come out and people outside could not go in. Internal and external information was isolated. The participants should work and rest inside according to established arrangement, and complete the experimental tasks and various physical fitness tests. During the experiment, the participants mainly engaged in three aspects:

1. carried out simulated voyage tasks according to the schedule.
2. conducted regular physical fitness tests with professional equipment and record data every few days, including hand muscle strength, upper limb muscle strength, lung capacity, body flexibility and body balance.
3. limited physical activities, daily living care and other recreational activities.

2.3 Participants

Eight participants were recruited to participate in this experiment. Their daily schedules were the same, despite of the leisure time. During the experiment, all of them completed the experiment and no one dropped out.

2.4 Experimental Facility

The experimental facilities are as follows (Table 1):

2.5 Experiment Procedure

Participants were assigned to the same duty hours. In the experiment, the participants completed the duty, test, and daily life in the isolated closed laboratory cabin. Physical fitness test was conducted every 6–12 days. They carried out and recorded the data by themselves in the confined cabin with limited space. In such limited space, the participants had some gym equipment such as power bicycle and dumb-bell, and were only allowed to do a small range of exercises.

Table 1. The introduction of experimental facility

	Facility	Unit of measurement	Accurate
Grip strength	Grip dynamometer	kg	0.1 kg
Push-ups	Second chronograph	Number per minute	1
Lung capacity	Spirometer	mL	0.1 mL
Eye-closed standing	Second chronograph	s	0.01 s
Sit-and-reach	Sit and reach tester	cm	0.2 cm

2.6 Data Analysis

Firstly, we performed descriptive analysis on the dependent variables, summarized a large amount of data preliminarily, and found out inherent rules. Secondly, we performed paired-samples t test to analyze the difference of participants' athletic data during the experiment.

3 Results

The descriptive analysis data of dependent variables is shown in Table 2. The data of baseline and T90 are compared below. The data of one day in experiment was labeled with 'T' and the test number, such as T12, T24, and T60.

Table 2. Descriptive analysis data of dependent variables

		Baseline		T90		Sig.
		Mean value	Standard deviation	Mean value	Standard deviation	
Grip strength (kg)	Left hand	41.69	3.49	46.47	3.94	.028
	Right hand	44.98	3.32	48.22	2.99	.272
Push-ups (number per minute)		24.78	4.37	25.78	3.83	.777
Lung capacity (mL)		4115.78	161.35	4581.78	200.08	.010
Eye-closed standing (s)		27.88	7.22	32.35	7.47	.583
Sit-and-reach (cm)		6.52	2.77	7.76	2.60	.498

By comparing the data of early and final stages of the experiment, the overall trend of change can be described:

1. The results indicated that the grip strength increased. During the whole experiment, the grip strength of left hand increased from 41.69 (kg) to 46.47 (kg) by 11.5%.

This trend is significant (Sig < 0.05). The grip strength of right hand increased from 44.98 (kg) to 48.22 (kg) by 7.2%. Although the difference was not significant, the trend was the same as that of the left hand. Two parts of data were highly relevant, which met the expectations of the research.

2. The data of lung capacity increased from 4116 (ml) to 4582 (ml) by 10.2%, which was significant (Sig < 0.05).

In terms of overall trends, different indicators showed different rules of change.

1. strength:

The grip strength of left and right hand showed an upward trend (Figs. 1 and 2), and the upper body strength did not show significant change trend (Fig. 3).

Fig. 1. The variation trend of grip strength (left hand)

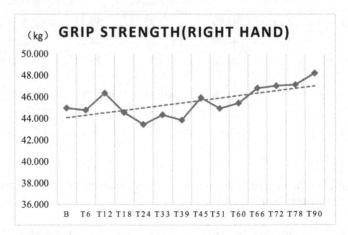

Fig. 2. The variation trend of grip strength (right hand)

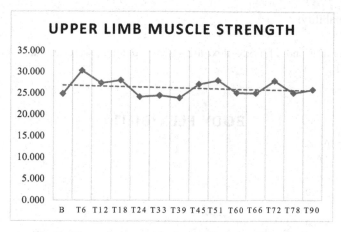

Fig. 3. The variation trend of upper limb muscle strength

2. breathing function:

The overall trend of lung capacity was rising, but not monotonous, which fluctuated in the medium term (Fig. 4).

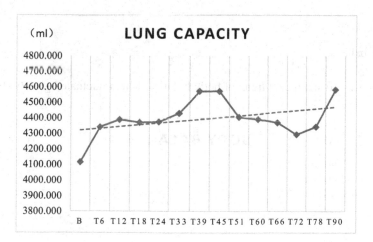

Fig. 4. The variation trend of lung capacity

3. body flexibility:

The overall trend of body flexibility showed an upward trend, which was not significant (Fig. 5).

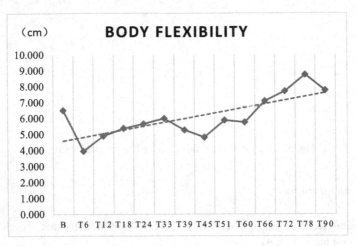

Fig. 5. The variation trend of body flexibility

4. body balance:

There was no significant trend of body balance, which fluctuated greatly (Fig. 6).

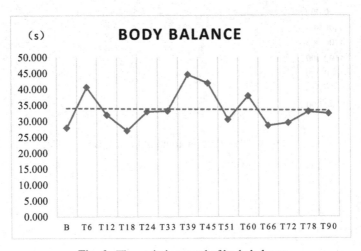

Fig. 6. The variation trend of body balance

Different from the experimental expectations, the strength data did not decline. On the surface, there was no negative impact of long-time simulated voyage (Fig. 7).

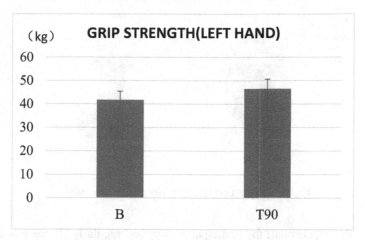

Fig. 7. The data comparison of baseline and T90 (grip strength)

Changes in physical fitness level are stratified. The same training stimuli have different training effects on people with different physical foundation, which will reflect on the data. Therefore, the data were divided according to different exercise habits (Figs. 8 and 9).

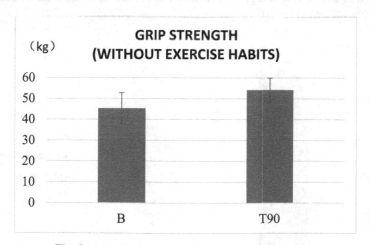

Fig. 8. The data comparison (without exercise habits)

Comparing the beginning and end data, the grip strength increased by 11.5%. The data of participants without exercise habits increased by 19.32%, and that of participants having exercise habits increased by 4.12%. The increase in data was mainly contributed by the former.

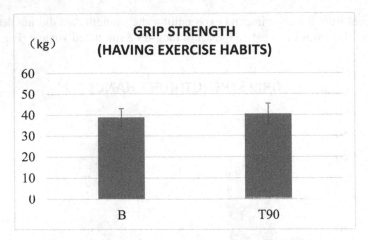

Fig. 9. The data comparison (having exercise habits)

During the experiment, the participants exercised regularly. There was a training effect between participants with different habits (before the experiment). The data of participants without exercise habits (before the experiment) was easier to increase than the ones having exercise habits. The increase in data was largely caused by the training effect. For the participants having exercise habits, the increase in data was very limited.

It could be inferred that the data would decline if the participants did not exercise during the experiment. In order to fight against potential physical decline, participants' willingness to exercise would gradually increase. Participants' exercise frequency was compared as follows (Fig. 10):

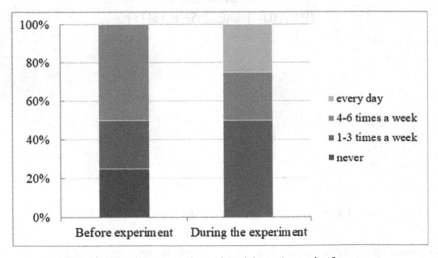

Fig. 10. The data comparison of participants' exercise frequency

In addition, Time series model fitting of data was also conducted by exponential smoothing method. The fitting equation was the Holt equation. The Holt equation is characterized by linear trends and no seasonal components. The data of strength was not periodic during the experiment. The stable r square of fitting was 0.88 (Fig. 11).

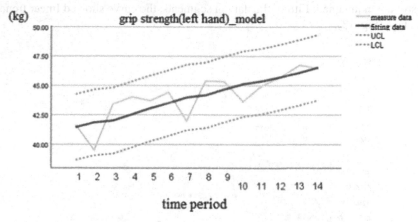

Fig. 11. Time series model fitting of grip strength

Based on the overall trend, the data of lung capacity was analyzed in more depth. The data was segmented in the time process. The data showed an upward trend from the baseline to T33, which increased significantly from 4116 (ml) to 4429 (ml) by 7.6%. The data showed an upward trend from T72 to T90, which increased significantly from 4300 (ml) to 4582 (ml) by 6.5% (Fig. 12).

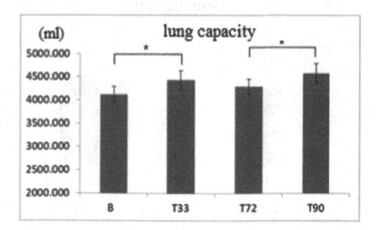

Fig. 12. The data comparison of lung capacity

The increase in lung capacity was related to irregular aerobic exercise (power bicycle) during the experiment. There was an inflection point during the second month. The data showed a downward trend since T33. The participants maintained or intensified their exercise in the second two months, but the overall lung capacity level still declined. Excluding pathological factors, the decline in this stage might be due to the decline in amount of exercise under long-time isolated environment, which resulted in the decline of respiratory muscle. While maintaining or strengthening exercise, the lung capacity was still not maintained. Fitting the data in segments, the curve showed linear trends in each stage (Fig. 13).

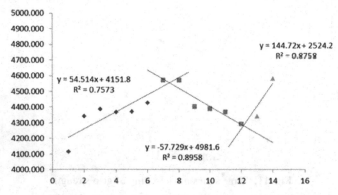

Fig. 13. Segmentation fitting curve (lung capacity)

The data showed a downward trend from the baseline to T45, which decreased significantly from 6.52 (cm) to 4.82 (cm) by 26.2% (Fig. 14).

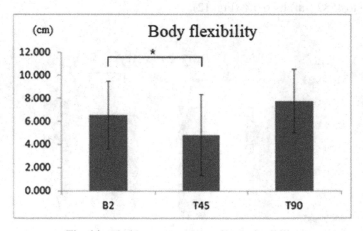

Fig. 14. The data comparison of body flexibility

During the experiment, participants' daily activities were restricted. The body flexibility would decline significantly in this environment for more than a month. In later stage of the experiment, the increase in data was related to strengthening the exercise.

4   Conclusion

In terms of strength, the experiment examined the strength of hand grip and upper limb muscle. Overall, the grip strength of both hands showed a monotonous upward trend, and the trend of left hand was significant (increased by 11.5%). The strength of upper limb muscle had no significant trend of change. The change rule of strength related to exercise habits and training effect. In terms of breathing function, lung capacity showed an overall upward trend (significantly increased by 10.2% from the beginning to the end), but without monotonous trend. The upward trend appeared in the stage of beginning and end. The data showed a significant increase in the first third of the time (increased by 7.6%), and a significant increase (increased by 6.3%) in the period of adjusting the sleep and rest pattern at the later stage of the experiment. In terms of body flexibility, the data showed an upward trend, but the trend was not significant. The significant downward trend appeared during the first half of the time (decreased by 26.2%). In terms of body balance, the indicator fluctuated greatly in the whole time, without a clear trend.

References

1. Zhang, R.P., Sun, X.C., Zhang, B., et al.: Advance in research of effects of ship environment on seamen. J. Prev. Med. Chin. People's Lib. Army 24(2), 149–151 (2006)
2. Fu, M.Z., Wang, M.K., Ba, J.B., et al.: Research progress on the influence of warship environment on the physical ability of shipboard personnel. Chin. J. Naut. Med. Hyperb. Med. 23(6), 483–486 (2016)
3. Le, X.: Effects of 60-day navigation on a new-type diesel submarine on physical tolerance and psychological ergonomics of submariners. J. Prev. Med. Chin. People's Lib. Army (1999)
4. Hu, J., Chen, G., Cong, Y.: Influence of a 60 days underwater voyage on Seamen's physical work capacity. Chin. J. Naut. Med. (2000)
5. Su, X., Zhang, H., Wang, J.X., et al.: Effect of navigation fatigue on static balance function of navy servicemen on a long-distance voyage. J. Prev. Med. Chin. People's Lib. Army (2018)
6. Sun, J., Xu, H.: Research progress on measuring methods and influence factors of pinch force. Sport Sci. Res. (2018)
7. Shen, W.M., Chen, H.S., Li, A.F., et al.: Effects of prolonged navigation on the pulmonary functions of sailors. Chin. J. Naut. Med. Hyperb. Med. 11(2), 68–70 (2004)
8. Ou, M., Xu, H.T., Lai, L.F., et al.: Influence of oceangoing voyage on the respiratory function of naval medical staff. Med. Pharm. J. Chin. People's Lib. Army 4, 89–91 (2015)
9. Yuan, J.F., Zhang, Q.X., Lu, A.M., et al.: One-legged standing with eyes closed in physical fitness testing. J. Clin. Rehabil. Tissue Eng. Res. 33, 6049–6054 (2013)
10. Yu, H., Xu, L.H., Hu, P.K., et al.: Influence of long-term navigation on mental health in crews. Med. J. Chin. People's Lib. Army 37(7), 745–748 (2012)

Author Index

Printed in the United States
by Baker & Taylor Publisher Services